Alternatives in Mobilization

What determines which identity cleavage, ethnicity or religion, is mobilized in political contestation, be it peaceful or violent? In contrast to
common predictions that the greatest contention occurs where identities
are fully segmented, most identity conflicts in the world are between
ethnic groups that share religion. *Alternatives in Mobilization* builds on
the literature about political demography to address this seeming contradiction. The book proposes that variation in relative group size and
intersection of cleavages help explain conundrums in the mobilization
of identity, across transgressive and contained political settings. This
theory is tested cross-nationally on identity mobilization in civil war
and across violent conflict in Pakistan, Uganda, Nepal, and Turkey and
peaceful electoral politics in Indonesia. This book helps illustrate a more
accurate and improved picture of the ethnic and religious tapestry of the
world and addresses an increasing need for a better understanding of
how religion contributes to conflict.

JÓHANNA KRISTÍN BIRNIR is Professor of Government and Politics
at the University of Maryland.

NİL SEDA ŞATANA is Visiting Associate Professor of Government and
Politics at the University of Maryland.

Alternatives in Mobilization

Ethnicity, Religion, and Political Conflict

JÓHANNA KRISTÍN BIRNIR
University of Maryland

NİL SEDA ŞATANA
University of Maryland

CAMBRIDGE
UNIVERSITY PRESS

CAMBRIDGE
UNIVERSITY PRESS

Shaftesbury Road, Cambridge CB2 8EA, United Kingdom

One Liberty Plaza, 20th Floor, New York, NY 10006, USA

477 Williamstown Road, Port Melbourne, VIC 3207, Australia

314–321, 3rd Floor, Plot 3, Splendor Forum, Jasola District Centre, New Delhi – 110025, India

103 Penang Road, #05–06/07, Visioncrest Commercial, Singapore 238467

Cambridge University Press is part of Cambridge University Press & Assessment, a department of the University of Cambridge.

We share the University's mission to contribute to society through the pursuit of education, learning and research at the highest international levels of excellence.

www.cambridge.org
Information on this title: www.cambridge.org/9781108412261

DOI: 10.1017/9781108304306

First published 2022
First paperback edition 2023

A catalogue record for this publication is available from the British Library

Library of Congress Cataloging-in-Publication data
Names: Birnir, Jóhanna Kristín, 1969– author. | Şatana, Nil Seda, 1976– author.
Title: Alternatives in mobilization : ethnicity, religion, and political conflict
    Jóhanna Kristín Birnir, Nil Seda Şatana.
Description: Cambridge ; New York, NY : Cambridge University Press, 2022. |
    Includes bibliographical references and index.
Identifiers: LCCN 2021053371 (print) | LCCN 2021053372 (ebook) |
    ISBN 9781108419840 (hardback) | ISBN 9781108412261 (paperback) |
    ISBN 9781108304306 (epub)
Subjects: LCSH: Political participation–Case studies. | Ethnicity–Political aspects–Case studies. |
    Religion and politics–Case studies. | Demography–Political aspects–Case studies. |
    Political geography–Case studies. | BISAC: POLITICAL SCIENCE / General
Classification: LCC JF799 .B57 2022 (print) | LCC JF799 (ebook) | DDC 323/.042–dc23/eng/20220206
LC record available at https://lccn.loc.gov/2021053371
LC ebook record available at https://lccn.loc.gov/2021053372

ISBN   978-1-108-41984-0   Hardback
ISBN   978-1-108-41226-1   Paperback

Maya, Óðinn and Sigþór

Contents

Figures

Tables

Acknowledgments

As is true of all scopious projects, this book has benefited from the input of multiple institutional and individual benefactors without whom it would not be the same and to whom we are boundlessly grateful.

The department of Government and Politics at the University of Maryland (UMD) and the Department of International Relations at Bilkent University provided vital institutional support, including research support and sabbaticals, over the course of this project. At UMD the National Consortium for the Study of Terrorism and Responses to Terrorism (START) funded our collection of the A-Religion data and supported Nil's writing sabbatical. While many START colleagues enriched this project, we want to thank especially Gary La Free, Bill Braniff, Gary Ackerman, Brandon Behlendorf, and Jonathan Wilkenfeld. We also thank the Snider Center and its director Rajshree Agarwal for Jóhanna's summer support, and the Center for International Development and Conflict Management (CIDCM) and its director, Paul Huth, for Nil's institutional affiliation and overall support of the project. The Global Religion Research Initiative Book Leave Award from the University of Notre Dame was instrumental to Jóhanna's writing as was the UMD Graduate School's Research and Scholarship Award (RASA). We thank the Dean's office in the College of Behavioral & Social Sciences – especially Wayne V. McIntosh for helping work out the administrative details and for steadfast support more generally. Similarly important was the support of the Folke Bernadotte Academy, and we thank especially Mimmi Soderberg Kovacs, Louise Olsson, and Sophia Wrede.

Despite the COVID-19 pandemic restricting travel in the last couple of years, this book or parts of it have been presented at multiple in-person conferences and workshops and some virtual ones. These include the Comparative/International Relations/Peace and Conflict workshops at the University of Michigan, Michigan State University; University of Texas, Austin, Washington University, St. Louis, Uppsala University, George Washington University,

Georgetown University, Daemen College, Indiana University-Purdue University Indianapolis (IUPUI), University of Maryland, University of Iceland, St. Mary's College of Maryland, and Florida Atlantic University, and the various professional conferences including those of the American Political Science Association, the International Studies Association, and the Midwestern Political Science Association. We thank organizers, discussants, and participants for their tremendous insights and contributions all of which have improved this work.

We want to express special gratitude for the early, ongoing, and enthusiastic support of Christian Davenport whose work continually inspires. Daniel Posner, we thank for generous guidance in the framing of the argument, Margaret Pearson for comments on the framing of the project, and Will Reed and Piotr Swistak for input about the formalization of the theory. We thank Jonathan Fox for the suggestion of the A-Religion name for our data set, for his feedback on the manuscript, and for his unfaltering support of our work throughout the years. We are similarly indebted to Monica Toft, Ragnhild Nordas, Jeffrey Haynes, Jocelyn Cesari, Joel Selway, and our anonymous reviewers for various types of input along the way, always of the highest caliber. Three Cambridge editors loom large in the production of this book: Lew Bateman, Robert Dreesen and Rachel Blaifeder – we are grateful for their contributions. At Cambridge multiple others contributed to the manuscript. We especially want to thank Vinithan Sedumadhavan, S. R. Saranya, and Claire Sissen.

Amy Liu, we can never thank you enough for introducing Jóhanna to Chicken S*** Bingo, but also for organizing outstanding workshops where the input from multiple participants including Ana Bracic, Lenka Busticova, Jonathan Ishiyama, William Mishler, Rahsaan Maxwell, Claire Adida, Raul Madrid, Kurt Weyland, and Michael Findley clarified ideas and improved the empirical analysis. We also thank Deniz Aksoy and David Carter for organizing an excellent workshop and to the discussants and participants – especially Barbara Walter, Laia Balcells, Navin Bapat, Jason Lyall, Kenneth Schultz, and Todd Sandler, whose comments and suggestions shaped the project in many ways.

We are indebted to several additional esteemed University of Maryland colleagues whose prints are on this manuscript in more ways than we can recount: Ernesto Calvo, Isabella Alcaniz, Kanisha Bond, John McCauley, Calvert Jones, Mark Lichbach, Kathleen Cunningham, Stella Rouse, Mike Hanmer, David Cunningham, Shibley Telhami, David Backer, and Jim Gimpel, thank you all for your invaluable contributions.

The Uppsala group – especially Erika Forsberg, Håvard Hegre, Hanne Fjelde, Sabine Otto, Magnus Öberg, and Guðlaug Ólafsdóttir, thank you for your insights on this project and identity politics more generally. We also want to express special gratitude to Isaak Svensson and Desirée Nilsson who in 2013 gave us the dependent variable for our test in Chapter 4, years before publishing, in 2018, the updated version they were working on. Their generosity in sharing data is a beacon we hope to pay forward.

We thank Lisa Parshall for inviting Nil to share our findings with the community interested in learning about recent approaches in the study of conflict in Buffalo, and SUNY Buffalo and Daemen faculty we thank for their terrific feedback. Tijen Demirel-Pegg, we thank you for an excellent workshop with undergraduates at IUPUI where we learned a great deal, and the faculty for their feedback.

For invaluable and early input, we also would like to thank Harris Mylonas, Henry Hale, Yonatan Lupu, Erik Cramon, Renat Shaykhutdinov, and Philip G. Roeder. The quality of feedback from the workshops organized by Ani Sarkissian, Ana Bracic, and Nazita Lajevardi gave us hope for the future of virtual meetings – and improved our work noticeably. Matthias Basedau, Davis Brown, Victor Asal, Stephen Saideman, Will Moore, Manuel Vogt, Dawn Brancati, Daniel Corstange, and Andrew Zaeske all contributed to our work at various points and for that, we are very grateful. For visiting scholar support in Iceland and early input during presentation of this work, we thank Baldur Þórhallsson, Silja Bára Ómarsdóttir, Stefanía Óskarsdóttir, Gunnar Helgi Kristinsson, Ólafur Þórður Harðarson, and Pia Elísabeth Hansson.

We thank Donald Horowitz for an insightful conversation about Indonesian politics. For help with setting up the research in Indonesia, we thank Teri L. Caraway and Julie Chernov Hwang who shared expert advice on completing the work in-country and put Jóhanna in contact with several Indonesian colleagues. Among the Indonesian scholars who contributed in many ways to this work and to the ongoing relationship building between UMD and Gadjah Mada University, we want to thank especially Najib Azca, Abdul Gaffar Karim, and Amalinda Savirani. Special thanks go to Ferry Kurnia Rizkiyansyah at netgrit.org who patiently answered far too many rounds of questions about Indonesian institutions and to the helpful staff at the Indonesian electoral commission (Komisi Pemiliham Umum, KPU) for assisting us in finding the pertinent laws and answering our questions. We are deeply indebted to Nathan Allen who read and commented on the Indonesia chapter with greater care than we could have ever hoped for. We are also grateful for all the help that was provided to Nil during her field research in Turkey throughout the years.

Several other colleagues with extensive country expertise read and critiqued our case discussions. Stella Rouse, thank you for your comments on the U.S. case, Trey Billing for your insights on Uganda, Ojashwi Pathak for your comments about Nepal, anonymous reviewers for feedback on Pakistan, and Zeki Sarıgil, Ekrem Karakoç, Tijen Demirel-Pegg, Burak Bilgehan Özpek, and Alperen Özkan for answers and comments about the Turkish case. Katherine Sawyer we thank for working with us on the early test in what is now Chapter 4 and Henry Overos for working through the replications of that analysis. We also thank Jessica Soedergo and Kai Ostwald who provided us with articles concerning the Indonesia case and answered our questions. We would also like to thank the numerous people – that go unnamed here – with whom we had informal conversations during our fieldwork in Indonesia and in Turkey. The importance of their insights to informing our understanding of local politics cannot be overstated.

To a very large extent the writing of this book also depended on the careful contributions of multiple students, some of whom have graduated, others who we still work with, and all of whom we have learned much from. Molly Inman and Agatha Hultquist made important contributions to the AMAR data that underpin the collection of the A-Religion data. Other exceptional graduate students that worked with us during the research and writing of the book and who contributed in multiple ways include Alperen Özkan, Anastassia Buğday, Mine Akar, Çağan Şatana, Pavel Coronado-Castillanos, Eric Dunford, and Tiago Ventura. We also thank graduate students for their in-class and in-house workshop comments about this project, as well as the multiple undergraduate students who have contributed to this work in so many ways as RAs and through insightful discussions in classes on the topic.

When committing to a project of this scale many personal debts of gratitude are also incurred. Nil would like to thank: My mother Şükran for motivating me to ask the hard questions and keep working until I get it right, my father Atilla for his peculiar sense of humor that always brings a smile to my face, my sister Rima, my brother Onur Alp, and brother-in-law Selçuk for being there for me even from 5000 miles away, niece and nephews, Selin, Alper, and Çağan, for bringing us joy when we most need it. Our family has come a long way from Mardin. I am also grateful to Mike and Midge Paulonis for welcoming me into their family with open hearts.

I am in debt to all the friends who have wholeheartedly supported me in one way or another over the years. Special thanks go to Burak Bilgehan Özpek, Chris Vaughan, Simon Dukstansky, Aruna Maruvada, Tijen Demirel-Pegg, Holly Cloer Rosario, Thom Rosario, Pinar Çebi Wilber, Steven Wilber, and Bahar Karaca. Burak and Tijen who have also coauthored articles with me during the writing of this book deserve plaudits for forgiving me as I asked them to bear with me more times than I can count.

Finally, I thank my husband Jay Paulonis for all the support and patience he has provided me, particularly for entertaining a mischievous toddler for many weekends at home during a pandemic so that I could finish writing. As Jóhanna and I started finally writing this book after many years of research, I had my daughter Maya, who watched countless Baby Shark videos on my lap and when she was able to speak, told me to keep working when I desperately wanted to stop and sleep. For her ability to find happiness in the smallest things, I dedicate this book to Maya and all the little girls who teach their moms not only that they can do it, but also it is okay to just prioritize and let go of what is not important. My hope is that Maya grows up in a world where not just girls, but all people feel that they can achieve anything they want.

Jóhanna would like to thank: My family and dear friends who, to some extent, overlap. My brother Bibbi – I thank you for his endless patience and close to daily conversations about how to best write and solve the model describing the political strategies at play in this book. My other siblings Tóta, Magna, Bía, and Ingi I thank for their support, friendship, and years of listening to descriptions of this and related projects. Other cherished friends that I am extraordinarily grateful for, some of whom I am so lucky to also count as colleagues, Christian, Margaret, Will, Isabella, Ernesto, Stella, Kanisha, Dawn, and yet others like Sif Margrét Tulinius, Maby Palmisano, and Holly Ridgeway Eckles who operate in different disciplines but who enduringly are available to listen, support, and share.

I would also like to thank those dearest and closest to me and to whom I dedicate this book. My husband and the perfect partner for me, David Matthew Waguespack, thank you for everything but especially for your resolute support and sense of adventure, and my sons, Óðinn Birnir Waguespack and Sigþór Birnir Waguespack, whom I thank for still keeping me focused on the truly important things in life, them.

Lastly, we want to give thanks for our twenty-plus years of collaboration and friendship that began at SUNY-Buffalo where Nil was Jóhanna's first Doctoral mentee. This manuscript represents the culmination of our collaboration and we are grateful for the opportunity we have had to work together, to learn from each other, and for our enduring friendship.

I

Introduction

When is ethnicity mobilized in political contestation? How about religion? Across the world, the answers to these questions seemingly vary across time and space. For example, scholars largely agree that Pakistan was founded on the idea of a "secular" Muslim cultural and/or ethno-national identity as opposed to a religious Islamic identity.[1] However, the success of this attempt at secular nation-building is debatable because, after independence, the country was plagued by ethnic separatism, with Bangladesh seceding in 1971, and the Baloch insurgency only recently abating (Akbar, 2015; Shah, 2016). More insidiously, some argue that, in the new millennium, Pakistani primary identity in political mobilization has shifted, and that it "has emerged as a center for global jihad" (Bajoria, 2011: 5) in a conflict increasingly cast as a battle over religion.

On another continent, in Africa, since Milton Obote (an ethnic Langi and a Northerner)[2] led Uganda's movement for independence in 1962, ethnic and regional identity mobilization largely dominated Ugandan politics (Atkinson, 1994; Tom, 2006). Obote was overthrown by Idi Amin (an ethnic Kakwa and Lugbara, also a Northerner) who set about purging the military of Langi (and Acholi) until Obote returned to power. Obote himself was later replaced by an Acholi general Tito Lutwa Okello who, in turn, was ousted by Yoweri Museveni (a Bahima and a South-westerner) (Green, 2009). However, in the late 1980s, Alice Lakwena and Joseph Kony (both Acholi Northerners),

---

[1] While the words of Pakistan's founding father Muhammad Ali Jinnah have been used to justify both religious and secular interpretations of the state, the idea of the two-nation state is predominantly considered a secular cultural idea (Cohen, 2004; Varshney, 2008).

[2] Obote was supported by the Acholi and he favored them as further discussed in Chapter 5.

mobilized a religious identity in a civil war that cost the country thousands of lives and unimaginable horrors (Allen, 1991; Behrend, 1999; Neethling, 2013; Ofcansky, 2018).

Further to the South East, Indonesia's recent history is replete with both ethnic and religious conflicts (Bertrand, 2008; Harsono, 2019; Schulze, 2017). However, in 2019, Indonesia's voters – close to 200 million of them – peacefully chose among roughly 245,000 candidates running for more than 20,000 national and local legislative seats across the country (BBC, 2019).[3] Even so, the elections were increasingly marked by mobilization of identity, especially religion. For example, the incumbent President Joko Widodo, who in 2014 ran a staunchly secular campaign (The Economist, 2019), picked Ma'ruf Amin, the supreme leader and chairman of the Indonesian Ulema Council, and reportedly "the country's most senior Islamic cleric" as his running mate in the 2019 election (Aditya and Abraham, 2019).

In all of these countries across peaceful electoral settings and more violent political contestation, political actors variously mobilize ethnicity and religion.[4] Fluidity in mobilization of ethnic and religious political identities extends well beyond these countries. For instance, while most civil wars are fought between ethnic groups (Fearon and Laitin, 2003; Denny and Walter, 2014), in the last half a century "religious civil wars have increased relative to non-religious civil wars" (Toft et al., 2011; Mason and Mitchell, 2016: 153).[5] Religion also exerts a strong influence across multiple domains of more conventional electoral politics (Grzymala-Busse, 2012), where ethnicity is commonly mobilized (Lijphart, 1977; Posner, 2005; Birnir, 2007; Birnir and Satana, 2013; Flesken, 2018).

What determines which is mobilized in political contestation, be it peaceful or violent? Addressing this question, the literatures on (shared) cleavages and the Minimum Winning Coalition (MWC) suggest that contentious identity contestation is increasingly likely when cleavages are segmented (for instance, when competing groups have different ethnic and/or religious identities), and that the identity groups mobilized are the ones that will form the smallest possible winning coalitions.

However, in contrast to the literature on cross-cutting (shared) cleavages, which predicts the greatest contention where identities are fully segmented, most identity conflicts in the world are between ethnic groups that share the same religion (Satana et al., 2013; Fox, 2016; Svensson and Nilsson, 2018). Furthermore, on the contrary to the MWC literature, which would predict preponderance of, and stability among identity-based MWCs, MWCs are

[3] The preliminary presidential results sparked some short-lived riots (Suhartono and Victor, 2019) but the election itself was by and large very peaceful and orderly (Kahfi, 2019).
[4] As we discuss further in the cases of Uganda, Nepal, Indonesia, and Turkey, multiple other cleavages, including but not limited to region, class, and migratory status, play a part in mobilization. For reasons discussed later in this chapter, we focus on ethnicity and religion in this book but acknowledge that our theory likely pertains to other cleavage types as well.
[5] See also Fox (2013).

actually not the most common types of ethnic coalitions (Bormann, 2019). The incongruences between predictions of the theory and the real-world observations are puzzling and remain under-explored in the literature.

To address these puzzles, we build on the literature about political demography, which draws special attention to the role of group size in political contestation (Weiner and Teitelbaum, 2001; Goldstone et al., 2011). While the current literature primarily focuses on segmented identities, the theory of *Alternatives in Mobilization* we propose in this book suggests that variation in *relative* group size and *intersection* of cleavages help explain the above and potentially other conundrums in the mobilization of identity, across transgressive and contained political settings. A formalization of this argument yields multiple testable implications including the hypothesis of the *Challenger's Winning Coalition (CWC)*. Where demographic conditions allow, our hypothesis posits that members of large minority identity groups that are left out of or under-represented through identity-based MWCs will seek access by redefining the axes of the identity competition to mobilize a potentially oversized CWC of an alternate identity, which is shared with the majority. In this book, we test this conjecture cross-nationally on identity mobilization in civil war and explore the mechanisms of this proposition across violent conflict in the cases of Pakistan, Uganda, Nepal, and Turkey. Finally, we examine whether the CWC hypothesis can be extended to a peaceful electoral setting in one of the most ethno-religiously heterogeneous countries in the world, Indonesia.

Importantly, the CWC implication does not contradict the idea of the conflict-mitigating effect of cross-cutting (shared) cleavages or the notion of majority leaders seeking to form an MWC. In contrast, the CWC hypothesis tested in this book refines the argument about the effect of shared identities to suggest that, conditional on the identity group's relative size, shared secondary cleavages *mitigate* or *motivate* conflict. Similarly, the CWC hypothesis builds on the premise of the MWC numbers game but further articulates when the assumptions of the MWC do not hold, conditional on demography, where and which minority CWC is more likely to mount a credible identity challenge to the MWC. Thus, the CWC implication accounts for why MWCs are sometimes unstable and short-lived.

Much is at stake in correctly explaining identity mobilization in contentious politics across the world. Specifically, most civil wars are fought between ethnic groups (Fearon and Laitin, 2003; Denny and Walter, 2014), and religious wars are on the rise (Toft et al., 2011; Mason and Mitchell, 2016: 153).[6] Success of peace-building depends on the accurate understanding of identity mobilization. For instance, substantial resources are spent on institution building, primarily of the power-sharing type, to resolve conflict and build peaceful post-conflict polities. However, it remains unclear whether these institutions are effective and under what conditions they reduce the likelihood of war

---

[6] See also Fox (2013).

recurrence (Sambanis, 2020). Without properly delineating the incentives for identity group mobilization, it is unlikely that this institutional puzzle ever gets resolved. Similarly, in electoral politics across the world, the representation of identity groups is variously sought because legislatures make policy and their makeup communicates the extent to which democratic politics are inclusive (Piscopo and Wylie, 2020), or suppressed in a controversial effort to decrease identity-based electoral contestation (Moroff and Basedau, 2010).[7] Regardless of which view one takes, and aims to either suppress or encourage identity representation, it is difficult to fulfill either without a better understanding of identity mobilization.

1.2 THE LITERATURE

One of the predominant answers to the question of what determines which cleavage is mobilized in political contestation is offered by the literature on segmented and cross-cutting (shared) cleavages. Specifically, "[a] near-canonical claim among observers comparing politics across highly-divided societies is that the degree to [which cleavages] are 'crosscutting' constitutes a critical stabilizing feature of those political systems" (Gordon et al., 2015). In other words, underlying demographic configurations condition between which identities political challenges are more likely to materialize. When at least some identities are shared (or cross-cut), for instance in Switzerland, where the French and Italians are both predominantly Roman Catholic, greater stability ensues. In contrast, when identities are segmented, as in Sri Lanka where the Sinhalese are mostly Buddhist but Tamils are predominantly Hindu, instability is more likely through political identity challenges, such as majority outbidding.[8] The notion that shared identities stabilize political systems and that segmented identities invite more identity competition cuts across contained electoral politics where shared identities are thought to reduce zero-sum contestations (Lipset, 1981; Lipset and Rokkan, 1967; Lijphart, 1977, 1999), and transgressive politics of violence where segmented cleavages are considered to facilitate recruitment for violent ends (Selway, 2011b; Gordon et al., 2015; Siroky and Hechter, 2016).[9]

---

[7] We return to this subject in Chapter 6 in the context of Indonesia's electoral politics.

[8] Majority outbidding here refers to the scenario where in competition for allegiances of the majority identity rank and file, the leadership of majority factions outbids each other in targeting a segmented minority. The case of Sri Lanka is commonly considered a classic case of majority outbidding (Horowitz, 1985). In turn, Toft (2013) describes a classic case of religious outbidding in Sudan.

[9] The increased conflict propensity of segmented ethno-religious groups has been tested cross-nationally (Ellingsen, 2005; Basedau et al., 2011; Selway, 2011b; Stewart, 2012; Toft, 2013; Sweijs et al., 2015). Moreover, the literature on horizontal inequalities shows that identity is not the only re-enforcing cleavage that increases conflict potential between segmented groups – so do economic inequalities (Stewart, 2008; Brown, 2008; Stewart et al., 2009; Ostby, 2008; Cederman et al., 2011). Indeed, Baldwin and Huber (2010) suggest economics are more

A complimentary answer in the literature, focusing on the question of which identity is mobilized within a country draws on Riker's idea of coalition size, which stipulates that in competition over finite resources "participants create coalitions just as large as they believe will ensure winning and no larger" (Riker, 1962: 32).[10] Applied to ethnic politics, the MWC theory has helped explain how and why competition for scarce resources takes on ethnic characteristics (Bates, 1983a), how ethnic parties win elections (Chandra, 2004), the onset of ethnic civil war (Choi and Kim, 2018), and why divergent identities are mobilized across different institutional settings (Posner, 2005, 2017).[11]

Furthermore, holding institutions constant, scholars have theorized the conditions favoring change from one identity MWC to the next. For instance, Chandra (2012) posits that underlying demographics, as constrained by institutions, produce a given number of identity groups of minimum winning size. These scholars argue that this underlying demographic condition determines whether a change in the identity composition of the MWC is possible within a given system. In contrast, focusing on alliances in civil war, Fotini (2012) argues that identity does not drive coalition formation. Instead, she posits that variation in the balance of group-relative power and intra-group fractionalization induces shifts between coalitions and that identity is often used in a *post hoc* justification of shifting allegiances. Thus, both accounts pre-suppose that underlying demographic identity configurations make mobilization of identity possible. However, they also suggest that, in a given setting, identity-based challenges to the status quo are either exogenously brought to the forefront by changing power balance (Fotini, 2012) or initiated among any of multiple possible contenders (Chandra, 2012).[12]

important – at least to public goods provision – than are cultural differences. While all of the above scholarship focuses on group politics, the behavioral psychology literature focusing on American politics also supports, at the individual level, the ideas about the increased potential for contestation resulting from segmentation and reduced contestation with cross-cuttingness (in this literature referred to respectively as low or high social identity complexity; Roccas and Brewer, 2002). Among other things, this literature points to a relationship between self-perception of belonging to highly segmented groups and lower out-group tolerance (Brewer and Pierce, 2005). More recently, Mason (2018) suggests an endogenous sorting mechanism where political parties pick up identity platforms, which in turn, induce sorting constituencies into increasingly polarized blocks based on multiple identity dimensions – contributing to the current polarization in American politics.

[10] Similarly, selectorate theory clarifies how authoritarian leaders secure a minimum winning coalition (Bueno de Mesquita, 2003).

[11] The literature using the idea of the MWC to explain outcomes pertaining to ethnic politics extends to multiple other outcomes including, for example, the distribution of clientelistic benefits (Fearon, 1999), and the amount of political aid a country receives (Bormann et al., 2017).

[12] Thus, in both accounts, the relationship of underlying identities to challenger mobilization is inconclusive with respect to predicting which identities get mobilized and/or superimposed in competition between the status quo coalition and the challengers mobilizing an alternate identity.

1.2.1 The Puzzles

We observe that much conflict occurs within cultural traditions between similar religious groups that differ in sect or school only, and not between religious families (Fox, 2002, 2004b; Tusicisny, 2004; Gartzke and Gleditsch, 2006; Toft, 2007; Akbaba and Taydas, 2011; Birnir and Satana, 2013; Satana et al., 2013; Fox, 2016; Gleditsch and Rudolfsen, 2016; Svensson and Nilsson, 2018). Furthermore, in contention with both the logic of the MWC and the literature about cross-cutting (shared) cleavages, recent empirical analyses suggest that oversized ethnic coalitions are actually more common than are MWCs, and that coalitions comprised of cross-cut ethnic groups are less stable than their more unified counterparts (Bormann, 2019).

It seems, therefore, that in the study of identity politics a number of issues remain unresolved. For instance, it is not at all clear that cross-cutting or shared cleavages deter political competition between identity groups in the way commonly postulated in the literature. Furthermore, while the MWC argument plausibly explains some cases of coalition formation, it also appears that MWCs may not be the most common, stable, or long-lived coalitions in identity politics. These observations present intriguing puzzles and, if correct, suggest some important questions moving forward including: Which identities are mobilized in political contestation and in what types of coalitions? These are the main questions that motivate this project.

1.2.2 Scope, Assumptions, and Terms

Scope
Comprehensive mapping of how political incentives change for mobilization of identity coalitions, as all cleavage combinations vary in size and intersection, is outside the scope of this study – if even possible.[13] Our goals are more modest. Specifically, within the study of identity cleavages the empirical scope of our study principally pertains to ethnicity and religion, though the case analyses in Chapters 5 and 6 pinpoint other identity cleavages that matter for mobilization, at least in the cases we examine. We acknowledge that multiple identity cleavages other than ethnicity and religion exist,[14] as do many more political cleavages of other types.[15] Furthermore, all types of cleavages – identity and beyond – are segmented or shared in innumerable different ways. In this book, we focus empirically on two variants of cleavage interaction: *groups*

---

[13] Changing mobilization incentives associated with the extensive variation resulting from inter-action of all cleavage types delineates the research agenda within which our inquiry fits - and our theory is developed with this in mind. However, the empirical scope of this study is far more circumscribed.

[14] Identity cleavages not specifically discussed in this book include, for example, gender.

[15] Other types of cleavages include class, native/migrant status, urban/rural dwelling, or political party cleavages, among others.

that are segmented on one or more dimensions, and *groups that are segmented on one cleavage but share a second identity.*

To be clear, the theory of *Alternatives in Mobilization* proposed in Chapter 3 is agnostic with respect to cleavage type, and can possibly be extended to account for other cleavage types and far greater complexity in cleavage interactions that lend themselves to mobilization. Other cleavage configurations may also be more relevant in the study of political outcomes that are not considered in this study. However, the empirical focus here on the demographics of segmented and shared ethnic and religious cleavage combinations is motivated by the literatures on cleavage intersection and the MWC as outlined above. In this scholarship, the demographics of shared or segmented ethnic and religious cleavage combinations feature prominently in electoral and conflict mobilization – but in ways that the above puzzles suggest – remain under-explained. Our general theoretical contribution consists of refining the role that demographics of segmented and shared cleavages play in mobilization for power within the state. In turn, the general theoretical contribution overlaps with the more specific contribution we hope to make, which is a better understanding of the role ethnicity and religion play in political conflict.

Finally, the scope of our inquiry is limited to exploring the incentives of actors that seek to alter power within the state in a way that grants them greater access to the spoils of office, within unaltered state boundaries. Identity is mobilized for multiple other purposes, including secession. However, the mobilization logic of secession possibly differs from the logic that drives groups to seek greater access within unaltered state boundaries. Rothchild (1983) divides these two types of claims respectively into internal, negotiable claims for re-distribution and external demands that are non-negotiable for the state. While external demands may often be disaggregated into negotiable claims for re-distribution (Rothchild, 1983), the process and consequences are sufficiently distinct to suggest that generalizing across the two types should be done with caution. This is an especially pertinent concern with respect to incentives for the mechanisms of identity bonding and bridging between majorities and minorities that are discussed further in Chapter 3. Therefore, explaining the logic of identity mobilization for purposes of secession is outside the scope of our study though we acknowledge that groups may pursue multiple objectives at the same time.[16]

Assumptions
To address the rationale for cleavage mobilization as conditioned by demographics and sharing or segmentation of identity among groups, we adopt some

---

[16] On this topic, see also Mason and Mitchell (2016). To be clear, we do account for secessionist movements in our empirical analysis, but the theory pertains to the logic of identity mobilization within unaltered state boundaries.

common assumptions from the literature. We assume that when excluded from access to power, a demand and/or opportunity for mobilization (voice) arises among the political actors in our story (Hirschman, 1970).[17] Furthermore, we assume that identity – both ethnicity and religion – is a common and useful heuristics for such mobilization.[18]

It is also assumed here that in a pursuit to secure voice by way of an increase in political power for their group,[19] sincere and/or instrumental political entrepreneurs recognize the opportunity to define and mobilize the emerging interest group, and to proclaim themselves leaders of the group (Brass, 1991; Chandra, 2004; van der Veen and Laitin, 2012; Huang, 2020).

Moreover, as is well established in the literature, in deciding whether to follow a political leader proposing a particular political strategy, individuals are anything but naive and manipulated. In contrast, multiple scholars argue that ethnic voters, for example, cast their ballot for ethnic parties because they believe the party is likely to succeed (Chandra, 2004) and will represent their policy preferences (Birnir, 2007). Similarly, in conflict situations, Fearon and Laitin (2000: 846) conclude that when information permits, "followers often are not so much following as pursuing their own local or personal agendas."[20] Therefore, we assume that when recruited – especially for potentially violent ends – individuals are agents in shaping political outcomes as they decide whether to support a political entrepreneur's proposed strategy based on whether it suits their own personal agenda. On this point it bears reiterating that beyond seeking greater access to resources, we make no assumptions about individual motives. For example, a devout individual may seek access to resources for reasons that further her faith, another may use religion for access to resources for purposes of public or private goods provision, and a third may seek access to resources for personal consumption. All of these goals are consistent with the mobilization logic we suggest in our theory of Alternatives in Mobilization.

---

[17] As explained by Wimmer (2013), we assume this demand and/or opportunity materializes for identity groups in much the same way as it does for other types of interest groups, where lack of access consolidates individuals as a group with a common interest. Furthermore, we assume that while the opportunity for mobilization is created by a lack of voice, demand may precipitate or follow entrepreneurial leadership's definition of group interests.

[18] Some classic examples that either explain why and how identity is used as a heuristic for mobilization or use examples of identity as heuristics for mobilization include Bates (1983a); Olzak (1983, 1992, 2006); Young (1976); Tarrow (2011); Tilly (1978); Gurr (1970, 1993a); Lipset and Rokkan (1967); Jelen and Wilcox (2002). This literature is vast. For recent overviews on mobilization of ethnicity see, for example, Fearon (2008); Vermeersch (2012); Cunningham and Lee (2016). On the mobilization of religion, see Birnir and Overos (2019).

[19] We adopt this assumption with the understanding that the precise reasons politicians wish to secure political power vary (Riker, 1986).

[20] Others have shown the same, specifically with respect to civil war (Kalyvas, 2006, 2009).

In other words, mobilization of identity is attractive to political actors – leaders and followers alike – for instrumental (Bates, 1974, 1983b; Chandra, 2005; Posner, 2005; Huang, 2020), sincere (or emotive) (Petersen, 2002), and symbolic reasons (Kaufman, 2001).[21]

When mobilized, we assume these political actors seek representation of their interests through the governing structures that determine the allocation of resources (Bates, 1983a). Furthermore, we follow the literature in assuming that, all else being equal, political actors generally would prefer to be represented by an MWC because it maximizes the political power of the actors' group while minimizing the division of political benefits. This is an important assumption because it allows us to articulate an example against which other types of coalitions can be compared so that we may gain a better understanding of when and why the MWC might not be an actor's preferred, or even a possible, vehicle for access. However, we also reckon political actors have a preference for access over minimum winning access. Thus, in a situation of great uncertainty, or when political actors believe the MWC only gives them tenuous access, a political actor will choose access over minimum winning access, even if that requires the construction of an oversized coalition.

The governing structures to which actors seek access need not be democratic (Schumpeter, 1992). Social movement theory explains how identity coalitions come into existence outside formal governing structures as "a network of informal interactions between a plurality of individuals, groups and/or organizations, engaged in a political or cultural conflict, on the basis of a shared collective identity" (Diani, 1992). Consequently, we expect identity is mobilized for access across regime types – even where formal channels are unavailable (Diani, 1992; Diani and Eyerman, 1992; Tilly, 1993). Furthermore, in line with the literature on social movements[22] the argument proposed here is neither exclusively an argument of supply or demand. In contrast, social mobilization is conceived as a political process involving both. Lack of access for identity groups generates an opportunity (explicit or latent demand) for voice that is recognized by political leaders who then call for mobilization of

---

[21] Kaufman posits that "political choices based on emotion and in response to symbols" (Kaufman, 2001: 29) is a better explanation of violent ethnic mobilization than are rationalist explanations. In our view the literature seems to support both notions. Similarly, in their discussion of the marketplace of religion, Stark and Finke are very clear that as opposed to "vulgar materialism," "faith and doctrine are central to our efforts to construct a model of the behavior of religious firms within a religious economy" (Stark and Finke, 2002: 32). In other words, a discussion of incentives in no way negates the importance of symbolism, including religious symbolism.

[22] See also, Wimmer's (2013: 111) discussion of the recent application of a "multilevel process theory" across the social sciences.

the identity group (supply). If that call resonates with followers – for a variety of reasons as explained before – contentious identity mobilization materializes. The contribution made here is to pinpoint which identities are more likely mobilized in this process.

Finally, we follow social identity theory (Tajfel, 1978; Tajfel and Turner, 1979, 1986) in that we treat divergent identity cleavages (ethnicity and religion in this book) as if they are comparable with respect to mobilization. The usefulness of this assumption is limited in predicting individual policy preferences within a given political environment (McCauley, 2014), as we discuss in greater detail below. However, overall similarities between mobilization of ethnicity (Vermeersch, 2012) and the mobilization of religion (Birnir and Overos, 2019) across divergent political outcomes support this assumption as a reasonable starting point.

Terms

Before outlining our argument, defining and clarifying some of the main terms of our inquiry, as they are used throughout this monograph, is helpful. Starting with the outcome, we are interested in examining the variation in the mobilization of identity types, empirically ethnicity and religion, in contentious politics. As explained earlier in this chapter, we assume excluded political actors seek access to governing structures that determine the allocation of resources (Hirschman, 1970; Bates, 1983a). These resources can be economic, related to security, symbolic, or any other type of resource that the state controls or has significant influence over. Thus, we define *political mobilization* as a process of activating a social movement for political ends (Tilly, 1978, 2004), and more specifically as "actors' attempt to influence the existing distribution of power" by way of interest formation, community building, and by employing available means of action (Nedelmann, 1987: 181). The means of action, in turn, is contentious politics.

To define *contentious politics* we rely on McAdam, Tarrow, and Tilly's definition of "[episodic, public, collective interaction among makers of claims and their objects when a) at least one government is an object of claims, ... and b) the claims would, if realized, affect the interests of at least one of the claimants]" (McAdam et al., 2001: 5). Our definition is slightly more narrow than theirs as we are not attempting to explain claims made by the government. Furthermore, relating claim-making to identity we follow Wimmer (2013: 109) who posits that an "Actor will choose those strategies and levels of ethnic distinction that will best support their claims to prestige, moral worth, and political power."

Like McAdam et al. (2001), we are interested in both *transgressive* and *contained* political contention. Respectively, these refer to collective claim-making using "means that are either unprecedented or forbidden within the regime in question" (McAdam et al., 2001: 8), such as civil war, and claims made through well-established means of claim-making such as elections. The claim-making of interest here can occur at various levels of formal or informal administration, including the national level and any sub-national levels where distribution of resources is vested in local authorities.

The identities of empirical interest in this book are ethnic and religious identities, though other types of identities – especially region, class, and migrant identity – also surface in the discussion of particular cases in Chapters 5 and 6. In thinking about identities, we find Brady and Kaplan's description of *identity* helpful. They describe social identity as a function of "The basic cognitive processes of self-categorization and self-schematization (Turner, 1985; Markus, 1977) [that] combine[s] with social interaction (Tajfel, 1978; Burke and Reitzes, 1981) to produce intersubjective agreement that (almost) every person can be placed in one of the *categories* (A,B,...,Z). These categories are described in terms of some easily perceived attributes X (e.g. language, race, or religion) such that the attributes can be used for classification (Laitin and Chandra, 2002). Moreover people attach themselves to these groups (Brewer, 2001)" (Brady and Kaplan, 2009: 34).[23]

Consistent with this way of thinking about identity, we join a long line of constructivists that posit identity groups are constructed and fluid (Barth, 1969; Berger, 1967; Fearon and Laitin, 2000; Chandra, 2012), and malleable (Laitin, 1986; Stark and Finke, 2002; Posner, 2005) for political ends. Malleability of identity here refers to the idea that individuals are simultaneously endowed with several identity attributes and that each of these attributes can be imbued with greater or lesser salience under given political circumstances and political leadership. For example, an individual's identity repertoire may include gender, race, ethnicity, religion, and several sub-sections of each of these categories.[24] This does not suggest identities are ephemeral or trivial. To the contrary, Wimmer (2013) explains that ethnic social boundaries are continually strategically negotiated as a result of distribution of power and interests, the reach of social networks, and the institutional setup that incentivize particular types of boundary making. In turn, the longevity of established boundaries depends on "the degree of power inequality and the reach of the consensus" about mutually beneficial exchanges and interests in society (Wimmer, 2013: 101), in some cases producing great fluidity and in others more static boundaries.

The crucial component in our theory is *political demography*, defined as the "study of the size, composition, and distribution of population in relation to both government and politics" (Weiner, 1971: 579). Because our inquiry centers on the interaction between groups that hold power and those that seek greater access to power by way of identity mobilization, it is important to clarify that when majority identity groups constitute less than 50 percent of the

---

23 We alternatively refer to identities as *cleavages* because an identity is used to cleave and sort members as belonging to either an in-group or out-group. While the above description refers to identity in general, we discuss the operationalization of ethnicity and religion further in Chapter 2.

24 For an overview of various definitions of ethnic identity in the literature, see Chandra (2012).

population, the common term denoting relative size for all identity groups is plurality. However, throughout this book we use the term *majority* in a slightly different way to denote the ruling group, and *minority* to denote the identity group not holding power and thus seeking access, even when both identity groups technically constitute a demographic plurality.[25]

Finally, the vocabulary of identity cleavage intersection[26] and overlap is reelingly varied across texts. Amongst the many possibilities, when referring to the intersection of cleavages we have chosen to use the terms *segmented* and *shared*. When discussing identity groups that are segmented along one or more identity cleavages, we mean groups that do not have an identity or identities in common. For example, Christian Dayaks and Muslim Malay in Indonesia are segmented on both ethnicity and religion. In contrast, Muslim Javanese and Muslim Sundanese Indonesians are segmented by ethnicity but share a religion. We discuss other common terms – especially the term of *cross-cutting (shared) identity* – and how they relate to our definition further in Chapter 3.

1.3 THE ARGUMENT

1.3.1 Alternatives in Mobilization: Demography of Identity as an Explanatory Variable

Identity outbidding among segmented groups and the MWC are very reasonable starting points for predicting which identities will be mobilized in politics. However, because identity groups are constructed, fluid (Barth, 1969; Berger, 1967; Fearon and Laitin, 2000; Chandra, 2012) and malleable (Laitin, 1986; Stark and Finke, 2002; Posner, 2005) for political ends, the core argument in this book presupposes that leaders of minorities that are targeted in majority outbidding or that do not gain access via the MWC will subsequently (or simultaneously) seek ways to re-define the relevant identity for political competition in ways that stave off targeting and afford access. Therefore, our principal proposition is that identity demographics influence the form minority challenges to the status quo take. Specifically, we argue that minority group size *relative* to the majority and the configuration of identity cleavage sharing

---

[25] In a select few cases the political "majority" as we use the term may even be a demographic "minority" as the term is only used to refer to numbers. We further discuss such groups in Chapter 2.

[26] The core idea in this book that political mobilization is better understood as a function of the multiple identity groups that an individual belongs to, and the position of those identities in the hierarchy of power, owes an intellectual debt to the literature on inter-sectionality (Collins and Bilge, 2016: 2). However, other than distinguishing between political majority and minority groups we do not theorize how intersecting vectors of power and oppression, across different contexts, differentially intervene in the mobilization dynamics that we propose. Consequently, we do not use the term inter-sectionality but rather refer to the intersection of cleavages and acknowledge the intellectual origin and possibilities for future study.

and segmentation incentivize minority leaders' choice of identity mobilization strategies. We refer to this argument as *Alternatives in Mobilization* to highlight the fact that group leaders and followers have a choice as to which cleavage is mobilized and how.

The study of political demography is already burgeoning and has substantially enriched our understanding of cleavage politics (Goldstone et al., 2011). For example, this literature supports the conjecture that communal group-mobilized quest for group representation often pits a new interest group against the *status quo*, and conflict at times ensues (Weiner and Teitelbaum, 2001). However, heretofore, existing studies primarily focus on the political demography of segmented groups or a single identity group over time (Goldstone et al., 2011), or examine the identity and absolute size of pivotal and/or majority groups, as discussed further in Chapter 3. In contrast, the argument proposed in this book directs attention to the demography of *minority relative size and cleavage intersection with the majority*. This refinement, in turn, helps explain the observed variation in mobilization of minority ethnic and religious identity in challenges to majority, and in majority outbidding and the stability of the MWC.

A Testable Implication: The Challenger's Winning Coalition

Chapter 3 formalizes the argument that relative minority group size and the configuration of underlying identity cleavages incentivize minority (and majority) leaders to pursue varying identity mobilization strategies. The formalization generates multiple testable implications, one of which is the *Challenger's Winning Coalition (CWC)*.

The CWC submits that relatively large minority groups segmented from a majority on identity A and excluded from an MWC founded around identity A will seek to mobilize a shared identity B to challenge the status quo MWC. In the context of ethnicity and religion, the idea is that leaders of large ethnic groups that are left out of, or underrepresented through, the majority's ethnic MWCs will seek to redefine the axes of identity competition to center on shared religion in a mobilization of an oversized CWC that affords them access. In other words, relatively large ethnic minorities may discern in a religious cleavage shared between the minority and the majority an opportunity to construct a new CWC by way of religious bonding, by bridging the majority/minority ethnic divide.[27] In doing so the objective of minority leaders is to recruit sufficient number of members from the majority rank and file that the new CWC gains access and the ethnic minority leadership is to some degree insulated from majority leader challenges for the leadership of the shared religion.

---

[27] Putnam (1995) distinguishes bonding from bridging social capital, respectively referring to socializing within and across cleavages. See also Paik and Navarre-Jackson (2011) on religion as a bonding social capital.

Ethnic minority leaders of the CWC can be expected to have reasonable hopes of success in recruiting members of the ethnic majority, at least from the rank and file, away from the MWC for two reasons. First, the greater distribution of material resources among a smaller group, which is a presumed stabilizer of preferences for the MWC, is more variable and in less competitive environments, sometimes more paltry than previously presumed (Corstange, 2018). Thus, it is plausible to expect that under-served members of the MWCs may be persuaded to join alternate coalitions. Second, emotive (Petersen, 2002) and symbolic identity rewards are of great importance for many political actors (Kaufman, 2001). The distribution of emotive and symbolic rewards is also not subject to the same constraints as material rewards, and may even be more credible when promised by leaders of an oversized coalition such as the CWC than by leaders of an MWC.

In turn, the reason the CWC challenge is expected to be led by large minority groups is that only leaders of relatively large ethnic minorities can reasonably anticipate success in leveraging their shared identity to recruit for mobilization enough co-religious supporters across ethnic lines to mount a credible challenge to the ruling majority. Furthermore, only leaders of relatively large ethnic minorities can reasonably expect to retain control of a coalition centered on religion mobilized across ethnic groups. This is especially important because minority leadership of the shared identity may be challenged by majority leaders in the event that the CWC is successful in reorienting identity competition from the segmenting identity to the shared identity.

Thus, consistent with the recent literature on MWC identity mobilization (Chandra and Boulet, 2012; Posner, 2005, 2017), the CWC suggests that minority choice to engage in an alternate mobilization of the shared identity is also a numbers game.[28] However, the numbers game suggested by the CWC differs from accounts of the MWC in some important ways. First, the CWC is led by the largest or one of the largest minorities rather than the majority or pivotal group that constitutes the core of the MWC. Second, it is the demographic majority/minority balance on the first cleavage and the sharing of the second identity that drive excluded minority decisions in mobilization, whereas absolute membership in the segmented identity group mobilized by the majority is what drives the strategy about the majority/pivotal group MWC.

Subsequent chapters then put to test the CWC across transgressive and contained political settings. Finally, as discussed in Chapter 3, the demographic variation within each type of cleavage configuration (segmented or shared) returns multiple additional testable implications that are not explored in this

---

[28] It bears emphasizing that the terminology "numbers game" does not preclude sincere preferences. Instead, the idea is that the underlying population numbers make certain mobilization strategies viable, regardless of whether the choice to mobilize is motivated by sincere preferences or instrumentality.

book.[29] Indeed, it is the central conclusion of this book that mobilization resulting from unexplored demographic variation among groups that share or are segmented by identity likely helps explain multiple puzzles across non-violent and violent outcomes in identity politics, suggesting an exciting new research agenda.

1.4 EMPIRICAL CONTRIBUTIONS

1.4.1 The New A-Religion Data and Case Analyses

The methodological objectives of the book are to provide evidentiary support for both the internal and external validity of our argument and especially for the testable implication of the CWC. To this end, we combine quantitative cross-national statistical testing with qualitative case narratives across cases (Pakistan, Uganda, Nepal, and Turkey) and within a case (Indonesia).[30]

To test the generalizability of our theory cross-nationally, we build on the new sample frame of 1202 socially relevant ethnic groups from the All Minorities at Risk (AMAR) data (Birnir et al., 2015, 2018), which we have coded for religion.[31] In the new A-Religion data set, in every country and for every majority-minority pair, in addition to group religion, we have also coded information about which ethnic groups share and which are separated by religion.[32] The cross-national analysis in Chapter 4 tests the group-level effect of the interaction of group relative size and the extent to which religion is shared on the probability of mobilization of religion in transgressive politics. The dependent variable operationalizes religious mobilization as minority religious claim-making, coded in the Religion and Armed Conflict (RELAC) data (Svensson and Nilsson, 2018) for the civil conflicts in the Uppsala Conflict Data Program (UCDP). Robust results strongly support our argument: approaching numerical parity increases the likelihood of minority religious claim-making in a civil war between ethnic majority and ethnic minority groups that share a religion.

Even so, multiple anecdotal accounts throughout the manuscript illustrate that the precise mechanisms of how religion gets activated in political conflict are highly dependent on context. Therefore, in Chapter 5, we probe the internal validity of our argument through narratives of four cases where religious claims

[29] We test some of these implications elsewhere, see for example, Birnir et al. (n.d.).
[30] Our case narratives adhere to many of the tenets set out by process tracing, including a standardized structured focused comparison across cases. However, while we discuss the cases in further descriptive detail elsewhere, (see e.g. Satana et al. [2019]), space constraints prevent us from providing sufficient descriptive detail for the cases to qualify as process-traced (George and Bennett, 2005). Furthermore, the cases are not intended to test the hypotheses (Ricks and Liu, 2018), rather they are intended to examine the plausibility of the mechanisms proposed by the theory. Consequently, the terminology we use when describing the qualitative analysis is case narratives.
[31] See also Birnir and Satana (2013); Satana et al. (2013).
[32] We thank Jonathan Fox for his suggestion of the name. "A" stands for "All."

are made in civil war between two or more ethnic groups. With internal validity as the objective, the cases were chosen to illustrate the mechanisms across religious doctrine, including Islam, Christianity, and Hinduism. While the logic of our CWC argument is consistent across doctrine with religious mobilization between ethnic groups in all the civil wars examined in this chapter, the case accounts also show how crucial context is to mobilization. Furthermore, the cases drive home the point that while the empirical focus in this book is on ethnicity and religion, across countries multiple other cleavage types play a role or at times are more important than ethnicity and religion in mobilization.

The second case study chapter (Chapter 6) explores the generalizability of CWC to contained political contestation in electoral politics through within-case comparisons across groups in Indonesia. As one of the most ethno-religiously heterogeneous countries in the world, and administratively an exceedingly complicated case, the political backdrop of Indonesia is useful for parsing out the interactive effect of minority size and mobilization of religion. While the exploration of cases in this chapter is a convenience sample that is far from comprehensive, the evidence shows that CWCs are common and predictable across administrative levels in Indonesia.

Finally, and perhaps most importantly, using our data on ethnic group religions in Chapter 2, we describe the ethno-religious landscape of the world cartographically and use the data to suggest answers to some additional puzzles in the literature that remain to be tested. Contrary to the conventional wisdom that envisions most ethnic groups as religious monoliths, A-Religion data illustrate that many ethnic groups are religious pluralists. Furthermore, far more ethnic groups share religion in part or entirely than might be assumed. One of the principal empirical contributions of the book, therefore, includes a more accurate empirical illustration of the complex tapestry of ethnicity and religion in the world.

1.5 ARGUMENTS OUTSIDE THE SCOPE OF THIS BOOK

1.5.1 The Onset or Success of Collective Mobilization

The objective of this project is to contribute to the theoretical explanation of why among multiple contenders a given identity is mobilized in contentious politics. Empirically, the aim is to scrutinize why religion and ethnicity are variously mobilized. However, this book does not purport to explain the onset or success of such mobilization.

Let us first think about onset as discussed by Lichbach (1994, 1998) in the context of rebellion, a particularly difficult type of mobilization onset. To paraphrase Mark Lichbach, in a response to Olson (1971), the literature has spent an extraordinary effort on solving the problem of collective action onset. As a consequence, there demonstrably exist at least some two dozen, highly context-dependent, solutions to collective rebellion, though any single solution likely explains only a part of the story. At the same time, the precise timing of the onset of aggregate dissent and particular outbreaks remains unpredictable because of the inevitable randomness of history.[33] Lichbach (1994: 31) continues to note that, therefore, the interesting challenges that remain are not further solutions to the question of collective action onset but, in contrast, include asking "Why?" certain solutions are adopted as "Why" questions "involve us in the politics of collective dissent."

In line with Lichbach's observations, this project does not ask how collective mobilization occurs. Taking our cue from Hirschman (1970), we assume that when groups sharing an identity lack voice, an opportunity for mobilization presents itself. Instead, we ask *why* mobilizing groups sometimes mobilize ethnicity and other times mobilize religion. This project suggests a general argument to answer this question: group-relative sizes interact with cleavage configurations to make certain types of identity mobilizations more or less likely. It then hones in on one specific type of mobilization strategy, the CWC, where large excluded ethnic minorities that share a religion see in the shared identity an opportunity for alternate identity mobilization.

Turning our attention next to success, this book does not purport to explain the success of a given type of identity mobilization. We assume the objective of mobilization is to increase access to state spoils. How increased access manifests is, however, context dependent and can take many different forms. For example, in an electoral context the election of a group's representative may be a descriptive measure of success. The passing of group-related policies as promoted by the representative may be a substantive measure of success. Distribution of clientelistic rewards by the elected representative to members of the supporting group is another possible measure of success. Similarly, in a conflict setting, there are many possible measures of success. Success might, for instance, mean that the group assumes political control of the state; thus, the identity, that is the catalyst of the mobilization, finds better representation in existing governing structures, and/or direct distribution of resources to the group is improved, and/or the state makes other concessions that benefit the group, and so on. Overall, this project does not attempt to measure success of mobilization and acknowledges that there is a wide range of possible success and failure outcomes associated with identity mobilization across politics. This topic remains a wide-open area for study.

1.5.2 Identity Groups' Pursuit of Peaceful versus Violent Strategies in Political Contestation

Scholars have long wondered what factors influence identity group choice between violent and non-violent transgressive political strategies. For example, Gurr's (1993) analysis suggests that divergent types of group grievances are

---

[33] Relying also on authors' recent conversations with Mark Lichbach.

differentially related to group choice to use violence or non-violent transgressive strategies. In a recent contribution to this literature, Vogt (2019) suggests that historically defined between-group hierarchization and integration condition the transgressive mobilization strategies selected by groups.[34] Scholars have also considered separately the effect of non-violent transgressive political strategies (Stephan and Chenoweth, 2008) on, for example, success of the civil rights movement (McAdam and Tarrow, 2000), and minority claims to autonomy (Shaykhutdinov, 2010).[35]

An equally large literature considers identity-related choice between contained and transgressive strategies (Horowitz, 1985; Birnir, 2007),[36] especially as these choices relate to divergent institutional configurations (Lijphart, 1977, 1984; Horowitz, 1985, 1990; Sisk, 1996; Selway and Templeman, 2012). For example, Fjelde and Höglund (2014) argue that violence is more likely in countries with large excluded ethno-political groups that employ majoritarian institutions because sizeable electoral constituencies represent threats to the incumbent party. Thus, in their account groups' choice to stay with contained political contestation or employ trangressive strategies of political violence is motivated by the interaction of identity, group size, and institutional configuration.

Our argument does not address identity group choice between contained or transgressive political strategies such as elections or rebellion, respectively. Nor do we purport to explain identity group choices between different transgressive political strategies such as peaceful protest and violent rebellion. In contrast, we explore the demographic incentive structures for mobilizing a given identity, ethnicity, or religion, in particular, holding the choice of strategy (transgressive or contained, or within the transgressive set, peaceful or violent) constant, to the extent that this is empirically possible.

1.5.3 What's in a Name? Religion or Religion, and Religion or Ethnicity

As previously noted, in this book, we follow social identity theory (Tajfel, 1978; Tajfel and Turner, 1979) in that for purposes of mobilization we treat

---

[34] For additional grievance-based explanations of group violent transgressive political strategies see, for example, Horowitz (1985); Wimmer (1997); Stewart (2008); Cederman et al. (2013).

[35] The literature on non-violent transgressive strategies that do not focus exclusively on identity groups is burgeoning. For instance, Stephan and Chenoweth (2008) show non-violent strategies win participants legitimacy and widespread support, while neutralizing the opposing security forces. They argue that in contrast violent campaigns are supported by few and serve to justify violent counter-attacks, among other things see also Schock (2005); Sharp et al. (2005); Chenoweth and Stephan (2011); Chenoweth (2020).

[36] For a recent piece on public approval of transgressive versus contained choices among different types of rebel groups, see Arves et al. (2019).

ethnicity and religion as if they were comparable identities A and B with respect to content. This bears some clarification. First, within the category of ethnicity the idea that divergent ethnic groups are more or less equivalently suited for mobilization is currently not a contested assumption.[37] Furthermore, the available evidence suggests that with respect to mobilization within the category of religions this assumption is warranted. For example, according to Young (1976), all religions potentially serve to provide the individual with continuous reaffirmation of membership while at the same time demarcating the group. Similarly, symbols across religions provide the basis for shared emotional reactions to real and imagined external threats, and call for defense of the faith as sanctioned by the divine (Jelen, 1993; Seul, 1999; Juergensmeyer, 2003). Furthermore, while the research shows organizational capacities of religious institutions matter for political mobilization (Kalyvas, 1996, 2000), it is less clear that such differences distinguish between mobilization across doctrines (Koopmans and Statham, 1999; Koopmans, 2004; Pfaff and Gill, 2006; Fox, 2006; Birnir and Overos, 2019). Consequently, with respect to mobilization we have no reason to believe that one religion differs qualitatively from the next in its capacity to unify members and mobilize them.

Second, and in contrast, emerging literature also contends that with respect to many political outcomes ethnicity and religion may differ substantively from each other. For instance, Brubaker (2015) finds that religiously-based, substantive regulation of public life is distinct. Similarly, McCauley (2014, 2017) argues that political entrepreneurs evoke religion for support of policy issues that differ from issues for which they seek ethnic support. Gerring et al. (2018) posit that while ethno-linguistic diversity increases the prospects of democracy, religious diversity decreases them.

The evidence which shows that each identity evokes distinct political preferences is persuasive and we acknowledge that future research will likely better delineate how ethnicity and religion are distinct. At the same time, we do not believe the evidence suggests one identity engenders political mobilization while the other does not. Rather the differences are possibly in the types of mobilization, such as contained or transgressive, for which each identity is best suited. Consequently, for the sake of simplicity, we feel justified in theoretically treating ethnicity and religion as if they were content comparable for mobilization. However, our empirical chapters also separate examination of different types of mobilization (transgressive, contained) to ensure that we are comparing apples to apples.

---

[37] To be clear, certain ethnic groups may lend themselves more easily to identification by in-and-out group members, or to mobilization for exogenous reasons such as resources. However, aside from such logistical issues the literature currently does not debate endogenous motivators of mobilization between ethnic groups in a way that it does with respect to religions.

1.5.4 A Panacea for Explaining Ethnic and Religious Mobilization

Finally, demography is by no means a panacea for explaining all identity mobilization. To the contrary, mobilization especially violent mobilization depends on a multitude of factors other than demography, including identity salience (Isaacs, 2017), group geographic concentration (Toft, 2002, 2003), repression (Davenport, 2014; Nordas, 2014b, 2015),[38] governments' regulatory involvement (Fox, 2008, 2015, 2016, 2020) or the decision to withhold protection from a population (Wilkinson, 2004), the institutional environment (Posner, 2005, 2017), and triggering events (Mecham, 2017) to name but some of the relevant factors.

This is especially pertinent with respect to the simplifying assumptions that are made such as the idea that ethnic and religious identities are equivalently suited for mobilization. In reality, identity cleavages likely have divergent features and levels of salience that may change over time in a given context and impact how demographic size contributes to political outcomes.[39] The case study chapters (Chapters 5 and 6) cast some light on the results of relaxing these simplifying assumptions and reveal that this is probably an especially fruitful venue for further study. At the same time, the focus of this book on the demographics of intersecting identities is an important stepping stone to research that more comprehensively accounts for all the factors that jointly influence identity mobilization. Moreover, this work makes a theoretical contribution to the consideration of identity mobilization as a dynamic process, which may begin with segmented cleavages and the MWC, but continues with overlapping identities of demographically balanced groups and the CWC.

1.6 OUTLINE OF THE BOOK

Following this chapter, Chapter 2 discusses the cross-national data set, A-Religion, coded for the book and uses this data set to speculate about the answers to some common identity puzzles in the literature. Chapter 3 is the main theory chapter, outlining the theory of *Alternatives in Mobilization* with an emphasis on the implication of the *Challenger's Winning Coalition (CWC)*. Chapter 4 tests the CWC hypothesis across civil conflicts, while Chapter 5 probes the mechanisms of the logic by way of four case narratives. Chapter 6 examines the CWC in Indonesia's electoral politics and Chapter 7 concludes. We recount the content of each chapter in some more detail below.

The principal objective of Chapter 2 is to outline a more nuanced view of the complex ethno-religious tapestry of the world made possible by the collection of the A-Religion data set, completed for this project. Thus the chapter describes the distinctly different account of the world that emerged during the coding of

---

[38] For a cross-national overview of repression of religion specifically, see Sarkissian (2015).
[39] Chapter 3 addresses the importance of changing social salience of identity.

the religions of the 1202 AMAR data groups. Each ethnic group was coded for every religious family and sect that is adhered to by at least 10 percent of the group's population. Among other things, these data show that many ethnic groups are far from being religious monoliths. For example, among non-politically dominant ethnic minorities, nearly a third are split between religious families. This includes such disparate groups as the indigenous in Guatemala, many of whom mix Animism with Christianity to varying degrees,[40] and in the United Kingdom the Chinese, some of whom are Buddhist while others are Christian, with a sizeable proportion of the group declaring no adherence to any religion. Similarly, in Indonesia the Ambonese are split between Christianity and Islam, and in Sri Lanka most Tamils are Hindu but some are Christian. The data also code within country the context of religious overlap between every political minority and majority. Interestingly, nearly half of all ethnic minorities overlap partly or fully with the religious family of the political majority in their country. Similarly, many minorities are split between religious sects and several overlap in part or fully with the religious sect of their respective majority. Majorities in turn are themselves sometimes split between religious families and sects, though this is less common. Because pictures often are worth a thousand words, the chapter describes this complex ethno-religious tapestry cartographically and ponders the theoretical implications.

Chapter 3 formalizes the theory of *Alternatives in Mobilization*. Considering the complex picture of ethnic and religious cleavages presented in Chapter 2, this chapter asks how divergent cleavage configurations structure political competition. It suggests that while extremely useful and informative, the literatures on cross-cutting (shared) cleavages and the MWC only scratch the surface of how identity is mobilized in contentious politics. The chapter further argues that demographics interact with divergent cleavage configurations to change incentive structures for mobilization in multiple additional, and, heretofore, unexplored ways. Next, it formally considers some prominent variations induced by demographics and articulates some of the multiple implications for both segmented groups that differ in ethnicity and religion, and for groups that share religion across ethnicity. In particular, the chapter highlights the testable implication of the CWC, that when a large ethnic political minority shares a religious identity with the ethnic majority, that minority can potentially mobilize co-religionists to form a CWC capable of challenging the state. In conclusion, the chapter explains how institutions interact with the testable implications of identity mobilization, setting the stage for the empirical exploration in the remainder of the book.

The remainder of the book endeavors to probe the external and internal validity of the CWC implication across transgressive and contained political settings. To this end, Chapter 4 specifies and tests cross-nationally a group-level implication of CWC in civil war. This implication pinpoints that in ethnic

---

[40] In our coding we also account for syncretic belief systems.

civil war within a country, minority mobilization of religious identity is more likely if the ethnic majority and minority that share a religion are closer to numerical parity. The test of this implication relies on the demographic data in the AMAR data coded for religion through the A-Religion data set, as described earlier in this chapter in conjunction with the RELAC data on religious claim-making, coded by Svensson and Nilsson (2018), of organizations in civil war as recorded in the Uppsala Conflict Data Program's (UCDP) data on internal conflicts that reach a yearly battle-death threshold of 25. The chapter introduces and describes the A-Religion data in detail and the methods used to test this implication, and consequently interprets the results of the analysis. The analysis shows strong support for the testable hypothesis. Increasing size of large ethnic minorities that share a religion with the majority has a significant and positive effect on the likelihood of religious claim-making in civil war. This result is consistent, across multiple model specifications, and while controlling for previously cited factors of rebellion and intra-state ethnic conflict provided by the literature.

Whereas Chapter 4 examines the external validity of the theory by testing the proposed relationship across cases in which the outcome (religious claim-making) did and did not happen, Chapter 5 delves further into the internal validity of the proposed mechanisms. The chapter achieves this by way of case narratives that "[examine] in detail how ethnic mobilization happened in order to determine whether the mechanisms suggested by [the theory] actually happened" (Kaufman, 2001: 460). Qualitative case analyses generally do not provide a crisp identification strategy but they do allow for a deeper examination of the internal validity of the theory (Laitin, 2002; George and Bennett, 2005). To this end, we stratified by doctrine[41] all cases where religious claims have been made and selected three cases (Pakistan, Uganda, and Nepal)[42] to examine the proposed mechanisms. Additionally, to vary the dependent variable, we examined one case where, according to the RELAC data, religious claims were not made despite the presence of a large minority that shares religion with the majority. Using a variety of primary and secondary sources, including field research in Turkey, in a focused and structured comparison, we then interrogated these cases to ascertain whether the story as it unfolds across the cases is consistent with the theory proposed. What we found was largely

---

[41] We made the choice to stratify by doctrine because of the attention doctrine has received in the conflict literature. To be clear, the empirical evidence by and large does not support the idea that doctrinal differences associated with religion cause violence in civil war (Fox, 2004b). However, because of the emphasis in the literature and because we frequently get asked this question when presenting this work, it is important to investigate this issue empirically by examining the process we propose across doctrines.

[42] Turkey was selected as a convenience case because of authors' prior knowledge, the other cases were selected 'randomly' within Islam and Christianity. In only one Hindu case, Nepal, do minorities make religious claims. Neither of the authors had prior expertise of the remaining three cases, and so country experts were consulted after the narratives were constructed to support the case interpretation.

consistent with the CWC, but this chapter also provided many more insights. For example, multiple alternate identities, other than ethnicity and religion and including region and migrant status, play a role in violent mobilization that centers on religion and – contrary to common assumptions – mobilization sometimes aims to decrease the role of religion in public life. Cases "on" and "off" the dependent variable suggest the state plays an important role in creating space for the mobilization of religion. Furthermore, while there are sound empirical reasons for separately studying transgressive and contained political outcomes, the case of Turkey suggests that jointly considering outcomes across the political space enriches our understanding of group overall strategy for increasing access.

The final substantive Chapter 6, is an in-depth examination of the generalizability of the CWC argument to an electoral setting in Indonesia. In a similarly structured and focused comparison to Chapter 5, we examine ethnic majority/minority relations with an eye to detecting mobilization of shared religion in CWCs. There are two major differences between the case analysis in this chapter and in Chapter 5. First, the structural and institutional factors mitigating the likelihood of contestation by groups vary internally in Indonesia as we examine contestation at divergent levels of administration beginning with the national level and then going on to examine contestation at subnational levels. Second, whereas three out of the four cases in Chapter 5 were selected on the dependent variable to examine the internal validity of the theory, in Indonesia we did not know *a priori* whether and then how a CWC would manifest in electoral politics at a given level. Furthermore, politics in contained settings allow for a more clear juxtaposition of the predictions of the MWC and the CWC than is possible in transgressive political settings. The examination of this case is, however, similar to Chapter 5 in that at each administrative level we used primary sources from authors' field research in Indonesia along with a number of secondary sources, to interrogate the relevant cases as to whether the story as it unfolds across cases is consistent with the CWC argument proposed. This case demonstrates that the CWC is, indeed, useful for predicting minority challenger mobilization strategies in electoral politics. At the same time, as with the other cases examined, Indonesian electoral politics highlight the importance of context and alternate political cleavages, including migration.[43] This case also revealed a number of less expected insights such as how quickly majorities adopt successful minority mobilization strategies of oversized CWCs.

Chapter 7, in conclusion, underscores the key claim of the book that to understand which identity is mobilized in political contestation and how, it is necessary to consider the complex incentives created by underlying demographics – especially as they relate to the interaction of identity cleavages and

---

[43] See Braithwaite et al.'s (2019) introduction and the other articles in the special issue for the effect of migration in politics, particularly political conflict.

group-relative size. The chapter highlights the principal empirical findings of the book. In sum, the nuanced view presented in this book allows scholars to see beyond the segmentation of divergent ethnic groups that also hold different religious beliefs to discover the potential for contentious mobilization in other cleavage configurations, notably, between divergent ethnic groups that share religious beliefs. We explain and show why among large ethnic minority groups, sharing a religion with the majority increases the likelihood that religious identity is mobilized. This is an especially important finding in the context of our descriptive data, which present that minorities and majorities worldwide often share religions. The chapter also highlights that while the MWC is likely a good starting prediction for identity mobilization, it is far from a static state of affairs – even holding institutions constant. Conditional on demographics, political leaders excluded from the MWC pursue a variety of alternate identity mobilization strategies in an effort to unseat the status quo MWC. Throughout the book, the prevalence of one of those strategies, the CWC, is tested and shown to have substantial explanatory power. Speaking directly to the real-world implications of our findings, this chapter also emphasizes the paramount importance of context. Cleavage configurations and demographics set up incentives for minorities to engage in or abstain from political identity contestation. However, multiple intervening variables influence whether those incentives come to fruition. This book unearths several additional questions for future scholarship, and the chapter concludes with some thoughts about new research directions that draw on the insights of the inquiry presented.

2

Demography of Identity in Political Conflict

2.1 INTRODUCTION

The overall contribution of this project is to focus attention on how group relative size and intersection of identity cleavages incentivize minority mobilization of particular identities, all else being equal. As our case study chapters (Chapters 5 and 6) explore in greater detail, mobilization is not deterministic and depends on the confluence of domestic and at times international processes and catalysts. However, the theory of *Alternatives in Mobilization*, that will be outlined in Chapter 3, suggests that the likelihood of certain empirical regularities in mobilization increases as a result of varying demographics, including cleavage configurations and group relative size.

Underlying cleavage structures generally consist of multiple identities, some of which over time become, or are made, increasingly salient for mobilization.[1] The objective of this chapter is to convince the reader of the importance of scrutinizing these identity demographics. We also aim to illustrate that, even with the narrowing of our scope empirically to ethnicity and religion, and setting aside the possibly varying effect of cleavage content, substantial demographic variance remains unexplored. This variation potentially helps cast light on some important puzzles in the literature beyond those highlighted in Chapter 1. To make this case, in this chapter, we use data compiled by other scholars as well as the new data that we have collected on the religions of ethnic groups and the intersection of ethnic and religious identities to speculate about the effects of demographics on political mobilization. This exploration, in turn, sets the stage for subsequent theorizing in Chapter 3 about cleavage-based political competition as conditioned by cleavage intersection and relative group size.

---

[1] For an in-depth discussion of the differences between cleavage structure and socially salient identities, see Chandra and Wilkinson (2008); Birnir et al. (2015).

To motivate the exploration of the role that demographics play in identity mobilization, we begin with three questions. The first brings attention to measurement, and the next two are substantive. The first question simply asks what difference divergent types of demographic measurements make in assessing the political role of demography. The second question stems from the observation that ethno-religiously segmented groups are shown to be especially conflict prone (Selway, 2011b; Basedau et al., 2011, 2016). While the evidence supporting this observation is strong, the literature does not explain why there is conflict between religiously segmented groups in some countries but not in others. The third question builds on recent theories explaining the increasing over-representation of Islam in conflict. This body of work explains conflict involving Islam mostly in relation to history, geography, and structure (Toft, 2007, 2021; Nordas, 2014a).[2] Following this emphasis on structure, we ask whether and how demographic features of Muslim ethnic groups contribute to our understanding of over-representation of Islam in civil conflict.

The chapter begins by describing the complex religious tapestry of the world cartographically. Speculating next about the answers to the question about why religiously segmented groups engage each other in violence in only some countries, we explore a number of observations. For example, the data show that religious heterogeneity across the world is quite varied in both degree and content. Consequently, our explorations focus on two continents where violence involving divergent religions is increasingly prominent. Seeking answers to the first question about measurement and the second about the role of demographics in conflict mobilization, we examine demographic change over time in Africa and South Asia. The maps suggest that while proportional population changes help illustrate the spread of religion, it is the change in absolute numbers of religious adherents that drives home the observation about how demographics likely induce mobilization by segmented groups in some countries but not others.

Turning next to the question of over-representation of Islam in conflict, we suggest that more granular data accounting for the religions of ethnic groups are necessary to properly tackle this question. After explaining our coding of the A-Religion data, detailing religions in the All Minorities at Risk (AMAR) sample frame of 1202 ethnic groups, we use these data to discern the internal diversity and overlap between ethno-religious minority and majority groups. Through this exploration, it becomes very clear that most ethnic majorities and minorities are far from being religious monoliths but are split and/or share religions in all manner of ways. With respect to our inquiry of why Islam is over-represented in conflict, we suggest that the demographics of how cleavages intersect provide at least a partial resolution to this perplexing puzzle.

---

[2] For an overview of the debate about the role of religion in conflict, see Birnir and Overos (2019).

In addition to cleavage intersection, the final piece of the puzzle highlighted in this chapter concerns the role of group size in motivating mobilization. To set the stage for the exploration of this question, we rely on visual representation of the A-Religion data as geo-coded in the GeoAMAR[3] data. Presented in this way, the data show the regional variation in the contemporary ethno-religious landscape across the world. The distinct differences between regions are especially noticeable when taking group size into account. Consequently, it is unlikely that identity mobilization will necessarily take the same form everywhere. Furthermore, this illustration suggests that, with respect to a number of outcomes political scientists care about, including identity mobilization, the demographic variation in group size and cleavage configurations is a fruitful venue for study in the remainder of this book and beyond.

2.2 DEMOGRAPHICS AND POLITICAL VIOLENCE BETWEEN RELIGIOUSLY SEGMENTED GROUPS

Mobilization for inter-religious conflict is increasingly common (Toft et al., 2011; Fox, 2013; Toft, 2021), especially where religious divide coincides with ethnic segmentation (Basedau et al., 2011). However, the reasons for why inter-religious conflict breaks out in some religiously heterogeneous countries and not in others are not fully understood. The literature suggests that, in part, our lack of understanding stems from too narrow of a scholarly focus on one religion or another, which does not account for the interaction between religions. For example, in Africa, while "the study of both Islam and Christianity is thriving ... these fields exist more or less independently from each other" (Janson and Meyer, 2016: 615). Consequently, Janson and Meyer (2016) renew Soares's (2006) call for a framework that allows for integrated study of the interactions of Islam and Christianity.

Pursuing the idea that better understanding of the interaction of religious groups is important, this chapter explores whether the demographics of those groups help us explicate why inter-religious conflict breaks out in some religiously heterogeneous countries but not in others. To explore this puzzle, we turn to the multiple available data sets that depict the size of distinct religious groups within countries across the globe (Hackett and Stonawski, 2017; Brown and James, 2018).[4] Using Brown and James's (2018) data,[5] we built the maps in

---

3 For further information on GeoAMAR, see Birnir and Coronado-Castellanos (n.d.).
4 For more, see the Association of the Religion Data Archives at www.thearda.com/.
5 Brown and James's (2018) selection criterion for inclusion is that the country be an independent state included in either the Correlates of War data (see www.correlatesofwar.org) or the Polity Project data (see www.systemicpeace.org/polityproject.html). For a dependency or sub-state entity, the inclusion criterion is that the entity has a UN code or that its inclusion be necessary to complete coverage of another state or a multi-state region. Thus, very small islands like Aruba are excluded.

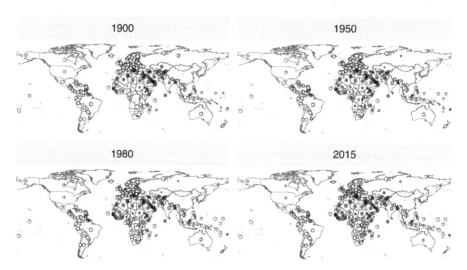

FIGURE 2.1. The change over time in proportion of a country's population belonging to any of the three most populous religious families (Christianity, Islam, and Hinduism) in the world

Figure 2.1 to illustrate the proportional size of religious groups within countries worldwide.[6] The radius of each circle corresponds to the proportions of the national populations that adhere to Christianity (white), Islam (black), and Hinduism (gray) by country. The panels, thus, depict the religious landscape of the world by proportion of national populations belonging to each religion in 1900, 1950, 1980, and 2015, respectively.

The comparison across panels in Figure 2.1 uncovers a couple of different phenomena. First, there is substantial variance in religion across the world, with Christianity predominating in the Americas and Western Europe, whereas Islam is more common in the Middle East and North Africa, and Hinduism in South Asia. Furthermore, the maps show that the national proportion of the populations adhering to the three main religions of the world has changed substantially in the last century. Christianity still predominates in Europe and North America, and Islam is still a more common religion in the Middle East and North Africa, but now Christianity commands a greater share of national populations. Another obvious change is the territorial spread of Christianity across sub-Saharan Africa. This variance in religious heterogeneity and content suggests that a closer look by continent is helpful. Therefore, we first examine Africa followed by South Asia, where much violence related to religion has occurred.

---

[6] To create the maps, we used Natural Earth data (see www.naturalearthdata.com) as available in R. We recovered each country polygon's centroid and plotted James and Brown's population data onto the centroid longitudes and latitudes using ggplot2.

2.2.1 Africa

Janson and Meyer (2016: 615) emphasize that much work remains before we understand the current interaction of religions, and rightfully so. At the same time, detailed historical accounts by Africanists (Voll, 2006; Nolte et al., 2016) of the interaction between Christianity and Islam on the continent help explain the role of demographics in the nature and timing of religious recruitment.[7] These accounts also elucidate why we see inter-religious conflicts in some parts of Africa and their absence in other parts over time. Furthermore, the analytic case histories highlight the great diversity in the expression of both Christianity and Islam in Africa, as each tradition integrated with local customs results in encounters that vary greatly depending on time and space. Thus, throughout modern history the interactions of the two religions were both "constructive and competitive" as each community "worked to win adherents" (Voll, 2006: 21).[8]

Explaining the political determinants of how Christianity spread on the continent, John Voll, for example, recounts that colonial rulers who feared that Christian missionaries would stir local resentment sometimes restricted missionary activity by territory.[9] Consequently, the Christian missionary activity on the continent "resulted in the conversion of virtually no Muslim but it did convert many from indigenous religious traditions" (Voll, 2006: 30–32). Later, the "Africanization" of Christianity[10] augmented the number of conversions while transnational Pentecostal and Evangelical institutions took greater hold at the expense of more traditional Catholic institutions.[11] In this environment, Voll (2006: 37) observes the development of "a strong sense of competition and potential open conflict among both activist Muslims and Christians in Africa." Voll's account, thus, elucidates how and why

---

7 For a discussion of the dearth of quantitative data on this topic, see Nolte et al. (2016).

8 In brief, Voll suggests that early conflict between adherents of Christianity and Islam seemingly resulted from expansion and consolidation of territory in what is modern-day Ethiopia. In contrast, encounters between adherents of the two religions in the early modern era were, to some extent, defined by the political economy of the slave trade. These were not necessarily characterized by religion, as some Islamic rulers collaborated with their European Christian counterparts in the trade, while in the Senegal Valley, Islamic political operatives consolidated and mobilized forces in response to this practice. Later encounters assumed the power asymmetry between Christian European colonial rulers and local Muslim Africans. In this context and setting the tone for the future, Islam at times became the unifying symbol – though not necessarily a very effective one – for resistance (Voll, 2006: 25–29).

9 For instance, North and South Sudan were divided up, and missionary activity was only allowed in the south.

10 Voll explains that the "Africanization" of Christianity resulted from expulsion of foreign missionaries during the years of struggles for independence when Christianity remained identified with the colonial powers, while Islam was more often identified with the establishment of the nation state.

11 For an account of the spread of Protestantism in Latin America and concomitant social changes, see, for example, Gill (2004).

inter-religious political competition between Christianity and Islam developed on the continent as political and demographic conditions changed from colonialism to independence.

What Voll's historical account does not fully explain is the recent global increase in religious conflict (Toft et al., 2011; Fox, 2013), including that in some African countries but not others. Following up on the idea that population changes affect the likelihood of political conflict (Weiner and Teitelbaum, 2001; Goldstone et al., 2011), we ask whether demographic changes can further inform recent intensification of conflicts involving religion in Africa. Figure 2.2 pulls out the African continent to further examine religious demographic changes. On the whole, the panels in Figures 2.1 and 2.2 clearly show that,

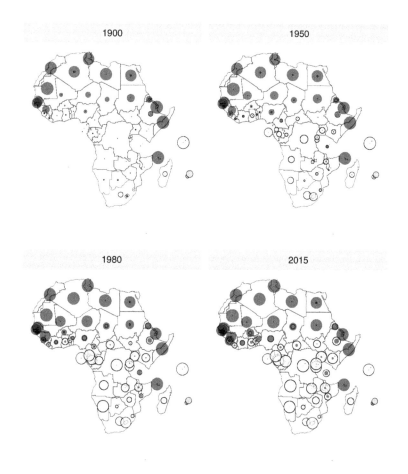

FIGURE 2.2. The change over time in proportion of a country's population belonging to any of the three most populous religious families (Christianity (white), Islam (black), and Hinduism (gray)) in Africa

in the last century, predominantly Muslim (population depicted with black circles) countries in Africa have become sandwiched between Christian Europe and increasingly Christian (population depicted with white circles or, where eclipsed by a larger Muslim population, with dark circles), south-western sub-Saharan Africa.

However, the reader will recall that the first question asked in this chapter was whether varying demographic measures help our understanding of political dynamics including mobilization. If so, then the national *proportion* of populations belonging to each of these religions reveals only one part of the story. A complementary view emerges in Figure 2.3 when considering the change in

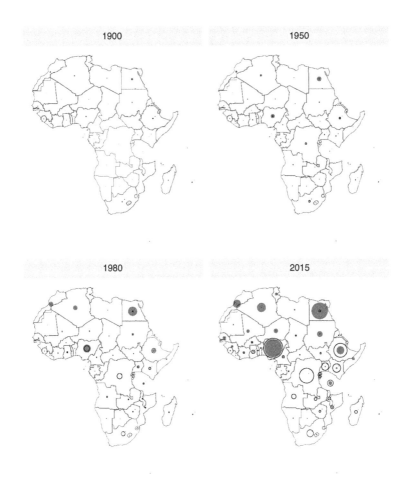

FIGURE 2.3. The change over time in absolute numbers of people belonging to any of the three most populous religious families (Christianity, Islam, and Hinduism) in Africa

the *absolute* numbers of people belonging to each religion, Christianity and Islam, in Africa. The panels again use increasingly large circles to indicate increasingly large populations. In this instance, however, rather than depicting the proportion of a country's population, the increase in size illustrates the change in the absolute numbers of people.[12] Similarly to the earlier figures, the first panel depicts numbers belonging to each religion first in 1900, second in 1950, third in 1980, and finally in 2015. Unlike the prior figures, we increased the transparency of the colors in Figure 2.3 to better show populations of both religions in countries where they co-exist. Thus, on the African continent the white circle shows an exclusively Christian population and the black circle demonstrates a Muslim population. A white circle containing a dark circle or visa versa a dark circle containing a white one, indicates that the population is split between religions as specified by the size of each circle.[13]

Figure 2.3 demonstrates a few interesting findings. First, religious demographics in Africa have changed very rapidly in recent decades, with adherents of Islam and Christianity rapidly growing. Second, on the border where the two religions split the continent, there are countries where population growth of both religions has been quite expansive – at least before these countries split. For instance, according to Brown and James (2018), the number of Christians in Nigeria grew from 93,906 in 1900 to 89,734,222 in 2015 while the number of Muslims grew from 4,200,000 to 79,737,210. In turn, in what is currently Sudan, the number of Muslims grew from 3,390,000 in 1900 to 24,330,380 in 2015, whereas the Christian population grew from 38,639 in 1900 to 1,363,651 in 2015. The opposite is true in what is currently South Sudan, where the number of Christians grew from 105 in 1900 to 7,146,486 in 2015, whereas the increase in the Muslim population was more modest, going from 87,672 in 1900 to 548,432 in 2015.

Importantly, Nigeria and Sudan/South Sudan are also countries where extremely violent conflicts involving religion have occurred, including the conflict after which Sudan and South Sudan split. Indeed, on our 2015 map, all of the countries in Africa that, according to Soares (2006: 1), have recently experienced conflict where "religion seems to have been a factor," show a large black circle encircled by an even larger white circle. Thus all of these countries now have large Christian and Muslim populations, and all are on

---

[12] The absolute number of people is, arbitrarily but consistently across groups, multiplied by $1.0E-8$ for each religious group. The reason this transformation was chosen – as opposed to log or some other transformation – is that it visually communicates in absolute numbers the drastic change in population size across Africa, in ways that can be compared directly to population sizes depicted for Asia in Figure 2.4.

[13] In addition, rather than mapping both religions right on the country's longitudinal and latitudinal centroid, we offset the circles symmetrically to better depict the size of each population. While all figures are in grayscale throughout the book, color-coded versions can be found at www.johannabirnir.com.

the border between majority Muslim and majority Christian parts of the continent.[14] Seemingly, therefore, the spread of Christianity in Africa and the increasing numbers of both Christians and Muslims in countries straddling the religious border suggest that, over time, more members of the two groups compete over the same resources. Therefore, the timing, increased frequency, and locations of conflicts between religious groups are not surprising, as religion historically defines at least some of the boundaries of inter-group competition as explained by Voll (2006). This is perhaps especially evident in countries where resources are scarce, in part because of high population growth and globally lower income.

2.2.2 South and South-east Asia

The content of religious heterogeneity (i.e. which religions are most common in a given region and within a given country) varies greatly across the globe. To examine whether similar demographic patterns are evident in other parts of the world where other religions predominate, we next turn the demographic lens on South and South-east Asia (including India, Pakistan, and Bangladesh). Demographic changes in this region provide another example of how, over time, changes in complex religious demographics resulting in part from political events have likely affected the location and timing of political mobilization of religious identities. Demographic changes in this part of the world may also help explain why the target populations are more receptive to the message of religious identity mobilization in certain places and at certain times.

Learning from Section 2.2.1 that absolute numbers are more informative in this context than are proportional numbers, Figure 2.4 shows the changes in absolute size of Christian, Muslim, and Hindu populations in this region. As in Figure 2.3, the panels in Figure 2.4 use increasingly large circles to indicate increasingly large populations, measured as the absolute number of people. Also similar to the earlier figures, the panels depict numbers belonging to each religion first in 1900, second in 1950, third in 1980, and finally in 2015.

The panels draw our attention to several demographic facts. First is the population explosion in the number of Hindus, primarily in India. According to Brown and James (2018), in 1900 the population of Hindus in India was 208,745,075, whereas in 2015 this population had increased to 1,004,491,268. Second is the great surge in the number of Muslims. In 1900 Muslims numbered 62,406,248 in India. After the territory was split into India and Pakistan, the

---

[14] Similarly, in the Ivory Coast between 1900 and 2015, the numbers of Christians rose from 700 to 8,112,133 and of Muslims from 50,000 to 8,952,187. In Kenya the numbers of Christians rose from 5000 to 38,126,051 and of Muslims from 100,000 to 6,901,153 between 1900 and 2015. Finally in Tanzania the numbers of Christians went from 89,864 to 28,792,270 and Muslims from 93,020 to 15,499,785 between 1900 and 2015.

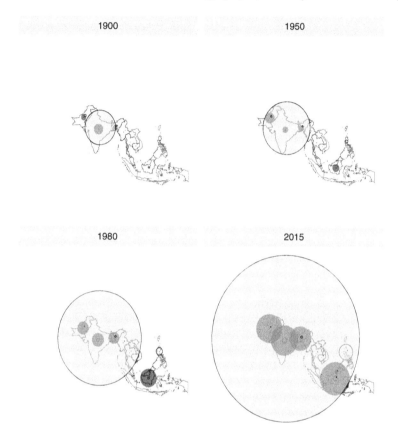

FIGURE 2.4. The change over time in absolute numbers of people belonging to
any of the three most populous religious families (Christianity (white), Islam (black),
Hinduism (gray)) in South-east Asia (including also India, Pakistan, and Bangladesh)

number of Muslims in India declined to 37,037,350 by 1950. However, by 2015
the number of Muslims in India had risen again to count 181,294,667 people.

To compare, the number of Christians in the United States in 2015 was
220,753,356 and Muslims in Indonesia numbered 201,961,620, while the
number of Christians in Indonesia stood at 26,335,283. On average, we
would expect the frequency of contention in competition among mobilized
identity groups over resources to increase as the populations sharing a territory
grow, especially where resources are scarce. Therefore, it is hardly surprising
that clashes between Hindus and Muslims are today again a prominent
feature of sub-national conflict in South Asia. This is especially true for India,
where the demographic contribution to the conflict is exogenous to doctrine
but likely associated with opportunistic mobilization of identity in political
competition.

In this way, national-level demographic data help clarify the context and broad changes over time and how these may contribute to changing global trends in political contestation between regions and countries. National-level data can also reveal some nuance in the way that identity groups intersect with each other and diverse cleavage types over time. Specifically, with respect to the questions posited, different types of demographic measures are clearly more or less appropriate for divergent analyses. Furthermore, demographic changes – especially explosive population growth in countries with groups that historically are segmented by religion – likely contribute to the explanation of where conflict involving religion is more likely to occur.

2.3 THE DATA: ETHNICITY, RELIGION, AND POLITICAL CONFLICT

National-level data clarify variation between countries or within a country over time, but cannot give the reason for variation within countries at a given point in time. For instance, there is significant sub-national variation in the seemingly religious conflict between Hindus and Muslims in India that national-level demographic changes cannot account for. However, using sub-national-level data, Varshney (2002) explains that at least some of the differences in the number and severity of conflicts between Hindus and Muslims across Indian communities result from variation in the presence of inter-communal civic associations across the country.

Similarly, the literature points out that there is significant variance in religious group representation in civil conflict. Specifically, Islamists are over-represented in civil war, arguably for reasons including overlapping historical, geographical, and structural factors (Toft, 2007, 2021; Nordas, 2014a). The third question asked at the outset of this chapter was whether demographics can further elucidate the over-representation of Islamists in civil conflict vis-à-vis other religious groups. Specifically, we are interested in investigating whether, at the sub-national level, group demographic structures vary in a way that may help elucidate Islamist over-representation in civil war.[15]

Voll's (2006) account certainly suggests that, across the African continent, there is a great deal of under-explored demographic complexity within each religious tradition in how Christianity, Islam, and Animism are segmented and/or shared. For example, he recounts how – for political reasons – Christianity remained segmented from Islam but integrated with native religions. This integration, in turn, paved the way for increasing intra-religious competition centering on Pentecostal and Evangelical conversions. Thus, Voll's story also shows that the internal religious diversity of ethnic groups in Africa likely

---

[15] Indeed, addressing questions about sub-national-level group propensities is, according to Birnir et al. (2018), not just reasonable also but necessary, because contradictory associations between heterogeneity and political outcomes can be found at the national level and group propensity and political outcome at the sub-national level, and both may be true at the same time.

varies between faith traditions, with more ethnic groups being split between Christianity and Animism, some adhering to syncretic versions of the two faiths, and a number of different denominations. In turn, if religion facilitates conflict recruitment and cleavage cross-cutting reduces political contention on average, as discussed in Chapter 1, internal group diversity has potentially important implications for conflict. The following sub-sections examine whether differences in internal demographic diversity of ethno-religious groups possibly explain some of the over-representation of Islam in civil conflict.

2.3.1 Existing Group-Level Data

Any dearth of inquiry into the political consequences of internal group diversity at the intersection of ethnicity and faith does not stem from a lack of data. Marquardt and Herrera's (2015) excellent review of prominent cross-national data on ethnicity discusses the breadth and complexity of current collections of ethnic group data.[16] However, they also highlight a recurring problem in the collection of data on ethnic groups, which is the endogenous selection of groups into data intended to explain political outcomes. Recent data – whose inclusion criteria center on including only "politically relevant groups" – constitute a significant step forward in the analysis of outcome variation between politically relevant groups (Posner, 2004; Wimmer et al., 2009).[17] However, as pointed out by Marquardt and Herrera (2015), this approach does not solve the concern about endogeneity of group selection to every outcome of interest. In other words, the problem regarding selection of groups into the data may be related to the outcome that the data are used to explain when the universe of relevant cases includes groups that are not "politically relevant" as defined by the Ethnic Power Relations (EPR) project (Hug, 2013; Marquardt and Herrera, 2015). Thus, the data on politically relevant groups can only be used to explain differences in relative propensity and trajectories among those groups. However, the sample of politically relevant groups cannot be used to explain, for instance, overall group propensity for violence, because the comparison set of groups that are not politically relevant according to the EPR data – but are

---

[16] Some of the difficulty in collecting data on ethnic groups highlighted by Marquardt and Herrera (2015) includes the inevitable incompleteness of any data on ethnic groups (see also Chandra and Wilkinson, 2008; Birnir et al., 2015), and inconsistency in the boundaries of ethnic markers across time, space, and levels of analysis. In addition to the complexities in measuring the concept discussed by Marquardt and Herrera, data based on particular markers are often a politically charged subject (Farkas, 2017), complicating the consistency of data collection efforts. For a critical review of the ontological debates over the nature of ethnicity, see, for example, Brown and Langer (2010).

[17] Since it was first created, the EPR data have released a number of versions, each time adding or deleting groups and linking to other useful data sets. For full information about the data, and the definition of "politically relevant," see https://icr.ethz.ch/data/epr/.

politically relevant in the sense that they constitute the unmobilized comparison group – is missing. Furthermore, a crucial feature of politically relevant groups may be a higher propensity to engage in violence (i.e. groups come to be defined as politically relevant for having engaged in the outcome to be explained).

Responding specifically to this concern about endogenous selection of the group list, a team of scholars constructed the AMAR data (Birnir et al., 2015).[18] The AMAR data consist of the AMAR sample frame of socially relevant groups, which currently includes 1202 groups over a certain population threshold and at a certain level of aggregation (Birnir et al., 2015), in addition to the AMAR sample data (Birnir et al., 2018).

The AMAR data code only group ethnicity and do not contain detailed information on faith. However, the religions of a given subset of ethnic groups are coded globally or in a given region in multiple other data sets. For example, nearly a decade ago, Akbaba and Fox (2011) began to compile information on the religions of groups in the Minorities at Risk (MAR) data.[19] Their data have expanded over the years to include additional groups and information about those groups (Fox, 2016). As another example, Basedau et al.'s (2011, 2016) data code ethnic groups for religion in a regional subsample (see also Basedau et al., 2017, 2019). For their analysis of the effects of religion among segmented groups that differ in both ethnicity and religion, they created a country-level index of religious diversity. Other scholars have constructed and examined national-level indicators of shared cultural characteristics, including religion (Selway, 2011a).

A recent data contribution by Toft (2021) describes key trends in religious civil war and tests whether Muslim or Arab Muslim groups are more likely candidates for religious conflict. In other studies of civil war, authors code the religion of conflict participants (Lindberg, 2008; Svensson, 2007; Svensson and Nilsson, 2018) but not necessarily their ethnicity – and not the internal demographic diversity within the faith of conflict participants. Even so, others have coded the ethnicity of these same participants defined by conflict (Forsberg, 2005, 2014; Vogt et al., 2015).[20] In sum, substantial information about subsets of ethnic groups and religions already exists, but we have not come across

---

[18] This does not mean that the issue of endogenous manifestation of identity is resolved in any absolute way. It does, however, mean that the identity recorded by the AMAR data is not systematically endogenous to particular national-level political outcomes. Identity is still likely endogenous to country-specific historical processes – but these vary between countries. For further information on the AMAR data, see amar.umd.edu.

[19] The genesis of the data about religions of MAR groups dates back even further to Fox's dissertation work at the University of Maryland under the supervision of Ted Gurr.

[20] One set of scholars (Bormann et al., 2017) use the Joshua Project's religious accounting in their assessment of the relative importance of language versus religious cleavages on conflict between ethnic groups. We do not use the Joshua Project data unless we can verify their coding for reasons discussed later in this chapter.

any global data of ethnic groups (including both groups that are and are not politically relevant), which also consider the internal diversity of faiths.[21]

2.3.2 The AMAR and A-Religion Data

To fill this gap in the empirical literature, we coded the entire AMAR sample frame of 1202 ethnic groups for religious family and sect in our A-Religion data. Collecting data on the universe of cases in a way that is unrelated to the outcome of interest is important for inference as discussed above. Collecting data on the universe of cases is also important for descriptive analysis because, for example, sub-sections of the data may differ in systematic ways. Therefore, in describing the ethno-religious landscape of the world, the AMAR data frame coded for religion in the A-Religion data is an appropriate set of cases for our purposes in this chapter.

However, as highlighted by Marquardt and Herrera (2015) and discussed further in Chapter 3, the group identities that matter for national political competition are not necessarily the same as the group identities that matter for regional-level competition.[22] Therefore, it is important to clarify the level of analysis and the use of pertinent data at each level. Specifically, the AMAR data are defined as nationally "socially relevant groups," and are intended for analysis of national-level group politics within or across countries. In contrast, the theory developed in this book likely has testable implications at various administrative levels of analysis. Therefore, we use national-level demographic data to explore national-level demographics in this chapter. However, the variation that we are interested in is between groups within a given country and between countries. Therefore, rather than examine national-level aggregate indicators of group composition overall (Selway, 2011a; Basedau et al., 2011, 2016), our analysis compares nationally socially relevant groups, within and across countries. Similarly, in Chapter 4, we test a group-level implication of our theory, using group-level demographic data of nationally socially relevant groups. In contrast, the case studies in Chapters 5 and 6 explore how variance in national *and* sub-national identities relates to identity mobilization.

---

[21] Multiple data sets on religion have been compiled within and across countries. The data discussed here by no means represent a comprehensive list of all such data. Instead, this chapter only highlights some useful data sets used in political science that either illustrate religious context across countries or specifically code the intersection of religion and ethnicity, often with an emphasis on clarifying conflict dynamics involving religion.

[22] Birnir et al. (2015) include suggestive and incomplete subgroup lists of identity categories that researchers examining contemporary regional politics and/or politics at different points in time may want to include in the universe of cases relevant to their study. Chapters 3 and 6 discuss how shifting the relevant institutional boundaries from the national level to the sub-national level changes incentives for mobilizing particular identities.

Coding of the A-Religion Data

Specifically, using the AMAR sample frame as our list of socially relevant ethnic groups, we coded the primary group religion, and all other group religions to which a sizeable segment of the group subscribes. Sifting through a great number of sources, it soon became clear that a precise and verifiable percentage is rarely available for either the primary group religion or other religions to which group members subscribe. Thus, the coding rules for the A-Religion data were to code the primary religion of a group: (1) if there is a published percentage equal to or more than the threshold of 50 percent; (2) if a reliable reference states that the number of the subscribers of a particular religion forms a majority or a predominant plurality.

For religions other than the group's primary religion, the coding rules were to code: (1) a group as adhering to a religion if there is a published percentage equal to or more than the threshold of 10 percent, or (2) a group as adhering to a religion if a reliable reference states that the number of the subscribers of a particular religion forms a significant portion (likely over 10 percent) of the group. The second rule was used more often than the former as reliable statistics on religion of ethnic groups are rarely available.

Examples of a reference that gets coded may be: "group X is predominantly Christian" or "significant percentage of group X is Christian" or "majority of group X is Christian." If we find that a reference to the number or percentage of subscribers to a religion is smaller than 10 percent, we make a note of the cite but do not code that religion for the group. In addition to a specific religion, we code a group as adhering to a syncretic belief system if our sources indicate this to be the case. Most commonly syncretic belief systems are combinations of Christianity and Animism or Islam and Animism, and found primarily – though not only – in Africa. Finally, we code a group as not adhering to any organized religion as per our sources.

Some groups were straightforward to code. For instance, according to the Croatian Bureau of Statistics (2011), accounting for the population of Croatia by ethnicity and religion, Croats are Christian Catholic with no other religions accounting for 10 percent or more. Coding of other country groups was more complicated and laborious. For example, according to Levinson (1995: 12), in the Ivory Coast "The Akan have largely been Christian since the nineteenth century, except for most kings, who have had to retain their indigenous religious status and practices." However, according to the Library of Congress, Ivory Coast country study, edited by Handloff (1988), most Ivorian Muslims are Sunni, while the largest Akan subgroups Baoulé (15 percent) and Agni (3 percent) are primarily Catholic, however, and have also evolved a number of syncretisms following prophets that promise fortune. Furthermore, according to Miran-Guyon (2012: 116), "Some 'mixed' Akan-Mandé societies of the eastern forest/savanna contact zone such as the Anno-Mango (related to the Baoulé) and Barabo (related to the Agni) are Muslim in majority, but they are the exception. On the village level, however, there are quite a few localities with a native Muslim majority." Based on all this information, we coded the Akan as primarily Christian Catholic but also with substantial numbers adhering to Islam (Sunni) and Animism.[23] For comprehensive information on coding rules, notes, and sources for each group by country, see the A-Religion Codebook 2021 and A-Religion Notes and Sources 2021.[24]

In some cases, a primary ethnic marker of an AMAR group is religion. This is true for only a small portion of the total number of groups and rarely is religion the only marker, as it is usually accompanied by other markers including language, race, and/or cultural traits. Out of a total of 1199[25] A-Religion groups, Appendix A, Table A.3 lists all 64 groups from 37 countries, where one of the primary identity markers is religion.

We also coded groups adhering to the most populous monotheistic religions of the world, Islam and Christianity, for sect/denomination.[26] Finally, to explore how commonly majorities and minorities share faith – as opposed to being segmented by faith – we coded the ethno-religious context for every minority ethnic group. The context coding accounts for whether the primary religion of any distinct minority in a country is shared with the most populous religion in the state as recorded by Brown and James (2018). In turn, the majority

---

[23] The Joshua Project (https://joshuaproject.net/) publishes precise numbers for religions of over 17,000 ethnic groups and articulates what they consider the primary religion. However, as this is an evangelical organization that does not explain how their numbers are gathered, provide sources for their numbers, or make public any procedures for ensuring that groups are consistently coded across countries, we do not rely on them unless we are able to independently verify their numbers. Furthermore, in the sample of 1199 A-Religion groups we work with, we have found over a hundred discrepancies between their coding of primary religion and ours. For instance, the Joshua Project codes the Mossi in Ivory Coast as majority Christian Evangelical. According to our sources, however, the Mossi primary religion is Islam (A-Religion Codebook 2021). We find that the number of discrepancies between our coding and the coding in the Joshua Project is particularly high where our sources indicate a group is majority Animist whereas they tend more often to code the same group as majority Christian Evangelical.

[24] The data and codebook are available at the interdisciplinary Laboratory in Computational Social Sciences www.iLCSS.umd.edu and at www.johannabirnir.com

[25] The overall number of groups coded in A-Religion data is 1199 because three AMAR groups in Taiwan were not coded due to complications surrounding Taiwan's status with respect to China. In addition, we did not have enough information to code religion for an additional twelve AMAR groups in nine countries because the groups were either large umbrella groups or there was not sufficient reliable information available for coding religions of the group. The groups we did not code for religion are listed in the Appendix A, Table A.1, along with the reason for why these cases were not coded.

[26] For coding of this data we classified the various Protestant sects according to the broader category of Protestant. Hinduism, the third most populous religion of the world (Hackett and Stonawski, 2017), is also monotheistic in the sense that the multiple deities are all a reflection of a single god. See, for example, Doniger (2014) on a discussion of why Hinduism can be considered both monotheistic and polytheistic. However, Hinduism is not organized into sects comparable to Christianity and Islam. Other religious families are significantly smaller and all except for Judaism are coded "not monotheistic."

religion is defined as the numerically most common religion in the country.[27] The second context coding, for Christian and Muslim minorities, accounts for whether the predominant sectarian affiliation of the minority is also the most populous sectarian affiliation in the country where the minority resides.[28]

2.4 DEMOGRAPHIC DIVERSITY AND OVER-REPRESENTATION OF ISLAMIC GROUPS IN CIVIL CONFLICT

We next turn to the third question we seek to answer: Can demographics – especially ethno-religious diversity – possibly help elucidate Islamist over-representation in civil conflict? To cast light on this question we use the coded data to explore the internal ethnic group religious diversity.[29]

The total number of groups in AMAR is 1202. In the A-Religion data we have coded information about the primary religious family of 1170 groups out of 1199.[30] To examine the distribution of primary religions across ethnic groups, Figure 2.5 tabulates AMAR groups by A-Religion's primary religious family. The figure shows that in the sample frame the primary religion of the

[27] An astute reader will notice that we code the context of the most populous religion in the country as opposed to the religion of the politically dominant majority. This nuance in definition is important for theoretical reasons. To foreshadow our argument, the central idea is that a large ethnic minority capitalizes on the opportunity to challenge the politically dominant group by enlarging or consolidating a following via the numerically most common religion that members of the minority share. Theoretically, therefore, it is not necessary that the numerically most common religion overlap perfectly with the religion of the politically dominant majority group.

Empirically, this nuance makes little difference because in all cases politically dominant groups share a religious family with the numerically most common religion, and in all but two cases (Bahrain and Syria) politically dominant ethnic groups overlap at least in part with the numerically most common sect. Often, when there is some difference, the politically dominant majority encompasses a mix of sects (and/or subscribers of no particular religion) that overlap partially with the numerically most common religion. Appendix A, Tables A.4 and A.5 list the country group details where religion of the politically dominant groups does not overlap perfectly with the religion coded as numerically the most common.

[28] In all but one case, Benin, according to Brown and James (2018), the predominant religion also contains the largest number of adherents to a given sect. In Benin the number of Christians (over 42 percent) is larger than the number of Muslims (over 29 percent), but the number of members of the largest sect (Catholics at 28 percent) is smaller than the number of members of the largest sect among the second-largest religion (Sunnis at 29 percent).

[29] To be clear this exercise is purely theoretical and descriptive in the sense that we do not test the relationship between the hypothesis proposed on group structure and groups that are in conflict. In this chapter, we simply highlight demographic differences between groups and propose a hypothesis in line with the literature about possible effects on conflict participation of groups.

[30] The data are missing for 29 groups. This number (29) excludes both the 12 groups which we have no information about religion and an additional 17 groups of which we have information on religion but cannot reliably distinguish which group religion should be considered primary. The 17 groups where we have information about religions but cannot determine which religion predominates are listed in the Appendix A, Table A.2.

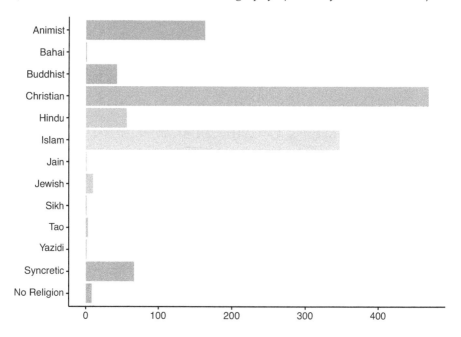

FIGURE 2.5. The number of socially relevant ethnic groups belonging to each of the coded families of religion

highest number of coded groups is Christian (467), followed closely by Muslim groups (347). Animist groups count third (163), followed by Hindu (57), and Buddhist (43) groups. Other religions count fewer groups but a substantial number of groups (68) practice a syncretic religion that blends elements from at least two religious families.

As noted above, we also coded groups adhering to the most populous monotheistic religions of the world, Islam and Christianity, for sect/ denomination, depicted by Figure 2.6. Excluding 68 groups that practice a syncretic version of Christianity and Animism (47 groups in Africa and Latin America), Islam and Animism (5 groups in Africa and Asia), Buddhism and Animism (14 groups in Asia or Latin America, thereof 10 also mixing in Taoism, Shinto, or Christianity), Animism and Hinduism (1 group, the Kirati in Nepal), or Christianity and Islam (1 group, the Roma in Serbia), a total of 814 groups in our data primarily adhere to either Christianity or Islam.

The figure clearly illustrates that among Christians, primarily Catholic groups are most numerous (209), followed by Orthodox (83) and Protestant groups (55), and other Christian sects (19). Importantly, information on primary sects of 101 Christian groups is missing (in the figure, unassigned), many of which are small ethnic groups and mostly in Africa. Even so, it is safe to argue that Catholicism predominates among Christians. Among Muslim

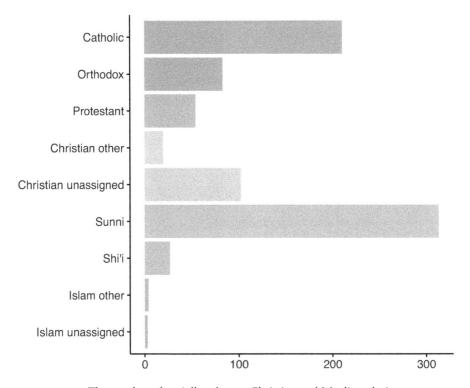

FIGURE 2.6. The number of socially relevant Christian and Muslim ethnic groups belonging to each of the coded sects

groups, Sunni groups are most numerous (313), with the number of Shi'i groups a distant second (27), followed by other Islamic sects including but not limited to Ibadhi Muslim and Druze Muslim (4), with sectarian information not coded for 3 groups.[31]

Importantly for our inquiry and the number of other studies that examine the cross-cutting and intersection of cleavages, variance in religion is found not only between ethnic groups but also within ethnic groups. What the above figures do not show is that while adhering to a predominant religious family, and in Christianity and Islam a predominant religious sect, many of the above ethnic groups are far from being religious monoliths. Tables 2.1 and 2.2 outline how

---

[31] We were able to determine the principal sect for all but two predominantly Muslim groups. These are Turkmen/Azerbaijani in Iraq and Romani in Iran. Both groups contain Sunni and Shi'i elements, however, there is no reliable information on which sect is to be coded as principal for the group. In addition, we did not code sect for the Ahmadis in Pakistan who by many are not considered Muslim because they follow a prophet that post-dates Muhammad (www.pewresearch.org/fact-tank/2013/09/10/in-pakistan-most-say-ahmadis-are-not-Muslim, last accessed on June 26, 2020). Finally, Alawites in our data are classified under Shi'i.

TABLE 2.1. *The numbers of minority ethnic groups adhering to a single religious family, or split between two or more religious families*

Political minorities	
One religious family	Two or more religious families
697	357
without "no religion" or "syncretic"	
709	283

TABLE 2.2. *The numbers of majority ethnic groups adhering to a single religious family, or split between two or more religious families*

Political majorities	
One religious family	Two or more religious families
88	28
without "no religion" or "syncretic"	
102	8

many of the groups we coded are cross-cut by two or more religious families. Table 2.1 accounts for political minorities. The reader will recall that for an ethnic minority to be coded as cross-cut by religion (adhering to more than one religion) a sizeable segment of the group has to adhere to a religion other than the primary religious family recorded for the group or subscribe to no religion.[32] The second set of numbers also account for internal group religious fragmentation, but this time the numbers leave out the category of "no religion" and minority syncretic practice of two or more religious families.

Table 2.1 also shows that around a third (357) of all minority groups coded in our data are split between two (288 groups) or more (69 groups) religious families. These include such disparate groups as the indigenous in Guatemala, many of whom mix Animism with Christianity to varying degrees, and in the United Kingdom the Chinese, some of whom are Buddhist while others are Christian. Similarly, in Indonesia the Ambonese are split between Christianity and Islam, and in Sri Lanka most Tamils are Hindu but some are Christian. Excluding groups that practice a syncretic religion or where a substantial segment does not subscribe to a religion, there are still 283 groups split between two or more religious families.

---

[32] As explained earlier, our conceptual reference number for coding a cross-cutting religion was 10 percent though a specific percentage is rarely available.

TABLE 2.3. *The numbers of predominantly Christian or Muslim ethnic groups that are unified or split by religious sect within each religion*

One religious sect	More than one religious sect
Predominantly Christian groups	
275	136
Predominantly Muslim groups	
327	19

Table 2.2 shows the same information for ethnic groups that are the sole politically dominant groups in their countries.[33] Proportionally the numbers of split majorities are similar to that of minorities with about a third of majorities split between religious families.

The politically dominant groups that are split include the Japanese in Japan, many of whom practice either Buddhism or Shinto or a syncretic version of the two, Estonians in Estonia who are either Christian or do not adhere to a religion, and the Swazi in Swaziland who are Christian and Animist. Notably absent are groups such as Whites in the United States because even though only around 70 percent of Whites adhere to Christianity, no other religion counts as members at least 10 percent of the White population.[34] However, when we exclude the categories of no religion and syncretic practice of religion (six groups), it becomes clear that the majority of dominant groups share a single predominant religion.

In addition to being split by a religious family, or alternatively, some of the above groups are split into different sects within the same religious family. For groups whose primary religious family is either Christianity or Islam, Table 2.3 details the predominant sectarian splits among these groups for which we can reliably code the predominant sect.[35] Specifically Table 2.3 shows – for the groups where we have these data – the number of predominantly Christian and Muslim ethnic minorities and majorities that adhere to a single sect or are split between two or more sects within a religious family.

The table shows that a large number of ethnic groups (155) are split between denominations or sects. This group is actually even more nuanced than the table suggests. While the table only shows sectarian splits within each religion, some of the minority groups in this category are split between sects but also split

---

33 For a definition of political majorities/minorities see Chapter 1.

34 US Census data at www.census.gov/data.html. See also www.pewforum.org/religious-landscape-study/racial-and-ethnic-composition/white, last accessed on July 3, 2020.

35 Coding of sect was more difficult for Christian groups – where we were unable to find reliable information on the predominant sect for 101 groups. In contrast we have information on the predominant sect of all but three Muslim groups in the sample. The numbers in Table 2.3 reflect this.

between religious families and even between sects in the second religious family. For example, while a majority of Mbunda in Zambia are Catholic, sizeable segments of this population also belong to other Christian denominations or are Animist. Similarly, some Arabs in Brazil are Muslims while others are Christian. Within each religious family Brazilian Arabs are also split between denominations, as earlier immigrants tended to be Catholic or Orthodox while later waves of Arab immigrants are more commonly Sunni or Shi'i (Karam, 2007). In contrast, majorities, which are predominantly Christian or Muslim, are less commonly split between religious families than are minorities though many contain large segments professing "no religion." When majorities are split between religious families, the split tends to be between Christianity and local Animist religions. Some exceptions include the Mossi in Burkina Faso and Albanians in Albania, both of whom are politically dominant groups that are cross-cut by Christianity and Islam with a sizeable Animist segment among the Mossi. In turn, Albanian Christians are further split into Orthodox and Catholics. More often, however, predominantly Christian or Muslim, majorities are split by sect only, such as the Dutch in the Netherlands, some of whom are Catholic while others are Protestant. Similarly, several minority groups belong to a single family of religion but are split into two or more sects. Examples include Afro-Brazilians, a majority of whom are Christians but split between Catholics, Pentecostals, Evangelicals, and other Christian denominations, and Kurds in Turkey and Iran, in each country containing both Sunni and Shi'i segments.[36]

Interestingly groups whose primary religion is Islam are far less commonly cross-cut by sect (19) than are groups whose primary religion is Christianity (136). Predominantly Muslim ethnic groups are also less likely to contain sizeable population segments that adhere to a different religious family than are Christian groups, though, this type of split is not very common among predominantly Christian ethnic groups either. These observations suggest an added explanation for Islamists' over-representation in civil conflict that bears further scrutiny. Specifically, if ethnic groups that adhere to Islam are more likely unified in religion than are other ethnic groups, this feature might facilitate conflict recruitment among Islamists above and beyond that of other ethnic groups, which may be more cross-cut by religion.

However, the likelihood of conflict also depends heavily on context. Specifically, the literature shows that countries with segmented groups that differ culturally on religion and ethnicity are especially conflict prone (Ellingsen, 2005; Basedau et al., 2011, 2016; Selway, 2011a; Toft, 2013). This means that inter-group conflict is more likely when ethnic majorities and minorities do not share faith. Using the information accounting for context or whether ethnic minority primary religion overlaps with or is segmented from the demographic

---

[36] For further information, see A-Religion Codebook (2021) and A-Religion Notes and Sources (2021).

TABLE 2.4. *The numbers of ethnic minorities that are segmented by religious family from or share religious family with the majority in their country*

Religious family	Segmented religion	Shared religion
Animist	163	0
Bahai	1	0
Buddhist	24	11
Christian	76	323
Hindu	26	30
Islam	118	199
Jain	1	0
Jewish	7	2
Sikh	1	0
Tao	3	0
Yazidi	1	0
Syncretic	60	2
Total	481	567

majority primary religion, Table 2.4 counts by religious family, groups that either overlap or are segmented from demographic majority groups in their country worldwide.

The table shows that the number of minority groups that share primary religious family with the majority in their country (567) outnumbers segmented groups (481). Furthermore, the table indicates that Muslim minorities living in countries where the majority religion is a different faith, outnumber other religiously segmented minorities substantially.

Taken together, our earlier observation from Table 2.3 that Islamic minorities are more commonly unified in religion than are minorities adhering to Christianity, and the observation in Table 2.4 that Muslim minorities outnumber minorities of other faiths that are segmented in religion from the majorities in the country where they live, casts an important new demographic light on the likely reasons for why Muslim minorities are over-represented in inter-religious conflict.[37] Specifically, it seems that *Muslim minorities are more commonly unified in religion than are other minorities and more likely to be segmented from the majority by religion.* Consequently, it is not unlikely that Muslim minorities may be more commonly the targets of segmented majority outbidding and more easily mobilized when targeted, contributing to an explanation for their over-representation in conflict between religions. Indeed, this idea resonates with Toft et al. (2011: 155) whose enumeration of

---

[37] To be clear, scholars such as Toft (2007) argue Islamists are overrepresented in both inter and intra religious conflict.

civil conflicts shows that by far the most common type of interfaith conflict between 1940 and 2010 is between Christian majority states and their Muslim oppositions (see also Toft, 2021).

2.5 GROUP SIZE, ETHNO-RELIGION, AND POLITICAL CONTESTATION

Another important observation that emerges from Table 2.4 is that nearly half of all ethnic minorities overlap in part or fully with the religious family of the political majority in their country. The reader will recall from Chapter 1 that instances of violence are not necessarily most common across religious families, but within them (Fox, 2002, 2004b; Gartzke and Gleditsch, 2006; Toft, 2007), although we have little in the way of explanation for why this is the case.

The final section of this chapter sets the stage for the remainder of the book by returning to this question and suggesting that one important piece of the answer to when conflict occurs within faith is group demographics – especially group size. Therefore, the final identity dimension we explore in this chapter is whether and then how identity group size varies across the dimensions of ethnicity and religion. To help illustrate the demographic variance in sizes of groups across these dimensions, we use the new GeoAMAR[38] that geo-references the AMAR sample frame of 1202 groups. We then use these data to map ethnicity, religion, and group size to illustrate the importance of accounting for varied group demographics in explanations of political phenomenon worldwide, including identity mobilization.

2.5.1 The GeoAMAR Data

There are two parts to GeoAMAR. The first part constitutes original geo-classifications and geo-referencing of AMAR group polygons, the second part builds on the existing GeoEPR data.[39] The AMAR sample frame contains both politically relevant groups and groups that have not mobilized politically. By design, the GeoEPR sample frame of only politically relevant groups is an imperfect[40] sub-sample of the AMAR sample frame of socially relevant ethnic groups. The difference in the numbers between the two data sets is around 4–500 groups depending on the version of the EPR. Because the GeoEPR data build on the MAR data classifications there is great overlap between GeoAMAR groups and groups included in the GeoEPR.

---

[38] The Geo-AMAR project is described in greater detail in Birnir et al. (2018).

[39] The GeoEPR data can be found at https://worldmap.harvard.edu/data/geonode:GREG_ovV. For the most recent version of GeoEPR, see Wucherpfennig et al. (2011); Bormann and Golder (2013). Data can be found at https://icr.ethz.ch/data/epr/geoepr/v2.0/

[40] By imperfect, we refer to the fact that the group aggregations and inclusion criteria do not match perfectly.

GeoAMAR also follows the original Minorities at Risk (MAR) data definition of the regional basis of group locations that are then mapped (georeferenced) and not mapped (not geo-referenced) by the GeoAMAR data, and additional GeoEPR definitions of group locations that are mapped and not mapped.[41] However, GeoEPR does not categorize its classifications according to whether groups are mapped or not. Therefore, the GeoAMAR classification of mapped and unmapped groups also diverges somewhat from that of the GeoEPR.[42]

Specifically, where GeoEPR has drawn group polygons because the groups are defined as either urban and regional, regional only, or statewide, GeoAMAR adopts the GeoEPR polygons.[43] For AMAR groups not in GeoEPR, GeoAMAR classifies the groups according to the criteria that establish their mappability (briefly regional, regional and urban, or statewide) or not mappable (urban, migrant, dispersed) and georeferences mappable groups as shown in Figure 2.7.[44] The first panel maps locations of majority groups only and the second panel maps locations of minority groups only.

2.5.2 The Religions of Ethnic Groups

Using the above GeoAMAR polygon data for mapping, Figure 2.8 illustrates the primary religions of groups (Political Majorities top panel, Political Minorities bottom panel) across the world. The polygons define boundaries of mappable groups within countries and the primary religion of each group is coded in alphabetical order on a grayscale with Animist religions coded the darkest. The very lightest shades represent groups who adhere to a syncretic religion and profess no religion.

Some interesting observations emerge from Figure 2.8. Because the top panel in the figure depicts the religion of a single politically dominant group where there is one (as opposed to say the majority religion), countries where more than one group rotate in and out of power are left uncolored. This reveals, for instance, the fact that sub-Saharan Africa is the only region where plurality groups are more likely to hold power than are single majority groups. Other observations include that Animist religions are more common among minorities than majority groups and Christianity predominates among

---

[41] See the GeoEPR codebook at https://icr.ethz.ch/data/epr/geoepr/GeoEPR-2014_Codebook.pdf (Vogt et al., 2015).

[42] For further discussion, see Birnir and Coronado-Castellanos (n.d.).

[43] The GeoEPR is time variant with respect to access to government. This has no bearing on our analysis. For further discussion, see Birnir and Coronado-Castellanos (n.d.).

[44] For each AMAR group not already mapped by GeoEPR but classified by the GeoAMAR research team as mappable, they have at least some regional base the team created a shapefile covering the area where the group predominantly resides. Country borders that delineate some group polygon boundaries come from Natural Earth Maps at www.natural earthdata.com. Furthermore, GeoAMAR uses Natural Earth Maps for urban areas to distinguish groups that are regional and urban (2) from groups that are regional only (1).

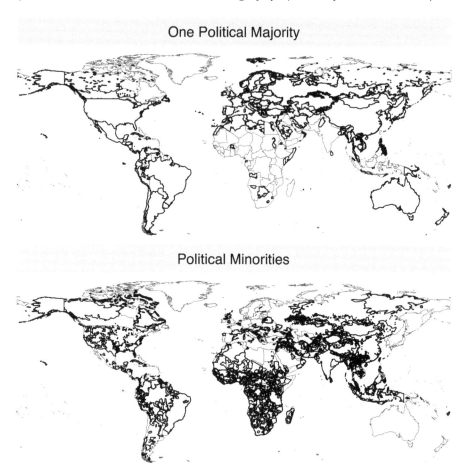

FIGURE 2.7. GeoAMAR polygons representing mappable groups across the world data

majorities in the Americas and the Northern hemisphere while Islam is the most common majority and minority religion in North Africa. Furthermore, ethnic group religions are clearly variable to the extent that they are likely better illustrated with more disaggregate regional mapping than globally.

Therefore, the next series of figures break out for a better view of groups and their religions in some of the more heterogeneous parts of the world, Africa (Figure 2.9), Asia (Figure 2.10), and Latin America (Figure 2.11). Religions are coded alphabetically on a grayscale followed by syncretic religion and no religion.

Some interesting observations emerging from the figures include the differences in religions and diversity of religions across these three regions, and the difference in the amount of ethno-religious diversity within each region.

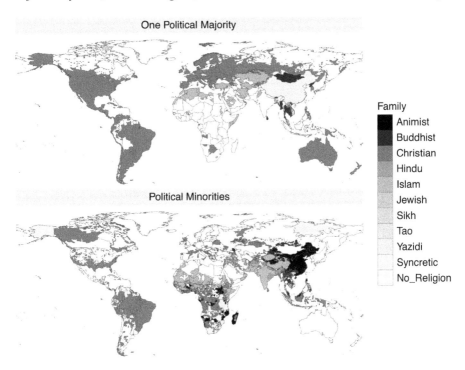

FIGURE 2.8. A-Religion as mapped in GeoAMAR

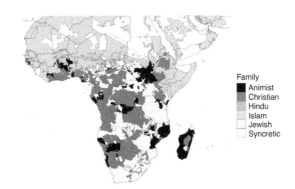

FIGURE 2.9. Ethnic group religions in sub-Saharan Africa

Specifically, predominantly Christian Latin America looks very different from Sub-Saharan Africa that is much more diverse in terms of religion but also contains groups of religions that are found in much smaller numbers if at all in Latin America. Similarly, comparing either Latin America or Sub-Saharan Africa to Asia the meaning of ethno-religious diversity clearly is very different by region. Aside from the predominance of Christianity in Latin America, there is the prevalence of people professing "no religion" in Asia. Animist

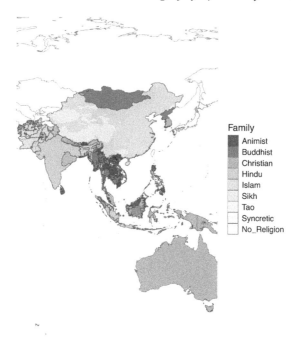

FIGURE 2.10. Ethnic group religions in Asia

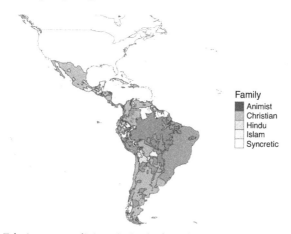

FIGURE 2.11. Ethnic group religions in Latin America

religions are also notable both in Sub-Saharan Africa and in Asia especially in China. Foreshadowing our discussion in the next section, the observation about Animist religions is one that changes quite dramatically when taking into account population numbers because the largest population segment in China subscribes to "no religion."

FIGURE 2.12. Ethno-religious group proportions of national populations in Africa

To illustrate some of the additional variance that group size brings to bear on our thinking of ethno-religious groups around the world, our last set of figures takes the data about group locations and their religions as depicted in Figures 2.9–2.11 and adds the population size dimension to the illustrations. To this end for Africa (Figure 2.12), Asia (Figure 2.13), and Latin America (Figure 2.14) they show a group's proportional size of the national population within each country. The polygons still represent distinct groups, the varying values of the grayscale represent differences in religious family, and the added population density dimension depicted with the raised surface represents the group's proportion of the national population compared to other groups in the country. Thus higher bars show that the group population in the country is larger compared to other groups in that country.

While depicting groups on whole continents in this way obscures much detail, this last set of figures, nonetheless, drive home the point that the demographic group contexts vary substantially within and between regions. For example, Figure 2.12 shows that groups in Northern Africa tend to account for a larger share of their respective country population than groups in Sub-Saharan Africa. Furthermore, the multitude of ethno-religious groups in Sub-Saharan Africa are less likely to live in countries where a single ethno-religious group predominates in terms of size. Most groups are relatively small,

FIGURE 2.13. Ethno-religious group proportions of national populations in Asia

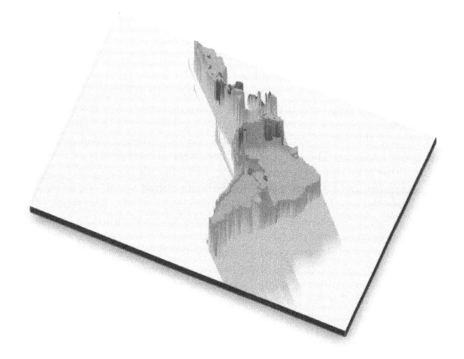

FIGURE 2.14. Ethno-religious group proportions of national populations in Latin America

and depending on location, either share religion or are divided by religion from multiple other groups of comparable sizes that live in the same country. Some other notable observations to emerge bear on the political context in which minority groups exist. For example, Figure 2.10 showed that a number of minority groups in China adhere to Animist religions. However, once we add in the population size dimension it becomes very clear that in terms of the population proportions shown in Figure 2.13, all minority groups in China are eclipsed by the Han Chinese who to a greater or lesser degree adhere to a syncretic mixture of Animism, Buddhism, and Taoism. Furthermore, while we know that in terms of population numbers Hinduism predominates in India, in Figure 2.13 no one ethnic group appears to predominate. This is an artifact of how groups in these cases are coded as the majority Hindu population is divided between multiple ethnic groups, most of whom are predominantly Hindu but none of whom constitutes a predominant ethnic majority.

In Latin America, yet another completely different picture emerges in Figure 2.14. There, minority groups do find themselves eclipsed by often much larger majorities. However, with the exception of the Andes represented by a valley on the map, those majorities tend to share religion with most of the minority groups as most all adhere to some variant of Christianity.

2.6 CONCLUSION

Contemplating the different types of information that emerge when considering a population's relative size as opposed to absolute size refers back to the very first question this chapter raised about whether divergent demographic measures help illuminate the varying roles of demography in inducing political outcomes. Again the answer is resoundingly affirmative, as accounting for relative size rather than absolute size seemingly brings to light certain inter-group dynamics that likely matter for group politics including mobilization.

Substantively, the last question asked in this chapter, about the likelihood of political contestation within religion as conditioned by group size in addition to cleavage intersection is the principal focus of the remainder of the book. Thus far we hope to have convinced the reader that, across the world, there is substantial variance in the sizes of ethno-religious groups, the relative sizes of majorities and minorities, and how these identities are segmented or shared. Chapter 3 develops a theoretical explanation to flesh out the argument about how group size and the intersection of cleavage types influence mobilization. Next, Chapter 4 tests a cross-national implication of this theory on the subset of groups in civil conflict. Chapters 5 and 6 further explore our answer at the more granular country and sub-country level and across transgressive and contained political settings.

3

The Theory: *Alternatives in Mobilization*

3.1 INTRODUCTION

This chapter addresses the pressing question: What determines which identity cleavage is mobilized in political contestation? The answer suggested here is that under-explored demographic variation in the relative size of identity groups and the intersection of cleavages shape the opportunity structures that incentivize group leaders to mobilize a particular identity across transgressive and contained political settings. We refer to this theory about the mobilization of identity as *Alternatives in Mobilization* to highlight the fact that where there are more than one identity cleavages, group leaders and followers have a set of options to choose from regarding which cleavage to mobilize in a particular context. The argument emphasizing *Alternatives in Mobilization* generates multiple testable implications. One of these is the *Challenger's Winning Coalition* (CWC), which suggests that among groups that are segmented on one identity and share a second identity, relatively large minority groups may find an opportunity for mobilization in the shared identity to challenge the majority controlling the state for political power.

The formalization of the theory at the end of this chapter takes the content-neutral approach of social identity theory (Tajfel, 1978; Tajfel and Turner, 1979). However, as explained in Chapter 1, the empirical scope of the book pertains to identity cleavages, in particular, ethnicity and religion. Thus, the remainder of the book explores the CWC as it pertains to the politics of ethno-religion across transgressive and contained political settings, including violent civil war and non-violent electoral politics.

In the rest of the chapter we first outline the central demographic intuition behind the theory of *Alternatives in Mobilization*. The next section engages the methodological literature to clarify the conceptualization of shared and segmented cleavages. Then we build on the literature about identity mobilization as a function of the Minimum Winning Coalition to flesh out the mechanisms of the *Challenger's Winning Coalition*, in the context of multiple identity groups and with respect to majority defections. The final section formalizes the argument and specifies testable implications.

3.2 SEGMENTED AND SHARED IDENTITY MOBILIZATION AND RELATIVE GROUP SIZE

The outcome theorized in this chapter – identity mobilization – occurs at the group level. The literature increasingly emphasizes the importance of studying outcomes at the meso-level of groups (Hale, 2004; Cederman et al., 2013) for a variety of reasons. For example, group processes are not necessarily a direct aggregation of individual preferences (Olson, 1971), and social movement theory (McAdam et al., 2001) shows that identity mobilization is not restricted to formal organizations, though the politics of organizations has contributed much to our understanding of ethnic politics.[1]

Group mobilization occurs across contained and transgressive political settings. Leaders representing divergent group segments and/or organizations may employ different strategies – including non-violent and violent political action (Weinberg and Perliger, 2008; Altier et al., 2014; Staniland, 2015). These strategies may be selected at the outset of mobilization or occur in response to state repression (Gurr, 1969; Davenport et al., 2005).

Furthermore, building on the existing literature we only consider two variants of cleavage configuration: groups that are segmented on one or more dimensions, and groups that are segmented on one cleavage but share a second one. In both instances we argue that the role segmented and shared cleavages generally play in mobilization, and specifically in the mobilization of ethnicity and religion, is better understood by considering demographic variation within the categories of segmented and shared cleavages.[2]

3.2.1 Segmented Identity

Explanations for contentious identity mobilization where cleavages are segmented are well developed for both the leadership and the rank and file. This is especially true for ethno-religious groups that are segmented along the lines of both ethnicity and religion so that neither identity is shared. Chiefly, the thrust of the principal argument is that threatened political elites attempt to enhance their identity credentials with their key domestic audiences to take over

---

[1] For example, the literature on rebel organizations – some of which are identity based – has burgeoned in recent years. See for instance Weinstein (2007); Asal and Wilkenfeld (2013); Fotini (2012); Staniland (2014); Cunningham (2014); Krause (2017).

[2] This chapter interchangeably uses the terms identity and cleavage. Thus, hypothetically the theory is not restricted to only identity cleavages, but empirically our inquiry is.

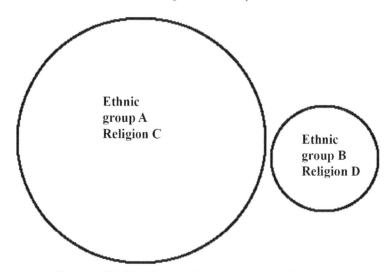

FIGURE 3.1. Classic outbidding demographics and segmented groups

and/or cement their hold on power. To this end, majority/plurality elite factions instrumentally outbid[3] each other (Rabushka and Shepsle, 1972; Horowitz, 1985) in targeting segmented minorities (Toft, 2013), which makes identity segmentation especially conflict-prone (Stewart, 2012; Basedau et al., 2011, 2016). Overlaying segmented identities such as ethnicity and religion increase group loyalties and strengthen social networks, which decreases the cost of recruiting rebels (Selway, 2011a; Ellingsen, 2005; Seul, 1999). This allows for the use of identity, including religion, as a mobilizing vehicle for conflict (Basedau et al., 2011, 2016; Juan and Hasenclever, 2015).[4]

The demographic foundations of this argument depicted in Figure 3.1 are underpinned, for example, in Horowitz's (1985) classic case of ethnic outbidding in Sri Lanka where the two Sinhalese majority parties, the United National Party (UNP) and the Sri Lanka Freedom Party (SLFP), outbid each other with Tamils as the target. Tamil parties then responded in kind and the conflict escalated into a decades-long civil war. More recently, Toft (2013) describes a similar case of classic religious outbidding in Sudan within the Arab plurality group, between Gaafar Mohamed el-Nimeiri, Sadiq al-Mahdi, and Omar Hassan Ahmad al-Bashir, which culminated in increasingly radical interpretations of Islam and targeting of southern tribes that primarily adhere to Christianity. This classic outbidding mechanism – intra-majority factional

---

[3] Outbidding here refers to the classic understanding of extreme and zero-sum positions taken by factions within two segmented ethnic groups.

[4] The microfoundations of increasing political conflict resulting from increasing segmentation are substantiated in political psychology in the American politics literature. See, for example, Mason (2018).

targeting of a segmented minority by emphasizing differences in ethnicity and religion – likely contributed to at least the second Sudanese civil war and arguably the secession of Southern Sudan. In addition to explaining contentious mobilization where the primary vehicle for mobilization was either ethnicity or religion, the empirical generalizability of this story has been verified across multiple countries.

Even so, as discussed in Chapter 2, segmented ethnic majorities and minorities are numerous, and most ethnic groups in the world live together peacefully (Birnir et al., 2018). This observation begs the question of whether there is something distinct about segmented majorities and minorities that engage each other in contentious mobilization by way of outbidding, which separates them from segmented groups that do not? Chapter 2 speculated that, over time, explosive population growth likely intensifies inter-group competition over resources making mobilization along established segmented fault lines increasingly probable. Taking a cue from the emphasis on measurement in Chapter 2, our proposition here adds some nuance to this suggestion. Specifically, we posit that it is not only the absolute population growth that matters. In addition, the *relative* size of segmented majority/minority pairs that mobilize identity through outbidding likely distinguishes them from majority/minority pairs that do not engage in contentious identity mobilization against each other.

Consider the political demographics of Sri Lanka where the Sinhalese majority constitute over 80 percent of the population while the minority Tamils, Sri Lankan, and Indian subgroups combined constitutes less than 10 percent. Similarly, while pre-war Sudanese population figures from the 2008 census are hotly contested (United Nations, 2018), the size difference between the predominantly Arab Muslim (now northern Sudanese) population at around thirty million and the South Sudanese Christian population of roughly eight million is striking. Both majority populations (Sinhalese and Arabs) who initiated the outbids, are at least twice as large as the target populations (both Tamils and the South Sudanese).

Compare next a very different hypothetical political demography depicted in Figure 3.2 and consider outbidding where the demographic size of the two segmented groups is substantially more even. Construction of a new factional winning coalition within the majority group by outbidding on identity, by definition, creates internal majority group fissures. If the fissures are substantial enough, the majority group may be irreparably cleaved risking that a unified minority, which is demographically larger than either majority faction assumes power. Of the two alternatives, majority factional challengers likely prefer to retain a majority winning coalition even if that winning coalition is led by a co-majority competitor, to the majority group losing political control to a minority-led winning coalition due to internal majority fissures. This is because when in control, minority leaders may enact legislation or take other measures that negatively impact all members of the majority. It stands to reason, therefore, that majority internal outbidding is not a very appealing strategy if it

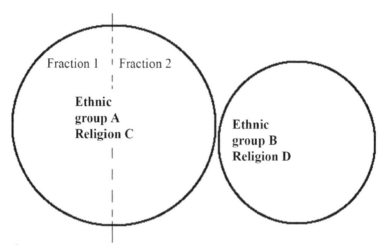

FIGURE 3.2. More balanced segmented groups

threatens the majority's absolute control when the minority is larger than either segment of a cleaved majority.

The principal point here is that even in cases or perhaps especially in cases of well-understood mechanisms of contention such as outbidding, we suggest that political demography allows for the refinement of predictions about when majorities and minorities, including segmented groups, are more or less likely to engage in contentious politics. In this book, this refinement is a building block for our argument about the role of shared cleavages. However, the implications of this refinement on segmented identities can be tested empirically and we do so elsewhere (Birnir et al., n.d.).

3.2.2 Shared Identity

Segmented cleavages are only one type of identity cleavage configuration. Identity cleavages including ethnicity and religion are also shared and cross-cut in all manner of ways across the world. The principal theoretical emphasis in this chapter pertains to the mobilization of a secondary identity where the primary segmented identity groups (such as two ethnic groups) share or are cross-cut by the second shared identity (such as religion).[5]

---

[5] To be clear we use the terms "primary" and "secondary" only to distinguish the identities from one another and not to indicate an order of importance with respect to content, salience, or mobilization. Thus, our use of "primary" is equivalent to calling the identity cleavage one and "secondary" is identity cleavage two. In the subsequent discussion "primary" refers to the cleavage that segments the groups (such as ethnicity), and "secondary" refers to the identity that the groups share (such as religion).

A large body of literature suggests shared identities increase political stability (Rokkan, 1967; Lipset, 1981; Lijphart, 1977, 1999). In this literature, the probability of war is also hypothesized to decline when identities are shared. The principal reason is that cross-cutting of cleavages reduces the number of zero-sum issues and the feasibility of recruiting combatants who share characteristics with the opponent (Selway, 2011a). At the same time – as we discuss in Chapter 1 and further elaborate in Chapter 4 – significantly more ethnic combatants in civil war share faith than are separated by it (Toft et al., 2011). Aggregate statistics about religious hostilities tell us a similar story. For instance, a report released by the Pew Research Center suggests that religiously motivated violence is substantial in many countries with high levels of cross-cutting identities. The report lists Afghanistan, Bangladesh, Central African Republic, Egypt, India, Indonesia, Iraq, Israel, Kenya, Nigeria, Pakistan, Palestine, Russia, Somalia, Sri Lanka, Syria, and Tanzania as the 17 countries or territories out of 198 classified with the highest level of social hostilities involving religion, with a cross-cutting score of 7.2 or higher on a scale from 0 to 7.2 or higher.[6]

To put these numbers in context, the average religious and ethnic cross-cutting score for the 150 countries in Selway (2011b) cross-national data on cross-cutting cleavages[7] is 0.726 (on a scale from 0 to 1). Excluding the outliers of Israel and Sri Lanka with cross-cutting scores of 0.05 and 0.31 respectively, Selway's average cross-cutting score of the seventeen countries classified by Pew as having high social hostility is 0.777. In other words, the countries with some of the highest religious hostility scores also have higher than average levels of cross-cutting cleavages. It seems clear, therefore, that all social hostilities involving religion are not ameliorated by cross-cuttingness. Within the category of cross-cut groups there is a seemingly abundant variation in conflict participation that merits further exploration. Thus, emerging literature, Selway and co-authors most prominently, is beginning to suggest that within the category of cross-cutting cleavages much variation in conflict potential remains under-explored. For example, examining conflict in Indonesia, Gubler et al. (2016) estimate that the conflict mitigating effect of cross-cutting cleavages may not be the same at all levels of conflict.

Additionally, Birnir et al. (2018) caution against using national-level indicators to make inferences about group-level politics. For example, they argue that aggregate relationships observed between identity and outcomes at the country level can be reversed at the group level. Thus, a very diverse country could be most likely in a cross-national comparison to experience conflict while at the same time any individual group in that country could in the

---

[6] See report, appendix 1 at www.pewforum.org/2015/02/26/religious-hostilities, last accessed on February 1, 2021.

[7] For data and a list of relevant publications, see https://politicalscience.byu.edu/directory/joel-selway

cross-national comparison be least likely to fight, and both things can be true at the same time. The logic is simple: If in country A one out of a total of two ethnic groups engages in violence, and in country B two out of a total of ten ethnic groups engage in violence, the absolute count of groups engaged in violence in country B is higher than the absolute count of groups engaged in violence in country A. An association between the absolute level of violence and a country-level index of heterogeneity would therefore show a positive association between heterogeneity and absolute levels of violence. At the same time the share of groups that engage in violence in country B (20 percent of the total) is lower than in country A where 50 percent of groups engage in violence. Therefore, probabilistically any individual group in country B is actually less likely (2/10) to engage in violence than any individual group in country A (1/2). Consequently, while studies finding a negative relationship between cross-cuttingness and conflict undoubtedly tell the correct story at the national level, there is likely more to this story at the sub-national level.

Shared Identity and Mobilization

Based on our discussion in the previous section, we argue that while aggregate indexes such as country cross-cutting scores communicate useful information about countries, they should not be confused with information on specific groups. Incentives of political operatives are shaped by their group's identity structures as available for mobilization and their group's size relative to other groups within the country in ways that elude country-level indexing. Our objective, thus, in this chapter is to elucidate the group-level story of the relationship between cleavage cross-cutting and contentious mobilization.

To this end, we draw attention to the great variety of demographic configurations within the category of groups that intersect on at least one identity cleavage. Furthermore, we highlight one specific variant among multiple possible demographic configurations to develop the core suggestion in this chapter. Specifically, holding institutions constant, we suggest that relatively large minorities segmented from majorities on an identity that forms a foundation of the governing coalition (such as ethnicity) may discern in a shared identity cleavage (such as religion) an opportunity to construct a CWC capable of competing with the majority for political power. We posit that the group-relative size is a primary driver in this type of mobilization because large ethnic minorities likely anticipate greater success in leveraging their shared religious identity to mobilize enough co-religious supporters across ethnic lines to mount a credible challenge to the ruling majority. Moreover, only large minorities can hope to retain control over such a coalition – especially when faced with competition for the leadership by the majority group.

Figures 3.3 and 3.4 illustrate the intuition about the variance in minority demographics that underpins our argument about where we would expect to see a CWC mobilize the shared cleavage in challenge to the status quo. The figures demonstrate the difference in mobilizing incentives of small and large ethnic minority groups that share a religion with the majority. Figure 3.3 depicts

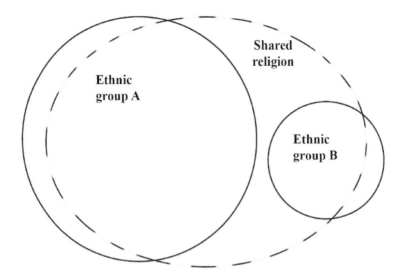

FIGURE 3.3. Classic cross-cutting, demographically less balanced ethnic groups that share a religious identity

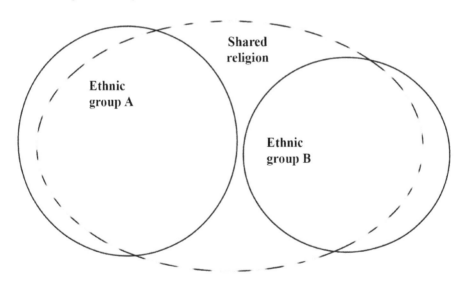

FIGURE 3.4. Demographically more balanced ethnic groups that share a religious identity

a case where there are substantial demographic size differences between the majority and the minority. In such instances, in line with the literature on the conflict-reducing properties of shared identities, we expect that small ethnic minorities have little incentive to mobilize a shared cleavage in competition with the ethnic majority because their anticipated success in recruitment for and control of such a coalition is small. In contrast, small ethnic minorities may find protection in emphasizing the unifying aspect of the shared religious cleavage because small minorities have much to fear from majorities if they are drawn into an asymmetric conflict. Furthermore, as the literature on cross-cutting cleavages (Lijphart, 1977; Selway, 2011a) suggests, when identity is shared, majorities have less incentive to outbid against minorities with whom they share the identity as such mobilization is more costly when politics is not perceived as a zero-sum game. This demographic configuration, therefore, likely dampens incentives of both minorities and majorities to engage each other in political conflict.

The demographic configuration of large ethnic political majorities and small ethnic political minorities that share a religion is quite common. For instance, many ethnic majority/minority pairs in Europe fall into this category. For the most part, these small ethnic minorities live with the majorities in their respective countries without attempting to mount political identity challenges to the majority over access to state power and resources. Where civil conflicts do break out between majorities and small minorities that share religion, these often center on the ethnic minority's goal to separate from the majority via secession.

In contrast, Figure 3.4 depicts a country where the population balance between the ethnic majority and minority is much more even, changing minority political incentives. In this scenario, the minority likely has a greater capacity to challenge the majority for power. This is especially true if the minority can shift political mobilization from the cleavage that separates the two groups to the cleavage that the groups share. In taking the lead in mobilizing a shared identity, leaders of the minority stand to gain the support of some majority constituencies while retaining their core minority constituency. The more salient the shared cleavage, the less the minority secular attrition and the greater the marginal benefit from recruitment of members of the majority. The more members of the majority that can be recruited under the alternate identity banner, the lower the chance that majority leaders can wrestle control back by counter-mobilizing the shared identity.

As noted above, majority outbidding that targets a minority is less likely to occur when there is a secondary shared (cross-cutting) identity (Lijphart, 1977; Selway, 2011a). Furthermore, in this scenario the demographic share of the minority segment on the primary cleavage is sufficiently large that majority outbidding along the segmented cleavage is not safe for the majority. If majority outbidding on the primary segmented cleavage identity is not safe because the majority fears competition from a large minority, majority-initiated mobilization of the secondary shared cleavage is even less likely[8] as it opens the

---

[8] This is obviously not always the case. For example, imminent fragmentation of the state or an exogenous threat may prompt majority leaders to mobilize the shared cleavage. For the sake of clarity we set those types of considerations aside here, and discuss variation in majority incentives further in our case studies in Chapters 5 and 6.

TABLE 3.1. *Selway, example one*

Blue (0.5)		Green (0.5)	
Alpha (0.5)	Beta (0.5)	Alpha (0.5)	Beta (0.5)

door to competing identity mobilization by minority (and majority) challengers that share identity. Therefore, in this scenario we expect that the minority will seek to mobilize the shared identity while the majority will refrain from doing so, at least until the secondary identity has come to constitute the principal political identity.

Importantly, our argument does not contradict the idea of the political conflict-mitigating effect of shared cleavages. In contrast, we seek to refine this idea to argue that conditional on ethnic groups' relative sizes, shared cleavages can serve as either conflict-mitigating or conflict-motivating. Furthermore, our argument complements the literature on the conflict potential between groups that are segmented on all relevant identities. Separate dynamics influence the two types of political conflict, within and between identities, and theoretically both can exist at the same time, even within the same country.[9]

Sharing and Cross-Cutting of Identity

To tell the story of sub-national variation with respect to groups that share identities and to explain why we expect some groups to mobilize politically along the shared cleavage while others do not, some clarification of the concept of "sharing" is in order. Selway (2011a: 51) provides a useful and thorough treatment of cleavage cross-cuttingness, which he defines as the degree to which "Group i on cleavage x is identically distributed among groups on cleavage y with all other groups on cleavage x."[10] As an example, Joel Selway depicts a hypothetical society of 1000 members where the secondary cleavage (Alpha/Beta) is distributed equally across categories of the primary cleavage (Blue/Green) as shown in Tables 3.1 and 3.2.

---

[9] A majority group could, for example, outbid against a segmented ethno-religious minority group while at the same time be engaged with another ethnic minority group in conflict involving shared religion.

[10] Selway's formula for aggregate cross-cuttingness is a normalized chi-square that defines the measure of cross-cuttingness as:

$$1 - \sqrt{\left[\Sigma \frac{(O - E)^2}{E} \right] / nm} \qquad (3.1)$$

where O is the observed group proportions belonging to a given cleavage, E is the expected proportion of group members belonging to a given cleavage (found for each group by multiplying the proportion of the relevant primary group by the proportion of the relevant subgroup and the size of the sample). N is the sample size and m is the smaller of either the number of columns minus one or the number of rows minus one in a contingency table displaying the observed sample numbers.

TABLE 3.2. *Selway, example two*

Blue (0.4)		Green (0.6)	
Alpha (0.2)	Beta (0.8)	Alpha (0.2)	Beta (0.8)

Plugging the numbers from Table 3.1 into Selway's formula for cross-cuttingness returns a perfect cross-cutting score of 1. As proportions change and individuals in the second identity cleavage become more unevenly distributed across the first cleavage (the Blues all become Alphas and the Greens all become Betas), the cross-cuttingness score decreases until at 0 the two groups are perfectly segmented on both identities. Selway then demonstrates that subgroups (Alpha and Beta) do not have to be identical in proportions for perfect cross-cuttingness, as long as they are evenly distributed vis-à-vis the primary identity. Thus, Selway's following example in Table 3.2 also returns a perfect cross-cutting score of 1.

Next, Selway (2011a) juxtaposes his measure of cross-cuttingness with Rae and Taylor's (1970: 537) measure, which Selway calls cross-fragmentation and accounts for the "proportion of all the pairs of individuals, whose two members are in the same group of one cleavage but in different groups of the other cleavage."[11] The primary difference between Selway's measure of cross-cuttingness and Rae and Taylor's cross-fragmentation[12] is that the latter measure is sensitive to secondary cleavage proportions as distributed across the primary cleavage. The greater the difference between sub-group proportions (Alpha and Beta) with respect to each primary identity, the lower the cross-fragmentation index.

Selway's focus is on aggregate national-level analysis. Where the score of cross-cuttingness is positive, the lower the cross-fragmentation score the more unbalanced the segments of the secondary (sub)cleavage. In contrast, our theoretical contribution to this discussion is to highlight how each measure (cross-cuttingness and cross-fragmentation) relates to theorizing about subnational political dynamics. Take the example of the political mobilization of Selway's secondary cleavage (Alpha and Beta).

The bigger the larger segment, it becomes more likely that Beta minority leaders of the primary cleavage (Blue) see the shared cleavage as a mobilizing opportunity across categories of the primary cleavage. Using the preceding population proportions in Selway's second example in Table 3.2, we would expect

---

[11] Selway adds the condition of "which different groups they must also share with members of other groups from the first cleavage."

[12] Selway's (2011a:53) simplified representation of Rae and Taylor's index is:

$$CF = 2F_C - F_X - F_Y \qquad (3.2)$$

where F_C represents subgroup fractionalization and F_X and F_Y represent the fractionalization score for each of the individual cleavages.

the leaders of the Blue Betas to have an incentive to mobilize the shared (Beta) cleavage because the total proportion of Betas $((0.4 \times 0.8) + (0.6 \times 0.8) = 0.8)$ is larger than the proportion of Green's overall (0.6), whereas we would not expect this to be true for the Blue Alpha's because the total proportion of Alpha's $((0.4 \times 0.2) + (0.6 \times 0.2) = 0.2)$ is smaller than the total proportion of Green's. Furthermore, we would only expect this incentive to grow as cross-fragmentation decreases, as long as cross-cuttingness remains positive. Therefore, while Selway's measure of cross-cuttingness yields useful information about the presence of cleavage intersection in the aggregate, much important sub-national variation eludes it. Similarly, while cross-fragmentation can pinpoint in the aggregate where intersecting identities are distributed in such a way as to create incentives for mobilization of shared identities, albeit by a decreasing value in the current definition, the aggregate measure does not pinpoint which groups are likely to mobilize.

We suggest one additional clarifying contribution to the discussion of the concept of cleavage intersection with respect to our specific theory.[13] Strictly speaking, an identity group is cross-cut/fragmented by a second identity only if the second identity has at least two categories. For example, ethnic identity group Blue is cross-cut by religion if the religious identity has two categories, Alpha and Beta. Similarly, religious group Alpha is cross-cut by ethnicity only if the ethnic group is divided into at least two groups, Blues and Greens. In contrast, ethnic groups Blue and Green may share a religious identity that does not cross-cut the groups because there is only one category of the religious identity.[14] In that case, the ethnic groups still cross-cut the religious category. Therefore, the order of cleavages – which is the primary group and which is the sub-group – in this discussion determines whether the cleavage classifies as cross-cutting or shared.

This clarification is important to the remaining theory developed in this chapter, which pertains to the mobilization of a secondary identity where the primary segmented identity groups (such as two ethnic groups) share a second identity (such as religion). The secondary identity, in turn, has at least one category (shared identity). This secondary identity can also be a cross-cutting identity cleavage (containing more than one category) provided that when tallied across the primary identity group the cross-cutting cleavage is cross-fragmented in such a way that the total proportion of members in at least one of the secondary (sub) identity categories approaches or exceeds the proportion of members belonging to the majority segment of the primary identity. In other words, if the cleavage is cross-cutting, rather than shared by all members of both groups on the segmented identity, we expect that incentives for mobilization of the secondary cleavage are generated only among the segment of cross-cut

---

[13] We thank Havard Hegre for pressing us to clarify this point.
[14] The measure of cross-cuttingness returns 1 even if there is only one subgroup.

groups, which fulfill the condition that together the size of the majority segment and the minority segment of the shared identity is larger than the majority primary identity, or more formally:

$$R_{\text{maj}} + R_{\text{min}} \geq C_{\text{maj}} \tag{3.3}$$

where R_{maj} and R_{min} respectively account for the majority and minority demographic shares of the largest secondary cross-cutting cleavage segment and C_{maj} accounts for the demographic share of the majority segment of the primary cleavage.

The idea here is that leaders of large ethnic minorities (such as the Blues) seek to mobilize a second cleavage because the total number of members belonging to that cleavage (all the Betas, both Blue and Green) are numerous enough to challenge Green's hold on power. Note that this condition may be satisfied even if the minority demographic proportion of the primary cleavage is small, if all or nearly all of the majority belongs to the same segment as the minority on the secondary cleavage. Therefore, though this is a necessary condition for minority alternative mobilization of the secondary cleavage it is not sufficient.

3.2.3 The *Minimum Winning Coalition* (MWC)

The literature on the MWC (Riker, 1962), as applied to identity politics (Bates, 1983a), helps further clarify our argument about the *Challenger's Winning Coalition* (CWC), especially when the identity competition involves multiple groups. Most recently, Posner (2017) argues that in a plurality competition the cleavage supporting the MWC determines the identity that the pivotal group elects to emphasize. In his example (that we have modified slightly here to better illustrate our story),[15] in Table 3.3, the South Asian Christian group is pivotal because they belong to a plurality coalition on both cleavages, ethnicity and religion. Posner (2017: 1475) suggests that "Christian politicians

---

[15] We thank Daniel Posner for recommending modifications to the example and other helpful suggestions about the theory overall. Specifically, the new example here is based on Posner's original example in figure 3 (Posner, 2017: 2009):

		Religion				
		Christian	Muslim	Hindu	Buddhist	
Race	South Asian	5	20	15	0	40
	African/Afro Caribbean	25	10	0	0	35
	Chinese	7	0	0	8	15
	White	10	0	0	0	10
		47	30	15	8	

The original example does not satisfy the condition that the MWC be larger than the combined size of excluded groups on the axis that the pivotal group (*w*) does not choose. The condition is that

$$w + x_i \geq y_i \tag{3.4}$$

TABLE 3.3. *Posner's example (modified)*

		Religion				
		Christian	Muslim	Hindu	Buddhist	
Race	South Asian	10	20	10	0	40
	African	25	10	0	0	35
	Chinese	7	0	0	11	18
	White	7	0	0	0	7
		49	30	10	11	

and community members will campaign strongly for [South Asians] to ally with their fellow Christians" to mobilize along the religious and not the ethnic cleavage. However, the demographics illustrated in the table and the logic of the MWC dictate that the South Asian group will seek to mobilize a coalition of forty across co-ethnics, ignoring the religious cleavage, because ethnicity satisfies the minimum winning condition. In other words "if what matters most is controlling the greatest share of resources that one can then the lobbying of fellow Christians will go unheeded"(Posner, 2017: 1475).

Furthermore, following the formation of the MWC, Posner also discusses how individuals who do not belong to either of the potential coalitions that include the pivotal South Asian Christians (i.e. African, Chinese, and Whites who are Muslim, Hindu, or Buddhist) will try to change the game by pushing for the introduction of a new cleavage dimension or by attempting to assimilate into the MWC. However, their bid to invoke a new cleavage dimension is restricted by the underlying ethnic structure[16] and their bid to assimilate is likely to fail because "insofar as membership in the winning category provides access to scarce resources, [new] attempts to claim membership in that category are likely to generate resistance from its members, who face the prospect of sharing the spoils with a larger number of people" (Posner, 2017: 1474).

	Identity 1		
Identity 2	w	x_j	x_i
	y_j		
	y_i		

where w is the pivotal group that chooses to align with a minimum coalition including $x_j \ldots, x_i$ and $y_j \ldots, y_i$ are excluded groups. According to Posner, "when $x > w + y$ or $y > w + x$ (i.e. when x or y are so large that they beat the minimum winning coalition of w + y or w + x) will individuals in w not necessarily do best by choosing the identity that puts them in the smaller winning coalition. In such a situation, whether the winning coalition is made up of a1s or b1s will be out of their control, so choosing membership in the smaller group is not necessarily advantageous" (Posner, 2017: 2008). The new modified example satisfies this condition and better illustrates our conjecture that the minority will seek to recruit also from members of the MWC.

[16] For a discussion of the differences between activated ethnic identity and underlying ethnic structure, see Chandra and Wilkinson (2008).

Posner's logic is sound and persuasive, and it illustrates that, the political mobilization of a given identity is a numbers game subject to opportunity. As he notes, in a plurality contest, as long as the MWC's underlying assumptions hold that what matters most in politics is access to resources, and that those resources are distributed equally among members of the power-holder's social group, and that individuals in society have information about, at least, the relative sizes of all competing groups (Posner, 2017: 1471), the identity mobilized will be that of the MWC.

However, recent scholarship questions the ubiquity of all of these assumptions, suggesting that for predicting identity coalitions the MWC is actually only the starting point. In particular, these challenges highlight that rather than being equal, there is frequently differential access to resources among members of the MWC; that members of society likely often lack information about just how big the MWC and alternative possible coalitions actually are; and rather than only resources determining support for a given coalition, the identity itself may matter in a deeper sense, which influences the selection of the coalition that group members choose to support.

First, recent research suggests that there is great under-explored variance in how clientelistic benefits are distributed within the winning coalition. For instance, Corstange (2016, 2018) shows that politicians have an incentive to spend their clientelistic resources to gain voters in highly competitive elections and to not spend as much in areas where they face less competition. Therefore, some of those "included" may not be receiving enough of the spoils to secure their loyalty to the MWC and the pocketbook opportunities afforded by the alternative mobilization are more attractive. To give one example, in some ethnically divided areas that experience high inequality and poverty, affiliation with religious leaders sometimes provides individuals with access to goods and services otherwise unavailable to them.[17]

Second, political actors may not have sufficient information to determine what the MWC is or which is more likely to win, the MWC or some alternative coalition. Some potential group members likely assess the probability of the redefined group's overall success based on an impression of the numbers of possible group members (Chandra, 2004; Stewart, 2012), and rightly or wrongly decide that the alternative coalition has as good or a better chance of assuming power than the MWC. Anticipating this criticism, Riker (1962: 88–89) himself points out that "the greater the imperfection or incompleteness of information, the larger will be the coalition that coalition-makers seek to form and the more frequently will winning coalitions actually formed be greater than minimum size."[18]

---

[17] See the case studies in Chapters 5 and 6 for further discussion and examples of individual recruitment.

[18] For a recent discussion of mobilization under the shadow of political instability – including the effects of information and average effects of relative group size, see Tyson and Smith (2018).

Third, for some of the individuals recruited to join alternative coalitions, the content of the alternative mobilization likely matters most. For instance, when the shared identity is religion and the separating identity cleavage is ethnicity the devout may prefer a religious definition of the state to an ethnic definition. Where the state already includes religion in its governance potential, recruits may, nonetheless, be drawn in by the alternative mobilization promise of increased religious intensity in identity mobilization.[19] Recruits may also relish the increased social capital resulting from the religious cultural bonding that bridges the ethnic cleavage.[20] Simply put, they prefer religion over ethnicity.

Supporting these challenges to the identity-based MWC, recent empirical analysis suggests that oversized ethnic coalitions are actually more common than are MWCs (Bormann, 2019).[21] In sum, therefore, the MWC is a good starting point and likely stable except where winner's resource distribution is less than even, where information is scarce or where group members simply prefer an alternative expression of identity. In such circumstances our explanation of political mobilization of a shared cleavage builds on the MWC numbers game to articulate where we expect a challenge to materialize as a function of demographic numbers lining up in a way that allows for a credible (e.g. religious) identity challenge to the (e.g. ethnic) MWC to emerge. It bears re-iterating that the terminology "numbers game" (Posner, 2017) as used here does not preclude sincerely held preferences. Instead, the idea is that the underlying population numbers make certain mobilization strategies viable, regardless of whether the choice to mobilize is motivated by sincere preferences or instrumentality. The next section further elaborates which groups we expect to lead the charge and why.[22]

---

[19] The religious marketplace paradigm notes "disadvantaged racial and ethnic minorities typically favor higher tension faith" (Stark and Finke, 2002: 36), which is consistent with our argument about minority leaders as suppliers of greater religious intensity.

[20] Putnam (1995) distinguishes bonding from bridging social capital, respectively referring to socializing within and across cleavages. See also Paik and Navarre-Jackson (2011) on religion as a bonding social capital.

[21] Earlier work, not specifically on identity, shows the same. Browne (1971) shows that Riker's MWC size principle does not do well empirically in predicting the size of legislative coalitions in Western Europe. Browne (1971: 407) argues that this is because when the assumption of perfect information is relaxed, the MWC size principle does no better in predicting winning coalition size than a coin toss. For a formal critique of Riker's size principle, see Shepsle (1974).

[22] Holding institutions constant, Chandra (2012) and Chandra and Boulet (2012) also predict where change in minimum winning identity coalitions will or will not occur. They argue that under majoritarian institutions any coalition of activated identities (k) that exceeds a threshold of 0.5 (defined by them as a "minimum winning threshold" of $k > 0.5$) but does not contain within itself a smaller majority group (any group independently $\geq k$), constitutes a potential winning coalition and change is possible. Their example of where change is possible and is not possible is depicted below. In "Changeland," Chandra (2012: 242–245) argues any of the coalitions that exceed the 0.5 threshold (Foreign [Black and White], Black [Foreign and Native], or White [Foreign and Native]) constitute a potential minimum winning coalition. In contrast to "Changeland," they argue that in "Nochangeland," because Black Foreigners by themselves

3.2.4 The *Challenger's Winning Coalition* (CWC)

The *Challenger's Winning Coalition* (CWC) argument explains how a minority with a segmenting identity (such as ethnicity), leads mobilization of a shared identity (such as religion) to challenge a majority controlling the state.[23] The mobilization of a CWC likely depends on the leadership's ability to make the case for a credible challenge. Only leaders of minorities that are relatively large when compared to the majority group holding power can credibly promise success in wrestling political power from the status quo coalition and retaining political control over the CWC. Therefore, we would only expect to see the formation of a CWC by leaders of relatively large minority groups that can credibly mount such challenges to the status quo coalition by recruiting members of a shared secondary identity.

To make this argument, we draw attention to the demographic share of excluded groups relative to the political majority. By mobilizing an oversized CWC relatively large excluded groups stand a reasonable chance of re-defining the relevant identity for political competition in a way that includes them. Indeed, we suggest Posner's (2017) modified example, which illustrates the mechanics of the CWC argument.

In the prior example in Table 3.3, relative to the forty South Asians, the thirty-five Africans constitute a relatively large racial group that is excluded from power when access is defined in terms of race. Even if accounting only for the numbers adhering to Christianity, at twenty-five the group of Africans is still more than half the size of the entire South Asian ethnic group. The African

constitute an MWC that cannot be further sub-divided, no other group or coalition that they are not a part of can challenge their MWC. Therefore, under this scenario, change is unlikely.

Changeland			
	Black	White	
Foreign	0.30	0.25	0.55
Native	0.20	0.25	0.45
	0.50	0.50	

Nochangeland			
	Black	White	
Foreign	0.60	0.10	0.70
Native	0.10	0.20	0.30
	0.70	0.30	

Our argument differs from theirs in that we would make the case that in "Changeland" the demographic data allow us to pinpoint which coalitions are more likely to form than others. Specifically, assuming that MWC is preferred by all we would expect Foreign Blacks as the pivotal group to first lead a coalition of Blacks (Foreign and Native), we would then expect White Foreign to mobilize an oversized CWC of Foreign (White and Black).

[23] It bears reiterating that our argument rests on the constructivist idea that identity groups are constructed, fluid (Berger and Luckmann, 1967; Barth, 1969; Fearon and Laitin, 2000; Chandra, 2012) and malleable (Laitin, 1986; Stark and Finke, 2002; Posner, 2005; Lynch, 2014) for political ends.

group is large enough to deter South Asian racial outbidding because outbidding would run the risk of cleaving the South Asian group allowing a unified African group to assume power. Therefore, the Africans constitute a group that could credibly lead and maintain control of an alternative religious coalition.

Posner explains that coalitions across group lines (i.e., across rows or across columns) are difficult to form because individuals will only support leaders they believe will share resources with them. However, the only relevant coalition for the Africans is the one that includes them, and religion is the only cleavage they could successfully recruit from to challenge the extant coalition of forty South Asians. Therefore, in this example, Christian leaders of the African racial group have nothing to lose and everything to gain from attempting to mobilize a CWC by shifting the emphasis on relevant political identity from race to religion.

Supporting the Challenger's Winning Coalition

Individuals are *not* just naive pawns playing into the hands of skilled political operatives. In contrast, when the objectives of political entrepreneurs align with the objectives of individual supporters, recruitment is successful. Thus, in line with the literature (Fearon and Laitin, 2000; Kalyvas, 2009), we assume individuals recruited from either the majority or minority groups make their choice in multiple different ways that are motivated by their own preferences and personal agendas.

In the example in Table 3.3, when politics is defined in terms of race, Chinese and Whites are also excluded. Neither the Chinese at 18 nor Whites at 7 is likely numerous enough to attain the numbers that would allow them to recruit enough of the majority to mount a challenge to the ruling coalition and/or credibly lead and retain control of an alternative religious coalition. Indeed, only a minority of the Chinese are Christian precluding them from mobilizing all of their co-ethnics around the only religious cleavage that is numerous enough to challenge the South Asian ethnic coalition. Moreover, the White and Chinese barriers to initiating a challenge to the MWC of South Asians are particularly high because majorities can counter-mobilize identity with the claim that they lead by a large margin on both cleavages. Were either group, Chinese or Whites, to attempt to lead an alternative religious Christian mobilization, South Asian factions could, without worry of losing absolute control, target them in an ethnic outbid. Therefore, in the absence of a viable leader of a large ethnic CWC (i.e. the Africans), small cross-cut ethnic minorities (i.e. the Chinese and Whites) may find protection in aligning with majorities by way of a shared cleavage. Consequently, we would not expect small minorities to lead the mobilization of a CWC. However, in joining a mobilization led by another ethnic group, small minorities have less to lose and much to gain by mobilizing as part of, in this example, a Christian CWC.

Leaders of the challenging minority (African) probably realize that over time one of their main competitors for leadership of the CWC may be the ethnic group currently leading the MWC. They also understand there will be some attrition across groups. Thus, leaders of the religious CWC will likely attempt to recruit members across all relevant racial groups, including South Asians.[24] Deciding whether to defect from the MWC to support leaders of the large minority group in their mobilization of the shared cleavage, individuals from the majority or pivotal ethnic group must choose between the primary and the secondary cleavages. Where the MWC assumptions of resource access and distribution, information, and indifference between cleavage types holds, members of the MWC are unlikely to defect. If, however, resources are unevenly distributed amongst members of the MWC, information about coalition sizes is scarce, or the alternative mobilization offers preferred expressions of identity, members of the MWC may defect to a CWC that they believe will better represent their interests and preferences.

To sum, across contexts varying demographic balances between majority and minority groups are likely associated with varying minority incentives for challenging an ethnic majority for political power. A shared cleavage presents a new opportunity to construct a minority-led CWC in a political contest. Whether the minority group leader attempts to do so, however, is contingent on demographic size of the minority group as segmented by the primary identity cleavage, because only sufficiently large minorities could plausibly expect to recruit enough supporters from among the majority group, and retain control over a new CWC constructed along the lines of the second and shared identity. The subsequent discussion formalizes our argument and outlines some of the expectations that follow, including the testable implications of the CWC.

3.3 FORMALIZATION: SEGMENTED AND SHARED IDENTITY MOBILIZATION AND RELATIVE GROUP SIZE

To set the stage, let us assume we have two distinct identity groups: a political majority, group A and a political minority, group B. A is in control of the government while B is not. The objective of both groups' political leaders is to maximize their group's share of political control under their leadership vis-à-vis the opposing identity group while also ensuring the safety of the members of their own identity group. Furthermore, we assume a basic political restraint in that leaders' concerns with the safety of the group supersede their desire for power.[25] In their quest to retain and/or win power, political leaders will consider

[24] In mobilization of race, attrition likely occurs among individuals who favor programmatic approaches over identity appeals, and among people who favor a different identity category. In mobilization of religion, individuals who favor secular approaches over religious appeals are likely alienated, as are people who favor a different religious identity expression. However, there is no reason to believe attrition is lesser or greater for one type of identity mobilization, race or religion.

[25] Clearly this is not the case for all leaders but comprehensively theorizing about the variation in leader utilities is outside the scope of our project. Consequently, we restrict our theorizing to leaders whose political objectives do not unnecessarily endanger the group.

all available strategies to mobilize their constituency's support for increased political access including identity mobilization.

3.3.1 Segmented Identity and Political Mobilization

To help us think more systematically through the implications of varying demographics of groups that are entirely *segmented* on identity so that if A and B are ethnic groups they also adhere to distinct religions, the following section formalizes our discussion. First, we define the relative size of each group in relation to each other as the *population balance*.

For segmented groups, we define the population balance (X) as the politically dominant majority (hereafter majority) proportional demographic size (C_{maj}) minus the politically non-dominant minority (hereafter minority) proportional demographic size (C_{min}), or $C_{maj} - C_{min} = X$. For simplification $C_{maj} + C_{min} = 1$, though in reality there can be more than two groups in society. In turn, X ranges between $-1 < X < 1$, because the politically dominant majority may be a demographic minority though this is more rare and for the purposes of our argument a less relevant scenario.[26] Furthermore, as the population balance increasingly favors one group over the other, the cost/benefit to each group from identity mobilization likely does not strictly change in a linear fashion but rather takes on some polynomial form that can be described more precisely by adding the appropriate power to the population balance (X^{α}). Importantly, in this story α is odd rather than even because the outcome for each group is asymmetrically linked to whether the population balance favors the group. Finally, majority and minority utility deriving from the population balance mirror each other so that a positive utility associated with X for the majority is a negative utility for the minority.[27]

For illustrative purposes Figure 3.5 shows the effect of group-relative size (X^{α}) cubed (X^3), on majority group leaders' incentives for identity mobilization as determined by the utility associated with a changing population balance.

However, relative size is not the only feature that influences the decision of majorities and minorities whether to engage in identity mobilization. We also suggest that each group weighs the risks of doing so. The risk assumption associated with identity mobilization differentiates majorities and minorities. With respect to a new identity mobilization, majority leaders are likely somewhat risk-averse because a change in their strategy – away from non-identity-based

---

[26] The reason this is a less relevant scenario is that among segmented groups when the political minority is a demographic majority, the minority demographic mobilization incentive may be to consolidate the cleavage for the mobilization of a new MWC. We are more interested in scenarios where the segmented political minority is also a demographic minority.

[27] Theoretically, we assume majority and minority utility are related. For instance, restriction of minority language rights decreases minority access to the bureaucracy while increasing access for the majority. Another example would be restricting minority access to resources in favor of majority access.

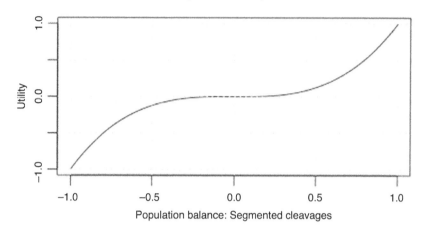

FIGURE 3.5. Majority utility associated with majority/minority demographic population balance when $X^{\alpha} = X^3$

mobilization toward identity mobilization – is risky in that it may adversely affect their hold on power.

In turn, minority identity mobilization against a majority, which controls the means of coercion, is quite risky because a miscalculated strategy in an asymmetric relationship could result in a very costly asymmetric conflict.[28] Thus, with respect to new identity mobilization, we assume both majorities and minorities are risk averse but unequally so.

More formally, we assume that majority utility grows faster than does minority utility. This difference is shown in Figure 3.6 where we take the square root of the absolute value of the majority utility, while minority risk aversion is modeled as the log of minority utility plus one,[29] because $\log(-X^{\alpha} + 1) <$ sqrt($|X^{\alpha}|$), setting $\alpha = 3$.

Furthermore, there is a social cost/benefit aspect to identity mobilization defined as p, which affects the decision to engage in this type of mobilization. This term (p) is positive when identity is salient and public[30] for non-political

---

[28] Rabushka and Shepsle (1972) examine group propensity for conflict assuming that the minority is always risk taking. Subsequent research has established that this assumption is not an accurate description of minority behavior as it leads to expectations that the minority is overly militant. For further discussion, see Birnir (2011).

[29] We take the absolute value off the majority utility and add one to the minority utility because the square root and logs cannot be taken of negative numbers.

[30] By public we mean that the identity is displayed and observable for signaling purposes in society. For instance, Mecham (2017) pinpoints variation in mosque attendance as a public signal about the mobilization potential of Muslims across countries.

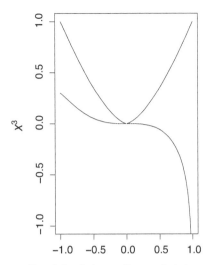

Population balance: Segmented cleavages

FIGURE 3.6. The effect of risk aversion on majority and minority utility where $\log(-X^\alpha + 1) < \text{sqrt}(|X^\alpha|)$

reasons and negative when there are strong social norms against identity mobilization and/or the identity is private.

Accounting for the exogenous social salience of identity (p) we would then expect the curves to be raised (increasing utility) when there is a positive exogenous benefit to identity mobilization such as increased identity salience or costs of collective action are decreased (e.g. in the case of religion, when worship is public). In contrast, the curves would be lowered (decreasing utility) where the cost increases (e.g. when worship is not public). This exogenous effect is captured in the probability term as illustrated in Figure 3.7, which shows the changing majority utility in identity mobilization as the probability of success associated with increasing or decreasing social salience of the identity (p) changes from low to high. The dotted, solid, and broken lines respectively account for probabilities (p) of 0.1, 0.5, and 0.9.

Having defined population balance, risk-taking, and social salience associated with mobilization, let us return to the idea of majority outbidding. For simplification, our earlier discussion around Figure 3.2 suggested that outbidding became a less attractive option when the minority is large relative to the majority. The reason is that outbidding cleaves the majority and if each half is smaller than the size of the minority then the majority could lose political control to the minority.[31] However, in reality, majority fissures resulting from

---

[31] This is likely not an entirely unrealistic assumption as political operatives contemplating outbidding strategies probably estimate their factional share with great uncertainty.

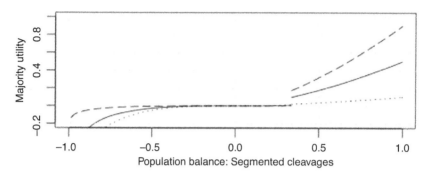

FIGURE 3.7. Change in majority utility as the exogenous social benefit/cost (*p*) of identity mobilization changes

factional outbidding targeting a minority likely occur between uneven segments of the majority so the majority challenger may not worry about this exactly at the point when the majority is twice the size of the minority but is likely to become more concerned as the population balance between the two groups is becoming more even.

To represent this idea more precisely, we introduce a contextual demographic tipping point (Lamberson and Page, 2012) that potentially has a large effect on competing majority leaders' decision to engage in identity mobilization.[32] Specifically, in our story outbidding is an attractive strategy to the political majority when the prospect of cleaving the majority (into advocates and adversaries of identity mobilization) does not threaten absolute majority control, because at least one majority segment is still larger than the entire minority. Under such circumstances an outbidding tipping point (Y) exists ($Y = 1$). The precise population balance (μ) where the tipping point emerges is an empirical question and may vary between cases. However, where it exists, this demographic tipping point entices competing leaders within the

[32] Extant work on cascades or tipping points, for instance predicting mobilization in Eastern Europe (Kuran, 1991; Lohmann, 1994), explains how mobilization within a context occurs as a result of a shock to the system. In the context of Islamic mobilization across the countries he studies, Mecham (2017: 62) calls the spark that ignites the mobilization a "focal point." This focal point can be a scandal or other type of internal crisis. In contrast, the idea of a tipping point here is more akin to Laitin's (1998) demographic tipping point in the sense that we argue demographics differentiate the types of mobilization that are more or less likely between contexts. Thus, two contexts can be stable on either side of the tipping point but only in one would we expect a positive probability of seeing the outcome, and the outcome may require a "cascade" or "focal point" to be set in motion. Furthermore, over time a single context can change to migrate from one side of the tipping point to the other because of changes in demographics. Specifically, therefore, our tipping point is the underlying demographic structure that allows or circumscribes the mobilization to occur following a spark.

demographic majority to initiate identity outbidding, targeting a segmented minority. This tipping point is defined as:

$$\begin{cases} Y = 0 & \text{where } -1 < X \le \mu \\ Y = 1 & \text{where } 1 > X \ge \mu \end{cases} \quad (3.5)$$

Thus the majority utility function for initiating a new identity mobilization when cleavages are segmented is better defined as:

$$U(M_{\mathrm{maj}}|S_e) = \sqrt{|X^\alpha \times Y|} \quad (3.6)$$

and the minority utility function for initiating a new identity mobilization when cleavages are segmented is defined as:

$$U(M_{\mathrm{min}}|S_e) = \ln(-X^\alpha \times (1 - Y) + 1) \quad (3.7)$$

Expected Majority Utility: Segmented Identity
Where majority and minorities compete for power and where identity cleavages are segmented (S_e), the majority expected utility is determined by the likelihood that the majority identity mobilization is successful, and majority power increases (majority utility increases), against the likelihood that it is not and majority power decreases (minority utility increases).[33]

$$E(M_{\mathrm{maj}}|S_e) = p \times \sqrt{|X^\alpha \times Y|} + (1 - p) \times \ln(-X^\alpha \times (1 - Y) + 1) \quad (3.8)$$

The exact shape of the utility α and the precise point of tipping μ are empirical questions. However, for illustrative purposes Figure 3.8 graphs the functions (solid lines) and their derivatives (broken lines) to show more precisely how utilities change as the majority/minority population balance changes, and to illustrate the maxima and minima. For this illustration we set $\mu = \frac{1}{3}$, cube X^α so that $X^\alpha = X^3$, and set $p = 0.5$.

Using these values, Figure 3.8 shows that there is a jump in majority utility (solid black line) from identity mobilization when the majority is at least two times larger than the minority $\frac{1}{3} \ge X > 1$. Following the jump, on the interval $[\frac{1}{3}, 1]$ the majority utility continually increases as the population balance becomes increasingly uneven until the majority is the sole ethnic group at 1. In contrast, on the interval $[0, \frac{1}{3}]$ majority utility is negative and approaches 0 as the population balance X approaches 0. The majority mobilization story we are interested in is on the interval $[0,1]$. Even so we include a sliver of the interval $[-1,0]$ to confirm that as the political majority passes from a demographic majority to a demographic minority, its utility in identity mobilization remains negative.[34]

---

[33] For calculations of expectations and their derivatives, see *Appendix B*.
[34] We do not elaborate further on the properties of the function with respect to the majority as we approach -1 but submit that this would be an interesting extension for future scholarship.

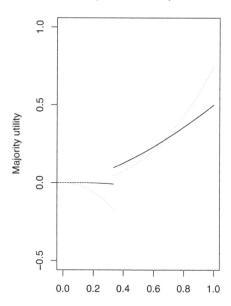

Population balance: Segmented cleavages

FIGURE 3.8. Change in majority utility of identity mobilization (solid lines) and derivatives (broken lines) as population balance changes from 0 to 1, between segmented cleavage groups

The figure also shows that none of the derivatives (broken lines) vanish showing that there are no local maxima or minima inside these intervals. The derivative of the first function is positive on the interval $\left[\frac{1}{3}, 1\right]$. However, the derivative of the second function is negative on the interval where X is $\left[0, \frac{1}{3}\right]$. Importantly, there is a sharp discontinuity at $X = \frac{1}{3}$ where the utility jumps. Furthermore, the derivatives emphasize the sharp decrease in the value of majority identity mobilization once the population balance favors the minority and, interestingly, show that the marginal utility decreases on the interval $\left[0, \frac{1}{3}\right]$ though this is difficult to detect from the equation (solid black) line.[35] For calculation and discussion of the values at the endpoints, see the Appendix for Chapter 3.

In this section, we first demonstrated how paying close attention to the details of the political demography of segmented identity cleavages allows for a refinement of extant expectations about mobilization. Specifically, we illustrated how expectations about majority outbidding change as the relative

---

[35] We do not investigate this further in this project but we have thought about the possibility that close to the tipping point the minority finds itself in a security dilemma. In that case any suggestion by the majority of identity mobilization might result in pre-emptive minority mobilization that could be very costly to the majority if it finds itself on the wrong side of the tipping point.

size of the targeted group shifts, arguing that there exists a relative demographic tipping point at which majority outbidding becomes increasingly likely/unlikely.

3.3.2 Shared Identity and Political Mobilization

Capturing more formally the idea that a shared identity cleavage becomes an opportunity for alternate identity mobilization, let us again assume we have two identity groups, a majority group A and a minority group B. A is in control of the government while B is not. Objectives of both groups' political leaders are the same as before; to maximize their group's share of political control under their leadership vis-à-vis alternative identity groups while also ensuring the safety of the members of the identity group they lead. In their quest to retain and/or win power, political leaders will consider all available strategies for mobilizing their constituency support to increase political power, including mobilization of available identities. Furthermore, unlike the groups we examined before, let us assume that in addition to the identity that separates them, A and B share a second identity.

The reader will recall the cross-fragmentation condition that across the primary cleavage of the majority and minority, the proportion of the segment of the secondary cleavage to be mobilized is at least as large as the majority segment of the primary cleavage.[36] Provided that this condition is satisfied, we define the contribution of the shared identity (Sh) to the minority utility calculation as the proportional population size of the minority (C_{min}) in relation to the majority/minority population balance X, or $\frac{C_{min}}{X}$.

Where the population difference is large (demographically large majority, small minority), the added utility from mobilizing the alternative (shared) cleavage is small but increases as the population balance X becomes increasingly even and approaches o (at o the political majority and minority are demographically equivalent in size, as we have previously discussed). Compare, for example, the difference in added utility for minorities that comprise 10 percent and 30 percent of the total population in countries 1 and 2. In country A the minority proportional size divided by the majority/minority population balance ($0.1/0.8 = 0.125$) is small. In country 2 the added utility ($0.3/0.4 = 0.75$) is substantially larger. Therefore, defined this way, larger minorities gain more utility from mobilizing the shared identity than do smaller minorities. Furthermore, mobilizing the shared cleavage likely is primarily an attractive option when the minority is smaller or equal in size to the majority ($o \leq X < 1$). The reason for this is the boundary set by the MWC logic. When a political minority exceeds a political majority in size on the primary segmented cleavage ($-1 < X < o$) an alternative CWC that also reaches out

---

[36] As formally defined p. 68:

$$R_{maj} + R_{min} \geq C_{maj} \tag{3.9}$$

to members of the majority to recruit on the secondary identity likely exceeds the necessary size of a CWC.[37]

The expected utility from mobilizing a shared identity for the political minority, states the minority size C_{min} in the form of X to facilitate illustration of change in the utility as the population balance changes. Because the proportional size of the majority and the proportional size of the minority together constitute the whole population $C_{maj} + C_{min} = 1$ and the population balance is calculated by subtracting the proportional size of the minority from the proportional size of the majority $C_{maj} - C_{min} = X$, the proportional size of the majority is $C_{maj} = 1 - C_{min}$.

Therefore, $1 - 2C = X$ and $C = \frac{1-X}{2}$ so that $\frac{C}{X} = \frac{\frac{1-X}{2}}{X} = \frac{1-X}{2X}$

The minority utility in mobilization of the shared (cross-cutting) cleavage then can be stated as:

$$U(M_{min}|Sh) = \ln\left(\left[-X^\alpha + \left(\frac{1-X}{2X}\right)\right] \times (1 - Y) + 1\right) \qquad (3.10)$$

It bears reiterating that we are mainly interested in values where X is positive. Where X is negative the minority is demographically larger than the majority and incentives for mobilizing an alternative cleavage likely change as noted previously. The majority segmented tipping point is still included in the equation because a majority that exceeds the minority in size as specified by μ and is faced with mobilization of a shared identity initiated by the minority, is more likely pushed to develop factional majority outbidding along the lines of the segmented cleavage targeting the minority as outlined in the previous section. This is a factor that necessarily features in minority utility calculation as majority outbidding along the segmented cleavage likely decreases the probability of minority success in mobilizing the shared cleavage, and therefore, minority expected utility.

Also as noted earlier, unless faced with an exogenous threat such as secession, the majority already holding power has little incentive to enlarge the minimum winning coalition by mobilizing an alternative cleavage. Consequently, the relationship of the shared cleavage to majority utility is negatively associated with X and increasingly costly as the minority grows in size.

$$U(M_{maj}|Sh) = \sqrt{\left(\left|X^\alpha - \left(\frac{1-X}{2X}\right)\right|\right) \times Y} \qquad (3.11)$$

---

[37] Empirically this is an interesting question. Madrid (2012) argues that despite constituting a demographic majority, only when Indigenous Bolivian leaders constructed a populist coalition across the ethnic divide, were they able to win. However, it is also possible that intra-indigenous cleavages hampered the consolidation of this identity in ways that necessitated alignment across ethnicity. In either case the question of identity mobilization among large demographic groups that remain political minorities constitutes an interesting venue for future study.

For this utility, we still take the absolute value because as C gets increasingly large (closer to 0.5) and X consequently gets increasingly small (close to 0) then $X^\alpha - C$ will be a negative number and we cannot take the square root of a negative number.[38]

Taking together the minority likelihood of success in mobilizing the shared identity cleavage and accounting for the probability that this mobilization is not successful, the minority expected utility in mobilizing the alternative identity or the CWC is:

$$E(M_{min}|Sh) = p \times \ln\left(\left[-X^\alpha + \left(\frac{1 - X}{2X}\right)\right] \times (1 - Y) + 1\right)$$
$$+ (1 - p) \times \sqrt{\left(\left|X^\alpha - \left(\frac{1 - X}{2X}\right)\right|\right)} \times Y \qquad (3.12)$$

When Y is 0 because X is on the range $-1 < X \leq \mu$, this gives the minority the following utility for mobilizing the alternative CW cleavage:

$$E(M_{min}|Sh) = p \times \ln\left(\left[-X^\alpha + \left(\frac{1 - X}{2X}\right)\right] + 1\right) \qquad (3.13)$$

In contrast, when Y is 1 because X is on the interval $1 > X \geq \mu$ the minority utility in mobilizing the alternate CW cleavage is:

$$E(M_{min}|Sh) = (1 - p) \times \sqrt{\left|X^\alpha - \left(\frac{1 - X}{2X}\right)\right|} \qquad (3.14)$$

For illustrative purposes Figure 3.9 shows the benefit to the minority from alternative mobilization when $\alpha = 3, p = 0.5$, and $\mu = 1/3$.[39] The figure shows that the minority utility (black solid line) in mobilizing the CWC is highest where the minority population is increasingly equal in size to the majority population (X approaches 0). Thus $E(M_{min}|Sh)$ is decreasing on the interval $[0, \frac{1}{3}]$ as a function of X. There is a substantial discontinuity at $X = \frac{1}{3}$ where the utility drops. For calculations and further discussion of endpoints, see Appendix B. Following the drop the minority utility in mobilizing CWC along the alternate cleavage is negative on the interval $[\frac{1}{3}, 1]$. This negative curve has a maximum at $X = 0.647$ because of the absolute value necessitated by the square root but the derivative does not exist (is infinite) at this point. The graph

---

[38] Specifically, when $X < C^{\frac{1}{4}}$ then $X^\alpha - \frac{C}{X}$ is a negative number.

[39] Consistent with the story we are telling the Figure 3.9 illustrates the negative utility associated with the square root. Therefore, the utility graphed is:

$$E(M_{min}|Sh) = -(1 - p) * \sqrt{\left|X^\alpha - \left(\frac{1 - X}{2X}\right)\right|} \qquad (3.15)$$

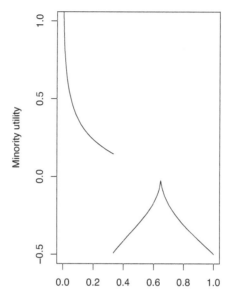

FIGURE 3.9. Change in minority utility of mobilizing the shared identity as population balance on the segmented identity changes from 0 to 1

shows that the closer X gets to 1 (increasing majority size, decreasing minority) the minority utility continues to decrease.[40]

3.3.3 Testable Implications

The principal usefulness of the preceding formalization lies in the clarity of terms and how they contribute to our thinking about the benefit of alternative mobilization. The model also highlights the fact that opportunities provided by one cleavage or another likely are linked and need to be considered together. Specifically, the tipping point of segmentation also sets up the boundary at which drawing on the majority for mobilization of a shared cleavage is either valuable or detrimental to the minority. Thus, the model makes clear predictions about when the shared cleavage becomes an opportunity for alternative mobilization by the minority and at which point it becomes a liability.

The implications of our argument for the types of competition we would expect to see in each of these instances are summarized in Table 3.4. The table summarizes the predictions resulting from varying majority/minority demographic balance on the primary cleavage and the interaction with the

---

[40] The derivatives of the functions are not informative and, therefore, not included in the picture. For discussion, see *Appendix B*.

TABLE 3.4. *Implications of varying majority/minority demographic balance and cleavage intersection*

	Demographic balance (X), on identity cleavage 1	
Sharing of identity cleavage 2	**Imbalanced.** (Majority substantially larger than minority. $\mu \leq X < 1$)	**Balanced.** (Majority and minority more similar in size. $0 \leq X \leq \mu$)
Segmented. (Majority and minority do not share identity 1 or identity 2)	Majority outbidding	Minority-initiated competition.[a] Majority accommodation.
Shared. (Majority and minority are segmented on identity 1 but share identity 2 and $R_{maj} + R_{min} \geq C_{maj}$)	Majority accommodation and minority cooperation	Minority Challenger's Winning Coalition

[a]While our scope conditions specify that minority-initiated secessionism is outside the scope of our theory, this is the demographic scenario that we would develop further with respect to explaining separatist minority movements. Moreover, it is possible that the relevant demographic balance is regional. We submit that these are fascinating questions for future study.

overlap on the second identity cleavage. Specifically, on the first identity cleavage the two groups are either imbalanced (small minority and large majority) or balanced (larger minority). On the second identity cleavage the groups are either fully segmented or cross-cut by a second identity that has at least one overlapping segment across the two groups that is equal to or larger than the majority segment of the primary cleavage.

Specifically, as shown in the upper middle quadrant our utility calculations suggest that where the two groups are demographically imbalanced $\mu \leq X < 1$ and segmented on both cleavages, majorities are the most likely to outbid at the expense of a minority. In contrast where the groups are segmented on both cleavages but demographically more balanced $0 \leq X \leq \mu$ the likelihood of majority factional outbidding targeting a segmented minority decreases substantially. This is a testable implication that we examine elsewhere (Birnir et al., n.d.).

This does not mean that where segmented groups are more balanced, there will not be any majority–minority conflict. However, the conflict mechanism will likely differ from majority outbidding. Where competition and conflict occur these may be minority initiated and perhaps center on autonomy or separatism because segmented minorities likely are not often successful in challenging majorities for access to the state – even if the larger minorities are closer to the majority in size. In such cases, another minority option is to separate and become a majority in their own state. However, we heed Rothchild's (1983) warning that the mobilization logic of groups that seek to secede possibly differs from groups that seek greater access within unaltered state boundaries. Thus, we simply note that generalizing across the two types should be done with caution and patterns across the two types need to be further investigated empirically.

In turn, where majorities and minorities share a second identity but are demographically imbalanced we would expect the lowest levels of competition and conflict. As noted in the literature, majorities find it more difficult to recruit antagonists where identities are shared. In turn, small minorities that have no hope of challenging the state fearing a costly asymmetric conflict, likely seek shelter with large majorities with whom they share at least one identity.

It is the last quadrant, in the lower right-hand corner, that is of most interest in this project. This is where a majority/minority dyad that is segmented on one identity cleavage shares a second identity. When this is the underlying demography, we expect that large minority leaders see in the shared cleavage an opportunity to initiate a successful alternative identity challenge, a CWC, against the leaders of the state in a bid for access to state power and resources. This is the implication that we test across the world in Chapter 4. Chapters 5 and 6 then explore this prediction further through in-depth case studies.

3.4 INTERVENING INSTITUTIONS

Before we turn to test the CWC hypothesis, one more clarification is in order. This clarification pertains to how institutions relate to identity cleavages in the contained or transgressive political contestations that we examine in subsequent chapters. State institutions determine the form of the competition for political access and interact with underlying identity cleavages to influence their expression in any given political contestation.[41]

First, contained political competitions vary greatly from one electoral democracy to the next. Moreover, authoritarian countries hold symbolic elections or no elections at all. Where institutions are weak and/or there is already violent conflict, political competition may be transgressive in that it takes place outside the formal internal institutional framework of the country altogether, while still occurring within country boundaries. The political contestations of interest in this project take place between identity groups within countries

---

[41] The importance of paying attention to the interaction of institutions and identity cleavages is amply illustrated in the electoral literature where the number of elected groups is jointly influenced by underlying diversity and institutions (Ordeshook and Shvetsova, 1994; Neto and Cox, 1997) and where institutions incentivize the expression of identity at different levels of aggregation in electoral competition (Posner, 2005). More recently, Selway (2015) even shows how underlying ethnic demography interacts with institutions to influence policy output. Specifically, he suggests proportional representation (PR) is better for public goods provision in countries with low ethnic salience (low fractionalization and/or high cross-cuttingness), while in high ethnic-salience countries (high fractionalization and low cross-cuttingness), majoritarian systems may perform better.

and we do not consider the role of cleavages in inter-state competition. However, we do believe our argument generalizes across strong and weak institutions. Where institutions are strong, we expect they clearly delineate the focus and actors relevant to the competition. Where institutions are weak, we expect that the competition often occurs outside formal state structures but that the focus and actors are delineated by the boundaries of the state, nationally or sub-nationally.[42]

The following examples briefly illustrate how the locus, form, and cleavage expression are influenced by strong institutions. Consider a simplified view of political races across the United States. First, the United States is a functioning electoral democracy, so political contestations for power generally transpire through the electoral system where voters vote for the candidates of their choice. For instance, candidates contesting the presidency of the United States likely seek to mobilize a winning coalition (and a CWC) drawing on the national population (or in this case, the segment with the most electoral college votes). In this contestation, therefore, the focus is on winning the office of the presidency and the relevant identity actors are nationally relevant identity groups. However, the relevant identity actors differ depending on the given competition. The United States is also a federal union and multiple electoral contests with distinct foci and boundaries take place within each state. For example, electoral contestants for governors mobilize state constituencies rather than national ones.

A simplified view across comparable races within a single country, such as mayoral races in the United States, helps illustrate how variation in the underlying constituency identity profile interacts with institutions to influence political entrepreneurs' choice of mobilizing strategies as they relate to mobilization of identity. In mayoral races in the United States, the focus is on winning the contestation for the leadership of the city and the type of competition is electoral,[43] and boundaries of the contestation delineate the locally pertinent identity groups that are registered to vote in city elections.

In Miami, for example, 70 percent of the city's residents are classified as Hispanic or of Latino origin.[44] Therefore, a politician whose goal is to become the mayor of Miami would presumably have to appeal to the Hispanic American vote to win. Furthermore, among Hispanics in Miami, 34.4 percent are of Cuban origin. Consequently, a politician would likely do well to select mobilization strategies that specifically incorporate references to and take into

---

[42] For example, while a violent conflict is carried out outside formal state structures such as elections it is still delineated at the national level by the boundaries of the state and at the sub-national level possibly by sub-state regional boundaries.

[43] A multitude of additional relevant institutional features bears on electoral competition, including district structure, party registration requirements, etc. However, the point that institutions structure the competition remains unaltered.

[44] For population figures, see data.census.gov. Breakdown by ethnic heritage is from the 2010 census.

consideration the distinct political preferences of Cuban Americans.[45] Seeking to unseat a Cuban incumbent a challenger in Miami might also mobilize a broader coalition of voters from all Central American countries including Cuba. In contrast, only 1.5 percent of Miami residents are of Mexican origin.[46] Therefore, references to the cultural heritage and needs and preferences of Mexican Americans likely would not provide any politician with much political leverage in Miami.[47]

Compare Miami to Los Angeles, where the population of Mexican Americans constitutes nearly 33 percent of the total population whereas the population of Cuban origin accounts for only a third of a percent.[48] Therefore, a politician aspiring to win the mayoral race in Los Angeles likely does so by specifically targeting the Mexican American vote with references to the unique features of Mexican American culture and the specific preferences and needs of this population or better yet with more general appeals to the Latino population that accounts for nearly half of all residents.

Juxtapose next Miami and Los Angeles with mayoral races in Oklahoma City to consider the effects of cleavage availability, salience, and size on political candidate mobilization strategies in Oklahoma. Race is a highly salient political issue in the country today. Whites account for 72.4 percent of the Oklahoman population statewide, Blacks constitute 7.3 percent, American Indian or Alaskan Natives constitute another 8 percent, and other non-White ethnicities less (U.S. Census, 2020a).[49] In Oklahoma City, Whites account for 67.7 percent of the population, Blacks number 14.4 percent but American Indian or Alaskan Natives constitute only 2.9 percent, Asians make up 4.5 percent, and other non-White minorities less (U.S. Census, 2020b). Clearly, therefore, non-White ethnic and/or racial groups, even if unified, do not constitute a large enough group to carry the vote either statewide or in the city.

Setting aside politicians' personal convictions, racial outbidding might seem like a tempting strategy for mayoral contests in Oklahoma but one that is risky

---

[45] Furthermore, while political partisanship and functional cleavages such as economic class may exert a stronger influence overall on the vote in the United States than does the ethnic–cultural cleavage, this is less the case for Cubans than other Latinos (de la Garza, 2004).

[46] In addition to coming from different countries with very different histories and cultures, Cubans and Mexicans are also divided in their predominant geographic locations and immigrant experience within the United States (Calderon, 1992; Oboler, 1995).

[47] At the same time salience of both Cuban American and Mexican American identities has varied over time in each location and in relation to local- and national-level politics making the emphasis on identity politics more or less effective at different times. Until recently, for example, ethnicity has been a good predictor of electoral outcomes in Miami. However, recent election results suggest this may be changing Mazzei (2018).

[48] Figures are 2010 census figures as reported along with 2019 estimates by the Los Angeles Almanac. www.laalmanac.com/

[49] Asian 2.3 percent, Native Hawaiian and other Pacific Islanders 0.1 percent, other races "alone" 2.3 percent and people of two or more races 7.6 percent.

for a number of reasons.[50] In contrast, religion[51] as a second salient alternative cleavage for mobilization, is demographically a very attractive option for Oklahoma politicians. Specifically, 79 percent of adult residents of Oklahoma City are Christians and thereof 47 percent identify as Evangelicals, including both Democrats and Republicans. Mainline and historically Black Protestants account for 22 percent and Catholics for 8 percent.[52] Numbers of adherents of all non-Christian faiths are negligible. The religious cleavage is by no means the only alternative identity available for mobilization in Oklahoma,[53] and religious voters are not necessarily any more fervent in politics than are their less religious counterparts (Rausch Jr., 1994). However, for a mayoral candidate who wants the Oklahomans' vote, courting Evangelicals across party lines is clearly an attractive mobilization strategy (Gaddie and Buchanan, 1998) simply because of their numbers[54] and apparent salience of this cleavage.[55]

This is not to suggest that the religious identity will be courted across race in US electoral politics (Calhoun-Brown, 1998; McKenzie and Rouse, 2013; Wong, 2018, 2019; Orcés, 2021). The point here is that even within the same country, in different states or cities, as constrained by institutions,

---

[50] One, overt racism is politically risky because of legislation prohibiting overt racism in many aspects of public life. Two, local racial outbidding could negatively affect a mayoral candidate aspiring to upward mobility beyond state boundaries. Three, racist mobilization might also be unpopular in a state where – despite their low proportions – non-White American Indian elected officials are prominent in state politics. For instance, in 2006, Oklahoma legislators created a Native American caucus and the current group of fifteen lawmakers "representing five of the state's nearly 40 federally recognized tribes meets monthly to discuss upcoming legislation, bridge communication gaps and share concerns" (Branch, 2020). See also Tribes (2006). Furthermore, for the first time in 2019 in the Oklahoma legislature the proportion of Black legislators rose to 5 percent with seven legislators, the highest number ever (Felder, 2019). In addition, historically of the twenty-two American Indians that have been elected to the US House or Senate, eight have been from Oklahoma, making Native American Oklahomans prominent in national politics. In contrast only one Black representative, Julius Cesar Watts Jr., has been elected to Congress from Oklahoma (House of Representatives, 2021). Finally, a large proportion of Oklahomans claim American Indian heritage, and American Indians constitute an increasingly important economic force in the state (Chavar, 2014) possibly deterring overt racist politics. Even so, in the United States, consolidating a White winning coalition vote by way of outbidding that targets ethnic and/or racial minorities is, still a strategy employed by politicians to win votes in elections (Major et al., 2018) and this clearly is a topic that merits continued attention.

[51] The history of Evangelical mobilization in the United States is intertwined with racial antagonism, though the primary religious social divide has shifted to LBQT rights in more recent decades (Wald, 2014).

[52] For these and additional data on religion across the United States, see Smith (2015).

[53] Urban/rural divide is another cleavage in the state (Krehbiel, 2017).

[54] Were an ethnic minority leader to attempt an alternative mobilization of a CWC in Oklahoma, religion would be a plausible available cleavage. However, because of low minority numbers relative to the majority, this is not likely.

[55] News reports about Oklahoma elections confirm that religion is not the only factor in Oklahoma voters' choice but it does matter (Lackmeyer, 2004; Felder, 2016).

the demographic configuration of available identities makes different types of identity mobilization in contained politics more or less likely. In some cases race and/or ethnicity may constitute an attractive platform for mobilization, in other cases religion provides a greater opportunity, and in some of those cases that opportunity cuts across race and/or ethnicity. The same is true in transgressive politics. The underlying demographic numbers condition the types of identity mobilization that likely emerges in that they make available and/or more attractive certain identities for mobilization while precluding others. Where transgressive politics take place at the state level – such as in civil war – the relevant institutions are the boundaries of the state and the relevant demographics are those of the national population.

3.5 CONCLUSION

To conclude, the overall contribution of this chapter is that it demonstrates how accounting for demography and the intersection of group identities allows for theoretical refinements, which assist in providing answers to persistent puzzles in the literature. Thus, one implication of our argument clarifies the role of fully segmented minority group size in majority leaders' choices to outbid. Specifically, this implication suggests an answer to the question of why outbidding dynamics only occur among a sub-sample of segmented identity groups.[56]

Another implication provides an answer to the persistent puzzles outlined in the introduction about shared cleavages and political conflict. Despite the fact that the literature leads us to believe shared cleavages decrease the likelihood of political conflict, non-violent and violent conflicts between ethnic groups that share religion are abundant. The answer we suggest to this puzzle in this book is that the conflict-dampening effect of shared identities varies with minority group demographic size. In particular, where ethnic minority groups approach majority groups in size, the shared identity becomes more attractive to minority group leaders as a vehicle to press the state for access. Because minorities operate in the realm of majority politics, we further expect that the tipping point associated with majority segmented cleavage only encourages minority mobilization of the shared cleavage when minorities approach majorities in size.

The objective of the remainder of this book is to examine and test the implication of the interaction of shared identity and political demography in various different ways. In particular we are interested in examining the types of mobilization outlined in this chapter across transgressive and contained

---

[56] We test this conjecture empirically elsewhere, showing that minority group size is strongly related to majority outbidding (Birnir et al., n.d.).

political environments. In Chapter 4, we focus on violent civil conflict to show that as majority/minority ethnic dyads, which share religion and are engaged in ethnic civil conflict, approach demographic parity, the more likely minority combatants are to claim the conflict is about religion. Subsequent chapters delve into case narratives to probe the conflict mechanisms we suggest – in Chapter 5 across transgressive politics and in Chapter 6 in a contained political setting.

4

Testing the *Challenger's Winning Coalition* Hypothesis on Mobilization of Religion in Ethnic Civil War

4.1 INTRODUCTION

The literature considers shared identities to stabilize political systems while segmented identities invite more identity competition (Lipset, 1981; Lipset and Rokkan, 1967; Lijphart, 1977, 1999; Selway, 2011b; Gordon et al., 2015; Siroky and Hechter, 2016). Therefore, one of the principal questions this book tackles is why conflict participants in civil wars share faith more often than they are separated by it. Chapter 3 provided the general theoretical insight that group-relative size and intersection of identities with the majority likely affect the strategies of identity mobilization that are chosen by minority group leaders. One testable implication of this general theory is the *Challenger's Winning Coalition* (CWC), which specifies that when groups that are segmented on one identity dimension become increasingly even in size, an additional shared identity presents leaders of the minority with an opportunity for alternative mobilization of the shared identity, across the segmenting identity.

The theory of *Alternatives in Mobilization* proposed in Chapter 3 is agnostic as to the content of the alternative cleavage being mobilized. Instead, the driver of the mechanism we expect to see is demography and shared cleavages.[1] In contrast, in this chapter, the empirical focus is on the strategic mobilization of religion across ethnicity, specifically asking whether the theoretical insight from Chapter 3 casts light on the observed role of shared religion in ethnic civil conflict across the globe.

---

[1] For instance, the theory would predict that separate religious groups sharing ethnic identity would be increasingly likely to mobilize the shared ethnic identity as their relative size becomes more even, *and* that evenly sized ethnic groups would mobilize a shared religion. Strictly speaking, we expect this prediction to be true, and in Chapter 6 on the politics of Indonesia, we return to the idea that demographic variation creates incentives for many different types of mobilization, including in electoral politics.

We already know a great deal about the role of religion in violent mobilization between ethnic groups that are also segmented by religion. Between segmented groups, religion is shown to reinforce in-group/out-group ethnic distinctions, decrease the cost of collective action, and provide the organization and symbols that help motivate mobilization (Toft, 2013; Stewart, 2012; Basedau et al., 2011, 2016; Basedau and Koos, 2015; Selway, 2011a; Ellingsen, 2005; Seul, 1999; Juan and Hasenclever, 2015). However, despite the fact that mobilization of religion in conflict is increasingly common (Toft, 2006, 2007, 2021; Fox, 2012; Mason and Mitchell, 2016; Svensson and Nilsson, 2018), and Islam is pinpointed as the most prevalent faith to engage in intra-religious conflict (Toft, 2006, 2021; De-Soysa and Nordas, 2007: 12),[2] we know much less about the role of shared religion in violent mobilization between ethnic groups. Therefore, the analysis in this chapter empirically explores whether large ethnic minority groups that share a religion with the majority are more likely to strategically use this shared cleavage to gain access to power. We believe this is one of the missing pieces of the puzzle on religion and conflict in the literature.

Notably, the CWC prediction is independent of the content of the particular religion that is mobilized. Furthermore, we expect the conjectures about the selection of strategies in identity mobilization hold across peaceful and violent political contestation, and we explore peace-time mobilization further in subsequent chapters. At the same time, identity mobilization is often endogenous to changing political circumstances such as institutions (Posner, 2005). Moreover, specifically speaking to conflict, Kaufman's (2001, 2015) theory of symbolism, for instance, explains how conflict processes harden identities that are mobilized for purposes of conflict in ways that likely influence subsequent identity mobilization later in the conflict.[3] Consequently, it is possible that collective identity mobilization, especially when it involves shifts from one identity category to another, is subject to different constraints across non-violent and violent settings. Therefore, in examining the role of identity cleavages in collective action,[4] we follow the convention in the literature and focus specifically on civil war in this chapter and the next, however, turn our attention to non-violent political contestation in Chapter 6.[5]

---

[2] The reasons for this are largely considered exogenous to doctrine.

[3] Importantly, Kaufman rejects the idea of "ancient hatreds" as the driver of ethnic conflict but explores how identities "harden" in a given conflict. Similarly, focusing on the role of emotion in ethnic conflict, Petersen (2002) rejects the idea of "ancient hatreds" while explaining how resentment contributes to ethnic conflict, in ways that likely influence mobilization throughout the duration of the conflict.

[4] Furthermore, as discussed in Chapter 1, it is possible that the identities themselves operate differently under different circumstances. Therefore, our examination in this chapter focuses on a particular cleavage mobilization under a comparable set of circumstances.

[5] To be clear the case we explore in Chapter 6, Indonesia, has seen its share of violence, which has been extensively studied. The outcome that we examine in Chapter 6 is non-violent electoral politics.

It bears reiterating that the outcome we purport to explain (mobilization of religious identity) is not the cause of collective action – but rather one identity strategy selected, given conflict mobilization. Specifically, in this chapter, we begin testing the implication pertaining to the role of group size and intersection of identity cleavages, in strategic mobilization by minority ethnic group leaders of a CWC centering on religion. To add historical nuance to the explanation of why among the multitude of possible shared identities, shared religion is increasingly a preferred mobilization strategy in civil war, the chapter begins with some contextualization of evolving identity conflict dynamics over the last century. Next, we undertake the cross-national test of the hypothesis predicting the emergence of a religion-based CWC among evenly sized ethnic groups engaged in civil conflict.

4.1.1 Why Religion and Why Now?

Pettersson and Wallensteen's (2015) historical overview of civil conflict after 1946 reveals an increase in the cumulative number of civil conflicts beginning in the 1960s, accelerating in the 1970s, and peaking in numbers after the fall of the Soviet Union. Thereafter, the number of civil conflicts decreases somewhat but still remains relatively high.

The conflicts, recorded by the Uppsala Conflict Data Program (UCDP), are of various types. Between 1945 and 1960 the number of extra-state or colonial conflicts was close to one for every two intra-state conflicts. Many of the conflicts after WWII also took on the ideological dimensions of the Cold War, likely in part because in a bi-polar world, ideology had the advantage of allowing for appeals to an external backer.[6] After the 1960s the relative number of colonial conflicts decreased, with the last recorded in the UCDP data terminating in 1974, while the number of intra-state civil conflicts rose steadily (Pettersson et al., 2019). Among intra-state conflicts the relative number of conflicts over the control of government increased beginning in the 1970s to rival the number of conflicts over territory, which had predominated earlier (Gleditsch et al., 2016).

Furthermore, according to Denny and Walter (2014), two-thirds of all intra-state conflicts since 1946 were fought between different ethnic groups though ethnic divisions were more common among secessionists.[7] Theoretically, ethnicity may be a straightforward first choice for a majority in conflict over government for a variety of reasons. For example, prior colonial conflicts may have activated ethnic consciousness making this identity easily mobilizable, or ethnic cleavages may on average lend themselves better to majority MWC mobilization for demographic reasons than do other identities such as religion. Minorities may then find themselves in a conflict defined by the majority MWC

---

[6] For a historical discussion of Marxist revolutionaries, see Balcells and Kalyvas (n.d.).
[7] See also Themner and Wallenstein (2014).

as an ethnic conflict. Alternatively, minorities may initiate ethnic conflict in response to perceived grievances with the objective of redress if not an outright takeover of government – especially when ethnicity overlaps ideological divisions. Furthermore, in intra-state conflict over territory, ethnicity is an attractive minority choice because of the frequent overlap between ethnicity and territorial concentration.

Whatever the reason for the prevalence of ethnic conflicts, Toft et al. (2011) point out that religion experienced a "political comeback" or "revival" after the Iranian revolution, which forcefully reintroduced this identity dimension into contemporary national-level violent political contestation in 1979. Thus the political "comeback" of religion coincided with the heyday and subsequent decline of bi-polar backing of governments and rebel groups where ideology sometimes reinforced ethnicity. Especially around the collapse of the Soviet Union in 1991, the popularity of Marxist mobilization waned, and many minority challengers likely searched for alternative ways to mobilize masses in their bid for political access.

It is, therefore, perhaps not surprising that after 1979 and especially after 1991, religion has become increasingly prominent as a mobilizing principle in conflict (Fox, 2003; Toft, 2006; Philpott, 2007; Toft et al., 2011; Satana et al., 2013; Svensson and Nilsson, 2018), including in ethnic civil conflicts for reasons that likely also include contagion (Fox, 2004a; Buhaug and Gleditsch, 2008; Kathman, 2011), and state collapse or economic decline (Hasenclever and Rittberger, 2000; Mason and Mitchell, 2016).

As a mobilization tool the attraction of religion is well understood. As explained by several scholars, religion has a distinct organizational advantage for mobilization due to its emphasis and enforcement of attachment to the community and its defense against any perceived attacks from outsiders (Tilly, 1978; Philpott, 2007; Mecham, 2017; Birnir and Overos, 2019). Furthermore, religion accommodates external supporters (Raphaeli, 2003; Crenshaw, 2017). Therefore, the role of religion in violent contestation between segmented ethno-religious groups since the 1980s has received considerable attention in the literature, and is well understood especially when initiated through a majority outbidding strategy among segmented ethno-religious identity groups (Horowitz, 1985; Toft, 2013).

However, to our knowledge, there are few explanations for why religion becomes an organizing principle between ethnic groups that share a religion in some violent conflict mobilization and not others. This is where our project contributes. We build on the understanding that violent conflict is best understood not as a discrete event, but as episodes (McAdam et al., 2001) in what is often a protracted struggle for power between communal groups (Gurr, 2000), in a complex and interdependent world (Azar, 1990). Taking this view of civil conflict over recent decades, it stands to reason that, if not earlier then at least beginning in the 1980s, members of ethnic groups who engaged in civil conflict with majority groups of the same religion are aware of the increasingly common use of religion as a mobilizing strategy in contentious politics.[8] Thus, leaders of ethnic minorities likely consider whether religion is a viable route to success in their group's bid for power, especially as Marxist mobilization loses its appeal. Our contribution is to clarify why, as conditioned by demographics, some ethnic minority groups that share religion with majorities take advantage of this attractive strategy in civil wars, while others do not.

Specifically, the idea we test in this chapter is the CWC, which applied to ethnicity and religion in that order, is that *in civil conflict between majority and minority ethnic groups of the same religion, the probability that conflict claims center on religion increases with greater population balance between the groups.* In violent national-level contestation such as civil war, we expect national-level identities, their relative size, and cross-cutting condition the numbers game that leaders (and followers) play in mobilizing conflict participants.[9] Submitting these implications to several empirical tests, the results in this chapter show clear support: when ethnic minorities share a religion with majorities, the probability that conflict parties claim religious incompatibility increases as the groups' relative size approaches parity.

The chapter next discusses in detail the cross-national data we use to test this implication. Then we turn to the series of tests used to probe our hypothesis across cases of civil conflict. Chapters 5 and 6 subsequently further explore, through in-depth case studies, the prediction of identity mobilization (religion) conditional on (ethnic) group-relative size.

4.2 THE DATA

The scope of our inquiry in this chapter – focusing on the strategies that group leaders promote for purposes of mobilization – pertains to all ethnic groups participating in civil wars. Taking into account the idea that group conflicts are embedded in regional and global politics (Azar, 1990), the period of time that we are interested in stretches back to at least 1979, when the Iranian revolution brought religious mobilization to the forefront of contemporary civil conflicts.

For some ethnic groups, mobilization of religion is a primary conflict mobilization strategy from conflict onset. For example, in the conflict between the government of Chad and the Beri, at least one minority-affiliated organization claimed religious incompatibility with the government at the outset of the conflict (Svensson and Nilsson, 2018). At the same time, the view of

---

[8] To be clear – and as the case analyses in Chapter 5 illustrate – in many cases religion was intermittently mobilized along with ethnicity long before the Iranian revolution. The point here is simply to draw attention to contagion in cases where religion may not have been previously mobilized.

[9] Where the political cost is loss of local control of resources, we expect that local identities, both their demographic shares and overlap, will condition incentives for local mobilization. These local identities may or may not mirror national-level identities. We explore local identity politics further in Chapter 6 where we study Indonesia in-depth.

civil conflicts as protracted social phenomena (Azar, 1990; McAdam et al., 2001) would suggest that the emergence of "new" organizations or "new" leadership of existing organizations in successive conflict periods, may reveal changing strategies among a more constant set of actors. Over time some of these strategies include mobilization of religion. Thus, for some ethnic groups, mobilization of a religious coalition is perhaps not the original strategy but one that is pursued by leaders seeking power at some later point after conflict onset, when other strategies have proven unsuccessful. For instance, the Tuareg and the government of Mali were engaged in civil conflict over the Azawad region long before any conflict participants began claiming religious incompatibility in civil war.[10] Indeed, prior to the founding of the Islamist Ansar Dine, the Tuareg leader Iyad Ag Ghaly, nicknamed "the strategist," is reported to have failed to secure a leadership position in the secular National Movement for the Liberation of Azawad (MNLA) (Beaumont, 2012).[11]

Organizations associated with ethnic groups enter and exit conflicts at different times. Sometimes many different organizations represent the same ethnic group, other times they do so sequentially. Over time one or more organizations often come to predominate mobilization, mostly only for a short time. At times, leaders of multiple organizations seek to mobilize members of the same ethnic group. In some cases leaders emerge and are only subsequently incorporated into an existing organization or alternatively, they split and establish a new organization. For instance, in a single conflict between the government of Afghanistan and several different ethnic groups, in different configurations depending on who controls the government, the largest ethnic group, Sunni Pashtuns, has been represented by nine different organizations that may include other co-religious ethnic groups.[12]

---

[10] This conflict is an excellent example of conflict where at times conflict participants seemingly pursued both secessionist goals and goals for greater access to the state. On account of groups often harboring multiple goals sequentially or at the same time, in the empirical analysis, we account for secessionist movements but do not specifically select out of the analysis groups that among other goals pursue secession.

[11] To be clear according to Svensson and Nilsson (2018: 1131), "Religious issue captures whether there is a religious dimension in the original incompatibility as explicitly stated at the onset of the conflict by the representatives of the primary parties." This is technically correct with respect to their data as coded at the organizational level, and when considering each organization as a new actor in a given conflict. It is only when taking the long-term view that is described above, of multiple organizations as representing a single ethnic group, that temporal variance in choice of group strategies becomes more apparent.

[12] According to the ACD2 (2018) data (Vogt et al., 2015), these organizations are Taliban, Jam'iyyat-i Islami-yi Afghanistan (Islamic Society of Afghanistan), Hizb-i Islami-yi Afghanistan (Islamic Party of Afghanistan), Hizb-i Demokratik-i Khalq-i Afghanistan (People's Democratic Party of Afghanistan or PDPA), Mahaz-i Milli-yi Islami-yi Afghanistan (National Islamic Front of Afghanistan), Ittihad-i Islami Bara-yi Azadi-yi Afghanistan (Islamic Union for the Freedom of Afghanistan), Harakat-i Islami-yi Afghanistan (Islamic Movement of Afghanistan), Hizb-i Islami-yi Afghanistan – Khalis faction (Islamic Party of Afghanistan – Khalis faction), and UIFSA (Northern Alliance or United Islamic Front for Salvation of Afghanistan).

This is not to suggest that civil conflict actors are necessarily only organiza-tions. Indeed, many organizations in the context of conflict are fluid and change rapidly to the point of being better described as transitory expressions of social movements than formal organizations with set leadership and administrative structures.[13] When observing claim-making at the group level as opposed to the organizational level in civil war, it becomes even more apparent that strategies of claim-making shift over time. For example, at some point in time multiple organizations representing minority groups that share religion with the majority come to claim religious incompatibility in conflict where conflict claims originally did not focus on religion. In addition to the Tuareg in Mali, such groups include, for instance, the Acholi, Langi and Teso in Uganda, Uzbeks in Tajikistan, the Luba Shaba in the Democratic Republic of Congo (Zaire), Sunni in Lebanon, Arabs in Libya and Sunni in Yemen, and Southern Shafi'i in North Yemen.[14]

Accordingly, the theoretical implication tested in this chapter is that within a country as the population balance becomes more even between ethnic groups that share religion and are engaged in civil conflict, the probability increases that conflict claims come to center on religion. The central premise of this argument is that *group demographics* create opportunities of which leaders of groups take advantage. Therefore, our test focuses on the mechanism that is changing incentives across groups as conditioned by relative group size.[15] This argument and test accommodate well the organizational fluidity in the emergence of leadership described above, as they pinpoint from which groups – and not organizations – leaders and followers emerge in alternative mobilization. These leaders can be members of more or less formal orga-nizations or may act as independent agents leading a movement. At some point they likely become involved with one or more organizations facilitating group mobilization, however, the part of the equation explaining how leaders come to participate in one organization or another is outside the scope of our inquiry.

Importantly, not all leaders and/or organizations representing the group need to agree that mobilization of religion is a viable strategy. Sometimes a group

---

[13] Event data that disaggregate conflict actors further than the organizational level, such as the Social Conflict Analysis Database (available at www.strausscenter.org/scad.html), better illustrate the actual variance of actors engaging in conflict mobilization. Our case studies in Chapters 5 and 6 pinpoint the same complexity.

[14] For example, the Lord's Resistance Army (LRA) in Uganda claims religious incompatibility in 1988 but the Langi and Acholi are previously represented by several organizations including the UNLF and the United People's Defense Army (UPDA), neither of which claim religious incompatibility with the majority. Another example, Uzbeks in Tajikistan are first represented by Forces of Khudoberdiyev that do not claim religious incompatibility, and later by the Islamist Movement of Uzbekistan (IMU) that does.

[15] Theoretically we should also be able to observe changing incentives for mobilization within a single group over time as group-relative size changes and we explore this further in Chapter 5.

is represented by multiple organizations only some of whom claim religious incompatibility with the state. Our theory is not deterministic; it only suggests that certain incentive structures make a given strategy more likely to be pursued by purported representatives of the group. Therefore, to capture mobilization of religion in contemporary conflicts at conflict onset or at any time subsequently, the unit of analysis in our study is the ethnic group in a given conflict year, beginning with the year of conflict onset.

4.2.1 The Universe of Cases

Ethnic groups that fight civil wars have similar reasons for fighting as other groups in civil wars (Denny and Walter, 2014), though the onset of ethnic civil war may also have some distinguishing features such as group grievances and repression (Sambanis, 2001). Our theory does not explain how collective action for civil war mobilization onset transpires, but it explores which strategies groups adopt, given mobilization. Mobilization onset and strategic trajectories, given onset, are analytically distinct and require different samples for empirical testing.[16] Since our focus is on the selection of strategies, given onset, the appropriate universe of cases for our inquiry includes all ethnic groups already engaged in civil war.

The strategy we are especially interested in is mobilization of shared religion in ethnic civil conflict. For information on the use of this strategy we rely on Svensson and Nilsson's (2018) coding of claim-making of religious incompatibility in civil war, in the Religion and Armed Conflict Data (RELAC).[17] RELAC's universe of cases is based on the Uppsala Conflict Data Program's (UCDP) Dyadic data.[18] Of these dyads, the RELAC data focus on the 420 government and rebel group dyads involved in armed conflict between 1975 and 2015 (Svensson and Nilsson, 2018: 1130).

As civil wars are ruinous on a very large scale, we are confident that they are comprehensively captured in the UCDP, and thus, in the RELAC data. However, in contrast to the group focus of the theory in Chapter 3 and in the A-Religion data introduced in Chapter 2, the RELAC data are coded at the level of the organization and do not include ethnic codes. Therefore, to identify ethnic

---

[16] For a recent discussion about appropriate samples for testing, in the literature pertaining to ethnic groups, see Birnir et al. (2018).

[17] We want to thank Isaak Svensson and Desirée Nilsson for their extraordinary generosity in sharing these data. When we contacted Isaak in 2013 regarding the first version of his data on religious claim-making (Svensson, 2007), he generously offered to send us updates to the data that he was then working on with research assistants. Therefore, we have been able to merge our original data with successive versions of his data in 2007, 2013, and 2018 and test our theory with all the versions. Our results remain substantively the same.

[18] Version 1-2016. For further information, see https://ucdp.uu.se/. The criterion for entering into these data is being an "active" conflict, which is defined as "at least 25 battle-related deaths per calendar year in one of the conflict's dyads" (see www.pcr.uu.se/research/ucdp/definitions).

actors in RELAC's universe, we use the ACD2EPR data (hereafter ACD2) (Vogt et al., 2015) coding of ethnic organizations in conflict from 1975 to 2015, as a bridge between RELAC and the A-Religion data and supplement the ethnic identification of groups when necessary with our original coding.[19] The ACD2 includes the latest coding of politically active ethnic actors in the Ethnic Power Relations (EPR) data, of UCDP's civil conflict organizational data.[20] In earlier versions of our tests, we used Forsberg's pioneering work that identifies ethnic actors in civil conflict (Forsberg, 2014), in conjunction with earlier versions of the ACD2 data.[21] Our results have remained substantively the same through multiple iterations of our tests, likely because the earlier Forsberg data and the later ACD2 data mostly code ethnic groups in both data sets in a similar way.

Complicating matters, while coding the same conflicts within a given time frame, the RELAC and the most recent version of the ACD2 data do not share dyad-identifying codes because ACD2 uses the most recent UCDP codes,[22] while the RELAC data uses 2016 codes. Thus the illustrative example in Table 4.1 shows how we used the organizational information in the ACD2 data to identify ethnic dyads in the RELAC data. The first five cells in the table represent RELAC coding of a unique Conflict identity code, Dyad identity code, Location of the conflict, and Side B organization name. The fifth, sixth, and seventh cells show the comparable information available for this case in the ACD2 data,[23] Side B organization name, ethnic Group affiliation, and ethnic Group id code.

We direct the reader to three main observations in Table 4.1 that illustrate how these two data sets fit together. First, the unit of observation in the RELAC data is the organization. Therefore, in the example of Pakistan where many organizations represent a single ethnic group, all the organizations shown on the RELAC side of the table are represented by separate dyadids. However, because the ACD2 centers on the ethnic group, all organizations that represent the same ethnic group are assigned the same group id on the

---

[19] Our coding matched additional cases and adjudicated differences in coding between various data sets. For example, the ACD2 (2018) data matches the United Islamic Front for the Salvation of Afghanistan (UIFSA) to Tajiks, Hazara, Uzbeks, and Pashtuns. In contrast, Forsberg's earlier coding (2005, 2014) matches the UIFSA only to Tajiks, Hazara, and Uzbeks. Other sources we consulted made clear that Tajiks, Hazara, and Uzbeks make up the bulk of the organization's members. However, a few sources do suggest UIFSA was also supported by some Pashtuns (Australian Government 2014). Consequently, we retain the ACD2 match. For additional detail on our coding see the AMAR website.

[20] The ACD2 data are available at https://icr.ethz.ch/data/epr/acd2epr/ For description of the data, see Wucherpfennig et al. (2011) and Vogt et al. (2015).

[21] We thank Erika Forsberg and Manuel Vogt respectively, for helpful discussions about the data.

[22] Personal conversation with Manuel Vogt, 2018.

[23] Specifically, we matched organizations on name and used 2014 ACD2 dyadid if there was a question ACD2 (2014) dyadids do match RELAC dyadids (Svensson and Nilsson, 2018). We also attempted to use organization codes found at ucdp.uu.se/downloads/ but did not find this to facilitate the match.

TABLE 4.1. *Accounting for ethnicity of RELAC conflict actors*

Conflict Id	RELAC			ACD2 2018		
	Location	Side B	Dyadid	Side B	Group	Groupid
1-129	Pakistan	BLF	544	BLF	Baluchis	77001000
1-129	Pakistan	Baloch Ittehad	638	Baloch Ittehad	Baluchis	77001000
1-129	Pakistan	BLA	639	BLA	Baluchis	77001000
1-129	Pakistan	BRA	774	BRA	Baluchis	77001000
1-209	Pakistan	MQM	340	MQM	Mohajirs	77003000
1-209	Pakistan	TTP	768	TTP	Pashtuns	77004000
1-209	Pakistan	TTP - TA	843	TTP - TA	Pashtuns	77004000
1-209	Pakistan	Lashkar-e-Islam	844	Lashkar-e-Islam	Pashtuns	77004000
1-209	Pakistan	IMU	10961	IMU		
1-209	Pakistan	Jamaat-ul-Ahrar	14227	Jamaat-ul-Ahrar		
1-95	Peru	Sendero	235	Sendero Luminoso	Indigenous peoples of the Andes	13501000
				Sendero Luminoso	Whites or Mestizos	13502000

ACD2 side of the table. Second, not all organizations represent ethnic groups. For example, in Pakistan, the IMU and the Jamaat-ul-Ahrar are not coded as ethnic organizations in the ACD2 data, therefore, they are not assigned an ethnic group identifier. These organizations drop out of our sample. Third is the example of Peru where a single organization in the RELAC data represents more than one ethnic group in the ACD2 data. Thus, the organization (Sendero) that is represented by a single dyadid in the RELAC data is split between two ethnic groups with two distinct group identifiers in the ACD2 data. For additional detail about this coding, see Appendix C as explained in greater detail below.

4.2.2 The Unit of Analysis: From Organizations to Groups

Because the testable implications resulting from the theory of *Alternatives in Mobilization* presented in Chapter 3 are at group level, we next match the ethnic RELAC organizations with the AMAR sample frame coded for religion in the

TABLE 4.2. *Collapsing or expanding RELAC organizational data to the A-Religion group level*

RELAC				A-Religion		
Conflict Id	Location	Side B	Rel. claims	Conflict Id	Group Side B	Rel. claims
1–129	Pakistan	BLF	0	1–129	Baluchis	0
1–129	Pakistan	Baloch Ittehad	0			
1–129	Pakistan	BLA	0			
1–129	Pakistan	BRA	0			
1–209	Pakistan	MQM	0	1–209	Mohajirs	0
1–209	Pakistan	TTP	1	1–209	Pashtuns	1
1–209	Pakistan	TTP - TA	1			
1–209	Pakistan	Lashkar-e-Islam	1			
1–209	Pakistan	IMU	1			
1–209	Pakistan	Jamaat-ul-Ahrar	1			
1–95	Peru	Sendero	0	1–95	Highland Indigenous	0
				1–95	Mestizo or White	0

A-Religion data discussed in Chapter 2. To this end, all RELAC organizations that represent a given ethnic group within a country in a given year are collapsed or expanded to the level of that group as coded in A-Religion data.

The resulting data structure, including both types of cases, collapsed and expanded organizations (as illustrated with the examples of Pakistan and Peru), is shown in Table 4.2. Again the first three cells in the data represent RELAC coding of a unique Conflict identity code, Location of the Conflict, and Side B organization name. The fourth cell on the RELAC side of the data in Table 4.2 is the indicator recording whether this organization made claims of religious incompatibility. This variable is coded annually for each organization in the RELAC data.[24] The fifth, sixth, and seventh cells show how the RELAC data are matched with the A-Religion data at the group level.

---

[24] In general, religious affiliation and coding of religious incompatibility of the ethnic group as associated with an organization is straightforward. There are, however, a few exceptions. For example, according to ACD2, the Lugbara are part of the Far North-west Nile (Kakwa-Nubian, Madi, Lugbara, Alur) coalition. This coalition is matched in ACD2 with several organizations, including the Alliance of Democratic Forces (ADF). All organizations they are matched with except for the ADF are Christian (Svensson and Nilsson, 2018), and none but the

The fifth cell accounts for the Conflict Id, the sixth for the Group name to which ethnic organizations were matched, and the seventh cell indicates whether any of the organizations representing a given ethnic group in a given year made religious claims in the conflict.

The reader will note in Table 4.2 that in cases such as the example of Pakistan from Table 4.1, where multiple organizations represent an ethnic group, all organizations are collapsed to the group level for a single group-level observation accounting for whether any of the organizations representing the group in a given conflict year claimed religious incompatibility. In contrast, in the example case of Peru where the Sendero represented both indigenous groups and Whites/Mestizos, the number of observations is expanded to account for both groups. The groups are then matched with the A-Religion data in a data set that includes the group year, from the time that any organization representing the group engaged in conflict.

Figure 4.1 summarizes the process of data matching including the numbers of observations in each set of data. Each transition is then discussed in greater detail in the following data probing section. Briefly, the original RELAC data contain 2044 organization year observations that are relevant to our inquiry.[25]

ADF claim religious incompatibility with the state. Thus, the religious incompatibility claimed by the Lugbara (who are coded as Christian in A-Religion) is only through an organization that is Muslim. Therefore, we code the Lugbara and other ADF-affiliated Christian groups in Uganda (Banyoro, Toro, Banyarwanda) as not making claims of incompatibility against their Christian co-religionists. The Acholi are still coded as making claims of religious incompatibility against their co-religionists because of their association with the Lord's Resistance Army (LRA). Another group that is rather complicated is the Chuvashes in Russia, which is coded as Christian in A-Religion. According to the ACD2, this group is represented by the Islamic State, which is noted by Svensson and Nilsson (2018) as Muslim. The Islamic state does claim religious incompatibility with the state but across religion not within religion. Consequently, we code the Chuvashes as not claiming religious incompatibility within religion against the state. Similarly, the ADC2 codes the National Liberation Front of Tripura (NLFT) in India as a Tripuri organization. The Tripuri are mainly Hindu but the NLFT "has also taken an assertive pro-Christian stance. At the core of their perception of the incompatibility stands resentment against the perceived political and economical supremacy of the Bengali immigrants" (UCDP, 2021). Consequently, the NLFT is coded in RELAC as a Christian organization and we code the Tripuri accordingly as not making claims against co-religionist state. Other cases are complicated for coding but in ways that have less implication for our test. For example, according to Svensson and Nilsson (2018), the Eritrean People's Liberation Front (EPLF) in Ethiopia shares Christianity with the governing majority. However, according to ACD2, the EPLF represents both Christian and Muslim Eritreans. The group does not claim religious incompatibility with the state and we match it with both Muslim and Christian ethnic groups in A-Religion. Other such cases are resolved on a case-by-case basis.

[25] The complete RELAC data contain 2812 organization years. However, these also include observations from conflicts where onset was prior to 1975, and those observations are not coded for religious incompatibility. Furthermore, the RELAC data include "Extrasystemic" conflicts, which are conflicts between foreign governments and a local group. For instance the data include conflicts such as that between the Khmer Issarak in Cambodia and the French Government in the 1940s and 1950s. Such conflicts are clearly outside the scope of this study and we drop them before matching.

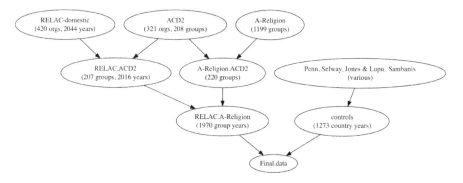

FIGURE 4.1. The data merging process (units and number of observations in parentheses)

The ACD2 data, in turn, code 207 relevant groups across 318 organizations in RELAC as ethnic.[26] However, many groups are represented across multiple organizations and the number of relevant observations in the ACD2 data is 420 when accounting for groups represented by multiple organizations. After matching the RELAC-ACD2 the number of unique relevant ethnic actors is 207 unique ethnic groups, represented by 318 unique organizations.[27] Next, the ethnically identified RELAC data are matched with the A-Religion data, resulting in a data set containing 2023 group-year observations of 201 ethnic groups.

4.2.3 Probing the Data: A-Religion and RELAC

Figure 4.1 highlights the two stages at which the numbers of observations are manipulated for the purpose of joining different data sources. The first is when organizations are collapsed or expanded to the group level when matching organizations with ethnic groups. The second stage is when ethnic groups are (1) expanded or collapsed or (2) included or excluded, because of differences in group definition and inclusion between data sets enumerating ethnicity.

---

[26] The complete ACD2 data contains information on 645 organizations. After removing organizations that are not coded as ethnic and organizations participating outside the temporal window we are examining (1975–2015), 207 ethnic groups across 318 organizations remain represented across 420 organization-groups observations; this number (420) includes groups repeated across organizations (i.e. same group represented by multiple organizations). This count does not include the "Other Arab Groups" in ACD2 represented by the National Front in Sudan, which is not an organization coded by RELAC. Finally, this count also excludes two organizations, the Donetsk People's Republic and the Lugansk People's Republic, representing Russians in Ukraine in a conflict that started in 2015 and is not included in RELAC. Both organizations are included through an earlier conflict.

[27] There are actually 208 unique relevant ethnic groups in the ACD2 data, represented by 319 organizations. The one ethnic group and organizational difference between RELAC and ACD2 is the Sudanese ACD2 category of "Other Arab groups" represented by the National Front, which as noted above is not an organization coded in the RELAC data and not a group represented by any other organization in the RELAC data.

When matching observations across data, especially through a process of reducing (by collapsing) and increasing (through expanding) the number of observations, the overarching research concern is that the match itself does not increase the likelihood of Type I error of a false positive (erroneously rejecting the null) in testing of the CWC hypothesis.

More specifically, assume our theory is correct that among ethnic minorities that share religion with majorities, relatively large ethnic minority groups more likely make religious claims for purposes of mobilization. If, by way of collapsing and expanding, we are increasing the number of observations for groups of types that contradict this hypothesis (large groups not making religious claims and small groups making religious claims), we run the risk that our analysis returns a Type II error and fails to reject the null hypothesis that there is no association. Taking the view of science as a cumulative endeavor, this is a risk we are not particularly concerned about because if the underlying relationship exists this will eventually be discovered. In contrast, if our hypothesis is incorrect, increasing the number of observations of types that support our hypothesis (large groups making claims, small groups not making claims) increases the chances of committing a Type I error and falsely rejecting the null hypothesis that there is no association. For the same reason – accumulation of knowledge – this is a very serious concern. Fortunately, because we are working with the universe of cases we can investigate and discuss each stage in turn.

Collapsing and Expanding Organizations to the Group Level

The ethnically identified group-level RELAC data contains 2024 group-year observations. Getting to that number requires collapsing and expanding RELAC organizations to the group level as noted above. At first glance collapsing RELAC organizations to the group level seemingly might cause concerns as the number of RELAC organizations representing groups in a given conflict ranges from 1 to 10 organizations[28] and a total of 82 groups (out of 207)

---

[28] For example, in their conflict against Israel, over time ACD2 records ten organizations purporting to represent Palestinian Arabs. These are the PLO (Palestine Liberation Organization), PFLP (Popular Front for the Liberation of Palestine), PFLP-GC (Popular Front for the Liberation of Palestine – General Command), Fatah, PIJ (Palestine Islamic Jihad), Hamas, PNA (Palestinian National Authority), AMB (Al-Aqsa Martyrs Brigades), PRC (Popular Resistance Committees), and Rejectionist Front. Similarly, in their conflict against the Afghan state, over time ACD2 reports ten organizations purporting to represent Pashtuns. These are the PDPA (Hizb-i Demokratik-i Khalq-i Afghanistan or People's Democratic Party of Afghanistan), Jam'iyyat-i Islami-yi Afghanistan (Islamic Society of Afghanistan), Hizb-i Islami-yi Afghanistan-Khalis faction (Islamic Party of Afghanistan Khalis faction), Mahaz-i Milli-yi Islami-yi Afghanistan (NIFA or National Islamic Front of Afghanistan), Ittihad-i Islami Bara-yi Azadi-yi Afghanistan (also known as Ittehad-e Islami, the Islamic Union of Afghanistan, and Islamic Alliance for the Liberation of Afghanistan), Harakat-i Islami-yi Afghanistan (Islamic Movement of Afghanistan), Hizb-i Islami-yi Afghanistan (Islamic Party of Afghanistan), Taleban, and UIFSA (United Islamic Front for the Salvation of Afghanistan). For further accounts of all of these organizations see the Uppsala Conflict Encyclopedia at: https://ucdp.uu.se/?id=1id=1.

have over time been represented by more than one organization in any given conflict.[29] In practice, however, when looking at how many organizations represent any given group in any given year, which is the unit of analysis in our final data and the unit within which organizations are collapsed to the group level, it becomes clear that this operation is much less problematic. Specifically, in the RELAC data for the majority of groups (156) and, after we match organizations to groups, also for the majority of organization-group-years (2024 out of 2352),[30] a group is represented by a single organization in a given year, which requires no collapse of organizations to the group level. For another 328 organization-group-year observations in the organization-level data, 51 groups[31] are represented by more than one organization.

For a complete list of all fifty-one groups whose organizations in any given year are collapsed to the group level, see Table C.1 in Appendix C. When we collapse organizations to the group level, we account only for whether *any* of the organizations representing a group in a given year claimed religious incompatibility with the state (the dependent variable). Therefore, for the 328 organization-group-year observations where a group is ever represented by more than one organization in a year, we are concerned about collapsing organizations to the group level, and thereby potentially decreasing the number of observations that run counter to our theoretical claim. To investigate, in the expanded data, we compared the proportions of groups represented by multiple organizations that claim religious incompatibility to that of groups represented by a single organization. The *t*-tests that we used for this comparison are detailed in Table C.2 in Appendix C. Briefly we discovered that minority groups represented by multiple organizations are in the uncollapsed data, indeed, statistically significantly more likely to claim religious incompatibility with the state than are minorities represented by a single organization. We could not

---

[29] This number includes the Tuareg in Mali, which have been represented by two different organizations in two separate conflicts. Over time across conflicts, a total of ninety-seven groups have been represented by more than one organization within a country.

[30] To reiterate the expanded data refer to the initial organization-level match where every RELAC organization is matched with every ethnic group that it represents according to the ACD2 data and our own coding. This initial match results in an organization-level data set where 51 ethnic groups (out of 207) are in a given year associated with more than one organization. This intermediary expansion results in 2352 group-organization-year observations. Out of that number of observations, 328 organization-group-year observations are of groups that are represented by more than a single organization in a given group year. A larger number of groups (97 in total) are at some point in their conflict history represented by different groups but we only collapse organizations to the group level for a given group in a given conflict year.

[31] Not all of those groups are relevant to the inquiry in this chapter. For example, because the theory is about political minority incentives, political majority groups coded in the RELAC data are not included in the analysis. In other cases groups and/or countries like the Africans in Zimbabwe are not coded in the A-Religion data and drop out when RELAC and A-Religion are merged as explained below. However, for this account we include a discussion of all groups in the RELAC data so as to give the reader a better sense of the overall structure of the data and the scope of this operation.

directly examine the effect of group size in the ethnically identified RELAC data because the ACD2 data do not include information on group size. Therefore, we coded in our final data groups represented by multiple organizations (that had previously been collapsed). The *t*-tests we ran on the final data (Table C.3 also reported in Appendix C) show that minority groups that were represented by multiple organizations are on average larger than groups represented by single organizations, and that this is also true within religion though the difference there was not statistically significant. Since within a religion a greater number of larger groups claiming religious incompatibility supports our hypothesis, we are very comfortable reducing the number of such observations by collapsing organizations to the group level and making for a more difficult test of our hypothesis.

Next we turn to the expansion of the organizational-level data to the group level. In expanding the data as described above we record a separate group year observation for every ethnic group represented by a multi-ethnic organization in a given conflict year. The concern here is to make sure that we do not unduly support the CWC hypothesis by increasing the number of observations with (1) large minority groups that share religion with the majority and claim religious incompatibility, (2) small groups that share religion with the majority but do not claim religious incompatibility. A total of 318 ethnically identified RELAC organizations represent 420 ethnic group-organization combinations in the ethnically identified RELAC. Of the 318, 272 organizations represent a single ethnic group. In a given year, another 46 organizations[32] represent multiple groups to be expanded to the group level.[33]

In the final data the number of ethnic groups that are expanded is fewer because the match between RELAC and the A-Religion data excludes some very small groups as discussed below. Table C.4 in Appendix C lists all the multi-ethnic organizations in the ethnically identified RELAC data and the groups they represent. To ensure that the expansion from the organizational to the group level for groups in the forty-six multi-ethnic organizations operating within countries does not unduly support the CWC hypothesis, we compared the proportions of groups represented by multiple ethnic organizations, which claim religious incompatibility, to proportions of groups represented by single ethnic organizations. The *t*-tests are detailed in Table C.5 in Appendix C. Briefly we found that groups represented in multi-ethnic organizations are statistically significantly more likely to claim religious incompatibility than are groups that are the sole groups represented by an organization. However, this is not the

[32] This count does not include the Islamic State (IS) as this organization operates across countries.
[33] Generally determining whether an organization is multi-ethnic is straightforward. There are, however, exceptions. For example, South-westerners in Uganda are counted as a single ethnic group in ACD2 but include the Ankole, Banyoro, Toro, and Banyarwanda. In A-Religion the Banyoro, Toro, and Banyarwanda count as separate groups. Thus, according to A-Religion, the Ugandan Alliance of Democratic Forces (ADF) is a multi-ethnic organization while it is not counted as such in ACD2.

case within religion. For groups that share religion with the majority when compared to each other, there is no difference in propensity to claim religious incompatibility between groups represented by single ethnic or multiethnic organizations. In line with the above comparisons, we coded groups in the final data for whether they have been represented by a multiethnic organization and then compared their average size to that of groups in organizations representing a single group only (results are detailed in Appendix C, Table C.6). Unsurprisingly, we found that groups that had been represented by multiethnic organizations (and expanded to the group level) were significantly smaller than other groups. Because small groups claiming religious incompatibility runs counter to our theory, we have no reason to suspect that our data manipulation of expanding observations from the organizational level to account separately for groups included in multi-ethnic organizations unduly supports our hypothesis by increasing the number of groups that share religion and claim religious incompatibility.

Furthermore, in conflict within countries, we expect some bandwagoning effects when smaller groups that share religion with the majority join larger groups in their religious contestation against the state. For instance, in Afghanistan depending on who was at the helm, every other Sunni ethnic group, even the Tajiks, at times joined the Pashtuns' bid to take over the state. The statistical analysis cannot distinguish between cases where an agent making claims of religious incompatibility is a bandwagoning small group (contrary to our expectation) or a large group (in support of our expectation). Therefore, independently coding smaller groups' claims of religious incompatibility makes for a more stringent test of our hypothesis: small groups that share religion with the majority and make religious claims contradict our hypothesis, as we do not expect small groups to lead the CWC. Consequently, we are confident that including separately each group represented by an organization, rather than factoring in only the largest ethnic group or averaging out group size to have only a single group representing this average does not unduly support our hypothesis.

Connecting Ethnic RELAC Data to A-Religion

The second question arising with the manipulation of the data pertains to the matching, at the group level, of the RELAC data and the A-Religion by way of the (group-identified) ACD2 data. The inclusion of cases and numbers of observations as they change through the data merging process is illustrated in Figure 4.1 displayed earlier. The reader will recall the figure showing that connecting the ethnically identified RELAC data to the A-Religion data return observations for 2023 ethnic group years. In this section we discuss the changing number of observations in light of support for the CWC hypothesis.

On its part the A-Religion data define the set of matched ethnic groups included in the analysis. The A-Religion data based on the AMAR, and the ACD2 data based on the EPR, have an imperfect overlap as EPR is conceptually akin to an independent sub-set of the AMAR data.[34] However, the inclusion criteria of AMAR and the EPR differ as the EPR only includes politically mobilized groups whereas the AMAR selection criteria are not tied to political outcomes but employ a population threshold. Because of these differences in aggregation or threshold for inclusion, AMAR includes a higher (more disaggregate) number of groups in some countries than does the EPR, and in other countries that number is lower. The question then is whether the AMAR data, that defines the universe of our A-Religion coding of religion and population balance, systematically skew the sample with respect to exclusion of cases from the EPR (and therefore RELAC as coded for ethnicity through ACD2), which could bias our results. For example, if in matching with the A-Religion data, the small ACD2 groups who do not share religion with the majority but claim religious incompatibility are excluded or subsumed under an ethic umbrella group, because of differences in aggregation and/or threshold of inclusion between the data, the CWC hypothesis could be unduly supported. Similarly, if the large EPR groups that share religion with the majority and do claim religious incompatibility are matched with several A-Religion groups because of differences in aggregation between the data, the CWC hypothesis might be erroneously supported.[35]

Fortunately, again because we are working with the universe of cases from both data sets, we can investigate this issue. Specifically, when the A-Religion data are matched with the ethnically identified RELAC data, the number of resultant groups is 201. The differences in aggregation leading to this final number of groups are outlined in Appendix C, Tables C.7 and C.10, respectively.

Appendix C also lists the *t*-tests that we conducted to examine whether, in the translation of RELAC to A-Religion, when compared to groups at large there was a significant difference in the size and proportion of groups expanded or collapsed, which claim religious incompatibility. These *t*-tests are reported in the Appendix, respectively in Tables C.8 and C.9. Briefly we found no significant differences in sizes between disaggregated ACD2 groups (where more than one ACD2 group were matched with (collapsed to) a single A-Religion group) and other groups in the data. We did, however, find that disaggregated ACD2 groups (a single ACD2 group was matched with (expanded to) more than one A-Religion group) tended to be smaller than

---

[34] To be clear the definition of what constitutes an ethnic group differs between the two data sets because AMAR defines groups that are "socially relevant" whereas EPR defines groups that are "politically relevant." The overlap stems from the fact that groups that are politically relevant are generally socially relevant, though not necessarily at the same level of aggregation. Similarly groups that are politically relevant are generally an expression of a social relevance though, again, sometimes at a different level of aggregation.

[35] This is less of a concern because the population data is coded for each A-Religion group. Therefore, larger EPR groups matched with several A-Religion groups will also be disaggregated in terms of population proportions.

groups in the data on average. This could have been a concern if the expanded (small) groups were all of a different religion than the majority and peaceful as this would have unduly supported the hypothesis. However, upon further inspection we did not find a cause for concern because, as shown in Table C.11 in Appendix C, most of the expanded small groups share religion with the majority and some of the expanded groups that do not share a religion do claim religious incompatibility. Consequently, we do not worry that this data transformation erroneously supports our conjecture.

Finally, seventeen ACD2 groups are "unmatched" because they either do not meet the AMAR criteria for a socially relevant ethnic group, or are in countries that are not in the AMAR data (Yugoslavia, South Sudan, Rhodesia), or are too small for independent inclusion in the AMAR data, or enter into the data in different configurations. The detailed discussion, enumerating all unmatched cases, can be found in Table C.11 in Appendix C. Briefly, for reasons explained in detail there, with one exception, the unmatched (excluded) cases discussed in the Appendix are not likely to increase the probability of Type I error because they do not contradict the CWC hypothesis.

The one excluded group that possibly contradicts our conjecture is the Nuer in their conflict with the Government of South Sudan.[36] South Sudan is excluded from the analysis because it was just becoming independent in 2011 during the configuration of the AMAR. The second-largest ethnic group in South Sudan, the Nuer, shares religion with the largest ethnic group Dinka, who account for around 35 percent of the population, in that both are Christian and Animist.[37] The two have long fought over land, before and after South Sudan became independent from Sudan following an inter-religious (Muslim–Christian) conflict. The conflict between the Dinka and the Nuer intensified when the appointed president of South Sudan, a Dinka, dismissed all his ministers and accused the vice president, a Nuer, of a coup attempt.[38] Scholars point out that while it is not evident that ethnic differences sparked the war, the conflict quickly took on ethnic (rather than religious) overtones (Radon and Logan, 2014). Specifically, the vice president Riek Machar, accused the president of moving toward authoritarianism and then "immediately fell back upon ethnic mobilization because it was very quick and it was very cheap. He [Machar] could call upon the [ethnic] Nuer militia and the so-called 'White Army' to mobilize almost overnight, because that's what they've done for some twenty years" (Noel, 2016) in the war against Muslims in Sudan.[39]

While the Nuer have not been completely excluded from access to the central government there is clearly an ongoing struggle for control of the state. However, current negotiations about the future institutional framework of the

---

[36] All other ethnic groups in South Sudan are small and conform to our expectations.
[37] See ethnic demographics in country file, South Sudan at www.cia.gov.
[38] For a brief conflict history, see ucdp.uu.se/#conflict/11345.
[39] The civil conflict in South Sudan has received significant scholarly attention. For a good overview of some principal theories used to cast light on the conflict mechanics, see Thiong (2018).

country – especially as it pertains to the federal framework (Radon and Logan, 2014; Schomerus and Aalen, 2016) – make it unclear what the focus of the contestation will be going forward, and what role religion will play. Basedau and Koos's (2015) survey work establishes some of the important correlates of support for inter-religious violence in South Sudan, and Zink (2018) details the increased importance of Christianity and movements away from Animism among the Dinka, in part, because of the ongoing conflict. However, as with other civil conflicts we know less about the intra-religious dimension of the South Sudanese conflict between ethnic groups adhering to the same religion or religions. Therefore, we note that South Sudan is a case that bears further examination with respect to our empirical conjectures about demography and mobilization of religion – especially as the institutional framework comes to clarify what are the most important loci of power in the country.

The final resulting unit of analysis then is, for 201 ethnic minority groups, the group conflict year in each pertinent conflict, from the time the group enters into the RELAC data in 1975 until its exit, for a total of 2023 group conflict years. Having clarified and probed the structure of our data, the following section describes in greater detail the variables included in the empirical analysis.

4.3 VARIABLES

4.3.1 Independent Variables: Demography and Shared Religion

For coding of the first set of independent variables pertaining to ethnic group religions, we use the new A-Religion data described in Chapter 2. The reader will recall that we code an ethnic group's primary religious *Family* as one of the religions listed in Figure 2.5 in Chapter 2, if (1) there is a published percentage of members of the group belonging to that religion equal to or more than the threshold of 50 percent or (2) a reliable reference states that the number of the subscribers of a particular religion forms a majority or a predominant plurality.

We also code ethnic group primary religious *Sect* if religious family is either Christianity or Islam, as explained in Chapter 2. We return to the discussion of sect later in the chapter. Next, we use information on the most populous religion in the state as recorded by Brown and James (2018), to code religious context of the demographic majority/minority *Shared Family* and *Shared Sect*. These variables are coded 1 if the primary religion of any distinct minority in a country is shared with the most populous religion in the country, and 0 otherwise.[40]

---

[40] To check our variable of shared religion we compared it to Svensson and Nilsson's (2018: 4) Codebook *relid* variable that accounts for "whether the religious majority of the constituencies of the conflict actors – the government and the rebel group – are separated in terms of their

In turn, the demographic independent variable is based on the group's proportional size of the national population within each country as recorded in AMAR (Birnir et al., 2015). Our conjectures about minority propensity for mobilization of the religious identity hinge on the minority group's relative rather than absolute size, in comparison to the size of the politically dominant majority. Thus, we use group proportional size to code *Population Balance*, which denotes the difference in demographic size between the ethnic minority and the politically dominant ethnic group. For ease in interpretation, this variable subtracts the proportional size of the politically dominant ethnic majority group from the proportional size of each minority ethnic group, by group.[41] When coded this way, a decreasing negative number approaching negative 1 (-1) indicates decreasing relative size of the minority, an increasing negative number approaching 0 indicates that the minority is closer in size to the majority. At 0, the groups are equal in size and an increasing positive number indicates that the population of the ethno-religious political minority is getting larger than that of the politically dominant ethnic majority population.[42]

religious identities. Hence, religious identity conflicts are those in which the constituencies of each of the conflict actors come from different faith traditions, and here we consider all the major world religions: Judaism, Islam, Christianity, Hinduism, Buddhism, and Sikhism. In addition, for those cases where both sides are culturally part of a major world faith tradition, we also provide information on whether they belong to different sub-traditions, specifically Shi'i and Sunni Islam, for the Muslim tradition, and Orthodox, Roman-Catholic and Protestant for the Christian tradition." By and large the RELAC religious id variable overlaps with our *Shared Family* variable with one significant exception. Svensson and Nilsson (2018) do not code religions as syncretic but in some cases code both religions that form the foundation of the syncretic religion. In the A-Religion data, syncretic is a classification that includes a large number of groups as illustrated in Chapter 2. However, because we also code information on the religious families that form the basis of the syncretic religions, we are able to account for whether at least one of the religions that are the foundation of the syncretic belief is shared by a majority in the country. Finally, RELAC only codes participants in civil war whereas the A-Religion data also code peaceful groups as noted in Chapter 2. This is important for the future comparisons of groups in and out of civil war.

[41] Note that this operation is the reverse of the operation that was used in the discussion of the model in Chapter 3. There, minority size was subtracted from majority size to avoid working with negative numbers in the space of theoretical interest, where the minority was smaller but approaching the size of the majority. The statistical setup is reversed because the CWC prediction is that the probability of the outcome (religious claims in civil war) increases as the minority approaches the majority in size. If our prediction is correct this setup (subtracting majority proportional size from minority proportional size) allows for an intuitive visual interpretation of a positive association where minority size increases going from the left to the right on the X-axis in tandem with the probability of claiming religious incompatibility increasing from bottom to top on the Y-axis.

[42] When there is not a single politically dominant group, we take the average of all politically dominant groups as the size of the politically dominant majority. The theoretical reason for taking the average is that any group leader mobilizing to challenge the current rulers of the state likely evaluates the chances of success of her group, as a function of group size, relative to the average size of other groups having held that position.

Finally, we expect that a slope change differentiates the conflict behavior of increasingly large minority groups which share a religion with the majority. Therefore, we interact the *Population Balance* variable with our variable of shared religion, *Shared Family*. The interacted variable takes on a value of 0 if the minority and majority adhere to distinct religions, and return the corresponding *Population Balance* variable, when groups share a religion.

4.3.2 Dependent Variable: *Religious Incompatibility*

To capture the idea of minority strategic mobilization of religion in civil war for intrinsic and/or instrumental motives, our dependent variable, *Religious incompatibility*, comes from the RELAC data, which accounts for religious dimensions in UCDP's civil conflicts. According to Svensson and Nilsson (2018: 1131–1132), their coding of religious incompatibility is based on "UCDP's coding of first stated incompatibility." They give as an example, Al-Shabaab's goal "to over-throw the Somali government, expel foreign troops from the country, and install a system of governance based on Sharia law." They also emphasize that conflict actors' religious positions do not necessarily reflect underlying sincere interests,[43] and remind the reader that "the parties in conflicts might strategically mislead or omit information about their true preferences or they can exaggerate or downplay religious aspirations in regard to the contested issue in conflict." This is an important point in that the veracity of combatants' religious claims (Barter and Zatkin-Osburn, 2016; Svensson, 2016) is not the focus of the data, while their strategy is. Toft (2021) highlights that not all civil wars where combatants make religious claims have religion as a "central" issue of contestation. She adds that "Religion is central to civil war if the rebels fight over whether the state or a rebel-dominated region will be ruled according to a specific religious tradition" (p. 1612). Importantly, our hypothesis does not address whether a religious message is central to the conflict, only whether religion is mobilized by way of claim making. Therefore, the RELAC variable of stated religious incompatibility is an ideal variable to use as our indicator of strategic mobilization of religion in civil war, which may be sincerely motivated but does not have to be. In Chapter 5, we will return to the content of the religious claims made by each of the ethnic minority groups that share religion with the majority and claim religious incompatibility in civil war. In the following tests, however, we adopt the RELAC variable accounting for claims of religious incompatibility as our dependent variable and recode it at the group level as described above.

---

[43] In support of this point, Svensson and Nilsson (2018) discuss the works of Fisher et al. (1981) and Rubin et al. (1994).

4.3.3 Control Variables

We control for some of the most common correlates of ethnic civil war (Denny and Walter, 2014; Mason and Mitchell, 2016; Forsberg et al., 2017). First is the effect of development or the standard of living across countries recorded in Penn World Tables 9.0. The variable we use accounts for the log of expenditure-side real GDP, per capita (*ln GDP per capita*), because this variable is the best suited for comparisons across space and time (Feenstra et al., 2015: 3151).[44] We also account for cross-cuttingness *National Cross-cutting*, which is a national-level index of ethno-religious cross-cutting cleavages from Selway (2011a),[45] and *Democracy*, a binary variable indicating whether or not a country is considered democratic, coded from the corrected X-Polity data (Vreeland, 2008) as updated to 2015 by Jones and Lupu (2018). We also include a binary indicator of the presence of one or more violent self-determination movements or *Separatism* in the country in a given year based on Sambanis et al.'s (2018) data.[46] Lastly, we account for issues of temporal dependence by including three time variables measured in years since the first conflict entry for a group, T_1, T_2, and T_3 (Carter and Signorino, 2010).

4.4 TESTING

4.4.1 Strategies in Civil War

Table 4.3 lists the descriptive statistics associated with our variables for the full data. The table shows that the dependent variable *Religious incompatibility*, is coded for 2023 cases (country-group-years). After excluding politically dominant groups because we are interested in the political minority claims against the political majority, we have information on our main independent variables, minority sharing of religious identity with the majority (coded as 0 or 1), and minority–majority population balance (ranging from −0.908 for the relatively smallest political minority to 0.471 for the relatively largest political minority) for 1846 country-group-year cases. Our control variables further restrict the number of available cases to 1450 for Selway's (2011a) measure of national cleavage cross-cuttingness (ranging from 0.054 to 0.995), 1608 cases for the log of GDP per capita (Penn World Tables 9.0, ranging from 5.821 to 10.954), 1703 cases for *Democracy* (Jones and Lupu, 2018; ranging from −6 to 7), and 1655 cases for secessionist movements (coded using Sambanis et al. [2018], as 0 or 1 in a given year). Our time variables are available for all cases.

---

[44] The variable is *rgdpe* (Expenditure-side real GDP at chained PPPs (in mil. 2011 US dollars) divided by pop (population in millions)).

[45] This is Selway's *ERC* variable, which measures Ethnic and Religious Cross-cuttingness at the country level.

[46] For this variable, we use the information to account for the presence of any separatist groups in the country in a given year.

TABLE 4.3. *Summary statistics*

Statistic	N	Mean	St. dev.	Min	Max
Religious incompatibility	2023	0.369	0.483	0	1
Shared family	1846	0.626	0.484	0	1
Population balance	1846	−0.263	0.327	−0.908	0.471
National cross cutting	1450	0.656	0.189	0.054	0.995
ln GDP per capita	1608	7.931	1.055	5.821	10.954
Democracy	1703	0.870	4.460	−6	7
Separatism	1655	0.754	0.431	0	1
T1	2023	9.507	8.110	1	47
T2	2023	156.120	265.392	1	2209
T3	2023	3,495.077	9,236.868	1	103,823

Before turning to our regression analysis, we first explore the data descriptively, using a cross-section of the data to examine the majority/minority demographic balance in civil war between ethnic groups at large and the ethnic groups claiming religious incompatibility with the state. The reader will recall that the theory of *Alternatives in Mobilization* explained in Chapter 3 suggested different ways a secondary cleavage (i.e. in ethnic wars, this could be religion) might be mobilized. One is through a large minority-led CWC challenging the majority for access to power. If the CWC accurately describes reality, we would expect that ethnic minorities, which share religion with majorities and mobilize religion in an ethnic civil war, are significantly larger than other minorities.

The means tests in Table 4.4a explore this core empirical implication. The means tests in the table compare, in the first column, the difference in population balance between groups that share religion with the demographic majority in their country and those that do not. As previously explained, the groups that are closer to 0 are closer in size to the demographic majority. The second column in the table illustrates the relative size differences between groups that claim religious incompatibility in civil war and those that do not.

The means tests show that ethnic groups that share religion with the demographic religious majority are highly significantly closer in size to the majority than are minorities segmented both on ethnicity and religion with a *Population Balance* of −0.19 and −0.37, respectively. The size difference between groups claiming religious incompatibility with the state is even more extreme between groups that do and do not share religion with the majority, with the former being significantly closer in size to the majority.

Furthermore, if we isolate groups that share family with the majority and claim religious incompatibility and compare their size to all other groups (sharing and not claiming, not sharing and claiming or not claiming), Table 4.4b

TABLE 4.4a. *t-tests, minority/majority* Population Balance *by* Shared Religion *and* Religious Incompatibility

Shared religion	All groups	Only groups claiming religious incompatibility
1	−0.19	−0.11
0	−0.37	−0.50
p-value	0.00	0.00

TABLE 4.4b. *t-tests, minority/majority* Population Balance *by* Shared Religion *and* Religious Incompatibility

Shared religion and religious incompatibility	−0.11
All other groups	−0.29
p-value	0.00

shows that at −0.11, the average size of groups that share religion and claim religious incompatibility with the state is also statistically significantly larger when compared to the majority, than that of all other groups at an average of −0.29. This descriptive analysis supports our conjecture but also suggests that demographics and claims of religious incompatibility tell more stories than only the one we are tackling in this book, which bodes well for future research.

4.4.2 Regression Analysis

Next, Table 4.5 details the results from our longitudinal test of the CWC hypothesis on the universe of all ethnic groups in civil war from 1975 to 2015: *As the population balance becomes more even between politically dominant majorities and ethnic minority groups that share religion, the likelihood increases that these minorities mobilize religion in civil war.*

We use logit analysis with robust standard errors to assess the likelihood that an ethnic minority strategically mobilizes religion in civil conflict, as a function of shared religion and group-relative size.[47] In addition to the dependent variable accounting for mobilization of religion as measured with claims of

[47] Specifically, we run a bivariate Generalized Linear Model in R and then use the sandwich package (Zeileis, 2006), to correct our standard errors and the margins package (Leeper, 2018) to calculate marginal effects. Our tables are formatted using stargazer (Hlavac, 2018), and all of our data management was performed using tidy (Wickham et al., 2018) both of which are packages for R.

TABLE 4.5. *Main regression results*

	Dependent variable: Claims of religious incompatibility		
	(1)	(2)	(3)
Shared family	−0.552***	0.431***	0.711***
	(0.100)	(0.140)	(0.212)
Population balance	−0.253*	−2.018***	−2.899***
	(0.147)	(0.232)	(0.354)
National cross cutting			−4.069***
			(0.478)
ln GDP per capita			0.008
			(0.079)
Democracy			0.103***
			(0.019)
Separatism			−1.736***
			(0.174)
T1			0.068
			(0.055)
T2			−0.007*
			(0.004)
T3			0.0001*
			(0.0001)
Shared family:Population balance		3.474***	5.388***
		(0.313)	(0.574)
Constant	−0.276***	−0.958***	2.022***
	(0.092)	(0.119)	(0.628)
Observations	1846	1846	1311

Note. $^*p < 0.1$; $^{**}p < 0.05$; $^{***}p < 0.01$

Religious incompatibility, the first model includes our *Shared Family* variable accounting for minority groups that share religious family with majorities, and the *Population Balance* variable accounting for minority group-relative size vis-à-vis the majority, with negative number approaching −1 indicating a small minority and a number closer to 0 showing more even groups. The second model adds in our interaction variable of *Shared Family and Population Balance*. The third model includes controls of *National Cross-cutting, log of GDP per capita, Democracy, Separatism,* and *Time*.[48]

Consistent with the literature the first model shows that on average religious *Shared Family* makes it less likely that a group mobilizes religion in civil war. Furthermore, model three shows a statistically significant decrease in claims of *Religious Incompatibility* overall as country-level cross-cuttingness increases. In other words, consistent with the extant literature, Selway most prominently, *countries* where identities are shared are less likely to experience mobilization of religion in civil conflict. At the same time, at the group level, our positive and significant interaction variable Shared.family:Population.balance in Models 2 and 3 shows that within countries larger minority groups that share religion with majorities are significantly more likely to mobilize religion in civil conflict than are other minorities.

Of the control variables countries with self-determination movements (*Separatism*), as one would expect, are significantly less likely to see minorities mobilize shared religion to bridge the minority/majority divide by way of shared religion. Mobilization of religion in civil war is significantly more likely in *Democracy*, but less in countries with lower *GDP per capita*, though not significantly so. Two of the time variables are significant.[49]

Because the non-linear effects of logit coefficients are difficult to interpret, especially in interaction, Figure 4.2 plots separately for groups that do and do not *Share Family* of religion with the majority, the marginal effect of changing *Population Balance* on the likelihood that the group engages in mobilization of religion in civil war by claiming *Religious Incompatibility* as shown in Model 3.[50] The figure clearly illustrates the interactive effect of *Shared Family* of religion and *Population Balance*. As minority groups that have *Shared Family* of religion with majorities become larger (more even population balance – closer to 0), they are increasingly likely to mobilize religion by claiming *Religious Incompatibility* in civil war. Conversely, for minority groups that are segmented by religion and ethnicity from majorities they are increasingly unlikely to claim religious incompatibility in civil war as their size increases, possibly for reasons discussed in Chapter 3.

---

[48] The number of observations in Model 1 is determined by the observations of minority groups that are not the politically dominant groups in their country. Control variables restrict the numbers of observations in Models 2 and 3 further.

[49] We also ran the analysis clustered on country. The results remain substantively the same. Coefficients are by and large of the same size and all in the same direction. The constitutive term accounting for shared family loses some significance but the interaction remains highly statistically significant. The time variables also lose significance.

[50] To interpret the coefficients, we use the margins package for R available at https://cran.r-project.org/web/packages/margins/index.html.

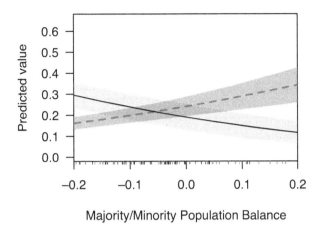

FIGURE 4.2. Marginal effect of *Population Balance* (o is parity) on probability of mobilization of religion in civil war for ethnic minority groups with *Shared Family* of religion with majorities (broken line) and ethnic minority groups that are segmented by religion from majorities (solid line)

4.4.3 Robustness of the Results

While we are confident that the data manipulation described earlier by and large increased the bar for rejecting the null hypothesis in support of our research conjecture, the nature of the data suggests a few additional robustness checks worth examining. Specifically, in this section, we outline our probing of robustness to numerical and demographic outliers, and show some additional analysis to support our main results.

The first question pertains to conflict dynamics in heterogeneous countries. Civil wars are ruinous on a large scale and ethnic groups may not be able to remain outside the conflict even if they wish to. Because of the limited size of the data, heterogeneous countries may therefore exert relatively undue influence on the analyses simply for numerical reasons. Again we are principally concerned with countries where large ethnic minority groups that share religious family with the majority claim religious incompatibility. Among the countries where ethnic minorities and majorities that share religion are in conflict, in two countries, Nepal and Uganda, several relatively large groups claim religious incompatibility. In Chapter 5 we delve into the case history of each of these countries but in the analysis below we account for them empirically.

A second issue we would like to address in our empirical analysis is how well it corresponds to our theory of *Alternatives in Mobilization*, which centers on the relative size of minority groups. The mechanism we propose for mobilizing a CWC in the case of ethnic civil war is that a minority uses the shared identity to build a cross-ethnic coalition to numerically challenge the politically dominant group. This mechanism is particularly compelling for groups that are smaller than and approaching the size of the majority group. At the same time, some political minorities are demographic majorities. In some cases, because of enduring structural disadvantages for instance, such groups may need to appeal to demographic segments of the political majority to build a coalition that is capable of challenging the political majority. For example, Madrid (2008, 2012) explains how the demographically more numerous indigenous groups were able to take power in Bolivia only after their political appeals incorporated segments of Mestizos and Whites by way of populism. This certainly suggests political minorities that are demographic majorities may in some cases only access power by building coalitions with political majorities.

However, when political minority groups are demographically substantially larger than the politically dominant group, the theory of *Alternatives in Mobilization* also suggests that the political minority does not necessarily have the same incentives to appeal to a segment of the majority in mobilizing the shared identity, which is religion in our empirical analysis. Because political minorities in several of the countries we examine are quite large, and in some cases, including Syria, Chad, and Iraq, claim religious incompatibility in civil war, we explore whether the results in this chapter are driven by political minorities, which are demographic majorities rather than the political and demographic minorities that are strictly within the scope of our theory.

Two additional models address these questions. The first model accounts specifically for Nepal and Uganda with dummy variables and the second drops all cases with a population balance exceeding 0. At 0 the political majority and minority indicate demographic parity; for any numbers exceeding 0 the political minority is demographically larger than the political majority. Table 4.6 shows that our concerns regarding Nepal especially, and Uganda to a lesser extent, are well founded. The coefficient for Nepal is very large, positive and highly statistically significant. Nepal is clearly an influential case where ethnic minorities sharing a religion with the majority, which they have engaged in civil war, make claims of religious incompatibility. However, accounting for Nepal and Uganda in this way does not change our substantive conclusions about the interaction of *Shared Family* of religion and *Population Balance*. Large minorities outside Nepal and Uganda that have *Shared Family* of religion with majorities are still significantly more likely to engage in mobilization with religious claim-making than are other ethnic groups.[51] Furthermore, we find that the cases of Nepal and Uganda account for some of the variance related to national cross-cuttingness, separatist violence, and level of democracy, although all these variables retain their signs. In contrast, our main interactive effect remains significant.

[51] We also ran a model where we dropped the case of Nepal and the results remained substantively the same.

TABLE 4.6. *The effect of* Shared Family *and increasing* Population Balance *on the likelihood that ethnic conflict parties claim* Religious Incompatibility *in civil war*

	Dependent variable: Claims of Religious Incompatibility	
	(1)	(2)
Shared family	0.338	0.974***
	(0.289)	(0.242)
Population balance	−3.017***	−3.010***
	(0.366)	(0.356)
National cross cutting	−1.807***	−3.597***
	(0.449)	(0.467)
ln GDP per capita	0.249***	−0.017
	(0.087)	(0.079)
Democracy	0.109***	0.120***
	(0.025)	(0.020)
Separatism	−0.295	−1.821***
	(0.237)	(0.189)
T1	−0.001	0.018
	(0.056)	(0.057)
T2	0.0001	−0.004
	(0.004)	(0.004)
T3	0.00002	0.0001
	(0.0001)	(0.0001)
Nepal	19.290***	
	(0.306)	
Uganda	1.136***	
	(0.318)	
Shared family:Population balance	4.687***	6.392***
	(0.703)	(0.832)
Constant	−2.797***	2.097***
	(0.877)	(0.665)
Observations	1311	1192

Note. *$p < 0.1$; **$p < 0.05$; ***$p < 0.01$

Finally, our robustness checks demonstrate that political minorities that are demographically larger than the political majorities in their countries are not driving the results. The second equation in Table 4.6 shows that dropping all cases that exceed population balance of 0 (demographic parity) has little effect on the original results from Table 4.5, other than to seemingly increase the magnitude of the coefficient accounting for the interaction between *Shared Family* and *Population Balance*. This relatively minor change is likely due to the fact that some of these cases where the political minority population is larger than the political majority may have been missing values on other control variables so they may already have been excluded in Model 3, Table 4.5.

4.4.4 Alternative Explanation: The *Challenger's Winning Coalition* or Sectarian War?

Given the resilience to robustness checks we are satisfied that our results accurately support the pattern proposed by our hypothesis. Evidently the probability of religious claim-making in civil conflict between majority and minority groups that share religion increases with greater population balance between the two groups.

However, our data are observational and a possible alternative explanation accounting for our result is that within religious families competition centers on differences between denominations or sects. For example, within Christianity, Catholics commonly battle Protestants and sectarian violence between Sunni and Shi'i is widespread. If the conflict pattern we observe is mostly between majorities and minorities that share a family of religion but differ in sect, the CWC mechanism of ethnic bridging by way of religion that we propose does not hold.

To examine this alternative explanation qualitatively in Chapter 5, we list all the groups that claim religious incompatibility in conflict and share religion with the majority, along with their religious family and sect. The table strongly suggests that the choice of religious claim-making is not due to sectarian differences between the mobilizing minority and the majority religion.

Even so, to rule out the alternative argument that our results stem from competition based on differences between sects within religious families, Table 4.7 examines the relationship between claims of religious incompatibility and group size among the subset of ethnic groups that *Shared Sect* within *Shared Family* of religion. For this test we use the independent variable that specifically accounts for the sect/denomination within the most populous monotheistic religious family, as discussed in some detail in Chapter 2. The reader will recall that this variable, *Shared Sect* is coded 1 if a substantial segment of the Christian or Muslim minority shares a sect or denomination with the majority, and 0 otherwise.

Substituting our sectarian variable *Shared Sect* for our religious family variable in Table 4.7, we run the same analysis shown in Table 4.5. Thus the

TABLE 4.7. *The effect of* Shared Sect *and increasing* Population Balance *on the likelihood that ethnic conflict parties make claims of* Religious Incompatibility *in civil war*

	Dependent variable: Claims of Religious Incompatibility
Shared sect	−0.142
	(0.328)
Population balance	−0.340
	(0.410)
National cross-cutting	−5.771***
	(1.246)
ln GDP per capita	0.350***
	(0.121)
Democracy	0.083***
	(0.031)
Separatism	−1.017***
	(0.292)
T_1	−0.008
	(0.121)
T_2	−0.008
	(0.012)
T_3	0.0004
	(0.0003)
Shared sect:Population balance	2.016***
	(0.751)
Constant	1.219
	(1.516)
Observations	684

Note. $^*p<0.1$; $^{**}p<0.05$; $^{***}p<0.01$

independent variable in the main regression Table 4.7 accounts for minority groups that subscribe to a *Shared Sect* with the majority in addition to *Shared Family* of religion, that is, if the shared religion is Islam or Christianity. If claims of religious incompatibility are driven by opportunities for alternative mobilization within sect, we expect to see substantively similar results across ethnicity, as in Table 4.5. In contrast, the alternative hypothesis suggests that religious claim-making stems from inter-sectarian competition, in which case our independent variables will not be significant.

Table 4.7 returns substantively the same results as the main regression Table 4.5. On average, shared identity, measured both at the group-level *Shared Sect* and the country-level *National Cross-cutting*, decreases the likelihood of claims of religious incompatibility in conflict, though only the national-level measure is significant in this model. Other control variables retain their sign and the variable measuring GDP per capita gains significance. Furthermore, the interaction term clearly shows that when the population balance between groups that share a sect becomes more even, the likelihood that combatants claim religious incompatibility in civil conflict increases. The number of observations is lower because groups that share a Christian or Muslim sect constitute a subsection of the data.

Once again, the CWC hypothesis finds support. As the population balance between majorities and minorities increases, it becomes more likely that parties to the conflict make claims of religious incompatibility. Furthermore, we now know that this increased conflict probability is not driven solely by inter-sectarian violence. In contrast, the likelihood of conflict increases as ethnic majority/minority population balance within sects becomes more even.

4.5 CONCLUSION

In this chapter, we cross-nationally examined the testable *Challenger's Winning Coalition* implication of the theory of *Alternatives in Mobilization* proposed in Chapter 3 that the demographic balance between majorities and minorities, which are segmented on one identity and share a second, influences the likelihood that the second identity is mobilized in contentious politics. Our theory is agnostic as to the content of the cleavages but in this chapter, we discussed why in the context of ethnic civil war it stands to reason that minorities look to religion for alternate mobilization strategies. Having thus contextualized our inquiry, we tested the conjecture that greater parity in the population balance between ethnic minorities and majorities sharing a religion increases the likelihood that minorities mobilize religious identity. The RELAC data we used includes information on organizations in all ethnic civil wars between 1975 and 2015 and is coded to account for religious claim-making. We paired these data diligently with the new A-Religion data collected for this project, which account for religions (family and sect) of ethnic majorities and minorities across the globe.

The results of our tests strongly support the CWC hypothesis: in civil conflict between majority and minority ethnic groups of the same religion, the probability that conflict claims center on religion increases with greater population balance between the groups. These results were robust to a number of checks based on influential cases and political minorities that are demographically larger than the majorities that govern them. Similarly, the results were robust with respect to a principal rival hypothesis asking whether the mobilization of religion within religious family could be explained away as a sectarian conflict. It cannot.

The substantive implications of these findings are significant. Multiple scholars argue, for example, that conflicts involving religion are more lethal overall (Hoffman, 1995, 2006; Juergensmeyer, 2003; Asal and Rethemeyer, 2008; Piazza, 2009). If the argument presented here is correct, then conditional on demography, political leaders can choose to mobilize religion with deadly consequences. The next chapter further probes the mechanics of the theory in the context of ethnic civil war by way of exploring four case narratives – Pakistan, Uganda, Nepal, and Turkey – where minorities and majorities that share religion have engaged in a deadly conflict.

5

The Internal Validity of the *Challenger's Winning Coalition* Hypothesis

5.1 INTRODUCTION

Our theory of *Alternatives in Mobilization* proposed in Chapter 3 predicts that demographics, relative group size, and the intersection of identity condition the identity mobilization strategies that minorities pursue. One testable implication of this theory, the *Challenger's Winning Coalition* (CWC), applied to ethnic civil war, suggests that among ethnic majorities and minorities that share a religion, leaders of large ethnic minorities are likely to use religion to mobilize a CWC across ethnicity. At the same time we recognize that each political contestation is unique in the timing and sequence of events and the catalysts that sometimes set violent conflict dynamics in motion. Thus, the argument about population balance and shared identity identifies a *common* strategy selected in civil war but not sufficient condition[1] for mobilization of religion in civil conflict.

The external validity of the CWC argument across cases is tested in Chapter 4. In contrast, the focus in this chapter is on internal validity of the CWC. In other words, this chapter aims to further probe the mechanisms of the hypothesis tested across cases in Chapter 4. This in-depth case analysis approach has several objectives. First, it seeks to confirm (or disconfirm) that the mechanism proposed in Chapter 3 about demographics driving strategic selection of mobilization is plausible. Second, it explores whether this mechanism holds across religious doctrine. The third goal is to uncover any omitted variables or alternative explanations that eluded our cross-national observational study so that the mechanisms at work may be refined for future testing.

---

[1] While this condition is arguably necessary for observing the mechanisms we propose, it is important to clarify that it is not necessary for all conflicts. Conflicts often occur between majorities and small minorities, for instance, when the minority seeks to secede. Furthermore, some small minorities make religious claims despite the low likelihood of success. However, mobilizing mechanisms in such types of conflicts likely differ from the mechanism of the CWC.

Consistent with the objective of probing the internal validity of the argument in this chapter, the focus here is on cases where a minority has claimed religious incompatibility, and shares religion with the majority.[2] Fearon and Laitin (2011) make a strong argument for a random selection of cases in lieu of selecting "good," "hard," "easy," or other convenience cases that illustrate mechanisms but convey little additional information, and may even have motivated the theory that they are intended to illuminate. Heeding this advice, Table 5.1 lists all the cases where according to the RELAC data used in Chapter 4, leaders of minority groups engaged in civil war with the majority controlling the state that claims religious incompatibility as one of the reasons for fighting. The coding of religion is supplemented by the A-Religion data in a way that is consistent with RELAC.[3]

A few important observations emerge from the table. First, and consistent with the literature discussed in Chapter 2, while Islamists are over-represented in conflict, claim-making of religious incompatibility in civil war clearly is a phenomenon that cuts across religious doctrine. Second, the table supports the robustness checks employed in Chapter 4 in that very few minority groups are demographically larger than the politically dominant majorities they fight. Thus, our results are not driven by a few outliers with extra-large populations. Furthermore, while in a number of cases like Syria, there are sectarian differences between at least some of the political minority and majority combatants in civil war; in most cases, combatants share both religious *Family* and *Sect*. Thus, the table reinforces the argument made in Chapter 4 that mobilization of religion in civil war is not explained solely by sectarian differences.

Only three families of religion – Christianity, Hinduism, and Islam – are represented among the cases in Table 5.1. The objective is to examine the plausibility of the CWC mechanism across doctrine. Therefore, our universe of appropriate cases is stratified by these three religions.[4] Because there is only one civil war where Hindu combatants make religious claims, Nepal self-selects to represent the Hindu doctrine. Only three cases represent Christianity – Congo, the Democratic Republic of Congo (DRC or Zaire), and Uganda. With no

---

[2] Fearon and Laitin (2011) caution against selecting cases on the dependent or the independent variable or some combination of the two because such cases may suffer from a lack of representativeness and omitted variable bias. Moreover, such cases do not allow for specifying the circumstances under which the hypothesized cause does not lead to the outcome. Since our theory is already tested across all groups in civil conflict in Chapter 4, and because the objective of this chapter is to examine the mechanisms leading to this outcome (minority claims of religious incompatibility), the dependent variable appropriately delineates the universe of relevant cases. Even so, to examine cases on the range of outcomes of the dependent variable, the last case that we examine in this chapter, Turkey, is selected to explore a case where the outcome, claim of religious incompatibility, is not recorded in the RELAC data.

[3] Specifically, RELAC data do not code sect for all groups. When this information is not recorded, we supplement with A-Religion data. The A-Religion data include information on more than a single religion per group but this information is not included in the table.

[4] An unintended benefit resulting from the stratification by doctrine is that the countries selected are all from different parts of the world.

TABLE 5.1. Minority groups that claim Religious Incompatibility in civil war (RELAC data) and share Religious Family with majorities (A-Religion data)

Country	Confl. Id	Group	Population balance	Family	Sect
Afghanistan	137	Hazara	−0.255	Islam	Shi'i
Afghanistan	137	Pashtuns (Pushtuns)	0.075	Islam	Sunni
Afghanistan	137	Tajiks	−0.075	Islam	Sunni
Afghanistan	137	Uzbek	−0.255	Islam	Sunni
Afghanistan	288	Pashtuns (Pushtuns)	0.075	Islam	Sunni
Chad	91	Beri	−0.122	Islam	Sunni
Congo, Republic of	214	Lari/Lali	0.0267	Christianity	Catholic
Congo, Republic of	214	Kongo	0.00667	Christianity	Catholic
DR Congo (Zaire)	254	Kongo	0.0346	Christianity	Catholic
Indonesia	171	Aceh	−0.401	Islam	Sunni
Iraq	62	Kurds	−0.148	Islam	Sunni
Iraq	62	Arab Shi'i	0.287	Islam	Shi'i
Iraq	62	Sunni-Arab	−0.139	Islam	Sunni
Lebanon	297	Sunni Muslims	−0.0393	Islam	Sunni
Mali	274	Touareg	−0.196	Islam	Sunni
Nepal	72	Dhanuk	−0.079	Hinduism	
Nepal	72	Gharti/Bhujel	−0.082	Hinduism	
Nepal	72	Magar	−0.017	Hinduism	
Nepal	72	Newar	−0.0333	Hinduism	
Nepal	72	Sanyasi	−0.0785	Hinduism	
Nepal	72	Brahmin – Hill	0.038	Hinduism	
Nepal	72	Tharu	−0.0208	Hinduism	
Pakistan	209	Pashtuns (Pushtuns)	−0.309	Islam	Sunni
Sudan	113	Nuba	−0.384	Islam	Sunni
Sudan	113	Darfur Black Muslims	−0.384	Islam	Sunni
Sudan	113	Beja/Bedawi	−0.379	Islam	Sunni
Syria	102	Kurds	−0.036	Islam	Sunni
Syria	102	Sunni-Arab	0.471	Islam	Sunni
Syria	286	Sunni-Arab	0.471	Islam	Sunni
Tajikistan	200	Uzbeks	−0.646	Islam	Sunni
Tajikistan	200	Kyrgyz	−0.788	Islam	Sunni
Tajikistan	200	Pamiris	−0.77	Islam	Shi'i
Uganda	118	Acholi	−0.0207	Christianity	Catholic
Yemen (North)	33	Sunni Arabs	0.162	Islam	Sunni
Yemen (North)	293	Sunni Arabs	0.162	Islam	Sunni

prior expertise in Africa we randomly chose Uganda. In contrast, Islam is over-represented in this group of cases. For the analysis in this chapter, also with no prior expertise in the politics of the country, we randomly selected Pakistan from the set of cases where Islam is the group religion.

If, across doctrine, the CWC is a valid argument, we would expect that in each of these cases where religion is mobilized: (1) the ethnic group leading the mobilization is excluded or underrepresented in the governing structures that determine the distribution of resources; (2) the mobilization has the purpose of making claims against a state that is controlled by an ethnic group other than the group leading the mobilization; (3) the political majority and the mobilizing minority share a religion; (4) mobilization of religion is led by the largest or one of the largest minority ethnic groups at the relevant level of administration;[5] (5) group leaders use religious claims for mobilization to appeal across ethnic lines.

The cases we examine in this chapter largely support our hypothesis that when excluded, large ethnic minorities that share a religion with majorities will mobilize the shared religion in a bid to form a CWC that affords them access. The cases also reveal a number of additional observations that clarify the precise mechanisms of how this mobilization comes about and suggest some directions for refining the theory moving forward. The first observation is that religion is a far more complex and nuanced concept than the data used in Chapter 4 captures. For example, RELAC data code Ugandan combatants as Christian and does not specify sect. The sectarian designation in Table 5.1 is supplemented by the A-Religion data, but this leaves out other coded religions and "sects" including Animism and Pentacostalism as well as Syncretism that cut across the Acholi and/or other ethnic groups aligning with or opposing them. Indeed, as the case narrative reveals, combatants in Uganda do not neatly adhere to religions and sects in a way that can be easily coded into discrete categories. Therefore, while there is seemingly a sectarian element to the conflict, the role of religion in Uganda is far more nuanced.

Another observation that gleaned from the cases is that mobilization claiming religious incompatibility does not always aim to increase the role of religion in politics. Indeed, the *raison d'être* of the Maoist mobilization in Nepal was to engender political change away from a system that up to that point was structured around religion and a monarchy that upholds it.

Some of the case insights suggest a different way of approaching the question of identity in mobilization across cases. For example, in all of the cases examined, ethnicity and religion were both socially very salient identities for the duration of the conflict and often much longer. In other words, at least in the cases examined here, politics did not so much induce salience as it activated an existing salient identity. We return to this observation in the conclusion to the book.

---

[5] In this chapter, we focus on the national level.

Similarly, along the lines of broader observation pertaining to all of the cases examined and likely beyond those, the narratives also clarify the mechanisms of mobilization that were theorized in Chapter 3, with respect to variation in the demographic landscape where the mobilization takes place. Specifically, the reader will recall the condition associated with predicting the composition of the Minimum Winning Coalition (MWC) that

$$w + x_i \geq y_i \qquad\qquad (5.1)$$

	Identity 1		
Identity 2	w	x_j	x_i
	y_j		
	y_i		

where w is the pivotal group that chooses to align with a MWC where $x_j \ldots, x_i$ and $y_j \ldots, y_i$ are excluded groups.[6] The argument we laid out in Chapter 3 posits that even where this condition is true and predicts the composition of the MWC, the CWC hypothesis still holds for large minorities because by recruiting from the majority on the shared identity, large excluded minorities can mobilize an oversized CWC.

What the case studies in this chapter reveal and add to our quantitative analyses is the importance of this condition for predicting the groups from which leaders recruit for mobilization of a CWC in a given context. Specifically, this condition suggests that minority recruitment depends not only on the population balance between the minority and the majority (the reader will recall X^α), but also on the relative size of the majority compared with the rest of the society. Therefore, where

$$w + x_i \geq y_i \qquad\qquad (5.2)$$

as in Pakistan,[7] leaders of the CWC will recruit co-religionists from their own excluded minority ethnic group and from the political majority, as suggested in Chapter 3. In contrast, in highly fragmented societies, like Uganda and Nepal, where majorities are relatively small, thus

$$w + x_i \leq y_i \qquad\qquad (5.3)$$

while the CWC leaders of the excluded minority are still expected to recruit co-religionists from across ethnic groups, they can do so without recruiting

---

[6] According to Posner "when $x > w + y$ or $y > w + x$ (i.e. when x or y are so large that they beat the MWC of w + y or w + x) will individuals in w not necessarily do best by choosing the identity that puts them in the smaller winning coalition" (Posner, 2017: 2008), under such circumstances it is more difficult to predict the MWC and/or the MWC will be unstable.

[7] This is also true in the case of Turkey discussed later in this chapter.

members from the ethnicity of the political majority. This, in turn, suggests important extensions of the theory to account specifically for when leaders operating in highly fragmented societies will include or exclude members of the majority from their recruitment efforts.

5.1.1 Cases That Do Not Conform

The objective of this chapter is to probe the internal validity of the theory by interrogating cases where the outcome is observed – minorities that share religion with majorities and claim religious incompatibility – to establish that the mechanisms proposed are a plausible description of reality. The theory is probabilistic hence we do not expect every case to conform to our expectations. Even so a remaining curiosity is why in some countries we do not observe the expected outcome. Why do the minority organizations leading the fight in some countries where large minorities that share religion with the majority that has engaged them in civil war not make religious claims as recorded by RELAC?

Because we do not have as clear expectations about what to look for in a case where the outcome – religious claims in civil war – is not observed, despite the presence of a large minority that shares religion with the majority, we select one additional case for a more organic theory generation. So as to best serve this purpose, following Seawright and Gerring's (2008) argument on unrepresentativeness of randomly selected cases when the *n* is small,[8] we chose Turkey, also a case of convenience on which we have substantial expertise.

The case of Turkey highlights the fact that civil war does not occur in isolation and raises a question about the separation of the study of civil conflict from studies of contentious processes of other types – including electoral politics. This case also illustrates that the same conflict actors that fight in civil war also cycle in and out of multiple other conflict processes, often simultaneously. For example, Kurds in Turkey have fielded political parties in every democratic interval while also fighting the state in a civil war (Karakoc and Sarigil, 2020). Therefore, while there are sound reasons for the isolation of the study of particular outcomes as explained in Chapter 4, such studies can only give an incomplete picture of contentious dynamics. Kurds, in their conflict with the state, do mobilize the shared religion and the Kurdistan Workers' Party (*Partiya Karkeren Kurdistan*, PKK) may yet openly proclaim a religious incompatibility with the state, taking advantage of the increased state tolerance of religious rhetoric, the organization has begun already to mobilize religion since an Islamist-led government came to power in 2002.

The remainder of the chapter discusses each case, Pakistan, Uganda, Nepal, and Turkey separately by following the same structure of narrative so as to

[8] Seawright and Gerring (2008: 295) note that "for a comparative case study composed of five cases (or less), randomized case selection procedures will often produce a sample that is substantially unrepresentative of the population."

facilitate comparison between the cases. The first section for each case puts the conflict in historical perspective, introduces demographics, and foreshadows our conclusions. The following section discusses the state's role with respect to religion. Next comes a discussion of the leading ethnic minority group and religion. The final section gives an account of how the minority alternative mobilization of religion (the CWC) occurs, if at all.

5.2 EXPLORING THE INTERNAL VALIDITY OF THE *CHALLENGER'S WINNING COALITION* HYPOTHESIS IN CIVIL WAR

5.2.1 Islam: Pakistan

Scholars largely agree that Pakistan was founded on the idea of a "secular" Muslim cultural and/or ethno-national identity as opposed to a more religious Islamic identity.[9] Thus, after the founding of Pakistan in 1947, during subsequent state consolidation, conflict involving the government primarily centered on ethnicity and territory, including Bengal's separation into Bangladesh in 1971, enduring insurgency in Balochistan and Sindhi nationalist violence against the state.[10]

Over time the leadership of the largest ethnic minority in Pakistan, the Pashtuns, came to play a central role in forming an alternative coalition around shared religion to challenge the majority Punjabi-led government over control of the state, first regionally and then nationally. In mobilizing the alternative coalition various Pashtun leaders appealed across ethnic boundaries to members of the Punjabi majority and to other Sunni ethnic minority groups[11] whose leaders shared prior experiences of religious mobilization in conflict.

The auxiliary factors that set in motion this course of events in Pakistan include regional geopolitics and internal state efforts to counter ethnonationalism, both of which augmented the salience of religion in an initially more secular state. Political centralization[12] and extreme poverty and underdevelopment in areas where the Pashtuns live, along with over-representation of the group in the state bureaucracy and military, likely helped direct ethnic

---

[9] While the words of Pakistan's founding father Jinnah have been used to justify both religious and secular interpretations of the state, his idea of the two nation-state is predominantly considered a secular cultural idea (Cohen, 2004; Varshney, 2008).

[10] This is in addition to intra-communal conflict such as that between Sindhi and Mohajirs in Sindh.

[11] We do not suggest Pashtuns were united in a religious mobilization as ethnic groups rarely are united in their political objectives (Asal et al., 2012; Gallagher Cunningham, 2014). Secular Pashtun ethno-nationalists competed bitterly with the "mullahs for votes" and over the political direction. Pashtun Taliban Islamists were also internally divided over policy objectives (Sheikh, 2012, 2016), though their overall political direction remains strongly tied to its tribal roots (Siddique, 2014).

[12] Decentralization promotes the creation of regional parties that have little stake in the central government, thereby fueling the flames of conflict and secession (Brancati, 2006). On the flip side, centralization likely directs political ambitions to the stage of state politics.

Pashtun's political focus over time to the national stage. This confluence of conditions likely also differentiated Pashtun incentives for mobilizing religion from incentives of other minorities in Pakistan including, for example, the Sindhis that are nearly equal in size. In turn, the Pakistani state's response to Pashtun mobilization alternated between repressive violence and reluctance to forcibly suppress a movement it assisted in creating. This resulted in a sputtering spiral of violence between the state and the alternative Pashtun-led coalition emphasizing religion.

Religion and the Pakistani State

While earlier heads of state were more committed to a "secular" Muslim cultural and/or ethno-national identity as opposed to a more religious Islamic identity, this changed under the rule of President General Zia in the 1980s. Concerned about continuing disintegration of the state, Zia used the idea of a unifying religion[13] to counter increasing social and administrative divisiveness[14] (Ahmed, 2013). Subsequently, in 1996 the Prime Minister Benazir Bhutto's support of the Taliban takeover in Afghanistan further "encouraged Pakistani Islamists to demand and agitate ... for a similar government in Pakistan" (Behuria, 2007a: 296; Ahmed, 2013). Indeed, during the better part of the conflict in Afghanistan, leaders of the Pakistani state, fearing resurgence in Pashtun nationalism and Afghan Pashtun claims to Pakistani territory, actively encouraged the religious aspect of the conflict in Afghanistan (Siddique, 2014). In brief, successive rulers of Pakistan consciously worked to increase the salience of Pakistani religious identity for both geopolitical[15] and domestic political reasons. This national mobilization of religion, in turn, set the stage for the alternative religious Pashtun-led coalition to challenge the state at the time of General Musharraf's renewed emphasis on secularism (Iqtidar and Gilmartin, 2011).

Religion and Pashtun Incentives

The Pashtun occupy chiefly the north-western part of Pakistan. The largest ethnic minority in Pakistan, Pashtuns constitute between 15–20 percent of the population according to the 2010 population census. The majority of Pashtuns are Sunni of the Hanafi School (Siddique, 2014) as are other Pakistani Muslims. Punjabis make up the majority of the Pakistani population constituting 46 percent of the total population. Much like other ethnic groups in the country,

---

[13] Zia's education reform spurred the proliferation of religious *madrassah*s especially along the border with Pakistan (Ahmed, 2013: 261–262). His administration also included Islamic parties and began the funding of religious militias (Belokrenitskii and Moskalenko, 2013: 264). Under his rule the military motto was changed to "Islamic faith, Piety and Jihad in the name of Allah" and religious observance was incorporated into the bureaucracy (Siddique, 2014: 127).

[14] "Decades of Pakistani investment transformed Pashtun Islamism into a formidable political force and reduced the Pashtun nationalist threat" (Siddique, 2014: 43).

[15] Pakistan's geopolitical concerns about India also played a role in the state's decision to align with Afghan *mujahedeen* and later the Taliban to gain "strategic depth" in a neighboring country (Barnett and Siddique, 2006).

their political objectives after partition initially focused on self-determination of an ethnically defined territory.[16] However, a few features differentiated the Pashtuns and their political situation from that of other Pakistani minority ethnic groups. The first difference is the porous border and shared ethnicity between Afghan and Pakistani Pashtuns. During the Afghan conflict, many Afghan fighters sought haven in Pakistan and many Pakistani Pashtuns fought alongside Afghanis. Furthermore, several Afghanis were educated in Pashtun government-funded *madrassah*s (Behuria, 2007a; Siddique, 2014) before returning to Afghanistan to fight. This extensive exchange increased the influence of local Pashtun religious leaders and the importance of religion at the expense of traditional secular tribal and political leaders in the area (Behuria, 2007a,b; Jaffrelot and Schoch, 2015).

Three additional features of Pakistani domestic politics likely encouraged the increasing shift from regional to national focus of Pashtun political contestation. First, the political centralization of the state without economic integration of Pashtun-occupied territory continually underscores the importance of controlling the Pakistani government.[17] Second, the great poverty, underdevelopment, and population displacement[18] in Pashtun territories likely increase the appeal of religious leadership for the rank and file[19] and for

---

[16] Before partition of India and Pakistan, Pashtun nationalists in Pakistan demanded an independent state because in Pakistan they would be dominated by the Punjabis, whereas in Pashtun-dominant Afghanistan they would have to give up nationalism. "After the creation of Pakistan they declared that their demand for Pukhtunistan did not mean an independent state but an autonomous province within Pakistan" (Khan, 2005: 96–98). As a result of state involvement, religious identity in Pakistan became intensely salient likely enabling Pashtun-led religious mobilization despite their relatively modest numbers overall.

[17] Pakistani Pashtuns primarily live in the Federally Administered Tribal Areas (FATA) along the Afghan border, and in Khyber Pakhtunkhwa and Balochistan provinces. Legally under direct rule of the president, in practice FATA is governed by the president's appointee Khyber Pakhtunkhwa's governor. Government-appointed political agents representing the FATA Civil secretariat and the federal Ministry of States and Frontier Regions handle daily administration of FATA (Siddique, 2014). "[T]he political agent is the judge, jury, police chief, jail warden, district magistrate, and public prosecutor.... He also oversees all development schemes and public service departments" (Barnett and Siddique, 2006: 13). Recently the federal cabinet approved to merge FATA with Khyber Pakhtunkhwa and repeal the Frontier Crime Regulation (FRC) (Sikander, 2017), including collective punishment. If implemented this may change the longer-term political incentives of FATA residents.

[18] Over two-thirds of people in FATA live in poverty (Ahmed, 2016), where per capita income is half that of Pakistan's national average and the unemployment rate is 60–80 percent (Barnett and Siddique, 2006). The rate of literacy is 45 percent for men, and less than 7.8 percent for women compared to a national average of 57 percent for adults (Ali, 2017). There are also tens of thousands of displaced people in the region (Barnett and Siddique, 2006: 12).

[19] Local leaders of *madrassah*s sometimes served as intermediaries between the poor and state services otherwise unavailable to them (Jaffrelot and Schoch, 2015). Parents who could otherwise not afford to educate or even feed their children in some cases sent them to *madrassah*s where they receive sustenance and shelter (Trivedi and Naqvi, 2016).

leaders, likely decreases the political desirability of regional autonomy vis-à-vis the pursuit of statewide political control.[20] Third, the disproportionate recruitment of Pashtuns into both the military and the civilian bureaucracy[21] likely inculcates a strong sense of ownership and capacity among Pashtun leaders with respect to the state.

Alternative Mobilization of the Pashtuns

For the relatively large ethnic Pashtun minority sharing an increasingly politically salient religion with the majority, 9/11 and the US-led invasion of Afghanistan served as a catalyst (Sheikh, 2012, 2016) that shifted the focus of the alternative mobilization centering on religion to a conflict over state control. After the United States backed military response to 9/11, Taliban fighters, Afghani and Pakistani alike, poured back into Pakistan from Afghanistan. There the Pakistani Taliban came to be represented by several different organizations that did not always agree on objectives and often competed for adherents. Early on the Taliban's most pressing objectives can be characterized as securing the region to conduct the war in Afghanistan (Siddique, 2014). As the conflict wore on, however, Pashtuns split[22] in their broad regional versus national focus resulting in the majority of Pashtun Taliban groups uniting to form the Tehreek-e Taliban (TTP)[23] in 2007 (Ahmed, 2013).

The TTP soon disassociated from the conflict in Afghanistan to focus on the fight against the Pakistani state, at times controlling large areas of territory in North-western Pakistan. The objectives of the TTP were explicit with respect to taking over the Pakistani state (Sheikh, 2012, 2016; Ahmed, 2013; Nellis and Siddiqui, 2018).[24] For example, a TTP pamphlet from 2010[25] reads "In this world our ultimate aim of '*sharia* or martyrdom' is now focused on the destruction of Pakistani rulers and army" (Siddique, 2014: 77).

---

[20] For an account of the recent history of the political contestation between religious leaders and the state in FATA where the rise of religious mobilization is "inseparable from the features of the land," see Jaffrelot and Schoch (2015: 547).

[21] Pashtuns constitute at least 19.5 percent of the army (Khan, 2005; Ahmed, 1998). Others put the number even higher at between 30 and 35 percent (Khan, 2005: 149).

[22] Internal splits and competition are common in social movements (Tilly, 1993).

[23] Urdu for Movement of the Pakistani Taliban (Siddique, 2014: 75). Several other groups were active in the area at the same time. They sometimes competed and other times aligned (Siddique, 2014).

[24] Sheik explains how the Pakistani Taliban used religion in multiple ways in mobilization, among others "as an object to be defended ... as the purpose of armed struggle ... as imagery and myth" (2012: 439). See also Sheikh (2016). In turn, Nellis and Siddiqui (2018) explain how the current struggle between secular and religious leaders plays out in local elections.

[25] In early 2007 Maulvi Faquir Muhammad, who in December that year became the TTP first deputy, described the opposition to the Pakistani state as one of trying to wrestle power away from those standing in the way of a change of the system (Siddique, 2014). See also Brumfield (2012).

The Pashtun Taliban also recruited and/or were joined by other ethnic leaders who shared a religious bonding experience from the Afghan conflict.[26] In recruitment the TTP was carefully clear about the pan-ethnic and even pan-national nature of their mobilization with the TTP leadership. Indeed, Sheikh (2012: 440) calls the cross-ethnic religiously-based outreach of the Pakistani Taliban "characteristic" of the movement, with the TTP leadership stating, for example, that "we are not fighting for the Pashtuns, the Punjabis, the Uzbeks or the Arabs … We advocate the unity of the [Muslim] nation" (Siddique, 2014: 79).

In turn, the rank and file recruited, likely joined the Taliban for a variety of different reasons. Some were mobilized through traditional, by and large Pashtun, ethnic, and tribal channels with an overlay of religion.[27] For those looking for a more intense religious experience within Islam, be they Pashtun, Punjabi, or members of one of the other Muslim ethnic groups, the Taliban likely offered an intense unifying religious experience with a credible opportunity for access to power (Brandt, 2010; Sheikh, 2012, 2016). Yet others likely joined because religious association afforded access to services otherwise unavailable to a very poor constituency (Jaffrelot and Schoch, 2015).

5.2.2 Christianity: Uganda

Uganda became a British protectorate in 1894 and gained independence from Britain in 1962 under the leadership of Milton Obote's Uganda People's Congress. Obote was an ethnic Langi and a Northerner who was supported by the Acholi ethnic group, and in return he politically favored them. The transition from colonialism was the only peaceful change of power in Uganda. Thereafter, ethnic and regional identity mobilization came to dominate politics (Tom, 2006; Atkinson, 2015) with "six changes of government and several institutional transformations" between 1966 and 1985 (Kasozi, 1994: 59).

Intertwined ethnicity and regionalism were traditionally the two cleavages in Uganda that motivated politics (Okuku, 2002: 23). In a similar vein, Weinstein (2007) argues that ethnicity was a very important part of Ugandan politics

---

[26] While religious intensity is not the only important factor to the Pakistani Taliban's political ambition, it is one of the mechanisms by which the minority Pashtuns have credibly appealed to Punjabis across ethnic boundaries. For instance, a veteran of the war in Afghanistan, Maulana Abdulla Ghazi, the founder of the Red Mosque in Islamabad, was Baloch from Southern Punjab (Ahmed, 2013). His sons Abdul Rashid Ghazi and Maulana Abdul Aziz, largely raised in Islamabad, led the resistance in the Red Mosque. The conflict over the Red Mosque is considered an important catalyst in the consolidation of the so-called Punjabi Taliban (Brandt, 2010).

[27] "Years of migration, cross-border tribal ties and the fact that most Taliban cadres had been educated in Pakistan madrassahs since 1980s, meant that Afghan Taliban networks were deeply enmeshed in the social fabric" (Siddique, 2014: 73). Some, including the establishment, likely supported the Taliban because they brought law and order to the region, especially as protection against the *mujahedeen* (Siddique, 2014).

before independence and remained as such post-independence.[28] Even so, religion was used as a mobilization tool during a civil war between the state and the Acholi Holy Spirit Movement (HSM) and Lord's Resistance Army (LRA), who claimed ethnic, religious, and regional grievances.[29] Similar to the Pakistani case, and the Turkish case discussed at the end of this chapter, the state and its discriminatory policies against certain ethnic groups and regions played a significant role in the mobilization of religion as a shared cleavage in violent political mobilization in Uganda. Thus, consecutive dictatorships, backwardness, and poverty of the northern Acholi provinces and favoritism of certain groups by each government likely facilitated the use of alternate mobilization around religion by the HSM and to a lesser extent the LRA, and differentiated Acholi (as well as Langi and Teso ethnic groups as we will further explain) incentives from other ethnic minorities.[30]

The historical context that set the stage for the mobilization of religion is that the colonial policies of the British led to divergent economic development of the North and the South, favoring the latter (Eichstaedt, 2009: 61). During the struggle for independence in 1962, despite being supported by the largest ethnic group in Uganda, the Baganda and their *Kabaka Yekka* movement, Obote, an ethnic Langi, eliminated Baganda from his coalition in 1964, which made his government a Northern-dominated regime.[31] Obote appointed a royal Northerner as the Inspector General of the police forces, which were already largely dominated by Northerners.[32] Subsequently, the army and police often clashed with the Baganda, including raiding the palace and driving the

---

[28] Haynes (2007: 307) finds that Uganda scores very high in both ethnic and religious fragmentation indices. To him, the root cause of civil war in Uganda is religious-ethnic competition for resources exacerbated by developmental failures and political instability.

[29] While the HSM and the LRA mostly advocated Christian practices, many members of their target groups also practice Animism.

[30] The founder and leadership cadres of both HSM and LRA are Acholi and in name Catholic. However, the organizations appealed across other Northern ethnic groups including the Langi and Teso, and in reality through a complex tapestry of shared syncretic religious practices that often combine Christianity with Animism. Specifically, while the North is predominantly Catholic, Pentecostalism has spread in the 1980s and 1990s in the region, particularly among the Teso, and across Uganda, and Animism is also widely practiced along with Christianity (Jones, 2007). Thus, despite the cult-like nature of the HSM and LRA, their mobilization appeals across ethnic groups who adhere to a mixture of syncretic Christianity (Christianity and Animism) and Christian sects (Catholic and Pentecostal). Therefore, while in rhetoric the HSM and LRA adhere to Catholicism, some of their practices, such as prohibiting consumption of alcohol for its members, bear more resemblance to Pentecostal practices. Similarly, some practices of the HSM and LRA, such as not fighting a battle on a day the spirits deem unlucky, have the undertones of Animist practices (Behrend, 1999; Bunker, 2016).

[31] According to Horowitz (2013: 487), the single issue dominating ethnic party politics in Uganda has been "the place to be occupied by the Baganda and their homeland, the Kingdom of Buganda, situated in the South of Uganda."

[32] Milton Obote (an ethnic Langi) and his successors, Idi Amin (an ethnic Kakwa and Lugbara), and Tito Okello (ethnic Acholi) were all Northerners (Ofcansky, 2018: 42).

138

5 *The Internal Validity of the CWC*

Kabaka of Buganda to exile (Horowitz, 2013: 488). Once the Baganda were eliminated as a threat, Obote eventually became suspicious of his Northerner coalition and came to trust only his own ethnic group, the Langi (Horowitz, 2013: 488).

His former army commander, Idi Amin, was supported by the Kakwa, Lugbara, and Alur from his own West Nile district and the Madi as well as Nubians who are a combination of Muslim groups such as the Sudanese (Horowitz, 2013: 489). In 1971, Amin mobilized and manipulated these groups to make sure he had a unit dominated by his loyalists, who helped him to topple Obote in a coup. Subsequently, Amin massacred Obote's supporters killing nearly 300,000 people (Eichstaedt, 2009: xvii), especially the Acholi and Langi soldiers, despite having offered them amnesty for returning to their barracks (Pirouet, 1980: 17). By 1971, "of the twenty four top military posts, only three were not held by West Nilers" (Horowitz, 2013: 489). While the Lugbara ethnic group dominated the military for a while under Amin, after unsuccessful revolts in 1974 they were completely replaced by the Kakwa (Hansen, 1977). Further elimination of ethnic rivals resulted in the domination of the Kakwa and Nubians, who are mostly Muslims, under Amin's rule (Horowitz, 2013: 492).

In 1979 with support from Tanzanian forces, the Ugandan National Liberation Army (UNLA), the military wing of the Ugandan National Liberation Front (UNLF), led among others by an exiled Obote, overthrew Amin. Subsequently, Obote returned to win the 1980 election but claims that the election was highly fraudulent increased opposition to his regime (Weinstein, 2007: 62). In 1981, a military commander, Yoweri Museveni (a Bahima and a South-westerner) (Green, 2009), who had lost in his bid for the presidency in the allegedly rigged election in 1980, formed the National Resistance Movement/Army (NRM/A) to fight Obote.[33] The ensuing struggle resulted in the loss of an additional 100,000 lives in the following five years. Obote was consequently toppled in 1985 by his generals and replaced with yet another military dictator, Tito Okello (an Acholi). The Okello government pushed for national reconciliation, however Museveni's NRM/A found the number of seats it was offered in the Military Council unsatisfactory and rejected partaking in it (Okuku, 2002: 23). Finally, in 1986, Museveni's forces captured the capital city, Kampala, and ended Okello's authoritarian regime only to build another semi-dictatorship in an economically devastated Uganda (Atkinson, 2018: 61). The country transitioned to multiparty politics in 2005. However, Museveni won the presidential elections in 1996, 2001, 2006, 2011, and 2016,[34] and his

[33] Museveni formed the National Resistance Movement with former President Yusufu Lule and led a guerrilla war against Obote after losing the 1980 presidential election race.
[34] See "Yoweri Kaguta Museveni." www.britannica.com/biography/Yoweri-Kaguta-Museveni, last accessed on August 8, 2019.

government has resisted providing the opposition with any real opportunities to launch an alternative to the current regime (Alava, 2017: 168).

To his credit, Museveni tried to revive the economy by "liberalization of the currency, and economy, so as to attract the badly needed foreign investments and businesses" (Twesigye, 2010: 203). However, the efforts to economically liberalize the country and build an inclusive coalition around Museveni's regime did not bring peace to Uganda. The Acholi ethnic group, first led by Alice Lakwena then by Joseph Kony (both Acholi Northerners), rallied an alternative CWC across the Acholi, Langi, and Teso ethnic groups on the basis of shared religion to challenge the Museveni government over control of the state. Since 1986, the Holy Spirit Movement, which later on merged into the Lord's Resistance Army, has fought against the NRM/A Government of Museveni from inside and outside Uganda (Amone, 2015: 130). As the war wore on, the LRA turned to abducting fighters from Acholi and Langi villages, by 2006 having kidnapped up to 38,000 children and 37,000 adults (Mukasa, 2017). As of 2019, the movement has only 100–150 fighters left; still, Kony continues to stir the borderlands of Uganda, the Central African Republic, the Democratic Republic of Congo, and South Sudan.[35]

Religion and the Ugandan State

Uganda is a Christian majority state, comprised of two main Christian factions: Anglicans (32 percent) and Roman Catholics (39 percent) (U.S. Department of State International Religious Freedom Report for 2016: 2). Furthermore, according to Pew, as much as 20 percent of the population subscribes to Pentecostalism and that number is growing.[36] There is also a small Muslim minority in the country (Pirouet, 1980: 13) and around 20 percent of the population follow local religions and subscribe to syncretic beliefs (Haynes, 2007: 310). The Northern Region – where the Acholi are from – and West Nile sub-region, are predominantly Roman Catholic (U.S. Department of State International Religious Freedom Report for 2016: 2).

According to Article 7 of the 1995 Constitution, Uganda does not have a state religion. Moreover, the constitution prohibits the creation of political parties based on religion. Nevertheless, religious cleavages have shaped the Ugandan political system even before its independence. For example, Milton Obote's Uganda People's Congress was known as the Protestant Party, whereas

---

[35] Kristof Titeca, "How Joseph Kony's notorious Lord's Resistance Army uses photographs as weapons," The Washington Post, December 9, 2019. Available at: www.washingtonpost.com/politics/2019/12/09/heres-how-joseph-konys-notorious-lords-resistance-army-uses-photographs-weapons, last accessed on June 6, 2020.

[36] Moreover, Pew reports that "Beyond electoral politics, pentecostalism has penetrated important sectors of African public life. In Uganda and Kenya, for example, pentecostals and other evangelicals control numerous radio and TV stations (Bengali 2006)." See www.pewforum.org/2006/10/05/overview-pentecostalism-in-africa, last accessed on May 27, 2020.

the opposition Democratic Party had a reputation as the Catholic Party. As a legacy of Anglican British colonialism in Uganda, Anglican political elites long dominated positions of power and marginalized Catholics, Muslims, and others from local and central government positions (Twesigye, 2010: 3). However, the Catholic and Anglican churches were also internally cleaved by ethnic factionalism (Pirouet, 1980: 13)[37] and the ethnic groups themselves are cross-cut by different religions (especially Animism and Christianity) and various Christian sects. Thus, it would be wrong to assume political contestation in Uganda plays out along strictly sectarian lines where a Catholic North is fighting a Protestant South. The religious landscape is far more complex and opposing sides cannot be cleanly distinguished along sectarian lines. For example, Milton Obote, a Northerner, who ruled two governments was Protestant but his cabinets included Protestants and Catholics, although the former were always in majority.[38] Moreover, in the 1980s and early 1990s, Museveni's government made efforts to appear non-sectarian by coalescing with diverse ethno-religious groups.[39] Similarly, the HSM and LRA use the teachings and practices from different sects of Christianity, including Catholicism and Pentecostalism, and other religions such as Animism and even Islam, to mobilize their following.[40] Consequently, although there are sectarian differences, political contestation in Uganda cannot be classified as strictly sectarian.

Religion and Acholi Incentives

Notably, the ethnic Acholi, leading the alternative mobilization of religion in Uganda, constitute only 4.4 percent of the total population and are, therefore, not one of the largest ethnic groups in the country.[41] However, as the historical overview illustrated political contestation in Uganda has not been only between the largest ethnic groups but has taken on an ethno-regional character, often spearheaded by leaders of smaller ethnic groups representing regional coalitions (Haynes, 2007). Thus, the average demographic size of groups included in

[37] Pirouet (1980) argues that due to all these tensions, the churches mostly stayed neutral or held an opposition role as political violence plagued the country, particularly during Idi Amin's dictatorial rule.

[38] See Isaiah Mwebaze, "Religion and tribe: the 'magic bullets' for Uganda's cabinet appointments," *Eagle Online*, March 21, 2017. Available at: https://eagle.co.ug/2017/03/24/religion-tribe-play-big-role-ugandas-cabinet-appointments.html, last accessed on June 5, 2020.

[39] Despite these efforts, Museveni is often accused of supporting the Pentecostals disproportionately, as his wife Janet Museveni is a member of the Covenant Nation Church, which is a Pentecostal church founded by one of her daughters (Kintu, 2018: 89).

[40] "Religious Beliefs of Joseph Kony's Lord's Resistance Army" New York Times, November 26, 2005. Available at: www.nytimes.com/interactive/projects/documents/religious-beliefs-of-josephkonys-lords-resistance-army, accessed May 27, 2020.

[41] According to 2014 estimates (The World Factbook 2019), larger plurality groups include the Baganda at 16.5 percent of the population, Banyankole at 9.6 percent, the Basoga at 8.8 percent, the Bakiga at 7.1 percent, the Teso at 7 percent, the Langi at 6.3 percent, and the Bagisu at 4.9 percent.

the government is only 6 percent,[42] and as the reader will recall, the theory in Chapter 3 suggests that it is the political minority group size relative to the political majority that motivates mobilization. Therefore, in Uganda, even though constituting only 4.4 percent of the population, the Acholi are not far off the average size for groups included in the executive. Furthermore, when seeking to stave off ethno-regional defeat by mobilizing religion, leaders of the group recruited across the Northern Acholi and Langi ethnic groups as well as the Teso people from the Eastern region (Haynes, 2007: 310). Together the Langi and Acholi constitute around 10 percent of the population, in size surpassing all but the Baganda ethnic group, and with the Teso at around 7 percent[43] the Acholi/Langi/Teso ethnic recruitment base surpasses the size of all single Ugandan ethnic groups.[44]

The Acholi have also intermittently been in governments, and like the Pashtuns in Pakistan, have been prominent in the military throughout the post-colonial history. During the colonial administration the Acholi were used as soldiers due to their purported "superior physique, habits of discipline, and unsophisticated outlook" (Atkinson, 2015: 6),[45] while most administrative tasks were given to other ethnic and regional groups, particularly Southerners. The common view was that "a soldier is northerner, a civil servant a southerner and a merchant an Asian" (Finnstrom, 2008: 64). Although the Acholi complained occasionally for being put on the front lines, they embraced this warrior identity which made them the "backbone" of Uganda. In fact, Doom and Vlassenroot (1999: 8) underlines that "when Milton Obote became the first prime minister of independent Uganda in 1962, he inherited armed forces dominated by Acholi, who saw the profession of arms as their natural vocation. Horowitz's (1985: 487) finding that the Acholi has comprised at least one-third to three-fourths of the army at the time confirms the weight of the Acholi perception of self-importance. Although they were hunted down by Amin, the Acholi not only dominated the Ugandan military until 1986, but also "exerted some degree of hegemony in the governments of Milton Obote and Tito Okello" (Amone, 2015: 130). Thus, leaders of the group may also have come to perceive the group as stronger than its numbers would suggest. Therefore, when

---

[42] AMAR groups that have been represented in the executive include the Acholi at 4 percent, the Alur 4 percent, Baganda 16 percent, Banyarwanda 5.9 percent, Banyoro 2.4 percent, Kakwa 3 percent, Karamojong 10 percent, Lango 6 percent, Lugabara 6 percent, and Toro 3.2 percent. For further information on ethnic access, see Ethnic Power Relations data by Vogt et al. (2015). Population shares come from the AMAR data.

[43] In AMAR, which does not take political mobilization as a selection criteria into the data, the Teso are included as a sub-group of the Karamojong. The Karamojong account for around 10 percent of the population and according to the World Factbook, the Teso constitute around 7 percent of that total.

[44] For regional population statistics see, for example, Uganda Bureau of Statistics, www .citypopulation.de/php/uganda-admin.php.

[45] The Acholi were at times portrayed as savages and warmongers by the Baganda and the British (Apuuli, 2011: 119).

the Museveni government took over in 1986, losing their remaining political and military power perhaps hit the Northerner Acholi harder than any other larger groups (Tom, 2006). When Museveni's NRM/A seized power in 1986, the Uganda National Liberation Army (UNLA), the majority of which was Acholi and Langi, retreated northwards to Acholi home districts of Gulu and Kitgum, as well as across the border, to Sudan (Apuuli, 2011: 118). Subsequently, these Acholi ex-soldiers formed the United People's Defense Army (UPDA), which then coalesced with Alice Lakwena's Holy Spirit Movement, to bring down the Museveni regime. However, by 1989 Museveni's forces had crushed not only Lakwena's movement but also the remaining UPDA rebels, and granted the remaining rebel forces a pardon (Eichstaedt, 2009: 68).

Had it not been for Joseph Kony, who had the reputation of "Wizard of the Nile" despite his young age of twenty (Green, 2009), Museveni might have had a shot at ruling in peace. Kony, however, claimed he inherited his cousin Lakwena's spiritual powers and invited her followers to join his forces (Allen, 1991), which they did either voluntarily or under coercion. Discontent with Museveni's regime was common in Kony's target audience including the Catholic youth, among others.[46]

In sum, the colonial divide and rule policies emphasizing the Acholi as warriors as well as the inherent North-South rivalry of various ethnic groups in Ugandan politics are crucial reasons that prepared the context for Acholi violent mobilization of religion.[47] Each dictator that came to power in Uganda manipulated ethnic groups and regionalism to build their own winning coalitions. We will next examine what made the Acholi leadership under Lakwena and her successor Kony consider religion as an alternative mobilization strategy to fight against the Museveni government.

Alternative Mobilization of the Acholi

Alice Auma, a twenty-seven-year-old ethnic Acholi woman, a "spirit medium" and healer, who lived in Opit village, Gulu in Northern Uganda claimed that she was possessed by a spirit called *Lakwena* (Messenger). Thereafter known as Alice Lakwena, she established a Christian-Animist syncretic rebel group called

---

[46] The Catholic Acholi youth finds no accountability in Museveni's rule, and in Alava's interviews they state that Milton Obote "came to show receipts – he made sure people knew where the money was going" (Alava, 2017: 167). Museveni's lack of transparency was further used by Kony and the Acholi leadership to manipulate the Catholic youth against the government as "… the Acholi community votes overwhelmingly anti-National Resistance Movement, and hence anti-Museveni, in local, parliamentary and presidential elections. During the 1996 elections, the LRA even declared a unilateral ceasefire to allow people to campaign and vote for the opposition" (Acker, 2004: 337).

[47] Part of the rivalry was due to the strategy of the Anglican British colonizers assigning important political positions to Anglican ethnic groups but not others.

the Holy Spirit Movement in 1985 (Behrend, 1999). Alice Lakwena capitalized on the perception of the Acholi that they are the most hated tribe in Uganda and when an Acholi dies at war, that is because of their past sins as the enemy for the Acholi is within (Behrend, 1999). Thus, Alice Lakwena's first and foremost strategy was to manipulate the Acholi through religion by way of using the group's historical role as soldiers and the need for retribution for the massacres committed by the Acholi.

Twesigye (2010: xv) details rural Catholics as the target base of Lakwena's Holy Spirit Movement. Although Museveni's NRM/A government tried to appeal across sects, it was predominantly ruled by Anglican political elites "covertly perpetuating the problematic British colonial structure of Anglican political hegemony. This elitist, autocratic, oppressive and sectarian Anglican hegemony had traditionally marginalized and excluded qualified Catholics, Muslims and the traditionalists from kinships and key political positions in the local and the Central Government" (Twesigye, 2010: 3). Therefore, the second strategy of Alice Lakwena's alternative mobilization involved pointing out the Anglican dominance of political elites in Museveni's winning coalition, regardless of how much Museveni's coalition attempted to appeal across sects and religions.[48] However, Lakwena's belief system also heavily emphasized Animism and in that sense was not sectarian Catholic (Behrend, 1999). Finally, the soldiers who ran from Kampala with heavy guns and equipment when a Southerner, Museveni came to power had the distinct memory of being tracked and killed by Idi Amin just for being Acholi. An Acholi parliamentarian Morris Latigo argues "the Acholi reaction was, this time we're not going to die like pigs" (Eichstaedt, 2009: 141). Thus, as a third strategy, Lakwena offered survival to these soldiers under the guise of religious mysticism.[49]

As Lakwena used religion to recruit rebels from all over the North, her cousin Joseph Kony, a witch doctor, positioned himself as a spiritual advisor for the rebels. When Lakwena waged war against Museveni's regime in 1986, Kony preferred to remain separate, which ultimately worked to his advantage. Lakwena's forces, which at first scored considerable victories believed to be due to the help provided by Lakwena's spirits, were defeated in 1987 and Lakwena fled to Kenya and spent the rest of her life there in a refugee camp until her death in 2007. After her defeat, Kony seized Lakwena's remaining forces and united them under the banner of the LRA.

---

[48] In 1995, the NRM/A Government, for example, formulated a new, religiously inclusive Constitution. It protected religious diversity and freedoms of conscience, religion, and its practice from the interference of the State.

[49] She often predicted where the enemy would come from during a battle and claim that her spirit would protect the fighters, which was part of the Animist part of her religious appeal to the rebels.

Kony, at that time the most charismatic leader of all the rebel forces in the north,[50] announced his aim to establish a religious state based on the Ten Commandments.[51] According to Finnstrom (2008: 108), Kony's stated religious and political goals were hardly original as missionaries have taught similar religious practices in Uganda for more than a century. Thus, Kony only sought to cement the work of missionaries spreading Christianity in Uganda.[52]

In addition to charismatic leadership as a self-proclaimed prophet, Kony followed in Alice Lakwena's footsteps, continuing the use of a combination of her strategies for recruitment. Former major Jackson Acama, after leaving the LRA in 2004, said in an interview (Eichstaedt, 2009: 100), that Kony emphasized two particular goals: following only God's path and overthrowing the Museveni government. Interestingly, the limited data on the religious practices of the LRA suggest that despite all that Kony preaches, the group does not strictly adhere to Catholicism but borrows rituals and beliefs from a variety of religions, including but not limited to Animism, Christianity, and Islam.[53] According to Acama, "Kony was both prophet and punisher of the Acholi," which is in line with Alice Lakwena's teachings. The Acholi, he argued, were also at fault for not following God's prophet – Kony's leadership and still practicing traditional religion. In this vein, the LRA's massacres and raids to the Acholi districts were justified as biblical punishment.

Finnstrom's study of the Acholiland reveals that fifteen influential Acholi clan elders denied that the rebellion against Museveni is an exclusively Acholi phenomenon (Finnstrom, 2008: 106). When Museveni called the Acholi "cannibalistic grasshoppers in a bottle," Acholi elders claimed "Now, in the

[50] Pamela Faber, "Sources of Resilience in the Lord's Resistance Army," Center for Stability and Development, April 2017, Available at: www.cna.org/cna_files/pdf/dop-2017-u-015265-final.pdf, last accessed on June 10, 2020.

[51] Specifically, the rebels declared under their former name United Democratic Christian Movement/Army that they want witchcraft and sorcery to cease and Ten Commandments to be promoted in the country (Finnstrom, 2008: 108).

[52] Doom and Vlassenroot (1999: 35–36) argue, Kony never aimed to change the system but "to replace it" by something 'higher', by a new way of living, but out of anger and frustration, because their [Acholi] lives do not fit into any system any more...." Their rebellion is political inasmuch as it is a result of the world political and economical system in place. It is, for those engaged, non-political inasmuch as they no longer believe in politics. For the majority of the rank and file, it is a survival strategy, a way to obtain things which are out of reach by all normal means: consummatory rewards as ideological drive. For those in charge, the brokers, it is a tool to acquire access to power, status, and some wealth: rebellion as a career. Twesigye (2010: 117) takes this as an unclear religious or political agenda "mainly due to its poorly educated leadership."

[53] Far from practicing Catholicism, "Kony delineated rules for his army's behavior, a sort of L.R.A. code of conduct that mixed derivatives of Christianity, Islam, Animism and what would seem a free association on guerrilla tactics, social justice, diet, marriage and capital punishment." See for specific examples of how different beliefs are adopted in Kony's rhetoric, "Religious Beliefs of Joseph Kony's Lord's Resistance Army," *New York Times*, November 26, 2005. Available at: www.nytimes.com/interactive/projects/documents/religious-beliefs-of-joseph-konys-lords-resistance-army, last accessed on May 27, 2020.

bush, the composition of rebels is composed of *all* the tribes of Uganda, except that the majority are Acholi, and leadership is again an Acholi leading ... Even Banyankole, Museveni's tribe, they are also there! (Gulu town, January 1998)" (Finnstrom, 2008: 106).[54] Thus, before the ceasefire in 2006, Kony's LRA has been able to mobilize, voluntarily or through force, a large coalition against Museveni, not only from the Acholi but also other groups in the North.

Several third-party conflict resolution attempts to negotiate peace between Kony and Museveni in the 1990s and 2000s failed. The civil war in Uganda cost hundreds of thousands of Acholi lives as the government moved Acholis into camps for protection but failed to protect the inhabitants from LRA's abductions and massacres. In the name of religion, the LRA abducted thousands of Northern children and used them as sex slaves and/or trained them as child soldiers (Eichstaedt, 2009), and continued recruiting across ethnic boundaries (van Acker, 2004: 347), particularly from Acholi, Langi, and Teso (Haynes, 2007: 310).[55]

In sum, in line with the expectations of our theory of *Alternatives in Mobilization* and the CWC hypothesis, Alice Lakwena's HSM and Joseph Kony's LRA offered a more intense religious (Christian and/or syncretic) experience to the Acholi and other groups such as the Langi and Teso, as well as a shot at retribution for the wrongs committed against them but also by them, particularly the wrongs that the Acholi as a tribe had committed during its reign in government and military. While the Acholi are not the largest ethnic group they were relatively similar in size to ethnic political majorities, and often predominant in administrative structures including the army. At the time of the HSM mobilization the Acholi were also politically marginalized. However, this case also revealed several unexpected factors. For example, while the Acholi shared a religious family with the majority the use of religion for recruitment was far more complex than anticipated – involving appeals across sect and other families of religion especially Animism. Furthermore, while the

---

54 The Ugandan government, like its counterpart in Turkey has done with the PKK, often claimed that the terrorist organization is a group of bandits and they do not have real support except for the child soldiers that they abduct from towns (Alava, 2017). Museveni government also assumed that the LRA could not survive without Sudan's aid. Kony was indeed supported and armed by Sudan to retaliate against Museveni who was supporting the Sudan People's Liberation Army in the Sudanese civil war (Eichstaedt, 2009: 175). The International Criminal Court passed indictments in 2005 for Kony and his four high ranking officers, which convinced them that there was no other viable option than to continue fighting, hence mobilization and recruitment continued (Eichstaedt, 2009: 174). The LRA thereafter has spread to neighboring countries including the Democratic Republic of Congo (Neethling, 2013) and no longer operates out of Uganda since signing a ceasefire with the Ugandan government in 2006. Scholars have since debated whether traditional restorative justice measures would have ended the conflict instead of the transnational justice ICC sought to implement upon the request of the Ugandan government (Clark, 2010).

55 Eichstaedt's (2009) interviews with Acholi ministers and parliamentarians pinpoint that the LRA's brutality and Kony's greed have eventually alienated the Acholi from the rebel movement.

story of the HSM seemingly supports the mechanism proposed this is less clear of the LRA. Most notably the HSM recruited voluntarily throughout its reign, LRA recruited mostly through abductions after 1994.[56] Indeed, in its current incarnation Vinci (2007: 337–338) argues that the "LRA's war cannot be considered using traditional models of ethno-political conflict. The LRA is not the armed representative of an ethnic group. Rather it now represents its own group, which is based on specific initiation and inclusion. As such, its 'political goal' is to continue existing as a separate unit, which necessitates continual warfare."

5.2.3 Hinduism: Nepal

Smaller kingdoms in Nepal were unified into one kingdom in 1768 under the Gorkha monarchy. The caste system, which is a hierarchical social stratification system based on Hindu beliefs and values,[57] was institutionalized by the 1854 *Muluki Ain* (National Legal Code) to solidify the power of the Rana ruling family, and the upper castes coalescing around its rule (Drucza, 2017: 162). When the Rana family took power in 1846, and for the century that it reigned, the Gorkha monarchy became *de facto* symbolic rather than the site of actual political power in Nepal (Svensson, 2012: 115). In 1951, anti-Rana rebels in the Nepali Congress Party ousted the Rana family and formed a government backed by the restored Gorkha monarchy. In 1960, King Mahendra of the Gorkha dynasty seized power and established the *Panchayat* (political system) where the King once again became the supreme ruler, political parties were disbanded, and limited power was delegated to local authorities (Svensson, 2012: 115). Despite widespread dissent and growing resentment against the state, the *Panchayat* survived for thirty years.

In 1990, the Nepali Congress Party and the United Left Front, a coalition of communist and leftist groups, organized the *Jana Andolan* (People's Movement) to voice grievances that included development failure and corruption of the ruling elite (Sharma, 2006, 2016), socio-economic inequalities stemming from poorly planned and governed development (Murshed and Gates, 2005), and

---

[56] We thank Trey Billing for making this point. The strategy of mobilization Kony used in the mid-1990s was to create exclusive membership. The LRA has indoctrinated recruits, voluntary or involuntary alike, into Kony's vision of religion and the world around them. No one was invited and no volunteers were accepted to the organization after mid-1990s, instead recruits were "chosen" by the prophet. Abducted boys and girls were taught that Kony is the messiah and they were his chosen people (Twesigye, 2010: 113).

[57] Subedi (2010: 135) uses the definition of caste in Nepal "as a small and named group of persons characterized by endogamy, hereditary membership, and a specific style of life which sometimes includes the pursuit by tradition of a particular occupation and usually associated with a more or less distinct ritual status in a hierarchical system" (Beteille, 1965: 46). Giving examples of several different definitions and regions the term caste has been used. Subedi concludes that caste system in Nepal is not exclusive to Hinduism and that many other societies have similar arrangements. See Whelpton (2004) for more on the history of caste system across Nepal.

repression of the opposition by a weak government (Kumar, 2005).[58] What was planned as a non-violent movement quickly escalated as the state forces killed protesters on the streets. This turn of events eventually forced King Birendra to transition from absolute to constitutional monarchy and declare a multiparty democracy (Davis et al., 2012: 120).

In practice, not much changed for the masses. The United National People's Movement, born out of dissatisfaction with the political elite gave way to the Communist Party of Nepal (Unity Centre), which remained an underground movement. However, its political front, the United People's Front of Nepal (UPFN) ran in the 1991 elections and became the third-largest party in the parliament. When the UPFN split in 1994, one of the political leaders Pushpa Kamal Dahal (commonly known as Prachanda, or "fierce") established the Communist Party of Nepal (Maoist) (CPN-M), which began an armed struggle that lasted until 2006.[59] The Maoists recruited across low caste and indigenous ethnic groups by appealing to them through their call for a secular government that would stop privileging the higher castes on the basis of the Hindu religion. Thus, in contrast to the other cases covered in this chapter where religion-based CWC sought to create a religious state (Pakistan, Uganda), or Marxist/Leninist/Maoists mobilized against a secular state (Turkey), the Communist Nepali CWC claimed religious incompatibility with the state in an effort to eliminate the role of religion in a state defined in religious terms. Their bid was apparently successful as on April 11, 2008, the CPN-M became "the first democratically elected Maoist party in world history" marking the demise of a 240-year-old Hindu monarchy (Cailmail, 2008: 2). On May 28, 2008, the Constituent Assembly voted for a federal democratic and secular republic, and officially abolished the monarchy.[60]

Religion and the Nepali State

The Gorkha king, Prithvi Narayan Shah, the founder of the kingdom of Nepal, declared it as a Hindu country. The Nepalese society consisted of four *varna*

---

[58] Do and Iyer (2010) find that poverty and geography explain where conflict starts and how mobilization/recruiting takes place. They also argue that ethnicity/caste relations, land inequality, and political participation are not correlated to the civil war. While this may be true in the disaggregate we suggest that high caste versus all other groups is a major cleavage that the Maoists capitalized on.

[59] Prachanda was born in the Hills to an upper-caste Brahmin lineage (Davis et al., 2012: 129) and was a high school teacher when he was indoctrinated in Maoism (von Einsiedel et al., 2012: 18).

[60] It was quite a shock for students of Nepali politics that the Nepali Congress, the mainstream political party that dominated the political scene since Nepal transitioned to multiparty politics in 1991, won only 19 percent of the seats in the elections. See the official web page of the party for further information: www.nepalicongress.org/index.php?linkId=2, last accessed on October 25, 2019.

(main castes) and 36 *jat* (ethnic and religious communities) (Cailmail, 2008: 6). This, in return, legitimized the supremacy of certain castes over others. Under this categorization, the higher castes such as the Chhetri, Brahmin, Thakuri, and Sanyasi held the economic and political power, while the lower castes and ethno-religious minorities such as the Dalits (Untouchables) and the *Janajati*[61] were politically and economically marginalized.

After a century of reign, when Rana rule came to an end in 1951, the situation for ethno-religious minorities and lower castes did not improve. Interestingly, as the Gorkha dynasty was restored to power, King Mahendra outlawed caste discrimination in an attempt to appease the public; however, Hinduism remained the state religion and the upper castes continued to rule (Adhikari, 2014: 116). The public in Nepal, thus, continued to perceive political parties as "tools of a high caste, corrupt, and nepotistic Kathmandu elite" (Davis et al., 2012: 121).

By 1990, Nepal was one of the poorest countries in the world with a small, wealthy coalition supporting the monarchy. Following the political tumult in 1990, a new constitution declared Nepal multiethnic, multilingual, and democratic, but still a *Hindu* constitutional monarchical kingdom (Ellingsen, 1991: 12). Thus, "Despite being a conglomeration of minorities, the 1990 Constitution maintained the hegemony of one religion (Hinduism), one language (Nepali), and one nationality" (Davis et al., 2012: 138). During this period of multiparty politics, the upper caste elite in the political parties did not include any of the ethno-religious and linguistic demands of the people in their programs for fear of disunity (Adhikari, 2014: 116). The continued lack of a more egalitarian system of governance and the positive discrimination of upper castes in the economic and political system at the expense of other groups set the stage for continued mobilization of groups for state control.

In 2001, the Crown Prince Dipendra allegedly murdered his family, including his father King Birendra, and killed himself, which decreased the legitimacy of the Hindu dynasty (Svensson, 2012: 117).[62] According to Khadka (1986: 431), the Nepalese people accepted the king as the "benevolent reincarnation" and this often legitimated the monarchy's repression. However, this incident shook the Nepalese people's faith. Shortly after, late King Birendra's brother Gyanendra, an unpopular successor, assumed power. When King Gyanendra declared a state of emergency in November 2001, dismissed the elected government in 2002, and established a dictatorship in 2005, the "people's movement" led by the Maoists initiated a violent conflict against the monarchy, often

---

[61] Janajati is a term used to legally define indigenous ethnic groups in Nepal. We will discuss these groups in greater detail in the following sub-sections.

[62] This incident is still controversial in the Nepalese public opinion since the investigation committee announced Birendra was responsible for the massacre, however, there was no further action taken.

through devastating terrorist attacks targeting civilians, that lasted until the 2006 peace accords were signed (Lawoti and Hangen, 2013: 6).[63]

While their demands in the first "People's Movement" of 1990 were multiparty democracy and a less influential monarchy, the goals of the Maoist insurgency in the second movement were more ambitious: a secular state and federalism (Lawoti and Hangen, 2013: 6). In this second movement, the coalition of the opposition included student movements, the Unified Marxist Leninist (UML) leadership as well as parties in the dissolved congress, in addition to the CPN-M, the main opposition, whose alternative mobilization strategy emphasizing the demand for less religion (or more secularism) forced the King to transfer power back to the parliament in 2008 (Pandey, 2010).

Since the Maoist takeover, abolition of the monarchy, and secularization of the state in 2008, the upper castes have used religious outbidding as a mobilization strategy against secularism; however, their right-wing Hindu activism has been weak and lacked countrywide organization (ICG, 2011: 20–21).

Religion and CPN-M Incentives

The Hindu religion and the monarchy were the foundations of the Nepali state for centuries but the Maoists eventually managed to change how the nation was defined by abolishing both and building a secular republic in 2008 (Adhikari, 2014: 244). Considering how salient Hinduism is to all castes as well as to some indigenous ethnic groups (like the Magar and the Newar) in Nepal, demanding secularization of the state was a seemingly risky strategy for mobilization. To understand why the Maoists pursued this strategy, it is important to outline the demographics of Nepal in some more detail.

According to the 2011 Census, the country is extremely diverse but also extraordinarily fragmented, with 126 widely dispersed caste and ethnic groups.[64] The caste system is strictly hierarchical and to some extent overlaps with several distinct economic classes, with "the privileged tagadhari at the top, composed of the higher castes such as the Brahmans (Bahun), the Thakuri, and the Chhetri; then come the Matwali, which designates all the castes that drink alcohol (meaning mainly, the tribal castes); next come those who answer to the rule *pani na calne choi chito halnu naparne* (which refers to all members of lower castes with whom a member of a higher caste can speak but from whom he cannot accept water); and the last are the Dalit, or untouchables"

---

[63] To curb the Maoist insurgency, King Gyanendra instituted the "Terrorist and Disruptive Activities (Control and Punishment) Ordinance (TADO), which publicly identified Maoists as 'terrorists' and deployed the Royal Nepal Army (RNA) against them" (Davis et al., 2012: 123). As a result, 227 people were killed in the first month following the royal coup (Kumar, 2005).

[64] The Central Bureau of Statistics (CBS) of Nepal recorded a list of 1250 ethnic/caste and 207 religious groups which is a significant improvement over the 2001 Census which listed "less than 350 ethnic/caste groups (excluding 3 unidentified categories) and 8 religious groups (excluding one other category) in Nepal" (Central Bureau of Statistics, 2014: 1–2). As such, many groups that have not declared their identity felt free to do so in the 2011 Census.

(Cailmail, 2008: 6).[65] Importantly, caste groups and ethnic groups (*Janajati*) are culturally and legally differentiated in Nepal, "as those who do not fall within the Hindu caste hierarchy and have their own language and cultural identity claim themselves as ethnic populations" (Paudel, 2016: 548). Furthermore, both caste groups and ethnic groups are often internally divided between regions and ethnic groups are sometimes also divided by religion, i.e. Hinduism, Buddhism, Kirat, etc.

As shown in Table 5.2, the ten most populous caste and ethnic groups comprise 70 percent of the total population of Nepal (Central Bureau of Statistics, 2014: 25). Of those, the Caste Hill Hindu Elite, the Chhetri, the Hill Brahmin, Thakuri, and Sanyasi constitute 31.25 percent of the total population.[66] Notably, as shown in Table 5.2 the high castes are the only groups that are unified in caste, religion, and region.[67]

Most other groups in Nepal are geographically more dispersed throughout three regions, the Hill, the Mountain, and the Terai; and some are divided between religions. For example, indigenous ethnic groups as well as immigrants from India, mostly live in the Mountains or the Terai region.[68] The Terai population, commonly referred to as Madhesi (meaning inhabitant of the Terai) and comprising almost half of Nepal's population, is internally divided between several different lower castes and ethnic groups as shown in Table 5.2. Demographically, according to a 2011 International Crisis Group (ICG) report, "even the dominant ethnic group in each area is likely to be in the minority," so much that "only in fourteen out of the 75 districts does any one group comprise more than 50 percent of the population" (ICG, 2011: 1).

By and large ethnic groups in Nepal, particularly the Madhesi groups in the Terai consider themselves marginalized for over a 100 years of dominance by the Pahadis (the hill-dwelling and mostly upper-caste groups) (Miklian, 2009: 3).[69] Consequent ethnic and regional conflict between varying coalitions

---

[65] See Subedi (2010: 152–153) for a more detailed account of castes and sub-castes in Nepal.

[66] Moreover, "Chhetri and Brahmin alone comprising the largest single cluster in 35 districts (46.7%) of Nepal, increasing their concentration in four more districts than in the 2001 census" (Central Bureau of Statistics, 2014: 25) points to the increasing demographic dominance of these two high castes in addition to their social, economic, and political hegemony.

[67] Thakuri (1.6 percent) and Sanyasi (Dasnami) (0.8 percent) are two of the four high caste groups (Central Bureau of Statistics, 2014: 27). Due to their smaller population size, they are not in Table 5.2, however, our discussion of high castes includes all four high castes living in the Hill region.

[68] According to Miklian (2009: 3), "The 'Terai'" is "the fertile strip of low-lying land sandwiched between the Himalayan foothills and the Indo-Gangetic alluvial plain, running from west to east throughout southern Nepal, and stretching to India and Bhutan." Overall, the Terai population is more heterogeneous than either the Hill or the Mountain region in terms of ethnic/caste structure, which "could be due to the heavy migration of Hill people as well as an uncontrolled flow of Indian people over the last 50 years" (Central Bureau of Statistics, 2014: 25).

[69] Interestingly, as we have seen with the other cases, "a government-sponsored resettlement program in the mid-1980s financed migration of Pahadis to the Terai in an attempt to solidify

TABLE 5.2. *Ten largest identity groups in Nepal, 2011 Census*

Group name	Identity type	Religion	% of Hindus	Region	# Pop.	% of Pop.
Chhetri	High caste	Hinduism	99.3	Hill	4,398,053	16.6
Hill Brahman	High caste	Hinduism	99.6	Hill	3,226,903	12.2
Kami	Low caste/ Dalit	Hinduism	96.4	Hill, Mountain	1,258,554	4.8
Yadav	Low caste/ Madhesi	Hinduism	99.7	Terai	1,054,458	4
Newar	Janajati, all 4 castes	Hinduism, Buddhism	87.38	Hill	1,321,933	5
Magar	Janajati, no caste	Hinduism, Buddhism	79.0	Mountain, Hill	1,887,733	7.1
Rai	Janajati	Kirat, Hinduism	32.6	Hill	620,004	2.3
Tharu	Janajati/ Madhesi	Hinduism	94.0	Terai	1,737,470	6.6
Tamang	Janajati	Buddhism, Hinduism	8.8	Mountain, Hill	1,539,830	5.8
Musalman	Cultural	Islam	0	Terai	1,164,255	4.4
Other	Over 116 Janajati/ Madhesi groups	Mainly Hinduism, Buddhism		Terai, Hill	8,285,308	31.3
Nepal Total					26,494,501	100

of these groups and against the state is historically the norm in Nepal, with twenty-five ethnic and caste-based mobilizations occurring between 1770 and 1979 (Lawoti, 2007: 32).[70]

After 1990, the change in institutional structures and political liberalization spurred a renewed opportunity for mobilization to rectify caste and ethnic group grievances. CPN-M capitalized on this opportunity by fomenting a mobilization strategy that unified all the lower castes across class and region, and ethnic groups across regions and religions, against the only common opponent and issue. CPN-M thus consolidated its opposition to the rule of the higher castes that continued by constitutional designation of the state as religiously based on Hinduism.

control over the valuable agricultural and industrial region" (Miklian, 2009: 3). Thus, as a result of decades of identity construction by Terai organizations such as Madhesi Janadhikar Forum, Terai Madhesh Loktrantrik Party, and Sadbhavana Party, several Madhesi groups now identify as "non-tribal, caste Hindus of Indian origin that live in the Terai. Thus adding racial/ethnic connotations in addition to the geographic association" (Miklian, 2009: 4).

[70] Reminiscent of other cases in this chapter and the next, some of the major reasons for these conflicts include loss of land to migrants, especially from upper castes, as well as centralization efforts of the state in the periphery (ICG, 2011: 3).

Alternative Mobilization for Secularism/Equality of Castes

The four higher castes in the Hill region monopolized the major positions in government from the birth of Nepal, disadvantaging particularly the Madhesi[71] (lower castes from the Terai region) and the Janajati[72] (indigenous ethnic groups) (Cailmail, 2008: 7). Despite making up only about 29 percent of the Nepali population, the Chettri and Brahmin "dominated the other castes and ethnic groups in terms of economic and social well-being and access to the top positions in the civil service" (Hachhethu, 2008). Other groups remained marginalized. For example, although untouchability or the status of Dalits was banned in early 1960s by the Constitution, it is still prevalent in the society as no governments enforced the ban before the Maoist victory in 2008 (Lawoti, 2005: 91).

In 1990, when the new multiparty system allowed for political parties, ethnic and class-based parties were established to represent people all over Nepal, and enjoyed considerable electoral success (Lawoti, 2013). In addition, these became more effective at pushing for and protecting ethnic demands and interests. In fact, Madhesis were the first to establish an ethnic party and have had the highest representation both in the parliament and the executive since 2008, and this coalition of groups has received concessions on issues such as citizenship, federalism, electoral reforms, Madhesi cultural rights, etc. (Lawoti, 2013: 229–230).[73] However, according to Davis et al. (2012), the first decade of democratization was also politically chaotic as nine governments were overturned in three parliamentary elections and "the fruits of democracy were being served to only a handful of Brahmin and Chhetri caste groups"(Davis et al., 2012: 121). Furthermore, the Constitution of 1990, continued to proclaim Nepal a Hindu state, still engendering severe opposition because of its marginalization of most of Nepal's population: the ethnic and religious minorities and lower castes (Cailmail, 2008: 6).

In this environment, the UPFN, one of the leading opposition parties in the country, split into the recognized and unrecognized factions of the political party. According to Davis et al. (2012), "Such inequalities among ethnic groups have given rise to various ethnic and caste movements in Nepal, especially after the opening of the political sphere in 1990. The Maoists have successfully mobilized this ethnic capital by giving existing and new ethnic movements a political framework for their demands." Thus, the unrecognized political faction led by Prachanda boycotted elections and consequently launched a guerilla war against the Nepali Congress Party-led coalition government in

---

[71] As noted above, Madhesis are peasants mainly from the southern Terai region and are considered a separate ethnic group as they originally migrated from India (Paudel, 2016: 548).

[72] "Nationality (Janajati) is that community which has its own mother tongue and traditional culture and yet do not fall under the conventional fourfold Varna of Hindu or Hindu hierarchical caste structure" (Central Bureau of Statistics, 2014).

[73] The Dalits were the last to establish an ethnic party and the least represented.

March 1995. In February 1996, "announcing that the government had failed to respond to its demands and that only a communist state could prevent Nepal from falling into an abyss," Prachanda started an insurgency that lasted a decade (Davis et al., 2012: 121). Later, Prachanda's unrecognized faction was renamed CPN-M and declared a list of forty demands that included elections for a new Constituent Assembly, the abolition of the King's and the royal family's privileges and establishment of a secular state, the abrogation of all discriminatory treaties with India in addition to sweeping social and economic reforms (Cailmail, 2008; Davis et al., 2012).

As expected, in line with conventional Communist rhetoric, the Maoist struggle prominently referred to class differences. However, aside from the privileged high castes, other classes in the Nepalese society are extraordinarily fragmented with lower-class divisions cemented and justified with what was the official state religion. Perhaps not surprisingly, therefore, the second appeal across lower classes was based on ethno-religious identity cleavages. This enabled the CPN-M to mobilize minority Hindu groups of different castes and indigenous ethnic groups across regional and religious differences together for a majority against the religious authority of the dominant high-caste Hindus. According to Paudel (2016: 549), the Maoists understood that "the issue of ethnic domination and marginalization was as important as class, gender, and regional discrimination." They knew the cultural grievances stemming from Hindu social hierarchies and thus aggressively incorporated these grievances and demands into their revolutionary rhetoric and practices. Moreover, the Maoists effectively mobilized the idea of ethnic autonomy to enroll the masses into the revolution, particularly in the Terai region.

For the purpose of mobilization, the Maoists strategically identified various target groups and provided them with resources to mobilize. Their targets were mostly "rural peasants and people of the hill tribes, especially in the Mid-Western Region of the country" (Davis et al., 2012: 134). Hence, mobilization of class and ethnicity became crucial to bring ethnic peasants into the revolution (Paudel, 2016: 549). These ethnic peasants had suffered from "exploitation and discrimination by the upper-caste Pahadi migrant communities (especially during the monarchy period) and the Nepali state," thus constituting the backbone of the Maoist insurgency (Nayak, 2011). As noted earlier, the Maoist focus was mostly on marginalized groups of two types: the Madhesi and Janajati, who were sympathetic to the Maoists as they both longed for a secular republic, language rights, and federalism, among other things (Cailmail, 2008: 6–7). Similar to the portrayal of the Acholi in Uganda, Janajati are alleged "unpatriotic, barbaric drunkards" who are not fit for political leadership by the Brahmins and Chettris (ICG, 2011: 13). Thus, the cultural alienation of the Janajati paved the way for their recruitment, particularly of those who practice Hinduism and belong to lower castes. As these indigenous ethnic groups mostly live in rural areas (Central Bureau of Statistics, 2014), it was easier to mobilize them outside the reach of the Kathmandu government.

Thus, "between 1998 and 2000, the Maoists formed seven ethnic-based organizations, and it was through these that the Maoists were successful in penetrating and expanding their activities in the eastern hills and terai regions of Nepal" (Hachhethu, 2008: 9). The Maoists have thus proved "their commitment to the 'ethnic' cause by making repeated demands for the declaration of Nepal as a secular state, equal treatment to all languages in Nepal, ethnic- and regional-based autonomy, and right to self-determination, among others" (Davis et al., 2012: 138).

Identity politics continue to be politically contested in Nepal. Indeed, after the Maoist electoral victory of 2008, "identity politics has become the most contentious issue in Nepal" as the first Constituent Assembly was dissolved after not being able to promulgate a new constitution due to "inability to settle contestations over the recognition of identities and autonomy to multiple ethnic groups" (Lawoti, 2015: 86). Even so, the alternative mobilization that brought together lower caste groups and indigenous ethnic groups from different regions, classes, and religions did succeed in secularizing the state.

In sum, while teaching multiple additional lessons, the case of the Maoists in Nepal suggests that the CWC mechanisms plausibly contribute to our understanding of this case. Specifically, compared to the set of higher-caste groups that controlled the government, multiple relatively large lower caste groups that shared religion with the politically dominant majority groups, along with ethnic groups some of whom shared religion with the politically dominant high caste groups, coalesced in mobilization to make religious claims against the majority in an effort to increase access.

Some of the additional lessons learned include that, as discussed at the beginning of the chapter, the extraordinary fragmentation of Nepalese society enabled challenger groups to mobilize a sufficiently large identity CWC without recruiting from the majority. Another lesson learned is that when discussing mobilization of religion, the theoretical mechanisms proposed in this book to explain support for the CWC mobilization of religion presuppose that mobilization of religion is for increased presence or intensity of religion. More accurately, however, religious claims can also be made by mobilizing actors pushing against religions for greater secularism in the state.[74] Thus, CPN-M used alternative mobilization in its fight against the Hindu Nepali state seeking less religion, not more.[75] However, when the objective of the mobilization is to oppose the identity at the foundation of the mobilization (religion), membership is not required.

---

[74] The Maoist PKK in Turkey also had an anti-religious discourse until recently, as will be discussed below in the case of Turkey.

[75] Svensson (2012: 114) argues the CPN-M is fighting against "religious status quo," "to decrease the role of a singular religion in a multifaith society," which is similar to how we think of religious claim-making in the context of Nepal. Thus, the religious claims made for more secularism (Svensson and Nilsson, 2018) cost more than 13,000 lives between 1996 and 2006 in the Nepali civil war (Lawoti and Hangen, 2013: 6).

5.3 CASES THAT DO NOT CONFORM: OR DO THEY?

While the CWC prediction is not deterministic and we do not expect it to explain every case, we still wonder why large ethnic minorities engaged in ethnic civil war with a majority with whom they share religion do not, according to the RELAC data (Svensson and Nilsson, 2018), make claims of religious incompatibility against the state. This last section explores this question in one such case: Kurds in Turkey. The objective of this narrative is to serve as theory generating or at the very least theory clarifying. Therefore, extensive *a priori* expertise allowing for the consideration of many different aspects of the case was important. Because we have extensive expertise relating to the politics of Turkey, the selection of this case was a convenient selection unlike the random selection across doctrine in the previous cases, where the outcome – religious claim making – was observed.

One organization of inquiry for the case of Turkey is the Kurdistan Workers' Party (*Partiya Karkeren Kurdistan*, PKK) with the claim to represent the Kurds in a civil war against the Turkish state. Both the majority of Kurds and Turks adhere to Sunni Islam. However, according to the RELAC data, the PKK has not made claims of religious incompatibility with the state. Because of the demographics and the shared religion between the majority and minority, the CWC hypothesis suggests that PKK leaders should see the shared religious identity as an opportunity for alternate identity mobilization. The question we ask in this section is why the PKK has not (according to RELAC) mobilized religion.

One possible explanation is that for the better part of its lifespan the PKK has focused on establishing a separate Kurdish state. As explained in Chapter 3, separatism is outside the scope of the theory of *Alternatives in Mobilization*, which focuses on groups that have greater access to the state at least as one of its aims. However, poverty and underdevelopment in Kurdish areas have driven Kurds to migrate across Turkey, and after the imprisonment of the PKK's leader in 1999, the demands of the population and the organization have changed to emphasize improved living conditions by way of access to the state. Therefore, while the early emphasis on separatism might explain why the PKK refrained from mobilizing religion, it is less clear that this condition applies today.

Another possibility is that the Turkish state has co-opted religion to such a degree that there is no space left for mobilization. A third explanation is that divergent types of identity mobilization are used in different types of contentious politics i.e. religious mobilization might be relegated to the electoral sphere where the spoils are shared between Kurds and Turks and that ethnic mobilization might be emphasized in the civil conflict with the objective of inducing separation.

The case of Turkey brings a number of observations to light. The first is the importance of McAdam, Tarrow, and Tilly's definition of political contention as "episodic, public, collective interaction among makers of claims and their objects" (McAdam et al., 2001: 5). To discern distinct empirical patterns across cases cross-national analysis such as that conducted in Chapter 4 is helpful. However, political contention, such as the conflict between Kurds and Turks, ebbs and flows endogenously over a long period of time. In many cases the majority sets and circumscribes the political opportunities that the minority then pursues. Therefore, to understand any given conflict from a longer and more nuanced historical view is helpful.

In a historical light it becomes clear that ethnic minorities often pursue multiple identity strategies at the same time and across multiple different types of political competition. This is certainly the case for the Kurds. Over the history of the modern Turkish state, Kurdish strategies of identity mobilization have included electoral and violent competition and emphasized ethnic, religious, and Marxist/Leninist identity. The PKK especially has pragmatically adapted over time from being a Marxist[76] ethnic organization to most recently incorporating religion into its arsenal of mobilization rhetoric. This observation, in turn, suggests that to fully understand how identity is mobilized in politics scholars should simultaneously examine the many divergent political strategies employed in a given context.

5.3.1 Turkey

Sharing religious family (Islam) and sect (Sunni) with the majority of Turks, Kurds constitute the largest ethnic minority in Turkey.[77] Turkish politicians and public intellectuals have long argued that surveyors manipulate the number of Kurds to support their own agenda.[78] The figures for the population ratio of the Kurdish population in three surveys carried out by one of the largest survey firms in Turkey, KONDA, estimated that Kurds accounted for 15.7 percent in

---

[76] Indeed the PKK's leader has been very strategic about ideology. PKK started out in the 1980s with Marxism, incorporated Leninism, and finally in the 1990s switched to Maoism in its rhetoric. See Unal (2014: 419), for example, who argues "PKK moves-particularly after 1994-are based on emergent (ex-post) pragmatic shifts rather than predetermined (ex-ante) strategic plans."

[77] The precise size of the Kurdish minority has always been a topic of controversy. Turkey officially recognizes only non-Muslim minorities in tandem with the 1923 Lausanne Treaty.

[78] Survey companies such as ORC, GEZICI, MAK, and KONDA are owned by business or political figures and are known to be pro/anti-government. See for a list of who owns which company, www.timeturk.com/hangi-anket-sirketi-kime-ait/haber-3433, last accessed on February 27, 2019. These survey companies are often accused of trying to manipulate election results or criticized for inaccurate predictions (Görmüş, 2015). For instance, some argue that Zaza speakers that are often included in the Kurdish minority are a different ethnicity since they have their own language, thus they should be counted separately. McDowall (1996: 10), on the other hand, finds a large overlap between Zaza speakers and Alevis, which may indicate that they are historically connected.

2006, 18.3 percent in 2010, and 17.7 percent of the total population in early 2013 (Özkan, 2017).[79] While their precise numbers are debated, overall, Kurds are a large minority in Turkey, whose numbers have been increasing at a higher rate than those of majority Turks (McDowall, 1996: 3).

The founder of Turkey, Mustafa Kemal Atatürk, was wary of identity politics, both Islamist movements and Kurdish mobilization. To break free from the legacy of the Islamic Caliphate and the Ottoman Empire, in 1923 Atatürk sought to establish a republic based on the six tenets of *Kemalism*: secularism, statism, nationalism, republicanism, populism, and reformism (Sakallioglu-Cizre, 1998).[80] However, the majority of his secular republican political and socio-economic policies were unpopular amongst both conservative Turks and Kurds[81] and subsequent political history of Turkey is characterized by political cycles where liberalization of party competition and mobilization of ethnicity and religion are followed by military repression of those very elements.

The secular and unitary Turkish state mostly repressed identity mobilization under the tutelage of the Turkish military, but at times also used religious bidding for electoral success and to curb growing Kurdish nationalism. In turn, Kurds themselves have over time used both ethnic and alternative mobilization strategies centering on religion, with the objectives to either separate from the Turkish state or to seek access to Turkey's unitary system. To achieve these goals, several Kurdish political parties have run in national elections, and the outlawed PKK has fought a civil conflict against the Turkish Armed

---

[79] Tarhan Erdem, "How many Kurds live in Turkey?" Hürriyet Daily News, April 26, 2013. Available at: www.hurriyetdailynews.com/how-many-kurds-live-in-turkey-45644, last accessed on February 23, 2019. Other estimates include: 19 percent in 1975 (van Bruinessen, 1992), 25 percent in 1990 (Izady, 1992), 23 percent in 1992 (McDowall, 1996), 12.4 percent in 1992 (Ozsoy et al., 1992), 13 percent in 1993 (Koc et al., 2008), and 14.5 percent in 2003 (Koc et al., 2008). See Özkan (2017) for more information.

   The CIA World Factbook, on the other hand, estimates the Kurdish population in Turkey at 19 percent in 2016. The CIA World Factbook, Turkey. Available at: www.cia.gov/library/publications/the-world-factbook/geos/tu.html, last accessed on March 9, 2018.

[80] Atatürk's worldview and these six principles are known as *Kemalism*, in which there is only one modernity to reach the standards of Western civilization that is the goal for the Turkish nation. Therefore, there is a single way to reach modernity and that is through secularism (Hanioglu, 2012). Unlike its Indonesian counterpart *Pancasila* discussed in Chapter 6, *Kemalism* embraces Western-style liberal democracy and secularism.

[81] The first attempts to transition from a single-party rule (1923–1946) to a secular multiparty democracy failed for a variety of reasons, among which were opposition parties' attempts to mobilize religion across ethnicities, including but not limited to Kurds, resulting in Atatürk's decision to disband the parties. For the various accounts of why the first opposition parties, *Terakkiperver Cumhuriyet Fırkası* and *Serbest Cumhuriyet Fırkası* were disbanded shortly after their foundation, see for example Karpat (2010) and Karaosmanoğlu (1992). A second attempt to liberalize did not come until after Atatürk's death in 1938.

Forces since 1984.[82] As we will discuss next, both the Kurdish political party and the PKK rhetoric oscillated between emphasizing Kurdish ethnicity or Sunni Islam, in response to the Turkish state's efforts to use shared religion to appeal to Kurds. Overall, and similarly to the Pakistani case, the centralization of the state and its discriminatory policies toward Kurds played a major role in the activation of religion as a strategy in political mobilization in Turkey. Thus, lack of political autonomy, backwardness, and poverty of the southeastern Kurdish majority provinces, as well as forced migration policies due to the conflict with the PKK likely facilitated the use of alternate mobilization by different Kurdish movements, and differentiated Kurdish incentives from other large ethnic minorities, including Turkey's Arabs, who are well assimilated.[83]

Religion and the Turkish State

According to a 2019 report,[84] 92.2 percent of Turkey's population is Sunni Muslim and 5.5 percent are Alevi,[85] with 2.3 percent classified as "Other," including very small Christian and Jewish minorities. With this demographic backdrop, Turkish state actors have, throughout the country's republican history, pursued a dual strategy of political secularization while at the same time mobilizing religion in an attempt to subsume rising Kurdish ethno-nationalism under the notion of "common citizenship" and (Islamic brotherhood) (Somer and Glupker-Kesebir, 2016: 8).

By and large the military has acted as the self-appointed "guardian" of the secular state while religion has found greater expression in electoral politics. Thus, the first free democratic election in 1950 brought about fierce competition centering on Islam and Islamic values, and set an electoral legacy of instrumentalizing Islam in Turkish politics for decades to come. Specifically, in the 1950, 1954, and 1957 elections the Democratic Party capitalized on the salience of religion among the peasants in the country, Turks and Kurds alike, which constituted roughly 80 percent of the population at the time, to sweep the elections (Pelt, 2008). Various Islamist political parties have followed

---

[82] The PKK leader Abdullah Öcalan was captured and imprisoned in 1999; however, despite periods of ceasefire (i.e. between 1999–2004 and 2013–2015), the organization is still active and operating from Qandil Mountains in Iraq.

[83] Arab Turkish citizens live mainly in south-east provinces, where Kurds dominate the population, as well as in the province of Hatay in southern Turkey, which became a part of Turkey following a referendum in 1939.

[84] KONDA Barometer 2019. Political and Social Survey Series Sample Report. Available at: http://konda.com.tr/wp-content/uploads/2017/02/KONDA-Barometer-SampleReport-2019.pdf, last accessed on February 20, 2019.

[85] There is an Alevi minority in the Kurdish population; however, most Kurds are Sunni of the Shafi School, who are more religious than the Turks that are mostly Sunni of the Hanafi School. The Alevi (or Qizilbash) religion "lies on the extreme edge of Shi'i Islam" and is "a mixture of pre-Islamic, Zoroastrian, Turkoman shaman and Shi'i ideas that became the basis of a religious sect during the fifteenth century CE" (McDowall, 1996: 10).

suit over the years but until 2002, rarely got into government. This is mostly due to the emphasis on the secular regime by the Turkish military, which perpetrated military coups in 1960 and 1980, and arguably to protect the secular nature of the republic, issued "memoranda" resulting in resignation of governments in 1971 and 1997.[86] Moreover, different factions in the military tried to overthrow the government in 2007[87] and 2016[88] with no success.[89]

However, for almost two decades since 2002, the overtly pro-Islamist AKP has enjoyed unprecedented electoral success and ruled an increasingly "competitive authoritarian" regime (Esen and Gumuscu, 2016; Satana and Özpek, 2020). In Turkey, similar to Indonesia, clientelistic patronage networks distribute resources to supporters. Thus, the AKP forms a "clientelistic linkage that functions not only as a problem-solving network, but also as a means to create a system of common identification. However, when courting voters of Kurdish origin, their religious identity also seems to be the major ground of common identification.[90] Yet, respect for their ethnic distinctness and opposition to the homogenization attempts of the republican institutions also constitute an

---

[86] Even so in a clear contradiction to its official stance, the military also used religion to mobilize public support for its involvement in Turkish politics (Satana, 2008).

[87] The military issued an e-memorandum against the Justice and Development Party (*Adalet ve Kalkınma Partisi*, AKP) government in 2007 weighing in the presidential elections of that year and raised its concerns about secularism declaring that it would continue guarding the secular nature of the republic. The controversy centered on the headscarf of candidate Abdullah Gül's wife since the military considered presidential office a neutral and secular institution. The so-called e-memorandum did not yield the results it was seeking and received criticism from both internal and external audiences (i.e. EU and the United States), which later led the military to take it off its website. This was a major milestone for civil-military relations in Turkey and as Gül got elected the president in general elections, his wife became the first to wear a headscarf in the presidential residence in Çankaya.

[88] In July 15, 2016, a religious cultist faction in the military loyal to a cleric called Fethullah Gülen, attempted a coup to topple the AKP government, which failed and resulted in purging of 1648 ranking officers from the Turkish Armed Forces (Satana and Demirel-Pegg, 2020: 10). According to Esen and Gumuscu (2017: 60), the AKP had "extensive access to public and private resources and control over both conventional and social media ... Deprived of both political and popular support and lacking access to mainstream as well as social media, the putsch failed."

[89] Satana and Demirel-Pegg (2020: 10) argue that a ceasefire between the PKK and the Turkish state between 1999 and 2004, as well as the EU accession process at the same time gave a breathing space to civil-military relations in Turkey, however, that did not last long.

[90] Akdağ (2015: 223–224) finds that "AKP motivates the voters and activists of non-Kurdish and Kurdish origin through the formation of a partisan network based on the distribution of the municipal resources" but with distinctly religious undertones. Specifically, when activists talked to those whom they knew were ideologically closer to AKP, they referred to the authoritarian bureaucratic state before AKP as repressive on religious rights. They also signaled religious belief in electoral campaigning activities by using expressions such as "'with the permission of God (Allah'ın izniyle)," "Thank God (Allah'a Şükür)," "Good deed (sevap)" "we came to have your prayer than your vote'" (p. 132). Still, the majority of messages were about access to resources, despite the religious undertone. Another interesting anecdote was a Kurdish AKP ctivist questioned by a Kurdish voter who asked how, as a Kurd, he could work for the AKP

important issue reformulated within the broader center/periphery dimension" (Akdağ, 2015: 252). Crucially, under the AKP's reign, the Turkish military's power deteriorated as the government changed the laws that previously had enabled the military to act as the "guardian" of the regime, and prosecuted various cadres in the military for coup plots (Satana and Özpek, 2020).

Overall, therefore, as much as the Turkish military has emphasized its secular nature, the state has had a symbiotic relationship with Islam in electoral politics where the main political actors have not refrained from religious outbidding when they found it beneficial. Responding to both of these state strategies Kurds have also mobilized around secular ethnic nationalism and when that has failed to yield results, they have alternatively used shared religion (Sunni Islam) as a mobilization strategy to access state power.

Religion and Kurdish Incentives

Kurds are the largest ethnic minority in Turkey and they share a religion with the majority Turks.[91] Generally, the Kurdish population in Turkey is increasing at a higher rate than the Turkish population (McDowall, 1996: 3).[92] This rate of increase is, among other things, due to reduced access to family planning services in the Kurdish provinces of south-eastern Turkey because of the decades-long conflict in the region between the Turkish security forces and the PKK (Yüceşahin and Özgür, 2008). As the size of Kurdish minority increases,[93] Kurdish votes matter more in national politics than they did in the past.

The Kurdish religious bloc consists of both Alevi and Sunni Muslim Kurdish groups, for whom religious identity trumps Kurdish national identity (Cicek, 2017; Sarigil, 2018). Furthermore, there is a large potential for swing voters among the Kurdish voters (Akdağ, 2015). Capitalizing on a strong religious identity among their people Kurdish leaders have a long history of mobilizing religion in Turkish politics. However, the emergence of modern

and his answer was to ask how the voter could vote for the Peace and Democracy Party (*Barış ve Demokrasi Partisi*, BDP) when its district president is an Alevi (p. 165). Also, the BDP did not refrain from using religious worship places such as mosques to mobilize the constituency.

[91] Kurds live throughout Turkey, however, their numbers are concentrated in the southeast provinces of Turkey. Over the years, the PKK attacks and counter-insurgency efforts of the state caused forced and voluntary migration of the Kurds from villages to larger cities like Diyarbakir in the south-east and Istanbul and Izmir in the west.

[92] Looking at the rate of the increase, most Turks, including President Tayyip Erdoğan, are afraid that Kurds could become a majority in Turkey within two generations. www.ibtimes.com/ Kurdish-majority-turkey-within-one-generation-705466, last accessed on May 8, 2021.

[93] In fact, President Erdoğan has not only made several derogatory remarks on cesarean births but also restricted them on the basis of the limitations of how many children one can have once giving birth via this type of delivery. See Elif Safak, "The silence hurts Turkish women," *The Guardian*, July 15, 2012. Available at: www.theguardian.com/commentisfree/2012/ jul/15/turkey-caesarian-ban-silence-hurts-womrn, last accessed on January 23, 2019. Parallel to socio-economic background, Turks have more access to hospital/cesarean births than Kurds who live in remote towns. Thus, Erdoğan's concern is that Turks have fewer children than Kurds do.

Kurdish nationalism is generally linked to the rise of the Turkish left in the 1960s and, like mobilization of the left more generally, during its heyday took on a secular character that at times even incorporated anti-religious rhetoric. Similar to mobilization of Pashtuns in Pakistan, the impetus of modern Kurdish at the national-level mobilization included the political centralization of the state without economic integration of the Kurdish minority, socio-economic backwardness of the Kurdish-dominated south-eastern provinces, and exclusion of Kurdish cultural and political identity from legitimate political outlets.[94] This mobilization culminated in the establishment of the PKK, a Marxist organization (Bozarslan, 1992; Kirisci and Winrow, 1997; Gunes, 2013) and gave rise to violence in 1984.[95]

However, as the AKP government curbed the military's hold on politics and decreased fears of military reprisals, religion also came to play a greater role again in Turkish politics. This includes a role in alternative mobilization led by Kurdish political leaders who, in this environment that is more permissive of religious expression, likely realized that mobilization of the shared religious identity could afford them greater access to state spoils.

In the following section, we trace the role of religion in mobilization of the Kurds back to three processes over time. First, to illustrate the historical roots of religion in Kurdish politics we briefly discuss Kurdish mobilization in the form of armed rebellions during the late Ottoman and early Republican eras (van Bruinessen, 1992, 2000; Yavuz, 2001). Second, to suggest that religion remained a proximate alternative after the turn to secular ethno-national politics in the 1960s we illustrate efforts of both Turkish and Kurdish political movements to mobilize religious Turks and Kurds in the 1990s and beyond (Sakallioglu-Cizre, 1998; Duran, 1998; Somer and Liaras, 2010; Akturk, 2018). Third, to drive home the strategic nature of the selection of identity for mobilization we outline the PKK's recent shift from a Marxist and anti-religious ideology to embracing religion and local religious Kurds in response to the declining appeal of socialism and rise of Islamist populism among Kurds (Sarigil and Fazlioglu, 2013; Sarigil, 2018; Türkmen, 2018; Kaya and Whiting, 2019; Gurses and Ozturk, 2020).

Alternative Mobilization of the Kurds
Early Kurdish mobilization, mainly in the form of rebellions, during the late Ottoman and early Republican periods (1923–1960s) stems from a combination of developing ethnic consciousness, religious reactionism, and dissatisfaction

---

[94] For example, Kurdish political parties, along with other smaller parties, have had a hard time passing the whopping 10 percent threshold in national elections.

[95] As in the case of Indonesia in Chapter 6, forced migration policies of the state, partly because of the ongoing counter-insurgency in the Kurdish areas in the last forty years, pushed Kurds to big cities and contributed to further identity mobilization (Kurban and Yeğen, 2012).

of semi-feudal Kurdish *aga*s (landlords) and *sheiks* (religious elders) with the centralization efforts of the state.[96]

Kurdish ethnicity and Islamic religious identity played an equally important role in mobilization of local tribal *aga*s and the population at large in early revolts against the state. These include, for example, the Sheikh Said Rebellion in 1925 during the establishment of a secular republic and after the abolition of the Islamic Caliphate in 1924, and numerous subsequent Kurdish rebellions (van Bruinessen, 1992, 2000; Yavuz, 2001). Indeed, van Bruinessen (1992: 297–300) argues that it is hard to disentangle ethnic and religious appeals in these rebellions – especially in the Sheikh Said rebellion. Sheikh Said was one of the most popular religious Kurdish leaders and during the rebellion named after him promised a more intense religious experience by way of bringing back the Islamic Caliphate. In support of the rebellion, local Kurdish[97] religious leaders used *tarikat* (religious order) networks to expand their social base and to appeal for support from anti-secularist Sunni Turks (Yavuz, 2001: 7). When the rebellion failed Said and the other leaders were executed by hanging and the mobilization came to be characterized as a Kurdish or Zaza rebellion, though in reality Said had led a coalition of Sunni Muslim supporters that included Turks as well as Kurds. Similarly, other Kurdish-led mobilization around this time centered on religion but failed to curb centralization and secularization of the new Turkish state, and led to increasingly repressive identity policies by the state including suppression of Kurdish identity.

In a secular state where religious expression was violently suppressed in the 1960s and 1970s, Kurdish mobilization efforts became largely ideological. The efforts of Turkish Workers' Party (*Türkiye İşçi Partisi*, TİP) to bring the Kurdish question to the forefront of Turkish politics and numerous Marxist Kurdish organizations such as the Revolutionary Eastern Cultural Hearths (*Devrimci Doğu Kültür Ocakları*, DDKO) that sprouted in the southeastern Turkey offered leftist Turks and Kurds an opportunity to coalesce in a socialist revolution against "the oppressive capitalist state" (Bozarslan, 1992; Kirisci and Winrow, 1997). Radical leftist ideology, in this context, facilitated a strategic coalition of Kurds and Turks excluded from government.

Throughout the 1970s into the 1980s, leftist Turkish/Kurdish coalition of youth organizations drew the ire of rightist/pan-Turkish political coalitions and the state under military tutelage intervened in 1971 and 1980 to protect the unitary and secular nature of the regime (McDowall, 1996: 411). Specifically, the 1980 military coup crushed Turkish and Kurdish leftist movements alike.

---

[96] Very little is known about the demographics of the Ottoman Empire. The best estimate to date is that Kurds numbered 1,000,000 out of a total of 35,350,000 people (Elibol, 2007: 153). However, taking into account the fact that the first census in the Empire took place in 1831 and was limited to some cities and only men, these numbers are fairly unreliable.

[97] This includes Zazas.

Mobilization of any sort became very difficult for leftist political actors, as the junta used repressive measures to install order in the country before the 1983 parliamentary elections. In response, various underground Kurdish groups mobilized the Kurdish masses using revolutionary and secular rhetoric and violence.

In the early 1990s, the Turkish led Islamist Welfare Party (*Refah Partisi*, RP) diverged from the mainstream view in center-right Turkish politics regarding the Kurdish question, in that it sought a compromise on the cultural demands of the Kurds espousing the notion of Islamic brotherhood (*ummah*) in their Milli Görüş (National View) ideology.[98] The strategy of the RP toward Kurds was not much different from that of Sheikh Said: emphasizing the Islamic brotherhood while blaming the Kemalist nation-state project and secularism for the grievances of the Kurdish population.[99] The RP achieved considerable success in the 1994 and 1995 elections, becoming the second-largest party in predominantly Kurdish provinces, including the expanding urban centers in the south-east such as Diyarbakır, Batman, Siirt, and Şanlıurfa,[100] and among religious and conservative Kurds living in poverty in the outskirts of Istanbul's poor suburbs (e.g. Sultanbeyli). In the 2000s, the AKP, established by a more moderate faction of the RP led by Tayyip Erdoğan, inherited this strategy and voter base. Since then, the emphasis on Islamic brotherhood between the Kurds and Turks has been one of the main characteristics of AKP's Kurdish policy both during periods of "openings" (negotiations) and resumption of conflict with the PKK after 2015. Somer and Liaras (2010) demonstrate the change in the rhetoric of Islamist newspapers with ties to the AKP as well as in more mainstream, secular media outlets at the outset of AKP's first Kurdish opening in 2005. The opening was initiated by then Prime Minister Erdoğan, declaring democracy and Islam as the solution to the Kurdish conflict.[101]

Overall, the RP's and later the AKP's strategy to court the Kurdish vote by way of religious mobilization worked for over a decade or until 2015 when conservative Kurdish politicians defected from the AKP to take on leadership in

[98] See Sakallioglu-Cizre (1998) for a very interesting examination of the intellectual underpinnings of this political transformation in the works of several Kurdish and Turkish Islamist writers affiliated with RP and its outreach to Kurds, such as Mehmet Metiner and Altan Tan, who later on joined the AKP cadres before shifting to the Kurdish-led Peoples' Democratic Party (*Halkların Demokrasi Partisi*, HDP).

[99] Burhanettin Duran, who has close links to both RP and AKP, defines RP's *Adil Düzen* (Just Order) as an "Islamist formula for ethnic coexistence" (Duran, 1998).

[100] Quite similar to the Indonesian case in Chapter 6, Kurds were forced to migrate from their villages all over the south-east due to the military counter-insurgency efforts against the PKK. Thus Kurdish voters have become increasingly available to various political parties, including pro-Islamist ones.

[101] The authors find that moderately Islamist newspapers with close ties to the government (*Yeni Şafak* and *Zaman*) have adopted a more positive discourse toward Kurds prior to the AKP's "opening policy."

the Peoples' Democratic Party (*Halkların Demokrasi Partisi*, HDP).[102] Prior to 2015, the HDP (and all of its banned predecessors) was a secular ethnic Kurdish political party, however, the electoral threshold of 10 percent in parliamentary elections and the rising repression of the AKP government, particularly toward the Kurds, provided the party with the incentive to try to strategically appeal to Turks and Kurds alike, by way of alternative religious mobilization, in an attempt to increase access to the government.

The HDP's strategic appeal to the ethno-religious Kurdish votes was particularly apparent in Kurdish-dominated areas. Kurdish votes depend on clientelistic tribal decisions and when clans change allegiance hundreds, if not thousands, of voters move with their elders (Kaya and Whiting, 2019; Whiting and Kaya, 2021). For example, in 2015, despite having previously consistently supported the majority rightist parties like the AKP, the Raman clan in Batman shifted 20,000 voters from the AKP to the HDP.[103] This is just one example of how the Democratic Society Congress (*Demokratik Toplum Kongresi*, DTK), an umbrella organization for Kurdish groups including the participation of the HDP, has been mobilizing large clans using Islamic rhetoric.[104] Another strategy of mobilization has been the politicization of the *mele*s, who are the local *madrasa*-educated Kurdish *imam*s (clerics), to support the HDP.[105]

The HDP is not the only party moving to capture the religious vote. State actors and multiple Kurdish Islamist groups, including PKK affiliates have more recently adopted Islamist rhetoric in fierce competition for the support of the religious constituencies. For instance, on March 25, 2011, as part of a larger *sivil itaatsizlik* (civil disobedience) campaign, the Kurdish-led Peace and Democracy Party (*Barış ve Demokrasi Partisi*, BDP)[106] initiated Sivil Cuma

[102] Akturk (2018) argues that the main motivation behind AKP's peace offerings to Kurds (as well as Alevis and non-Muslim minorities) is an effort to establish a new religious national identity. AKP's religious rhetoric aims at activating intra-group differences among the Kurds (religious-conservative versus urban-secular) to curb separatist demands. Moreover, Sakallioglu-Cizre (1998) notes that even though they advocate recognition of cultural rights, Islamist Turks reject a separatist solution to the Kurdish question because it would divide the *ummah*. Similarly, Houston (2001) distinguishes Statist Islamist, Islamist, and Kurdish Islamist stances to the Kurdish question and argues that the first two are not willing to extend a status to Kurds as a separate people because it will damage the state and Islamic brotherhood, while only Kurdish Islamists interpret religion as supporting Kurdish ethnic demands. See Gurses and Ozturk (2020) for more on the relationship of religion and Kurdish ethnic demands.
[103] Fehim Taştekin, Kurds abandon AKP, Al Monitor, May 20, 2015. Available at: www.al-monitor.com/pulse/originals/2015/05/turkey-pious-kurds-abandon-akp-in-droves-hdp.html, Last accessed on February 1, 2019.
[104] Moreover, the HDP "fielded candidates such as former Diyarbakir *mufti* (religious authority) Nimettullah Erdogmuş and Hüda Kaya, an activist who has campaigned against the ban on the hijab, making a positive impact on the pious electorate" (Taştekin, 2015).
[105] The *mele* are quite influential on the Kurdish votes, thus, all political parties have been competing for their votes. See Sarigil and Fazlioglu (2013) Karakoc and Sarigil (2020) for more on the influence of *meles* and *madrasas* in Turkey's politics.
[106] The BDP joined with the HDP in 2014 after running locally in the 2014 local elections.

(Civilian Friday Prayer), which boycotts Friday prayers at state-controlled mosques. Party officials argued that they did not want to stand behind state-appointed *imams* because they feel that state *imams* propagated pro-state, pro-government views and Turkishness (Sarigil and Fazlioglu, 2013: 556). However, Türkmen's (2018) interviews of sixty-two Islamic clerics, both state-appointed *imams* and *meles* who were at the forefront of the Civilian Friday Prayers, pinpoint how different elites diverge wildly in their conceptualizations of the relationship between identity and religion, while all basing their reasoning in Sunni Islam.

Parallel to the emergence of Kurdish Islamist movements like the Hüda-Par and the efforts of the Turkish Islamist parties to co-opt Kurds by referring to religious bonds, the PKK has moved from an anti-religious stance to a rhetoric that embraces traditions and beliefs of the people.[107] Sarigil and Fazlioglu (2013) discuss the changing rhetoric of the PKK as the push from the Kurdish political elites to gain popular support and legitimacy. Their interviews of several figures from Mustazaf-Der, the civil society branch of Kurdish Hizbullah, show that the budding movement aims to "establish an Islamic and pro-Kurdish political party to challenge the ruling, conservative AKP and the secular, ethno-nationalist Peace and Democracy Party."[108] In an era where Marxism has been on decline and religion was no longer suppressed by the state, Sarigil (2018) further suggests that the PKK has recreated the threat to the Kurdish nationalist cause and found the solution in making peace with Islam. Perhaps the most notable change in rhetoric from secular ethno-nationalism to the use of Islam was that of PKK leader Öcalan's attempts to increase the declining legitimacy of the organization in the eyes of conservative Turks sympathetic to the Kurdish cause.[109] Gurses and Ozturk (2020: 330) note that Ocalan was able to keep his secular image by reaching out to influential Kurdish religious leaders to establish religious political organizations to pressure the AKP government.

In sum, despite the purported secular nature of the regime, continuous state involvement in religion has made religious identity an overtly politically salient cleavage in Turkey. For example, to mobilize the Kurdish constituency, the Turkish-led AKP government has incorporated religious Kurdish intelligentsia into their ranks. In response, Kurdish political leaders have sought to build a coalition of nationalist and religious Kurds and to obtain political support from

[107] This is in striking contrast to the previous PKK st ance. Kirisci and Winrow (1997) and Yavuz (2001) note how both the PKK and precursors of the PKK not only declared *imams* as well as the sheiks and *agas* as enemies of Kurdish national consciousness, but also violently targeted Diyanet (Directorate of Religious Affairs)-appointed *imams* as representatives of assimilation efforts of the Turkish state through religion. Please see Ozturk (2016) for more on *Diyanet*.

[108] The BDP was the predecessor to the HDP and was dissolved in 2014.

[109] Another factor was the internal rivalry between the PKK and Kurdish Hizbullah whose stated goal was to change the regime of the state to *shari'a*. The PKK fought the Kurdish Hizbullah in the 1980s and 1990s, before the latter was crushed by the security forces in early 2000s (Hermann, 2003; Yavuz and Ozcan, 2006). Also see Kurt (2017) for a detailed account of the Kurdish Hizbullah.

religiously conservative Turks in electoral politics (van Bruinessen, 2000; Sarigil and Fazlioglu, 2013). Even the PKK, despite its Maoist and atheist leadership, in an effort to survive, has adapted to the rise in Kurdish Islamist movements and alternated its strategy to emphasize religion at least in the electoral arena.

5.4 CONCLUSION

The cases of Pakistan, Uganda, and Nepal examined in this chapter support the hypothesis of the CWC in that in all instances minorities mobilized religion across multiple ethnic and/or caste groups for violent ends in an effort to gain access.

In the case of Turkey, while religion was not mobilized by the PKK in its fight against the Turkish state, at least not until recently, this case shows that Kurds did use religion to mobilize support for their cause in electoral politics across ethnicity through various Kurdish political parties.

Overall, these cases are complex and raise as many questions as they answer. Most prominently, we were left to wonder whether the deviations from the expected causal path of recruitment, appealing also to members from the ruling ethnic group, was driven by the extreme demographic fragmentation of minority groups in Nepal and Uganda in the face of much more unified ruling groups. Similarly, we wonder whether the representation of Pashtuns and Acholi in the administration, and especially the military, contributed to their perception of viable size in challenging the majority. This and the other questions raised by the cases warrant much further exploration and we return to this topic in the conclusion to the book. However, before we conclude, the following chapter pushes further the inquiry started with the Turkish case, of the plausibility of the CWC in electoral politics in the absence of civil war.

6

The *Challenger's Winning Coalition* in Indonesia's Electoral Politics

6.1 INTRODUCTION

The theory of *Alternatives in Mobilization* proposed in this book elucidates the role of demographics in conditioning the choice of identity mobilization strategies in political contests. As discussed in Chapter 4, transgressive political mobilization arguably differs from contained collective action, and the focus of political contestation in civil war is often about national politics. Therefore, the cross-national empirical test in Chapter 4 and the tracing of mechanisms across cases in Chapter 5 were restricted to only the cases of identity mobilization in civil wars.

This chapter returns to the idea that, conditional on institutions, group demographics influence which identity mobilization strategies, if any, political competitors choose in contained political contestation. The reader will recall that the CWC implication suggests that when a minority and majority that are segmented along a given identity cleavage share a second identity, *the probability that minority leaders mobilize the shared identity increases as the demographic balance of the two groups becomes increasingly even*. This testable implication does not change between transgressive and contained politics but the conditions for testing do.

The goal of the qualitative analysis in this chapter is to investigate the generalizability of the CWC to electoral politics while at the same time probing the internal validity of the CWC's causal mechanism in electoral politics.[1] Specifically, the in-depth qualitative case analysis selected for this task allows for a detailed consideration of electoral contestants' counter-factual political strategies against which the actual strategies adopted by these political actors

---

[1] This is in contrast to testing the prevalence of CWC in electoral politics, which would require collection of data on all contestants in elections and the demographics of all of their identities and mobilization strategies, across all relevant institutional boundaries.

can be evaluated to reveal the accuracy of predictions made by the CWC and the MWC in a limited number of electoral contests.

The Indonesian case explored in this chapter also highlights a central feature of the theory of *Alternatives in Mobilization* as articulated in Chapter 3, that there is not a natural sequence to identity mobilization, i.e. ethnicity is not necessarily mobilized first, followed by mobilization of religion. In many cases including Indonesia, and also other cases explored in this book such as Turkey and Pakistan, ethnicity and religion are both salient identities and contestants likely consider both (and possibly other salient identities) whenever they mobilize. The theory only suggests that when a majority group uses an identity cleavage to instill and uphold political dominance, a second identity shared by majority and minority groups may offer an opportunity to the segmented minority for alternate mobilization of a CWC.

The Indonesian case also contextualizes and reveals omitted variables and processes (Seawright and Gerring, 2008; Seawright, 2016) not articulated by the theory of *Alternatives in Mobilization* or highlighted in the discussion of the empirical scope of the book. For example, the primary focus in this chapter – as in the rest of the book – is on ethnicity and religion. However, this case also pinpoints the important role that place of origin i.e. the politically salient identity cleavage of *migrants* versus *natives* plays in Indonesian politics.[2]

Indonesia was selected as a case study for this chapter because of its extraordinary demographic and institutional diversity.[3] Indonesia features multiple overlapping and intersecting identity cleavages and exceptional institutional complexity, including a multitiered administrative system with a variety of electoral rules that have changed over time across several levels. Indonesia[4] is, therefore, an excellent case for evaluating the plausibility of CWC in electoral politics. The ethno-religious diversity and the complexity of the administrative system is important because it affords us within-case comparisons of different identity groups across multiple institutional boundaries.[5] To trace the role that ethno-religious cleavages play in political mobilization in Indonesia, the chapter surveys the secondary data published by Indonesia country experts as well as

---

[2] It bears re-emphasizing that defining who is a migrant and who is a native is subject to all the tenets of constructivism. In Indonesia, for example, many "native" communities have, if not emerged then at least consolidated, in response to institutional changes as discussed later in the chapter, and migrants often have lived for generations in the place where they are still not considered natives.

[3] Most of Indonesia's identity groups live together in peace. Consequently, Indonesia provides an extraordinary backdrop for parsing out the interactive effects of ethnic minority group size and religion on peaceful political mobilization. At the same time, many groups have engaged in intra-religious, inter-religious, ethnic, ideological, and/or separatist conflict, and thus conflict politics of Indonesia have received a disproportionate share of the academic attention (Bertrand, 2004).

[4] We are deeply grateful for the generous advice and time that many of our colleagues with expertise in the politics of Indonesia have devoted to discussing the case with us and to reading and providing feedback for this chapter before and during our fieldwork in Indonesia.

[5] This is in addition to the advantage of holding multiple potential independent influences such as history and prior politics constant in comparison between groups.

the 2000 and 2010 Census information and a variety of primary legislation pertaining to the administrative structure and local governance. In addition, the case study in this chapter relies on information collected during authors' field work in Indonesia in summer 2019, including interviews with experts at the Indonesian electoral tribunal in Jakarta, *Komisi Pemilihan Umum* (KPU), Indonesian academics with expertise in election matters, and experts at non-profit organizations that specialize in electoral oversight.

The remainder of the chapter proceeds as follows. After a brief introduction, for a backdrop to the story told here, we survey the political history of Indonesia as it pertains to identity cleavages. Next, we describe Indonesia's current administrative and electoral system in some detail, followed by an account of Indonesia's demographic data. The subsequent section addresses expectations of CWC at three administrative levels in Indonesia, as conditioned by demographics and the pertinent institutional features. At these three administrative levels, we present evidence (or lack thereof) comparing expectations and actual mobilization of MWCs and CWCs. These case accounts represent an available convenience sample based on secondary sources and are not intended to test the prevalence of the mechanism but, as intended, are an illustration of the generalizability of the theory to non-violent electoral settings and an examination of the internal validity of the mechanism.[6] Even so, the results of the elections examined adjudicated which of the mobilization expectations (CWC versus MWC) better account for the actual strategies employed by contestants. The final section concludes.

6.2 INDONESIA

Spread across an archipelago of more than 17,000 islands in South-east Asia, Indonesia is home to at least 300 distinct indigenous ethnic groups that speak over 700 local languages and dialects, and officially adhere to six religions (Fox and Menchik, 2011: 2). With over 260 million inhabitants, Indonesia is one of the most populous and ethno-religiously diverse countries in the world, and is also inhabited by the world's largest Muslim population. Java, albeit not the largest island and only as big as the state of New York, is home to more than half the population of the country.[7] Other larger islands are Sumatra, Kalimantan (also called Borneo), Sulawesi, and Papua (Indonesian part of New Guinea).[8]

---

[6] We collected additional case data that illustrate evidence of the CWC but in the interest of space we were only able to include a limited number of cases.

[7] Sumatra for example is much larger than Java but has less than a third of its inhabitants. See recent population figures available at: www.embassyofindonesia.org/index.php/basic-facts, last accessed on November 19, 2018. Java, on the other hand, has only 6.77 percent of Indonesia's habitable land (Arifin et al., 2015: 242).

[8] Like Java, the inhabitants of these islands as well as the Outer Islands, are very diverse but have received far less scholarly attention than inhabitants of Java, and particularly of Jakarta (Schulte Nordholt and van Klinken, 2007).

Immediately following President Suharto's forced resignation in 1998, Indonesia re-democratized[9] and decentralized in an effort to curb secessionism and violence, and to improve economic and government performance.[10] A concurrent change in the party law, followed by a change of the electoral system, and several updates since then, simultaneously discouraged identity fragmentation in national-level politics by mandating national presence of parties and encouraged local identity politics by decentralizing the local administrative framework by way of direct election of local heads of government. Together these institutional changes fundamentally altered politics in Indonesia (Horowitz, 2013). While clientelism and corruption are common complaints lodged against the new system, the widespread large-scale violence that followed Suharto's downfall declined after the reform. In turn, lower-scale violence has increased (Barron et al., 2016; Pierskalla and Sacks, 2017) and political Islam has been on the rise (Hadiz, 2010; Hefner, 2018).

Multiple case studies throughout this book illustrate that the precise mechanisms of how any identity cleavage, including ethnicity and religion, get activated in identity politics is highly dependent on context. The case of Indonesia is no exception, and this case highlights important variables other than demographics and shared identity that influence whether and how groups mobilize. At the same time, overall, the case evidence also does demonstrate widespread use of the CWC mechanisms by several large minority groups seeking greater access by way of mobilizing an identity shared with the majority.

6.3 IDENTITY IN INDONESIAN POLITICS FROM INDEPENDENCE THROUGH RE-DEMOCRATIZATION

In the national emblem of Indonesia, *Garuda*, a legendary bird holds a banner with the motto *Bhinneka Tunggal Ika*, which translates as "Unity in Diversity." When leading Indonesia's bid for independence from the Dutch in 1945, President Sukarno formulated the ideology of *Pancasila* to create such unity in a diverse society. *Pancasila* refers to the "Five Principles" of the Indonesian state ideology that appeared in the preambles of 1945, 1949, and 1950 constitutions[11] with the goal that "sovereignty that is based on wisdom through consultation and representation becomes the core democratic value enshrined

---

9   Indonesia went through a brief period of *Demokrasi Liberal* (Liberal Democracy) between 1950 and 1959, until Sukarno declared martial law and introduced his *Demokrasi Terpimpin* (Guided Democracy). Building on the literature on Indonesia (McDonald, 2015), we refer to the transitionary period after Suharto's fall as *Reformasi* (Reform) and the ensuing period involving attempts to decentralize and build democratic institutions as re-democratization.

10 Indonesia was plagued with civil conflict between 1998 and 2003, which killed at least 10,000 people in mere five years (Bertrand, 2004: 1).

11 The 1945 Constitution was repealed and replaced by the Federal Constitution of 1949 when the United States of Indonesia officially gained sovereignty from the Netherlands. Later in 1950, the constitution was replaced by a provisional constitution, which returned Indonesia into a

in the idea of Demokrasi Pancasila" (Sofjan, 2016: 53). These five principles are belief in one supreme God, social justice for all people, the unity of Indonesia, democracy through deliberation and consensus among representatives, and a just and civilized society.[12]

In the context of Indonesia's diverse archipelago, *Pancasila*'s stipulation of belief in one God is meant to equate the majority religion in the country, Islam, with four others: Christianity (specifically Protestantism and Catholicism), Buddhism, Hinduism, and Confucianism.[13] It also guarantees the same citizenship rights to the believers of these minority religions as to the majority Muslims. The main objective of Sukarno, therefore, was to bring together a nation divided by ethnic, religious, and ideological cleavages around a common goal.[14] Consequently, the 1945 Constitution embodied the unifying notion of *Pancasila* despite considerable controversy behind the scenes.[15]

After independence, the first legislative election of 1955 was the only free national election Indonesia held for the new People's Representative Council

unitary state. In 1959, the 1950 constitution was abrogated by Sukarno who restored the 1945 Constitution. *Pancasila* was articulated in all these constitutions as the state ideology (Butt, 2018: 61).

[12] Adherence to *Pancasila*'s five principles is still legally mandated for all political parties, lawmakers, and bureaucracy as well as the society in Indonesia. *Pancasila* principles are often inaccurately considered unalterable by jurists (Butt, 2018: 61).

[13] Confucianism was de-recognized in 1979, only to be reintroduced into *Pancasila* by former President Abdurrahman Wahid under his Reformasi (Reform) policy (Ananta et al., 2013).

[14] His version of *Pancasila* was based on "a culturally neutral identity, compatible with democratic or Marxist ideologies" (Worden and Frederick, 1993: 236). Sukarno was not the first to promote nation-building. As early as 1928, to raise political awareness and steer away from the Dutch colonial rule, the Indonesian *priyayi* (aristocrat class) declared *Sumpah Pemuda* (Pledge of Youth) for one fatherland, one nation, one language (McDonald, 2015: 15–16). Furthermore, the Javanese secular nationalist organization *Budi Utomo* (Highest Endeavor) and the Muslim-devout but also nationalist *Sarekat Islam* (Islamic Union) were established in 1908 and 1911, respectively, as a result of growing contempt for the colonial rule. Similarly, the Communist Party of Indonesia (*Partai Kommunis Indonesia*, PKI) joined in the anti-colonialist movement in the early 1920s eventually leading to an uprising against the Dutch. However, it was Sukarno and his friends, who founded the Indonesian National Party (*Partai Nasional Indonesia*, PNI) in 1927 to amalgamate under one banner all these different factions subscribing to Islam, Marxism, and nationalism. As the World War II and the Japanese invasion of Indonesia (1942–1945) came close to an end, Sukarno and his political coalition in PNI declared independence on August 17, 1945.

[15] The Jakarta Charter, which required all Muslims to observe Islamic law, was omitted from the Constitution the day after independence not to alienate Christian minorities (McDonald, 2015: 19). Acquiring independence, at the time, was more important for the Islamic leaders than any *sharia*-based institutional arrangements. Still, this omission has long been treated by Islamists as catastrophic for Muslims in Indonesia (Elson, 2009: 105) as the Islamic movement under *Sarekat Islam* was pivotal in organizing masses to support an independent Indonesia (Kahin, 1952). However, Sukarno's notion of *kebangsaan* (nationalism) did not mesh with Islamic unity of ummah in Indonesia (Effendy, 2003: 20). See van der Kroef (1950) and McDonald (2015) for a detailed account of Indonesia's struggle for independence.

(*Dewan Perwakilan Rakyat*, DPR) until re-democratization in 1999. Although more than twenty political parties and social movements, including various Islamic parties i.e. *Nahdlatul Ulama* (NU, The Awakening of Muslim Scholars) and *Majlis Sjuro Muslimin Indonesia* (Masjumi, Consultative Council of Indonesian Muslims) as well as two Christian parties and political parties representing Dayak and Sundanese ethnic groups got in the parliament, Prime Minister Burhanuddin Harahap's cabinet did not reflect the ethnic and religious diversity in the new parliament (Feith, 1957).

In 1957, democracy gave way to Sukarno's *konsepsi* (concept) of a "Guided Democracy" (Liddle and Mujani, 2007: 834), justified as a system of governance that aligned better with the objectives of Indonesia's culture of unity and solidarity. Indeed, one of the goals associated with *Pancasila* was to discourage political mobilization of identity cleavages that challenged Sukarno's repressive rule. This policy seemingly worked to curb ethno-nationalist violence. "[I]n spite of a spate of ethnic rebellions in almost all parts of independent Indonesia between 1950 and 1964, 'Indonesia' survived" (Anderson, 2006: 134). Anderson further suggests that at that time nearly all major ethnolinguistic groups in the archipelagos accepted their role in the nation-state.[16] Moreover, *Pancasila*'s pillars persist to this day (Piccone, 2016: 192). For example, the various laws on decentralization and local governance begin with a reference to the 1945 Constitution and *Pancasila* explicitly. The same reference is made in the electoral law, and candidates for various offices are legally required to respect *Pancasila*. Accordingly, during his re-election campaign for the April 2019 presidential elections, President Joko Widodo (commonly referred as Jokowi) called for a renewed emphasis on *Pancasila*.[17]

Approximately a decade after the institution of "Guided Democracy," former Army Chief of Staff Suharto rose to power after a thwarted military coup eroded Sukarno's power.[18] Suharto reigned as the second president of

---

[16] The South Moluccans, who had aided the Dutch during the anti-colonial struggle and still had separatist ambitions post-independence were an exception.

[17] The minorities who were supportive of Jokowi Widodo's second term supported his efforts to bring *Pancasila* to the forefront. For instance, "At Buddhist temples in Bandung, Indonesia's third-largest city, banners were draped calling on all Indonesians to respect the rights of minorities to worship because it was a principle of Pancasila." See https://religionnews.com/2018/08/30/indonesian-president-invokes-pancasila-to-counter-rising-islamism/, last accessed on October 8, 2018.

[18] Allegedly, in 1965, the PKI, acting under the name of 30th September Movement, kidnapped and murdered six high-ranking army officers (and one lieutenant who was mistaken for a general). The following two years witnessed a military-led crackdown on the PKI and anyone with leftist inclinations, which culminated in massacres of almost a million people (Melvin, 2018). Suharto's regime rewrote history to glorify the military's efforts to save the nation from the communists and commemorated the day of the failed coup as *Hari Kesaktian Pancasila* (Sacred Pancasila Day) every year at the spot where the generals were killed and dumped in a well (Robinson, 2018: 258).

Indonesia from 1968 to 1998, a period which is known as the "New Order."[19] Suharto's selective interpretation of *Pancasila* where "decisions are reached by *musyawarah mufakat* (consensus through deliberation) rather than through a conflictual voting model" (Bertrand, 1997: 443), legislated party politics to limit their function.[20] For example, the legislative elections, held every five years officially recognized only three parties/groups including "Golkar, the government-sponsored association of functional groups, a *de facto* political party; the Unity Development Party (PPP), representing Muslim interests;[21] and the PDI, an amalgamation of Sukarno's old Nationalist Party and small Protestant and Catholic parties."[22] Suharto supporters were installed in all associations that organized the public collectively[23] and by law that was passed in 1975, parties were banned from organizing below the regency level (Ward, 2010: 29) so as to minimize the "distraction" from economic activity.

Finally, Suharto used a policy called *asas tunggal* (sole basis) which required all social and political organizations, regardless of ethnic and religious goals, to adopt *Pancasila* as their sole ideological foundation. This was to suppress identity-based organizations "by depicting all parties as SARA affiliations of tribe, religion, race and class (*suku, agama, ras antar golongan*)" (Xue, 2018: 3).[24]

[19] Suharto, who was a US-backed anti-communist and nationalist, believed that social conflict would stall the economic development that Indonesia so desperately needed (Ward, 2010). Therefore, he sought to further curb opportunities for meaningful mobilization of identity at any level.

[20] Also, Suharto allowed the military to enjoy political and territorial presence so much that "over two-thirds of provincial governors and half of all *bupati* (heads of Regencies or large rural districts) and city majors were military officers" (McDonald, 2015: 51). During Sukarno's "Guided Democracy" the *Tentara Nasional Indonesia* (Indonesian National Armed Forces) served a *dwifungsi* (dual function), first of which was to defend the country against external enemies, and the second was to aid in the country's social and economic development. This second role meant civilian control of the military was out of the question, and the military was free in its reign to suppress identity mobilization. This is similar to the notion of guardianship Turkish military leveraged after the 1980 coup to curb Kurdish mobilization attempts (Satana, 2008).

[21] The PPP was an amalgamation of various Islamist parties, including the *Partai Muslimin Indonesia* (Parmusi, Muslim Party of Indonesia) and NU that ran on their own in 1971 legislative elections. PPP is currently a nationalist and moderate Islamist party.

[22] Bertrand stresses, "The latter two [PPP and PDI] are not considered as opposition parties but merely as different avenues for political expression." Similar to the legislative elections, "conflict is avoided in the election of the president and vice-president by the People's Consultative Assembly (MPR), which convenes every five years for this purpose and reaches its decision by consensus" (Bertrand, 1997: 443).

[23] A good example is the Indonesian Journalists' Association. Similarly, the All Indonesian Workers Union was established in 1992 as a government-controlled umbrella organization under which trade unions became centralized.

[24] This policy infuriated Islamists and led to riots resulting in massacres of Muslim protesters by Indonesian armed forces on the outskirts of Jakarta in 1984 (Singh, 2007: 63).

6.3.1 From the "New Order" through Re-democratization

For over thirty years, until right before the 1997 parliamentary election, Suharto maintained a tight grip on the regime and his political coalition. These included *abangan* (Javanese syncretic) masses, Chinese business groups, Christian clergy and aristocrats, military and the bureaucratic elite (Hadiz, 2016: 105).[25] Due to the close-knit relationship between middle-class interests and the patrimonial regime in Indonesia, no one really anticipated Suharto's fall in 1998 (Bertrand, 1997: 443). However, despite the continuous annual economic growth of 7 percent since 1965, more than half the population lived below the poverty line (McDonald, 2015: 65). Besides, the Asian economic crisis hit Indonesia hard. When protesters took their frustration to the streets, the military shot at them, which only exacerbated unrest in the country and distrust in the government.

To make matters worse, anti-Chinese sentiment was on the rise and Chinese businesses were scapegoated as a source of the economic crisis.[26] In 1997, widespread violence broke out with Muslims attacking Christian churches, and in 2002 radical Islamist terrorists attacked the touristic Kuta district in Bali, killing 202 people, mostly Australian tourists.[27] Islamists, however, were not the only culprits of violence in this period in Indonesia. Other perpetrators included, for example, Christian Dayaks in Kalimantan attacking transmigrant Muslim settlers from Madura (McDonald, 2015: 63), and Muslim Malays cooperating with the Christian Dayaks in 1999 and 2001 to massacre and force mass migration of the Madurese from West and Central Kalimantan (Davidson, 2008).[28] While authors disagree on the reasons for the violence,[29] the fact remains that around 10,000 people were killed in the archipelago in a mere

[25] Suharto excluded Islamists because of his fear of their "potential capacity for political mobilization on the basis of a common identity founded on membership of a socially and economically marginalized" (Hadiz, 2016: 104).
[26] For example, more than 1000 people were killed in two-day anti-Chinese riots in Jakarta only a week before Suharto was removed from office in May 1998 (Tadjoeddin, 2013: 25). For a thought-provoking digital graphic novel about the violence, see Rani Pramesti's https://thechinesewhispers.com/, last accessed November 23, 2019.
[27] Sidel (2006) argues that there is "a shifting pattern of religious violence in Indonesia from riots in 1995–1997, to pogroms in 1998–2001, and to globalized jihad in 2002–2005" as exemplified by the Bali attack.
[28] Also see "Violence in Indonesian Borneo Spurs the relocation of Ethnic Madurese," Cultural Survival Quarterly Magazine, June 1999. Available at: www.culturalsurvival.org/publications/cultural-survival-quarterly/violence-indonesian-borneo-spurs-relocation-ethnic, last accessed on April 9, 2017.
[29] Bertrand attributes ethno-religious violence in Indonesia between 1998 and 2001 to systematic ethnic discrimination before and after Indonesia's independence, engendering economic, cultural, and political grievances (Bertrand, 2004). Similarly, to explain variation in rioting across Indonesia's districts during democratization, Risa Toha (2021) argues that where ethnic groups lack access and exit is prohibitive, the regime is relatively open to accomodation, and local networks for mobilization of ethnic challengers are in place, ethnic leaders will foment riots

five years (Bertrand, 2004: 1).[30] By 2001, Indonesia was also home to over 2 million *pengungsi* (refugees/internally displaced persons), especially in Aceh, Maluku, East Timor, Central Sulawesi, Central Kalimantan, Papua, and West Kalimantan (Hugo, 2002: 298).[31]

During this violent transition, Suharto's successor B. J. Habibie and his interim government pursued *Reformasi* (Reform) of the political system. According to Bertrand's historical institutionalist argument, these political actors had to renegotiate several elements of nationhood: "the role of Islam in political institutions, the relative importance of the central and regional governments, the access and representation of ethnic groups in the state's institutions, as well as the definition and meaning of the Indonesian 'nation.'" (Bertrand, 2004: 3). In 1999, Suharto's *asas tunggal* regulation was repealed and parties were now free to adopt other ideologies than *Pancasila*.

Once *asas tunggal* was repealed, many marginalized ethnic communities (such as the Betawi in Jakarta), sought collective rights, often "ethnicizing" their cause (Brown and Wilson, 2007: 375). Several Islamist parties also sprouted, emphasizing a greater role of religion in Indonesia's politics.[32] For example, the Islamist *Partai Bulan Bintang* (PBB, Moon and Stars Party) and PPP proposed to amend the constitution in 2000–2001 so that *sharia* law would be enforced for Muslim citizens in Indonesia. However, the two largest Muslim associations Muhammadiyah and NU opposed the proposal (Hefner, 2018: 213). When efforts to install *sharia* law nationally failed, Islamist parties sought implementation of *peraturan daerah* (regional bylaws) in provincial, district, and city governments, which aimed at restricting dress, worship, entertainment, etc. at the local level (Hefner, 2018: 214). However, despite rise in religious conservatism in Indonesian society,[33] Islamist parties and their proposals have not had substantial success for reasons that are widely debated in the literature (Tanuwidjaja, 2010; Hicks, 2012; Satana et al., 2019).[34]

---

to signal their political clout. In contrast, according to van Klinken (2007: 7), "the violence was just part of normal politics" in Indonesia, particularly in the five cases that he studied in West Kalimantan, Poso, Ambon, North Maluku, and Central Kalimantan. van Klinken further argues that migration and change in demographics between Christian and Muslim Ambonese explain the sudden seemingly religious conflict between two communities that had peacefully lived together for ages (van Klinken, 2007).

[30] Varshney et al. (2008: 379) attribute 9612 deaths or 89.3 percent of all casualties to ethnic communal violence between 1990 and 2003.

[31] We thank Nathan Allen for pointing out that many residents moved within their provinces i.e. Aceh to North Sumatra. Thus, displacement occurred *within* as well as *between* provinces.

[32] Habibie's *Reformasi* freed political prisoners, installed freedom of press, and abolished the three-party system, which gave rise to many Islamist political parties (Azra, 2004: 140).

[33] In 2009, the Centre for Strategic and International Studies (CSIS) in Jakarta conducted a survey that found rising levels of conservatism in Indonesian society. Also see Ufen (2008) on how Muslim Indonesians that practice pre-Islam Animism have been becoming more devout Muslims and dropping traditional syncretic beliefs.

[34] See Hadiz (2016: 14–18) for a literature review on Islam and Indonesian politics.

Initially, to distance themselves from Suharto's legacy,[35] *Pancasila* was not prominent in the discourse of political leaders between 1998 and 2001. However, Indonesia's political leaders reverted back to emphasizing the nationalist ideology of *Pancasila* to curb the surge in identity-based politics and ethno-religious conflict. For example, Habibie's successor and Indonesia's first president elected by the legislature, Abdurrahman Wahid, a former leader of NU, did not subscribe to the idea of Indonesia as an Islamic state. He argued religious freedom included not having to subscribe to any religion and allowed for the belief in local spirits as most Javanese did (and some still do) before Islam came to the islands. A renowned Islamic scholar, Wahid did not consider Islam and nationalism incompatible, and was a *Pancasila* enthusiast (Intan, 2006: 112–113).

Indonesia's fifth President Yudhoyono went even further as he assigned the counter-terrorism agency *Badan Nasional Penanggulangan Terorisme* (BNPT, National Agency for Combating Terrorism) to hold *Klinik Pancasila* (*Pancasila* clinics) about the nationalist state ideology and educate impressionable young Muslims, who were deemed under the threat of radicalization by jihadist groups like the Islamic Defenders Front (*Front Pembala Islam*, FPI). The BNPT also distributed "a pamphlet titled *Buku Cinta NKRI* (Book of Devotion to the Unitary State of Indonesia)" (McDonald, 2015: 164–165).[36] Similarly, the reformist President Jokowi, who first came to power in 2014 and recently got re-elected in 2019, emphasized *Pancasila*[37] to counter rising conservative Islam in the country.[38]

To sum, notwithstanding recent economic stagnation, corruption (Tomsa, 2018: 95), and ongoing low-level violence (Barron et al., 2016; Pierskalla and Sacks, 2017),[39] Indonesia successfully re-democratized (Horowitz, 2013;

---

[35] Leo Suryadinata, "Indonesia's ideological war," *The Straits Times*, December 2, 2016. Available at: www.straitstimes.com/opinion/indonesias-ideological-war, last accessed on December 4, 2019.

[36] To clarify, NKRI stands for Negara Kesatuan Republik Indonesia or the Unitary State of Indonesia.

[37] Margauerite Afra Sapiie, "Jokowi wants Pancasila to be 'nation's way of life'," The Jakarta Post, June 1, 2018.

[38] Even so, as we discuss further below, Jokowi resorted to religious outbidding against his opponent in the 2019 electoral race.

[39] Both religious and ethnic mobilizations are prominent in recent violence. For example, in 2011, three members of the Ahmadiyya were beaten to death in West Java and two churches were set on fire in Central Java during a protest about blasphemy. Moreover, in 2017, Basuki Tjahaja Purnama, known as Ahok, former Jakarta governor and a close ally of President Jokowi, was sentenced to two years in prison for blasphemy when he quoted a Qur'anic verse during his re-election campaign. Ahok, a Christian with ethnic Chinese roots, was the first non-Muslim governor in fifty years and both the blasphemy sentence and his imprisonment for it sparked widespread violence between political Islamists and Ahok's supporters, before he was released early after twenty months in prison. Recent riots in West Papua, in turn,

Aspinall, 2018). This success, in turn, rests on an unfaltering belief in elections, a thriving civil society (Aspinall, 2018: 85), and a culture of tolerance (*Pancasila*), albeit without liberalism (Menchik, 2006).[40]

6.4 INDONESIA'S INSTITUTIONS

It is the post-*Reformasi* electoral setting that is the focus of our exploration of CWC dynamics in Indonesia's electoral politics. Indonesia has undergone numerous administrative changes since the start of *Reformasi*. Because the spoils of office arguably engender electoral competition at many different administrative levels as discussed below, we presuppose that CWC electoral mobilization also occurs at many different levels of the Indonesian electoral scene.

The testable implication of the CWC articulated in Chapter 3 is that within a given institutional setting (be it national or sub-national) leaders of relatively large unrepresented or underrepresented minority identity groups seek to mobilize a secondary identity that they share with the majority in a challenge for greater access. Therefore, as in prior case chapters and focusing on ethnicity and religion, conditional on the specified demographic conditions, we expect to see minority mobilization of a shared identity at each relevant administrative level in Indonesia. Furthermore we expect that the minority group leading the mobilization: (1) is excluded from or underrepresented in the governing structures that determine distribution of resources; (2) makes claims against a state that is controlled by a political majority other than the group leading the mobilization; (3) shares a second identity with the political majority; (4) is the largest minority or one of the largest minority groups segmented from the majority at the relevant level of administration; and (5) has group leaders using claims pertaining to the shared identity to appeal across lines of the segmented identity to individuals belonging to the majority and minority.

Furthermore, the interaction of the institutional configuration with the demographics at each administrative level allows for *a priori* specifications

---

were triggered by racist comments against Papuans followed by the burning of the Indonesian flag. Tens of Papuan civilians were killed. The Indonesian military is accused of committing gross human rights violations to curb all ethnic mobilization attempts in the island. See "West Papua: Day of violence sees at least 27 dead," BBC, September 24, 2019, available at: www.bbc.com/news/world-asia-49806182, last accessed on December 2, 2019.

[40] Menchik (2006) explains the unique practice of *demokrasi* in Indonesia with the presence of what he calls "tolerance without liberalism" that he finds in all Islamist organizations, and the society in general. In this context, liberal democracy was never a goal of the regime during Suharto's New Order, neither has it really been since then. As is common in other Muslim democracies, such as Turkey, Indonesians tolerate differences as long as they do not threaten the "Indonesian way of life."

across Indonesia regarding in which administrative units we expect the CWC will materialize, and what group is expected to mobilize which identity cleavage.[41] While our focus is on ethnicity and religion, qualitative case analysis is also sufficiently flexible to allow for the manifestation of other relevant identities.

To examine these conjectures, in the following section we discuss in some detail the current administrative structures of Indonesia and the incentives influencing political competition at each administrative level. Next we outline the overall demographics of Indonesia. This is followed by three case accounts of political competition that illustrate the mechanics of the CWC at different administrative levels.[42]

6.4.1 Administrative Divisions and Elected Bodies

In contrast to the consolidation of centralized power under the New Order,[43] decentralization since re-democratization has aimed to devolve both administrative and budgetary authority to the local level. The first law to this end was enacted in 1999, with the last revision passed in 2014 (Rudy et al., 2017).[44] Generally speaking, while the central government retains most fiscal authority related to taxation, lower levels of government are authorized to set their own budgets and receive large transfers directly from the state to pay for expenditures.[45] Furthermore, the amounts transferred have increased significantly over time. For instance, Anshari's (2017: 305, 311) case study of the Banjar regency reveals that on average, villages in his study receive around two-thirds of their revenue from the state and the amount of transfers grew nearly tenfold between 2011 and 2016 (2017: 305 and 311). This type of direct budgetary devolution raises the stakes of the political competition at lower

---

[41] Depending on the demographics where we would not expect a CWC, another type of mobilization might be expected. For specification of additional mobilization strategies see Chapter 3, Table 3.4.

[42] Importantly, this chapter only outlines the official rules of the game and does not account for variations and/or how widespread clientelism and corruption subvert the process. On this topic, see for example Aspinall and Sukmajati (2016); Aspinall and Berenschot (2019); Nasution (2016). However, even if the process is marked by clientelism and corruption, we would still expect that the interaction of institutions and demographics influences which identities candidates seek to mobilize to challenge the status quo.

[43] To be clear, legislation for decentralization existed under the New Order but scholars largely agree that implementation of the law aimed to consolidate the power of the central government (Hidayat, 2017; Rudy et al., 2017).

[44] Law 23/2014 on Local Government.

[45] One of the changes in redistribution of funds includes changing the law from transferring funds hierarchically down the administrative ladder to being directly transferred from the central government. This includes the village level, which after 2014 receives transfers directly from the central government.

levels of the administration. Consequently, it is safe to assume that in Indonesia there is significant competition for political office across administrative levels.[46]

Earlier work outlines many of the administrative structures and changes before, during (Hicken and Kasuya, 2003; Reilly, 2007a), and after re-democratization (Shair-Rosenfield, 2012; Butt, 2017; Allen, 2018), of which there have been many. Currently, Indonesia is divided into roughly five main administrative units. Representatives are elected in three and a half of these and appointed in one and a half. Figure 6.1 illustrates the current administrative structure.

At the national level, the office of the President (*Presiden*) is filled in an election of pair of a presidential and vice-presidential candidates that are nominated by political parties. The president and vice-presidential candidates are elected with more than 50 percent of the national vote, having obtained at least 20 percent of the vote in half of Indonesia's provinces.[47] At the national-level, elections are also held for the (lower) House of Representatives (DPR) and the (upper) Regional Representative Council (DPD).[48] The number of representatives elected to the DPR in each of the 80 constituencies across Indonesia varies from 3 to 10 depending on population size, whereas the number elected to the DPD is the same from each Province. Together these two chambers constitute the People's Consultative Assembly (*Majelis Permusyawaratan Rakyat*, MPR). The National Government collects most taxes, which it then re-distributes to local-level governments, and retains sole authority over the areas of finance, foreign affairs, defense, security, religion, and state administration and justice.[49]

At the second administrative level are the Provinces (*Provinsi*), depicted in Figure 6.2,[50] each represented by a Governor (*Gubernur*), elected by plurality.[51] The provinces also elect representatives to the Provincial Houses of Representatives (*Dewan Perwakilan Rakyat Daerah Provinsi*, DPRD Provinsi) and the number of elected representatives varies depending on the size of the population in each province. These bodies govern areas other than those

---

[46] A substantial body of literature already examines the consequences of decentralization in Indonesia. For some examples, see Aspinall and Fealy (2003); Pepinsky and Wihardja (2011); Allen (2014); Lewis (2015); Pierskalla (2016); Vel et al. (2016); Anshari (2017); Tajima et al. (2018); Talitha et al. (2019).

[47] Article 416, Law 7/2017.

[48] The lower house has the powers to legislate, in addition to budgeting and oversight. The upper house can propose bills pertaining to regional government. For further information, see www.dpr.go.id.

[49] Article 10, Law 23/2014.

[50] Administrative divisions depicted in all figures are from 2017 and based on https://data .humdata.org/dataset/indonesia-administrative-boundary-2017.

[51] The minimum of the plurality rule for Governor changed from 25 percent in Article 107, Law 32/2004 to not being specified in Article 33, Law 22/2014 to 30 percent in Article 109, Law 1/2015, to be eliminated again in Article 109, Law 10/2016.

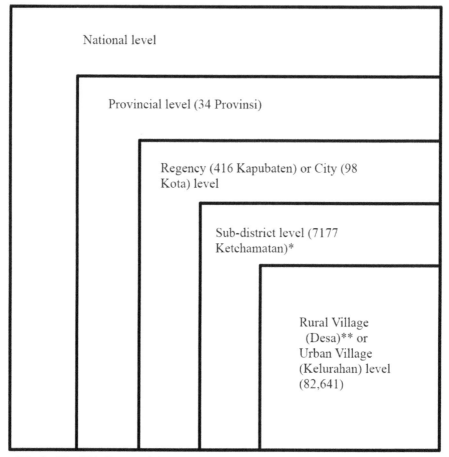

*District (Distrik) in Papua and West Papua.
**Other terms are used for villages in some parts of the country.
Source: Indonesia statistics office.

FIGURE 6.I. Indonesia's administrative structure

articulated as under the sole purview of the central government and because
of the "'concurrence functions'[52] ... whatever and whenever the central government exercises its power ... provincial authorities and the authorities of the
regency/municipality have the similar power to exercise it, only its scale is different" (Hidayat, 2017: 4).[53] However, while Provincial governments in Indonesia are, thus, both the regional representatives of the national government
and autonomous regional governments they currently have no hierarchical

[52] Law 32/2004.
[53] Part 3, Law 23/2014.

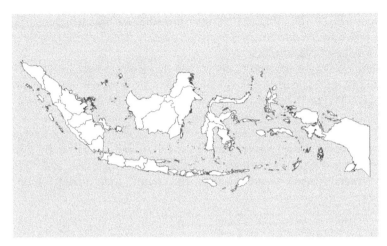

FIGURE 6.2. Indonesia's Provincial boundaries (white areas show the locations of Indonesia's provinces and the lines between them show provincial boundaries)

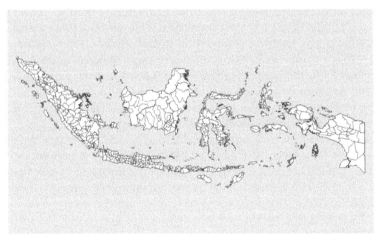

FIGURE 6.3. Indonesia's Regency and City boundaries (The white arears show the location of Indonesia's regencies and cities and the lines between them show regency and city boundaries)

authority over subordinate governments, i.e. their role is akin to that of a coordinator of the activities that they are charged with implementing at lower administrative levels (Nasution, 2016).

Below the Provincial level is the level of the Regencies (*Kabupaten*) and Cities (*Kota*) depicted in Figure 6.3. Each is represented by elected Regency/Municipality-level DPRDs and an elected Regent (*Bupati*) or a Mayor (*Walikota*), also elected by plurality.[54] With respect to the Provincial level of government, the level of the Regency is quite powerful as the Regency/City has

---

[54] Same law that regulates elections of governors specifies rules for elections of regents and mayors.

the responsibility and authority to determine the size and structure of its own budget expenditure, and receives transfers directly from the central government to pay for these (Nasution, 2016).

Each of the Regencies and Cities is then divided into sub-districts. The sub-districts are represented by district heads that are civil servants appointed by the Regent/Mayor.[55] Sub-districts are further divided into Rural and Urban Villages (respectively *Desa and Kelurahan*).[56] The former is led by directly elected Rural Village Heads (*Kepala Desa*)[57] and elected Village Consultative Councils (*Badan Permusyawaratan Desa*, BPD), and the latter by appointed Urban Village Heads (*Lurah Desa*).[58] Similar to Regencies and Cities, the villages receive transfers directly from the central government for operating expenses.

6.4.2 Party and Election Law

In addition to the election law, the parties law that was passed during re-democratization and last amended in 2011[59] is arguably one of the more important laws for influencing electoral competition (Reilly, 2006, 2007b; Allen, 2012; Horowitz, 2013) in Indonesia. This series of laws directly conditions subsequent electoral competition in Indonesia. Over time, one of the most notable features of this law is the increasingly stringent party registration requirement.[60] In the latest iteration of the law, to register, parties must have a national presence with chapters in all Provinces and a deep penetration with chapters in no less than 75 percent of all Regencies/Municipalities, and in no less than 50 percent of all sub-districts.[61]

With respect to identity politics, Table 6.1, which elaborates the election rules at each administrative level including candidate nominations, drives home the importance of the parties law. Both the presidential candidates and legislative candidates are nominated by parties, though in selection of legislative candidates lists are open; thus, voters have some direct influence over ordering on the lists proposed by the parties. Even so, to get on the list in the first place, candidates must be nominated by parties with a national presence. Furthermore, accounting for the presidential voting requirement of 50 percent

---

55 Article 224, Law 23/2014.
56 The village is further split into community unit (*rukun warga*) or urban village unit (*orrukun tetangga*).
57 Article 31, Law 6/2014.
58 Article 229, Law 23/2014.
59 The parties law in Indonesia passed during and after *Reformasi* includes Laws No. 2/1999, 31/2002, 2/2008, and 2/2011.
60 For a discussion about the importance of party registration laws with regional requirements, see Birnir (2004). Specifically on the reasons for the increasingly stringent registration requirement in Indonesia, see for example, Reilly (2006, 2007b) and Allen (2012).
61 Article 3, section C, Law No. 2/2011.

TABLE 6.1. *Electoral rules at each administrative level in Indonesia*

Elected candidate /assembly	Nominating rule	Term length and limits	Election rule	Timing of election
Nation				
President (*President*)	A party (or a coalition of parties) that won at least 20 percent of seats or 25 percent of vote in last legislative election nominate a pair (President and Vice-President)	5 years, 2 term limit	Pair wins with over 50 percent of votes, and with at least 20 percent of votes in more than half of the provinces. Runoff between 2 top pairs if no pair meets the above conditions	Simultaneous with elections to DPR, DPD, DPRD-Province, and DPRD Regency/City
DPR (575 members)	Parties	5 years	Open list PR. 3–10 representatives (determined by population size) elected in 80 constituencies. Sainte-Laguë, 4 percent party vote threshold	Simultaneous with elections to Presidency, DPD, DPRD-Province, and DPRD Regency/City
DPD (4 members from each of the 34 provinces)	Independent (non-partisan) candidates. To register candidates submit copies of identification cards of between 1000 and 5000 voters depending on the number of registered voters in each province	5 years	Single non-transferable vote system, 4 independents with the highest number of votes elected in each province	Simultaneous with elections to Presidency, DPR, DPRD-Province, and DPRD Regency/City
34 Provinces* (Provinsi)				
Governor (*Gubernur*)	Parties clearing a vote threshold in DPRD elections nominate a pair (Governor and Vice Governor). Independent candidate pairs can run if meeting a registration requirement ranging from 6.5 to 10 percent of registered voters, in an inverse relation to the number of voters in the province and those are divided between at least half of the Regencies/Cities in the province	5 years, 2 term limit	First past the post	Staggered by group in which the elections are simultaneous with election of Regents/Mayors

(continued)

TABLE 6.1. *(continued)*

Elected candidate /assembly	Nominating rule	Term length and limits	Election rule	Timing of election
DPRD Province (34 provinces electing 35–120 members depending on population size)	Parties	5 years	Open list PR, 3–12 representatives (determined by population size) elected in 272 constituencies. Saint-Lague, no threshold	Simultaneous with elections to Presidency, DPR, DPD and, DPRD Regency/City
514 Regency (*Kabupaten*) /City (*Kota*)				
Regent (*Bupati*)/ Mayor (*Walikota*)	Parties clearing a vote threshold in DPRD elections nominate a pair. Independent candidate pairs can run if meeting a registration requirement ranging from 6.5 to 10 percent of registered voters, in an inverse relation to the number of voters in the province and those are divided between at least half of the sub-districts in the Regency/City	5 years, 2 term limit	First past the post	Staggered by group in which the elections are simultaneous with election of Governors
DPRD- Kabupaten/ Kota. (508** Regencies or Municipalities electing 20–55 members depending on population size)	Parties	5 years	Open list PR, 3–12 representatives elected in 2206 constituencies. Saint-Lague, no threshold	Simultaneous with elections to Presidency, DPR, DPD, and DPRD- Province
7177 Sub-districts (Ketchamatan)*				
Sub-district head (*Camat*)	Civil servant appointed by Regent/ Mayor			

Elected candidate /assembly	Nominating rule	Term length and limits	Election rule	Timing of election
82,641 Rural villages (*Desa*)/ Urban villages (*Kelurahan*)				
Rural Village head (*Kepala Desa*)*	Independent candidates	6 years	First past the post. Direct election by villagers	Simultaneous in all sub-districts of the Regency/City
Village Consultative Council (BPD)	Candidates screened by an appointed committee	6 years, consecutive 3 terms	Direct election by villagers	Simultaneous in all sub-districts of the Regency/City
Urban Village civil servant (*Lurah*)	Civil servant appointed by Regent/Mayor at the suggestion of the regional secretary	No term limit. Subject to rules regulating civil service	Answers to the sub-district head (Camat)	

*Five provinces have special administrative status. These are Aceh, Yogyakarta, Papua, West Papua, and Jakarta.
** Excluding six Regencies or Municipalities in Jakarta that do not have DPRD at the municipality level.
*** District (*Distrik*) and headed by *Kepala Distrik* (district head) in Papua and West Papua.

Special thanks to Ferry Kurnia Rizkiyansyah at netgrit.org for answering several rounds of questions about Indonesia's electoral framework. For other sources, see various election laws.[62]

and over 20 percent of votes in at least half of the Provinces, it is very clear that at the national level only candidates supported by parties with a broad national appeal have a chance at being elected to the presidency.

The implication for identity mobilization in presidential elections is that only identities with broad national resonance are viable contenders in presidential competition. Because of the open list selection, local identities may play a greater role in the legislative election but only in a way that can be subsumed

[62] This includes:

Person/Body	Current Law/Regulation	Prior Law
President	7/2017	42/2008 and 8/2012
DPR	7/2017	8/2012
DPD	7/2017	8/2012
Governor	10/2016	1/2015
DPRD-Province	7/2017	8/2012
Regent/Mayor	10/2016	1/2015
DPRD-Kabupaten	7/2017	8/2012
Sub-district	23/2014	
Rural Village	6/2014*	
Urban Village	23/2014	

*Additional regulations including Law 43/2014 and 47/2015 further flesh out the selection mechanics.

under national party politics. In contrast, in elections to the Regional Representative Council or the upper house of the national legislature (DPD Provincial), identities likely play a larger role as candidates are independent and selected in the Province. But because this is a less consequential body with far more limited powers, the electoral competition may be less intense.

At the Provincial level and the Regency/Municipal level, local identity politics likely play a greater role than in national elections because candidates for governor/regent/mayor can run as independents. Furthermore, legislators at this level are selected through an open list system. However, the candidates to the legislatures (and some gubernatorial/regent/mayoral candidates) are also nominated by parties, which must register nationally. This likely dampens overt emphasis on local identity in favor of identities with national penetration.

In contrast, at the Village level candidates are independent and there is no specified role for parties. The same is true for the Village Consultative Councils. Therefore, at the Village level local identity politics likely play a more overt role in the election than at any other administrative level.

6.5 DATA ON ETHNICITY AND RELIGION

The argument explored in this chapter is that underlying demographic conditions, as delineated by the institutional boundaries of the pertinent political competition, incentivize particular mobilization strategies. The literature makes it very clear that ethnicity and religion are important identity categories in Indonesia. Therefore, as in other empirical analyses in this book we focus on the role of ethnicity and religion in mobilization while at the same time exploring additional identity categories that may have special significance in Indonesian politics.

After the first population census carried out by the Dutch colonial government in 1930, no demographic information was collected until the Central Statistics Office (*Badan Pusat Statistik*, BPS) of Indonesia started conducting censuses again in 1961, 1971, 1980, 1990, 2000, and 2010. Furthermore, because the governments of Sukarno and Suharto believed "knowing the 'truth' about ethnic composition could result in social and political instability" (Ananta et al., 2015), no official statistics on ethnicity were collected between 1930 and 2000 (Arifin et al., 2015: 234). At the same time, questions about religion were allowed and this information was systematically collected.

In an effort to decipher the very complex census data on ethnicity and religion Ananta et al. (2015) studied the 2010 Census, which provides a more accurate and comprehensive coverage of identity demographics than the 2000 Census. Specifically, relying on expert knowledge of the principal ethno-religious fault lines in Indonesia, they reclassified the 1331 ethno-religious categories from the 2010 Census[63] into more than 600 ethno-religious

---

[63] For the most part these data are consistent with their classification of the ethno-religious groups listed in 2000 Census, except for the underestimation of the Muslim Malays and Christian Dayaks in 2000 (Ananta et al., 2015: 85–86).

groups,[64] and tracked changes to populations of 15 major[65] ethno-religious groups in 33[66] provinces.

Consequently, we use Ananta et al.'s (2015) classification for information[67] about the demographic influences in national-level elections – such as the presidency – where the overall distribution of ethno-religious groups affects the majoritarian election of the president. Similarly, we use their information in our examination of provincial-level elections though we do supplement with other sources because the census measures used and classification of ethnicity varies between the 2000 and the 2010 Censuses.

At lower administrative levels, it is the demographic distribution of groups within each administrative boundary that influences the electoral mobilization of identity, as illustrated in the comparison of presidential and mayoral elections in the United States in Chapter 3. However, below the provincial level Ananta et al. (2015) do not provide systematic re-classified ethno-religious data for all sub-national administrative units. Suryadinata et al. (2003), for example, analyze eleven major ethno-religious groups in eleven selected provinces. Ananta et al. (2004), using the 2000 Census data, calculate numbers of aggregated groups and describe ethnicity and religion, but the data cover only Javanese versus others at the District level. Subsequent sections, therefore, supplement the examination of the influence of demographics at the relevant administrative level with available data from other sources as specified in each section.

6.6 THE CWC IN NATIONAL-LEVEL POLITICS

6.6.1 National-level Demographics

Overall Indonesia's demographics are extremely diverse and geographically varied. By 2030, Indonesia's Muslim majority is projected to comprise 86.8

[64] A group of scholars have jointly published the bulk of the work that aims to make the 2000 and 2010 Census data more user-friendly. See for example, Suryadinata et al. (2003); Ananta et al. (2004); Ananta (2006); Arifin et al. (2013, 2015); Ananta et al. (2015).

[65] The Census data are very complex with ethno-religious group, sub-ethno-religious and sub-sub-ethno-religious group, and alias categories. Ananta et al. (2015) match all sub and sub-sub ethno-religious groups and aliases that people name themselves in open-ended census questions, to a smaller number of aggregate ethno-religious groups. This way we are able to discern demographics of the large ethno-religious groups in provinces.

[66] As noted in the above section, there are currently thirty-four provinces in Indonesia. However, there were only thirty-three provinces at the time of the 2010 Census. North Kalimantan is the youngest province formed in 2012. Since we use the Ananta et al. (2015) data on ethnic and religious demographics, which relies on the 2010 Census, we only examine thirty-three provinces in this chapter.

[67] Depending on their research objectives and the necessary level of aggregation other researchers rely on alternate sources for demographic data. Pierskalla (2016), for example, uses the BPS or PODES (*Potensi Desa*, Village Potential) statistics on plurality ethnic groups and officially designated transmigration communities in sub-districts. Similarly, Tajima et al. (2018) use both the 2000 Census data and the PODES data.

percent of the national population, Christians account for 10.5 percent, Hindus for 1.5 percent, and Buddhist, Animist, Jewish, and other religions in the country for less than 1 percent.[68]

The island of Java, where the largest number of Indonesians live, can be divided into three parts: Central Java, Eastern Java, and West Java. Central Java is the homeland of the majority Muslim Javanese ethnic group. Ethnic Javanese have also voluntarily or as a result of forced migration policies of the state (as discussed later in the context of the Kepri case study), migrated over time to many other islands in the archipelago. East Java is home to large Hindu Balinese and Muslim Madurese migrant communities from the islands of Bali and Madura. West Java, on the other hand, has a majority Sundanese population.

The island of Sumatra is home to the Muslim Acehnese in the north. Other large minorities in the archipelago include the Muslim Minangkabau and the mostly Christianized Bataks. Kalimantan, on the other hand, is dominated by Muslim and Christian Dayaks, Muslim Malays and Christian and Buddhist ethnic Chinese, along with Muslim Madurese migrants. Christian and Muslim populations, i.e. Muslim Buginese, Javanese, and Butonese migrants, and Christian and Muslim Ambonese inhabit the Moluccas (also known as Maluku Islands). Sulawesi hosts Muslim Buginese and Makasarese in the south, and Christian Minahasans and Manadonese in the north. Finally, 800,000 indigenous Christian Papuans belonging to hundreds of different sub-groups live on the island of Papua.[69] Table 6.2 lists the population share of the fifteen largest ethnic groups in the re-classified Indonesian National census data from 2010. Overall Javanese comprise right around 40 percent of the population, the Sundanese 15.5 percent, Malay 3.7 percent, Bataks 3.58 percent, and other groups less.

6.6.2 National-level Institutions

As noted above, National-level elections are held for the (lower) House of Representatives (DPR) and the (upper) Regional Representative Council (DPD) and the office of the President (*Presiden*). In these sections we focus on the election to the Presidency as an illustrative example of the interaction between institutions and underlying demography in shaping the electoral competition. The Presidency is filled in an election of a pair of presidential and vice-presidential candidates that are nominated by political parties. The president and vice-presidential candidates are elected with more than 50 percent of the national vote, having obtained at least 20 percent of the vote in half of Indonesia's provinces.[70]

---

[68] "The future of world religions: Population growth projections, 2010–2050," Pew-Templeton Global Religious Futures Project, available at: www.pewforum.org/2015/04/02/religious-projections-2010-2050, last accessed on May 27, 2019.
[69] Indonesia. World Directory of Minorities and Indigenous Peoples, available at: https://minorityrights.org/country/indonesia/, last accessed on July 17, 2019.
[70] Article 416, Law 7/2017.

TABLE 6.2. *Demographics of the fifteen largest ethno-religious groups in Indonesia, 2010*

Ethnicity	Religion	Population (%)
Javanese	Islam	40.05
Sundanese	Islam	15.5
Malay	Islam	3.7
Madurese	Islam	3.03
Betawi	Islam	2.87
Minangkabau	Islam	2.73
Buginese	Islam	2.71
Bantenese	Islam	1.96
Banjarese	Islam	1.74
Acehnese	Islam	1.96
Sasak	Islam	1.34
Batak	Islam and Christianity	3.58
Dayak	Islam and Christianity	1.36
Balinese	Hinduism	1.66
Chinese	Christianity and Buddhism	1.2

Referring to the parties law discussed earlier, Horowitz notes that despite geographic concentration of many of these groups "Regional and ethnic parties were effectively prohibited.... This was not due to explicit provisions to that effect, but rather because of the requirements that parties establish branches virtually all over the country" (Horowitz, 2013: 143 and fn 82). This law has had substantial ramifications for national-level elections, including the Presidency. Specifically, as a result of the parties law compounded with the rules regulating nomination in the election law, presidential contests are now limited to candidates backed by parties with significant national following. As intended, and substantiated in Table 6.2, no one ethnic group is sufficiently large or geographically distributed (not even the Javanese) that they can support party chapters in half of all sub-districts in three-fourths of all Regencies and Cities in every single Province.

Not surprisingly, therefore, most presidential teams include a Javanese candidate but often appeal beyond the Javanese ethnicity. Indeed, with the exception of the transitional President Bacharuddin Jusuf Habibie, who was of Buginese origin, every president since re-democratization has been Javanese,[71] but often paired with vice-presidents from different ethnic backgrounds, including Malay Hamzah Haz and Buginese Muhammad Jusuf Kalla (Mujani et al., 2018: 99).

Furthermore, at the national level religion only came to play a substantial role in the 2019 presidential election but not because of a CWC, but rather as a result of intra-Javanese competition over leadership of a largely

---

[71] The Presidents are Abdurrahman Wahid, Megawati Sukarnoputri – who assumed power when Wahid was impeached, Susilo Bambang Yudhoyono, and Joko Widodo.

Muslim constituency.[72] In contrast, the 2009[73] and 2014 elections, were contested mostly by career politicians, businessmen, and former army generals, and
won by Javanese candidates who emphasized economic growth (Rondonuwu
and Davies, 2008) and stability, and none of whom were particularly noted for
emphasizing religion.[74]

This lack of emphasis on religion in the 2009 and 2014 presidential
elections is much in line with recent research that shows that Indonesia's pious
population does not care only about religious issues but consider a range
of policies when deciding which party to support (Pepinsky et al., 2018).
Consequently, Indonesian religious parties have had limited success in electoral
politics (Satana et al., 2019).

The CWC in Electoral Competition for the Presidency

However, for the 2004 presidential election the electoral regulations about
candidate nominations and the party law about party registration were less
stringent. Specifically, for the 2004 election a one-time exception was made in
the 2003 election law[75] to allow parties that obtained at least 3 percent of the
number of legislative seats or 5 percent of valid votes nationally to propose
candidates for the election (Article 101, Law No. 23, 2003).[76] Moreover,
according to the party law, at the time, parties only had to be registered in half
of all provinces, and in those provinces in half of all Regencies and Cities and
in those Regencies and Cities in a quarter of the sub-districts.[77] Consequently,
in the 2004 election five different candidate pairs were supported by parties
to take part in the election, including a pair of large ethnic minority group
representatives that attempted to challenge the ethnic Javanese for control of
the presidency by way of mobilizing a religious CWC – albeit unsuccessfully.[78]

---

[72] At the national level the prosecution of Jakarta's mayor Ahok and Prabowo's emphasis of his
running mate's religious credentials are more likely causes for Jokowi's change from secular
electoral strategies in 2014 to his emphasis on religion in 2019.

[73] Interestingly, despite the global economic crisis which caused Indonesia's economic decline of
2 percent from 2008 to 2009, voters in 2009 election surveys reported economic satisfaction
under the incumbent government (Mujani and Liddle, 2010: 43).

[74] The main candidates for the 2009 election were the incumbent Yudhoyono (Javanese)-
Boediono (Javanese) against Megawati (Javanese)-Prabowo (Javanese), and Kalla (Buginese)-
Wiranto (Javanese). The main candidates for the 2014 election were Prabowo (Javanese) and
Rajasa (Malay) running against Jokowi (Javanese) and Kalla (Buginese).

[75] We thank Nathan Allen for bringing this to our attention.

[76] According to the general provisions of the law regulating the 2004 election, candidate pairs
could be proposed only by parties that had won 15 percent of legislative seats or 20 percent of
the national vote in the preceding election (Article 5(4), Law 23, 2003). This requirement was
increased further in the 2008 election law.

[77] Article 2(3b), Law 31, 2002. Subsequent revision to the party law was passed in 2008.

[78] As the rules for nominations in the election law have become increasingly restrictive the number
of candidate pairs contesting the election dwindled to 3 in the 2009 presidential election, and
2 in 2014 and 2019 following the increase in the nomination requirement in the election law
passed in 2008. Article 9, Law 42/2008.

The ethnic minority candidates were Hamzah Haz, an ethnic Malay born in West Kalimantan (and a former minister in Megawati Sukarnoputri's government and vice-president from 2001 to 2004),[79] and Haz's running mate Agum Gumelar, a Sundanese general and former minister under Wahid and Megawati cabinets.[80] The Haz-Gumelar pair was supported by the Islamist PPP, and in the otherwise secular campaign Haz strongly set himself apart by emphasizing his Islamist credentials (Mujani et al., 2018: 99, 100). Indeed, some opined that "Hamzah … is widely seen as blatantly vying for support from among Indonesian Muslims, including the militant groups, to strengthen his run for the presidency in the country's next general elections in 2004" (Guerin, 2002).

While the Malay constitutes less than 4 percent of the population, at over 15 percent, the Sundanese are the second-largest ethnic group in Indonesia and both share with the Javanese Islam as their religion. It is not an unrealistic expectation, therefore, that together and by mobilizing religion across ethnicity this pair could present a real challenge to Javanese monopoly of the presidency. Seemingly, however, Indonesia's voters at the time cared more about the economy than religion when electing their presidents (Freedman and Tiburzi, 2012: 155), and voted for a Javanese president supported by secular parties, including the PDI-P and Golkar (Mujani et al., 2018: 86, 99).

To sum, therefore, the Haz and Gumelar coalition is evidence that institutions permitting leaders of relatively large ethnic groups have sought to mobilize shared religion for a CWC to challenge Javanese monopoly of the executive after re-democratization. Increasingly stringent registration law and learning about which political strategies make success more likely make it unlikely that future challenges be mounted that do not include the Javanese, but this case suggests that even under the most restrictive circumstances minority political leaders consider various available options for identity mobilization including a CWC.

6.7 THE CWC AT THE PROVINCIAL LEVEL

Under current institutions, Islam[81] is the only identity numerous enough to garner the minimum number of votes necessary for the Presidency in Indonesia.[82] However, lower on the administrative ladder in Indonesia, the rules of election change in terms of the number of votes required for election and to

---

[79] Other challengers included Megawati and her running partner Hasyim Muzadi.

[80] During re-democratization, Gumelar originally supported Megawati's political campaign defying Suharto, contributing to his ouster (Kingsbury, 2003: 155).

[81] Recently, the salience of religion in national elections in Indonesia is confirmed by an early 2018 survey where "a plurality of voters considered presidential and vice-presidential candidates' religious identity to be the most important determinant of their support" (Power, 2018: 311).

[82] Elections to the national legislature are different from elections to the presidency because representatives are elected in districts so it is plausible that the party plays ethnic politics in the district.

incorporate independent candidates. Furthermore, parties can appeal locally –
at least implicitly – to other identities that are sufficiently numerous to win
local offices. Therefore, following the logic of the MWC that politicians will
appeal to whichever identity wins them office with the lowest number of supporters, we should expect that overall in Indonesian politics ethnic appeals are
substantially more common in sub-national politics than they are in national-
level elections.

Indeed, Fox and Menchik (2011) demonstrate that in comparison to parties
operating at the national level, when operating at the regional level parties are
more likely to reinforce regional and/or ethnic identities, pass legislation in
favor of their ethnic groups, and mobilize ethnic groups to engage in conflict.
Explaining why this is so, Allen (2012) argues that subnationally where ethnic
diversity encourages rent-seeking, decentralization draws multiple local elites
into a competition emphasizing local goods and ties while diminishing the value
of national party platforms.[83]

Our objective is to examine whether there is also evidence at the Provincial
level that candidates representing large segmented minority identity groups
that are underrepresented by the majority MWC seek to mobilize a CWC
of a shared identity for access. Substantively, in Indonesia both ethnicity and
religion are salient and there is not necessarily a natural sequence to the
mobilization of ethnicity and religion. Rather the argument we make is that the
interaction of institutions and the underlying demographics condition whether
challengers attempt to shift identity mobilization from a segmented identity to
a shared identity. However, in Indonesia Provinces are more often segmented by
ethnicity than religion and Governors are elected by plurality. Therefore, on the
assumption that all else being equal political actors prefer an MWC we should
expect a politician to first consider ethnicity as a mobilization strategy and
religion second because ethnicity likely offers a smaller winning coalition than
does religion, which more often is shared across ethnic groups. For the same
reason, we would expect the CWC more often center on religion than ethnicity
in a segmented minority effort to beat an MWC with an oversized coalition of

---

[83] Moreover, Fox and Menchik's analysis of local and national political parties' electoral campaign
material in Aceh further supports the idea that sub-national political competition is to a much
greater extent ethnic, but in a non-generalizable way. Specifically, the electoral law governing
elections in Aceh allows local parties to run in elections – in contrast to the electoral law
mandating parties with a national presence elsewhere in Indonesia. The reasons for this can
be traced back to the insurgency between the Free Aceh Movement and the Indonesian state,
which ceded in 2004 after the devastating Indian Ocean earthquake and tsunami cost tens of
thousands of local and military lives. The peace agreement, signed in 2005, reinstated Aceh's
provincial status, appointed a local Acehnese governor, and allowed local political parties to
run in elections. For more on Aceh before and after the peace agreement see Robinson (1998);
Aspinall (2007a,b); Drexler (2008); Aspinall (2009); Barter (2011); McDonald (2015). Fox and
Menchik's analysis shows that in Aceh candidates of national parties "use religious symbolism
much more (34% versus the average of 23%), and nationalist symbolism much less (16% versus
the average of 39%)" than local parties (Fox and Menchik, 2011: 18).

the shared identity. To probe the plausibility of these expectations in this section we first examine in detail the underlying demographics in each province with respect to what types of mobilization we would expect to see. Next we turn to a case example that illustrates the logic of a CWC mobilization as compared to the logic of mobilizing an MWC in one of the Provinces.

6.7.1 The Provinces

Indonesia has thirty-four provinces as of 2019.[84] Each province elects between 35 and 100 members to a Provincial legislature, depending on the population size of the province. The chief executive of a province is a Governor, who is elected with a Vice governor for a five-year term with a plurality of the vote (50 percent in Jakarta).[85] The candidates are nominated by national political parties or run as independents.[86]

Across several tables, Ananta et al. (2015) categorize the thirty-three provinces covered in the 2010 Census in terms of their ethnic homogeneity. We combine this information into a single table (Table 6.3) and from the same source add the information on religions of each ethnic group. Thus, Table 6.3 lists the ethnic majority and largest ethnic minority group and their group sizes by Province. The table is organized around ethnicity rather than religion only because all Provinces are home to more than one ethnic group and most of the ethnic groups are not internally divided by religion. In the cases where ethnic groups are divided by religion we note the group share of each religion in a table note. Furthermore, Table 6.3 organizes the Provinces into Ananta et al.'s (2015) spectrum of six categories ranging from Provincial homogeneity to heterogeneity.

To predict from which identity a CWC could be expected to emerge we first have to establish what is the majority MWC in terms of identity and then show minority mobilization of the shared identity in challenge to the rule of the segmented majority. To this end we next delineate the underlying demographics of the Provinces.

Central Java and Yogyakarta are "homogeneous" provinces as over 95 percent of the population in these provinces are Muslim Javanese and the largest minority, Muslim Sundanese constitute less than 2 percent. In terms of ethnicity, Gorontalo, West Sumatra, and Bali are "almost homogeneous"

---

[84] As previously mentioned, since we use the Ananta et al.'s (2015) data on ethnicity and demographics, which relies on the 2010 Census, we only examine thirty-three provinces in this section.

[85] The minimum of the plurality rule for regional heads changed from 25 percent (Article 107, Law 32/2004) to not being specified (Article 33, Law 22/2014) to 30 percent (Article 109, Law 1/2015) and was then eliminated again (Article 109, Law 10/2016).

[86] Independent candidates may run provided they collect a sufficient number of signatures. Independent candidates must gather 6–10 percent of registered voters and those have to be divided between at least half of the Regencies/Cities in the province.

TABLE 6.3. *Demographic majority/minority ethnicity, religion, and size in thirty-three Indonesian provinces, 2010 Census*

Homogeneity	Provinces	Majority ethnic group/religion	Majority group size (%)	Largest minority ethnic group/religion	Largest minority group size (%)
Homogeneous	Central Java	Javanese/Muslim	97.72	Sundanese/Muslim	1.40
	Yogyakarta	Javanese/Muslim	96.53	Sundanese/Muslim	0.69
Almost homogenous	Gorontalo	Gorontalo/Muslim	89.05	Javanese/Muslim	3.39
	West Sumatra	Minangkabau/Muslim	87.33	Batak/Christian and Muslim*, Javanese/Muslim	4.61/ 4.49
	Bali	Balinese/Hindu	85.50	Javanese/Muslim	9.59
Less homogenous	East Java	Javanese/Muslim	79.72	Madurese/Muslim	17.53
	South Kalimantan	Banjarese/Muslim	74.34	Javanese/Muslim	14.51
	West Java	Sundanese/Muslim	71.87	Javanese/Muslim	13.28
	Aceh	Acehnese/Muslim	70.65	Javanese/Muslim	8.94
	West Nusa Tenggara	Sasak/Muslim	67.58	Bima/Muslim	12.70
	Lampung	Javanese/Muslim	64.06	Lampung/Muslim	13.54
Less homogenous	Bangka-Belitung	Bangka/Muslim	52.73	Belitung/Muslim	16.14
	Central Kalimantan	Dayak/Christian and Muslim*	46.62	Javanese/Muslim, Banjarese/Muslim	21.67 21.03
	West Sulawesi	Mandar/Muslim	45.42	Buginese/Muslim	12.49
	North Sulawesi	Minahasa/Christian	45.16	Sangir/Christian	20.27
	South Sulawesi	Buginese/Muslim	45.12	Makassarese/Muslim	29.68

	Region				
	North Sumatra	Batak/Christian and Muslim*	44.75	Javanese/Muslim	33.40
	Banten	Bantenese/Muslim	40.65	Sundanese/Muslim	22.66
	Jambi	Malay/Muslim	40.35	Javanese/Muslim	29.09
Almost heterogeneous	Jakarta	Javanese/Muslim	36.16	Betawi/Muslim	28.29
	West Kalimantan	Dayak/Christian and Muslim*	34.93	Malay/Muslim	33.84
	East Kalimantan	Javanese/Muslim	30.24	Buginese/Muslim	20.81
	Riau	Malay/Muslim	33.28	Javanese/Muslim	29.20
	Riau Archipelago	Malay/Muslim	30.23	Javanese/Muslim	24.55
	Bengkulu	Malay/Muslim	32.12	Javanese/Muslim	22.64
	South Sumatra	Javanese/Muslim	27.41	Malay/Muslim	20.54
	Papua	Dani/Christian	23.32	Auwye or Mee/Christian	11.32
	South-east Sulawesi	Butonese/Muslim	22.80	Buginese/Muslim	22.28
	Central Sulawesi	Kaili/Muslim	21.45	Buginese/Muslim	15.62
Heterogeneous	East Nusa Tenggara	Atoni/Christian	19.85	Manggarai/Christian	15.57
	West Papua	Javanese/Muslim	14.76	Arfak/Christian	9.18
	Maluku	Butonese/Muslim	12.74	Ambonese/Muslim	12.13
	North Maluku	Tobelo/Christian	10.78	Galela/Muslim	9.70

* According to Ananta et al. (2015: 268), the Batak demographics in Indonesia are as follows: 49.56 percent Protestants, 6.07 percent Catholics, 44.17 percent Muslims, 0.11 percent Buddhists, and 0.07 percent "Others." Ananta et al. (2015: 272–273) reports Dayak demographics as: 30.18 percent Protestants, 32.50 percent Catholics, 31.58 percent Muslims, 0.38 percent Hindus, 0.54 percent Buddhists, 0.02 percent Confucians, and 4.79 percent "Others." These numbers are Ananta et al.'s (2015) calculation from the raw data set of the 2010 Indonesia Population Census.
Source: Ananta et. al. 2015. We compiled this table based on several tables the authors reported for their categorization of ethnic groups in the 2010 Census.

since Gorontalo, Minangkabau, and Balinese ethnic groups account for more than 85 percent of the population with many small and evenly sized migrant communities accounting for 3–10 percent of the population. In terms of religion and group size these Provinces are more diverse as the Balinese are Hindu and the Batak are split between Christianity and Islam. Even so we would not expect a minority religious CWC (mobilizing religion across ethnicity) or an ethnic CWC (mobilizing ethnicity across religion) in any of these provinces for the following reasons. In Gorontalo the segmenting ethnic identity is very uneven and we would not expect to see a CWC led by a very small minority. In West Sumatra it is the ethnic minority that is segmented by religion. Therefore, ethnic mobilization across minority religions would not improve minority access unless the minority also appealed to members of the majority but the overall size of the minority is too small to expect this.[87] In Bali both religion and ethnicity are segmented. Therefore, in all of these provinces we would expect an MWC to be formed within the majority ethnic group, and in none of these provinces would we expect to see evidence of a CWC.

The six "less homogeneous" provinces, East Java, South Kalimantan, West Java, Aceh, West Nusa Tenggara, and Lampung are inhabited by the majority populations of Banjarese, Sundanese, Acehnese, Sasak, and Javanese, respectively ranging from 64 to 80 percent and their largest minorities account for about 9–18 percent. All of these ethnic minorities are Muslim. As applied to ethnicity and religion in Indonesia, the CWC suggests that within the province, leaders of relatively large excluded minority ethnic groups that share a religion with the ruling majority may see in the shared religious identity an opportunity for mobilization to challenge the status quo (MWC) for access. Furthermore, the expectation is that CWC mobilization is more likely where the population balance between the majority and the minority that share religion is increasingly close. Chapter 3 suggested a tipping point for the population balance where a CWC becomes more likely but subsequent case analysis (including the case of mobilization for the Presidency discussed above) suggests that this tipping point may be more contextual than the model suggests. Consequently, it is possible that at least the larger minorities in the "less homogeneous" provinces attempt to mobilize a religious CWC though this expectation is not as strong as where the population balance is more even.

The next two categories, "less heterogeneous" and "almost heterogeneous," include eight and ten provinces, respectively. The "less heterogeneous" provinces are Bangka-Belitung, Central Kalimantan, West Sulawesi, North Sulawesi, South Sulawesi, North Sumatra, Banten, and Jambi with majorities being the Bangka, Dayak, Mandar, Minahasa, Buginese, Batak, Bantenese, and Malay constituting 40–52 percent of the province and large minorities ranging 12–33%. The "almost heterogeneous" provinces, in turn, are Jakarta, West

---

[87] See Soedirgo's (2018) work on Ahmadis in Indonesia for small minority-majority group dynamics.

Kalimantan, East Kalimantan, Riau, Kepulauan Riau (Kepri), Bengkulu, South Sumatra, Papua, South-west Sulawesi, and Central Sulawesi, with majority groups including the Javanese, Dayak, Malay, Dani, Butonese, and Kaili with size in the range 21–36 percent, and minority groups including the Betawi, Malay, Buginese, Javanese and Auwye/Mee, whose populations are anywhere from 11 to 34 percent.

These eighteen provinces present two demographic scenarios. In most the ethnic majority and minority share a religion, for example, in North Sulawesi the Minahasa and the Sangir are both Christian and in South Sulawesi the Buginese and the Makassarese are both Muslim. In all such Provinces ethnic groups are increasingly even in size and we would expect to see instances of ethnic minority-led religious CWCs challenging the majority ethnic group for political power. In others (Central Kalimantan, North Sumatra, and West Kalimantan), ethnic majorities are split by religion. Here we would still expect majorities to prefer ethnic MWCs but minority-led religious CWCs are especially appealing because of the religious fault lines within the ethnic majority.

Finally, "heterogeneous" provinces are East Nusa Tenggara, West Papua, Maluku, and North Maluku inhabited by the majority Atoni, Javanese, Butonese, and Tobelo ranging only from 11 to 20 percent with numerically relatively very large minorities such as the Manggarai, Arfak, Ambonese, and Galela that constitute 9–16 percent of the population. Among heterogeneous provinces, in East Nusa Tenggara and Maluku ethnic majorities and minorities share religion, whereas ethnic majority and largest minority groups in West Papua (Muslim Javanese and Christian Arfak) and North Maluku (Christian Tobelo and Muslim Galela) are segmented by ethnicity and religion.[88] Consequently, we would only expect to see minorities mobilize religious CWCs in the former two provinces.

To sum, within the Provincial administrative boundaries we would only expect CWC mobilizing religion is possible where at least one ethnic minority group is large enough to mount a challenge to the majority. As per the logic of the MWC we would expect majorities to prefer ethnic mobilization to that of religion because ethnicity allows for smaller coalitions. Thus, the possibility of a CWC applies to the twenty-six provinces where the majority and the largest minority share religion, and includes Muslim-Muslim majority-minority pairs, as well as two Christian-Christian majority-minority pairs (in East Nusa Tenggara and Papua). Furthermore, for such pairs the expectation of a religious CWC is stronger in the heterogeneous, almost heterogeneous, and less heterogeneous categories because of relatively even distribution of the population between the majority and the largest minority. However, there are possibly one or two provinces in the less homogeneous category where such

---

[88] West Papua and North Maluku are, therefore, Provinces where we might expect to see segmented ethno-religious political mobilization between groups. However, that mechanism is outside the empirical scope of the examination in this chapter.

mobilization might take place because there ethnic minorities are large enough to challenge the majority by way of a CWC.

The objective of this chapter is to probe the plausibility of a CWC mobilization where the demographic balance between the majority and minority produces the appropriate incentives. Table 6.3 and the majority-minority grouping gathered from Ananta et al.'s (2015) data enable us to identify potential cases where CWC mobilization may take place. While this is not a test of the prevalence of such mobilization, examination of the evidence does reveal a number of cases where large minorities that share a religion with the majority do mobilize in a challenge to the status quo. The next section delves into one such case: the Javanese in Kepri.

6.7.2 The Case of Kepri

The discussion of CWC in provincial politics centers on the Riau Islands (or Kepulauan Riau, hereinafter referred to as Kepri).[89] This is an important case because it allows for the juxtaposition of the predictions made by the CWC and the MWC both when considering only ethnicity and religion and also when taking into consideration another politically salient identity cleavage created by transmigration.

The Kepri depicted in Figure 6.4 lies between the islands of Sumatra and Kalimantan.[90] Kepri has "a particularly unusual regional economy, with a large oil enclave, a cash crop economy, a relatively wealthy capital city, and a strong export-oriented manufacturing and service economy" (Hill et al., 2013: 117) and enjoys the advantage of its close proximity to Singapore (Choi, 2007: 333). Before separation into two provinces as Riau and Kepri in 2004, Riau was the third richest province after East Kalimantan and Jakarta. In 2000, it accounted for 23 percent of Indonesia's total export income and 28 percent of Indonesia's oil revenue. Even so, over 40 percent of the population lived below the poverty line and only 16 percent had high school education (Ford, 2003).[91]

The Muslim Malays claim to be the *putra daerah* (sons of the land) in Kepri. Arguably their vision for Kepri was to build a pure Malay province by splitting the original Riau province; however, this vision was far from realistic, as the newly split province was still not predominantly ethnically Malay (Faucher, 2005, 2007). Indeed, figures from Ananta's (2006: 48–56) demographic study of Kepri in Table 6.4 show that in 2006 the Malay comprised 37.44 percent of the total population of the province. However, it appears that proportionally

---

[89] Due to space constraints, we could not tell the stories of all the cases where we found evidence of CWC but were left to pick cases that clearly illustrate the point.

[90] With the passing of Law No. 25 in 2002, Riau province was split into two provinces as Riau and the Kepulauan Riau, and the split formally took effect by 2004.

[91] Until 1998 Suharto used the Batam Industrial Development Authority (BIDA) to extract revenue from Kepri as did Habibie until 2001. See Choi (2011: 53), for a detailed account.

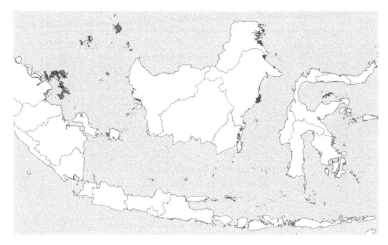

FIGURE 6.4. Kepulauan Riau (Kepri)

the ethnic Malay population decreased after the split as in 2010, they constituted only 30.23 percent of Kepri's total population (Ananta et al., 2015).

All but 1.71 percent of the Malay in Kepri are Muslims but one-fifth of the total population in the province is now non-Muslim. The second-largest identity group in the province of Kepri are the predominantly Muslim[92] Javanese migrants that constituted 22.20 percent of the Riau population in 2000 and 24.55 percent in Kepri in 2010. The third-largest group is the Christian and Buddhist Chinese comprising 9.73 percent of the population in the Province. Along with the Malays, the Chinese are considered the natives of Kepri (Ananta, 2006: 56) as most of them lived in the province for generations and "with migration as the criterion, Chinese Indonesians, like the Malays, may not be regarded as *pendatang* [migrants] either in the province" (Ananta et al., 2018: 42). The fourth and fifth largest ethnic groups were the Muslim Minangkabau who migrated from West Sumatra (9.24 percent – only 0.58 percent non-Muslims) and the Christian Batak (8.84 percent, of which 64.11 percent were Protestants) from North Sumatra. The Javanese, the Minangkabau, and the Batak are considered *pendatang* (migrants) in the province.

The following examination of the first gubernatorial elections in Kepri in 2005 relies heavily on Choi's (2007, 2011) account. The rules of the gubernatorial election at the time stipulated a plurality (first past the post) contest where the candidates with the most votes won the office even if they had less than 50 percent of the votes, as long as they received at least 25 percent of the vote.[93] Three party coalitions nominated three pairs of candidates for the election.

---

[92] Only 2.99 percent were non-Muslim (Ananta et al., 2015).
[93] Law 32/ 2004.

TABLE 6.4. *Demographics in Kepri, 2010*

Ethnic group	Religion	Population (%)
Malay	Muslim	30.23
Javanese	Muslim	24.55
Batak	Christian and Muslim	12.48
Minangkabau	Muslim	9.72
Chinese	Christian and Buddhist	7.7
Sundanese	Muslim	2.96
Buginese	Muslim	2.22
Flores	Christian	1.79
Palembang	Muslim	1.76
Banjarese	Muslim	0.71
Others		5.9

Before discussing the details of the races, let us think about the incentives for building various types of coalitions as conditioned by the underlying demographics. Accounting only for ethnic and religious demographics, Table 6.5 suggests that in this competition the Malay should strongly have preferred a mobilization of an MWC of the Malay vote only, and could have won had they succeeded in making the election about ethnicity because they command 30.23 percent of the population and no other group is large enough to challenge them on ethnicity. One caveat is that, accounting for the condition that $w + x_i > y_i$ as discussed in Chapter 3, the pivotal Malay group (w) might also recognize that a Malay MWC might not be stable because the Javanese (y_1) and the Minang (y_2) together are more numerous than the Malay alone. In contrast, the Javanese, not being able to compete on ethnicity, should, according to the CWC, have pursued mobilization of an oversized Islamic coalition. As Muslims, the Malay, Javanese, and Minangkabau together constitute around two-thirds of the population (64.5 percent) (Choi, 2011: 63).[94]

However, as a dwindling population, the Malay's hold on power is greatly threatened by migration to Kepri by the Javanese and other migrants. Therefore, the Malay strongly emphasize not just their ethnicity but also their nativity in Kepri. Before completing our account of the CWC in Kepri it is, therefore, important to elucidate the relevance of this political identity constructed by forced and voluntary migration, in Kepri and Indonesia at large.

Forced and Voluntary Migration in Indonesia
As in the case of Turkey, discussed in Chapter 5, population movements in Indonesia in the form of forced and voluntary migration fundamentally altered the demographic landscape of the archipelago over a century. Despite the end

---

94 The MWC does not speak to minority/non-pivotal group incentives but if it did would likely recognize that Javanese incentives would be to pursue an oversized religious coalition.

TABLE 6.5. *Kepri CWC*

		Religion		
		Islam	Other	Total
Ethnicity	Malay	30.23		30.23
	Chinese		7.7	7.7
	Javanese	24.55		24.55
	Minang	9.72		9.72
	Batak		12.48	12.48
	Total	64.5	20.18	

of forced migration policies after re-democratization, the long-term effects of these policies are still relevant for political mobilization in Indonesia.

The island of Java, and particularly the capital Jakarta, is grossly over-populated. This led to various government programs, known as *Transmigrasi* (transmigration), which originally stipulated resettlement of farming populations from densely populated Java (and Bali) to the Outer Islands, dating back to 1814 when Indonesia was still under Dutch colonial rule (Abdoellah, 1987: 180). Dutch strategy to forcefully shift around labor to more efficiently extract resources was not the only reason for early population movements. Local populations that wanted to avoid Dutch taxation or earn better wages in cities also migrated of their own volition (Hugo, 2006: 60). In addition, some groups chose to move to the Outer Islands for better opportunities (Hugo, 2000; van Klinken, 2003) or due to natural disasters such as eruption of many of the volcanoes in the archipelago (Hugo, 2006).[95] Moreover, poverty, that "manifested in low agricultural incomes, landlessness, low productivity, and underemployment" pushed many members of the two largest ethnic groups in the country, the Sundanese and the Javanese, to voluntarily migrate (Abdoellah, 1987: 183). Accordingly, "geographical features such as regional contrasts in soil fertility, terrain, and availability of water" encouraged migration of populations looking to improve their standard of living (Hardjono, 1977: 36).

Thus, the increasing heterogeneity or the presence of multiple minorities in every province in Indonesia can be explained both as voluntary migration and as coming about by way of historical conflicts with the Dutch, which forced and/or incentivized many groups to move away from their home-regions. This accounts for, for example, the large numbers of Acehnese in Maluku

[95] Food shortage and change in environmental factors also drove populations away from their home-regions dating back to pre-colonial times. For example, Javanese movement from wet rice (*sawah*) areas in Central Java to dry field cultivation (*ladang*) areas in West Java where Sundanese heavily lived changed demographics even before the Dutch colonization and implementation of forced migration policies (Hugo, 2006: 58).

(Gooszen, 1999: 29), the Madurese in Kalimantan, and the Javanese in Lampung and North Sumatra (Ananta et al., 2015: 137).[96]

Transmigration policy did not change much after Indonesia's independence
in 1945. Several Indonesian governments adopted the same forced migration
policy to not only relieve population pressure in Java but also to assimilate
and integrate marginalized regions of the country that were economically
underdeveloped (Hugo, 2002). While often mismanaged and poorly run,[97]
these transmigration programs relocated up to 10 million people until they were
finally terminated in 2000 (Tirtosudarmo, 2001).[98] Through transmigration
policies the state attempted to extend its sphere of influence beyond Java into
the country's margins, or as Elmhirst (1999: 813) aptly puts it "extend a
particular imagined geography across the archipelago."

The migrant experience across the archipelago was decidedly mixed (Barter
and Cote, 2015). For example, in forced migration for agriculture, the wet rice
(*sawah*) type agricultural methods associated with Java were often introduced
in locations that were not appropriate for the cultivation of this crop to the
great frustration of local populations (Hugo, 2006). Similarly, "sites were
often selected without the necessary prerequisite surveys of soil and other
determinant ecological factors; settlers lacked clear title to the land allotted
to them; often there were prior claims on the land which had not been
investigated" (Hardjono, 1977: 36). Indeed, Adam (2010) suggests that insecure
access to limited land exacerbates poverty and social exclusion in agricultural
societies, which jeopardizes the relationship between the groups that were
forced to migrate and the host/indigenous populations that have to share
land/income with outsiders.

In other instances, the influx of Javanese migrants was perceived as a
colonial encroachment of the state. Indeed, indigenous populations in the Outer
Islands have long interpreted the government's transmigration program as a
continuation of colonial policies and considered it an attempt at Javanization
of the nation as the newcomers mostly came from Java and Bali, and shared
access to land, services, and other resources (Hugo, 2002: 300).

---

[96] Lampung used to be a central destination for transmigration; hence 5.12 percent of the
population in the province is Javanese (Ananta et al., 2015: 139).

[97] Hardjono's 1977 study of transmigration shows that both Sukarno and Suharto governments
aimed at moving a couple of million people out of Java annually. However, the overall results
were not all intended. For example, Hardjono finds that "frequent changes in departmental
structure, problems of interdepartmental cooperation, and specific policy shifts in such areas as
the setting of targets, types of settlement areas, and classification of transmigrants" led to the
failure of forced migration policies (Hardjono, 1977: 26). Moreover, security force negligence
made the problem worse as at times police and army competed to "tax" migrants or refugees
fleeing from conflict zones (Davidson, 2009a).

[98] Potter (2012: 272) suggests that under the guidance of the rebranded Ministry of Manpower
and Transmigration, there is a new system in place evaluating applicants from "'sending
districts' (in Java, Bali and the poorer provinces of East and West Nusa Tenggara) being matched
to requests from 'receiving districts' (in Sumatra, Kalimantan, Sulawesi, and Papua)" to address
the growing need in the past decade for labor on palm oil plantations.

Many of the migrants also failed to assimilate into the local communities and were perceived negatively due to cultural differences with the host populations. For instance, the Madurese who voluntarily migrated to West and Central Kalimantan for at least a century (Hugo, 2002: 316), were, as an insult, called "middle-aged and treacherous" by ethnic Malays that claim indigeneity to the Sambas district in West Kalimantan (Davidson, 2009b: 121). Variations in the practice of Islam across different ethnic groups were also a cause of conflict. While the Javanese are historically syncretic in their interpretation of Islam, for instance, Sumatrans are more conservative, if not fundamentalist (Abdoellah, 1987: 189). Similar clashes occurred in Aceh, which received large numbers of Javanese migrants that migrated with their syncretic beliefs to the historical home of the religious Darul Islam rebellions[99] of 1953–1957 and 1959–1961, which had aimed to make Indonesia an Islamic state (Hugo, 2002: 303).[100]

In other cases, the migrant populations distinguished themselves socio-economically to the chagrin of locals. For example, over time Buginese, Butonese, and Makassarese from South Sulawesi, came to dominate small- and medium-scale commerce in many areas they emigrated to in eastern and western parts of the Outer Islands (Hugo, 2002: 302). This increased tension considerably between the hosts and the migrant communities. In response to the influx and increased competition over resources, the local ethnic groups often stigmatized the "newcomers" regardless of how many generations the settlers had inhabited the area (Diprose, 2009: 118–119). Claims of indigeneity are frequently used to justify rights and privileges for a particular ethnic group, as well as being used as a tool for political mobilization (Tirtosu-darmo, 1997).

Alesina et al. (2018: 37–38) argue that the constant demographic trans-formation over the last century explains why ethnic and religious cleavages have remained salient in Indonesia since pre-colonial times. Whatever the reason, anecdotal evidence collected during the authors' fieldwork in Indonesia confirmed that in addition to religion, which is indeed very salient in Indonesia, ethnic identification and migrant versus native origin seem quite salient identity categories across the archipelago – at least superficially. For example, during our fieldwork, we found that in casual conversations Jakarta respondents often identify themselves by the region they or their parents are from or as "Indonesians," distinct from members of the various ethnic immigrant communities in the city (who often retain a distinct character though some trace their migration back generations). In Bali and Lombok, inhabitants some-

---

[99] *Darul Islam* was established in 1942 under Sekarmadji Maridjan Kartosuwirjo's charismatic leadership during the Indonesian National Revolution against the Dutch colonial rule. This was a militant Islamist group that challenged the Indonesian state after independence until its defeat in 1962, and called for *jihad* (holy war) to establish an Islamic state in Indonesia (Solahudin, 2013).

[100] The rebellions caused 215,700 refugees to flee out of conflict zones between 1951 and 1956 (Hugo, 2006: 73). A lot of these groups were Buginese and Makassarese of South Sulawesi that migrated to Jakarta and the east coast of Sumatra and Kalimantan.

TABLE 6.6. *Kepri CWC versus MWC*

		Religion			Native/Migrant
		Islam	Other	Total	Total
Ethnicity	Malay	30.23		30.23	37.93
	Chinese		7.7	7.7	
	Javanese	24.55		24.55	**46.75**
	Minang	9.72		9.72	
	Batak		12.48	12.48	
	Total	64.5	20.18		

times describe each other in ways replete with ethnic characterizations, and consider themselves distinct linguistically and culturally. In Flores inhabitants of the center make a clear distinction between themselves as the "native" Christians and the Muslim migrants who inhabit the shore, to name but a few examples.

6.7.3 Natives, Migrants, and the CWC in Kepri

Returning to our discussion of political strategies in Kepri, Table 6.6 adds the demographics of the politically salient migration cleavage and contemplates the resultant mobilization strategies. By the logic of the MWC, as the plurality group the Malay in the 2004 election should still have emphasized ethnicity and had they succeeded in framing the election in ethnic terms, they would have won with a plurality of the votes (the caveat still holding that this might be an unstable coalition). However, it is now more clear that the Javanese had a choice to make. They could only beat the Malay by mobilizing a religious coalition or a coalition of natives versus migrants. By the logic of the MWC the Javanese competing in this election should have embraced Malay rhetoric about the migrant versus non-migrant cleavage to form an MWC of migrants (Javanese, Minangkabau, and Batak) with 46.75 percent of the population beating out a coalition of non-migrant Malay and Chinese at a total of 37.39 percent or the ethnic Malay by themselves at 30.23 percent.

However, the idea of the CWC presupposes that the large minority perceives the ethnic majority (in this case Malay plurality) as its principal competitor. Therefore, the Javanese realize that if they mobilize the migrant coalition of 46.75 percent, the Malay, knowing that they do not have the numbers to challenge the Javanese on the migration cleavage, can choose to mobilize the shared religion instead. Therefore, it is imperative to gain the first-mover advantage to undercut the possible subsequent counter-mobilization for leadership of the shared religious identity. In Kepri, this means that the

Javanese are aware that if they do not take leadership of shared religious cleavage, the Malay may. Therefore, in contrast to the MWC, the CWC suggests the Javanese will seek to mobilize the shared religious cleavage in a way that undercuts competition from the Malay for leadership in mobilizing religion. The results of the election adjudicate between which of the mobilization expectations (CWC or MWC) better account for the actual strategies employed by contestants.

Choi (2011: 55–56) argues that political parties were insignificant in the election after the nomination process, and instead of policy debates, candidates depended on *sosok* (personality or charisma) and personal spending in their campaigns. Contrary to the expectations of the MWC, the Javanese contestants did not align with the Minangkabau and Bataks but opted for an oversized CWC that emphasized piousness while de-emphasizing ethnicity. Thus, the Javanese candidate who won, Ismeth Abdullah, selected as his running mate a Malay, Muhammad Sani, who was a devout Muslim (Choi, 2007: 340). Abdullah appealed across ethnicity and capitalized on Sani's piousness to build a CWC around religion instead of an MWC emphasizing native versus migrant identity.

This is particularly interesting because originally from Cirebon of West Java, Abdullah was the acting governor, appointed in 2004 when the 2002 decree on the formation of the new province of Kepri came into effect. Therefore, he did not represent a group that had no prior access to power. Still the 2004 election was the first direct election for Governor and because the Javanese were an ethnic minority and the Malay sought to marginalize the Javanese as migrants and colonizers, the Javanese harbored a realistic fear of losing access.[101] At the same time, Abdullah was also very wealthy, politically connected and the former head of the Batam Industrial Development Authority (BIDA). He was also supported by the largest party in the provincial assembly, Golkar. With all those advantages he should have been able to put together an MWC of migrants only but instead chose to mobilize a religious CWC.

The strongest opponent of Abdullah and Sani was Nyat Kadir who ran with Soerya Respationo, supported by another large coalition of PDI-P, PAN, and a few smaller parties.[102] A Malay and "local boy," Kadir was mayor of Batam, which makes up more than half of Kepri's population, during 2001–2005. His running mate, Soerya Respatiano, was a Catholic Javanese who migrated from Yogyakarta in Central Java and was the chairman of the Batam municipal assembly from 2004 to 2009. As the "underdogs" of the election, compared

[101] Kimura (2013: 96) explains that due to its economic value, Suharto regime appointed only Javanese and Minangkabau governors to Riau. This created resentment against the Javanese and once Kepri became an independent province, the Malay wanted the islands to remain solely native (Choi, 2007). While this goal did not materialize, the Malay rhetoric of nativity threatened all migrants in Kepri, including the Javanese.

[102] The third pair, Rizal Zen and Firman Boisowarno were not well known in the local population (Choi, 2007: 335), and thus not likely winners from the outset.

to "BIDA heavyweights" Abdullah and Sani (Choi, 2007: 336), Kadir, and Respatiano focused on local poverty.[103] However, although Respatiano was popular among the lower social classes, his popularity was not sufficient to counter the CWC mobilizing Muslims across ethnicity.[104]

In earlier accounts, the CWC is initiated by a minority out of power. In this case, however, the appointed governor seemingly recognized that the migrant Javanese by themselves could not retain power through elections. However, rather than responding to the mobilization of sons of the land/native coalition to build a migrant MWC, he opted for an oversized multiethnic coalition based on common religious identity.

6.8 CWC AT LOWER ADMINISTRATIVE LEVELS

Thus far, this chapter has outlined some demographic incentive structures in presidential contests, and a gubernatorial contest at the Provincial level. The final case illustrates the building of an oversized CWC in a mayoral election, to drive home the point that where the spoils of office engender political competition, demographics will condition the identity mobilization in competition at all levels of administration. Furthermore, where the population balance is increasingly even between the majority and a marginalized minority we expect that the likelihood of mobilization for an oversized CWC increases, capitalizing on an identity shared by the minority and the majority.

6.8.1 The City of Medan, North Sumatra

The city of Medan, depicted in Figure 6.5 is a multiethnic, multireligious metropolitan of over 2 million inhabitants according to the 2010 Census, and the capital city of North Sumatra. The 2010 Mayoral election in Medan is a good illustration of CWC mobilization at this administrative level. The case of Medan is particularly important because it shows "how in conditions where citizens may identify with overlapping and multiple identity categories, political actors can choose to select and emphasize those identities that confer maximum political advantage in a given setting" (Aspinall, 2011: 30). Specifically, similar to Kepri, Medan is also divided between *natives* (Batak and Malay) and *migrants* (Javanese and Chinese) but the largest native ethnic group in Medan, the Batak, is also cross-cut by religion. Around a third of Bataks are Muslim while at least two-thirds are Christian. This case, therefore, illustrates how

---

[103] Ananta (2009: 18) argues that Kadir's focus on his nativity was a mistake as the numbers in the island reflected that the natives were no longer the majority.

[104] An oversized inter-ethnic coalition proved to be a winning formula in Kepri. In 2010 another Malay-Javanese pair won the election: Muhammad Sani was elected governor and Soerya Respatiano became his deputy governor. This time, however, Christian votes were also targeted as Respationo was Christian. Then in 2015, Muhammad Sani ran with Nurdin Basirun, another Malay native and former regent of Karimun, against Soerya Respationo with another native and prior regent of Bintan, Ansar Ahmad, as his running mate.

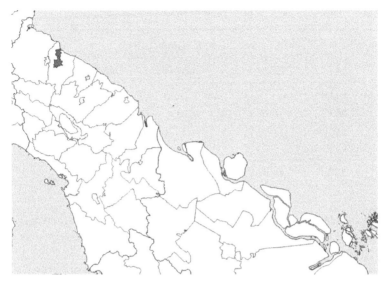

FIGURE 6.5. Medan, North Sumatra

the complex underlying demographic tapestry of cleavage intersection helps elucidate the political strategies employed by local political actors.

Similar to elections for Governors, heads of cities are elected in pairs consisting of the Mayor (*Walikota*), and the Deputy Mayor (*Wakil Walikota*). Parties clearing a vote threshold in DPRD elections nominate the pairs but independent candidate pairs can run if they meet a registration requirement. The mayoral pair is elected for a five-year term with a plurality of the vote.[105] Same as at other administrative levels, the argument here is that, in each electoral contest the interaction of the institutions and the underlying identity demographics, including intersection of cleavages incentivizes contestants as to whether and then what identity they should attempt to mobilize. Furthermore, where a marginalized minority approaches the majority in size and the two share a second identity, the CWC suggests that the minority will attempt to mobilize the shared identity to challenge the status quo.

In Medan, the Mandailing Batak typically dominated local politics and governorship. Furthermore, Malays had access to city politics beginning in the second half of the New Order era. For example, Bachtiar Djafar was mayor from 1990 to 2000 and Rizal Nurdin was appointed as governor from 1998 to 2003, and served a second term until his death in 2005 (Reid, 2010: 111), both were Malay. In contrast, the Javanese and the Chinese were completely marginalized in the city during the New Order (Aspinall et al., 2011: 39). As new migrants that came to North Sumatra during the colonial era to

---

[105] Depending on the version of the regional electoral law, in some elections there was a minimum vote threshold the candidate pair was required to clear.

TABLE 6.7. *Ethnicity and religion in Medan*

		Religion				
		Islam	Christian	Buddhist		
Ethnicity	Batak		34		40.6	Native
	Malay	6.6				
	Javanese	31.9			43.1	Migrant
	Chinese			11.2		
	Total	approx 49.8	approx 22.3	11.2		

work in plantations, according to Bruner (2013: 258), "the Batak regarded the Javanese as a lower segment of humanity, and referred to the men as coolies and to the women as prostitutes."[106]

As shown in Tables 6.7 and 6.8, the Batak, who are native to the highlands of North Sumatra, are mostly Christians with a significant Muslim minority, and constitute the largest ethnic group in the city (about 34 percent of the population). According to the 2000 Census cited in Aspinall et al. (2011: 31) and Damanik (2016: 71), Batak sub-groups include Tapanuli Bataks (0–1.7 percent of the population and split 55 percent Muslim, 35 percent Protestant and 9 percent Catholic); Toba Bataks (17.4 percent and 79 percent Protestant, 12 percent Catholic and 9 percent Muslim); Karo Bataks (5 percent, and 56 percent Muslim, 28 percent Protestant and 15 percent Catholic); and the Mandailing Bataks (9.9 percent of the population and 99 percent Muslim). Muslim Javanese, who constitute 31.9 percent of the population, Buddhist Chinese at 11.2 percent, and Muslim Malay at 6.6 percent of the population are the largest ethnic minorities that migrated to Medan.[107]

Given the demographics displayed in Tables 6.7 and 6.8, the MWC argument would suggest that as the politically dominant and the largest ethnic group,

---

[106] Bruner (2013: 261–262) also suggests that "there were alliances that crosscut ethnic boundaries," however, these attempts of rallying natives (i.e. Malays and Bataks) against the migrants (i.e. Javanese, Minangkabau, and some Batak sub-groups that migrate) was not successful. To be clear, of the migrant groups mentioned by Bruner (2013), the Minangkabau are not in our table since demographics have changed in Medan in the last few decades.

[107] The general numbers are cited from Aspinall et al. (2011: 31), who use the 2000 Indonesian Population Census as the source and the Batak sub-groups numbers are from Damanik (2016: 71). Since the Tapanuli Batak numbers were not available, we estimated them in the remaining Batak population which makes up to 1.7 percent. According to the World Directory of Minorities and Indigenous Peoples, Bataks, numbering around 6 million in the 2000 Census in Sumatra province, are primarily Christian with a Muslim minority. See "Batak," World Directory of Minorities and Indigenous Peoples. Available at: https://minorityrights.org/minorities/batak/, last accessed on December 28, 2018. Ananta et al. (2015: 104) put Bataks in North Sumatra at 44.75 percent, followed by Javanese at 33.40 percent in 2010.

TABLE 6.8. *Batak sub-groups and their religions, 2000*

Population (%)	Sub-group	Muslim (%)	Christian (%)
0–1.7	Tapanuli	55	45
17.4	Toba	9	91
5	Karo	56	34
9.9	Mandaling	99	1

Bataks should mobilize ethnicity because ethnicity is less numerous than the Islamic identity cleavage (which is the plurality religious cleavage), while at the same time Batak ethnic identity is more numerous than any other ethnic identity group. Furthermore, the MWC logic would suggest that the best mobilization strategy of the Javanese would be an attempt to mobilize the native/migrant cleavage because, with the Chinese, migrants constitute a larger number than natives. In contrast, due to their ethnic minority size, historic marginalization, and the understanding that their primary competitor for political power is the majority ethnic group the Batak, the CWC argument would suggest that the Javanese candidates in the 2010 mayoral election should strategically mobilize an oversized coalition of religion to appeal across all Muslim ethnic groups.[108]

In the 2010 mayoral election, twenty candidate pairs from a total of ten tickets ran for the mayor and deputy mayor positions representing over ten ethnic and sub-ethnic groups (Aspinall et al., 2011: 29). Indeed, rather than mobilize an MWC of migrants and natives in the contest, Javanese candidates by and large mobilized oversized religious coalitions appealing across ethnicity to include also Malay and Muslims from among the majority Batak.

For example, Sigit Pramono Asri, an ethnic Javanese born in North Sumatra, ran with a Muslim female deputy-mayor candidate Nurlisa Ginting, who is a Karo Batak. Asri was a representative in the provincial parliament and a founding member of the *Partai Keadilan Sejahtera* (PKS, Prosperous Justice Party), which is one of the largest Islamist parties in Indonesia. Asri was also an advisor to the oldest and largest Javanese ethnic organization in North Sumatra, *Pujakesuma (Putra Jawa Kelahiran Sumatera*, Sons of Java born in Sumatra) and had good relations with many other ethnic Javanese organizations in the province. Thus, Asri's mobilization strategy was not only to appeal to Javanese and Batak votes, but also to activate religion.[109] In fact, according to Aspinall et al. (2011: 39), "The press covered many public declarations by Muslim youth organizations and leaders in support of their campaign, which Nurlisa described as being 'shaped by courteous [santun] politics and Islamic politics'."

[108] Supporting the view that the Javanese political strategies aim to bridge ethnicity, Aspinall et al. (2011: 33) report that Javanese organizations are open to all ethnicities.

[109] In addition, according to Aspinall's interview with Asri, he chose Nurlisa Ginting because of her gender in an effort to also appeal to women as the Karo are not a large minority in the city, constituting only 5 percent of the Batak population.

Other Javanese candidates such as Supradikno, an ethnic Javanese running with a Mandailing M. Arif, or Javanese, Joko Susilo who ran with a Muslim Batak, Amir Hamzah Hutagalung, similarly emphasized religion over ethnicity in their campaigns.[110]

The winner of the Mayoral race was Rahudman Harahap, an ethnic Mandailing Batak Muslim who was the acting mayor at the time, supported by the Governor of North Sumatra Syamsul Arifin, and teamed up with a Malay Muslim Dzulmi Eldin (Nasution, 2014). Aspinall posits that candidates in Medan think "they must build coalitions of the biggest ethnic groups in a particular locality if they wish to win office there" (Aspinall et al., 2011: 28). Therefore, in contrast to the Javanese candidates, in the first round at least, the (Batak and Malay) winners, "believed the mobilization of ethnic symbols and ethno-religious organization to be a necessary and profitable endeavour" (Aspinall et al., 2011: 44).[111]

All of the Javanese candidates dropped from the race after the first round for various reasons.[112] The runoff pitted Rahudman Harahap and Dzulmi Eldin against the Buddhist Chinese candidate Sofyan Tan and his female Minangkabau Muslim running mate Nelly Armayanti. Interestingly, in this second round, the winning pair switched to emphasizing inter-religious competition. They even went so far as to get the *ulama* (Islamic scholars) in Medan to issue *fatwa* (Islamic ruling) for people not to vote for the *kafir* (infidel) (Aspinall et al., 2011: 47). For them, this may have seemed like a reasonable strategy in the second round because even though the emphasis on Islam might alienate the Christian Batak votes (approx 1/2 of Bataks in Medan), the backing of Javanese Muslims would more than make up for Batak defection.

In terms of the theory proposed in Chapter 3, the political strategies of most of the Javanese candidates did not conform to the expectations of the MWC that they align with the Chinese in a migrant versus native political alliance. In contrast, as a marginalized group in a contest primarily with the majority

---

[110] Javanese candidates were not the only ones emphasizing religion in the first round. Mandailing Batak and Malay candidates such as Hasrul Azwar and Ikrimah Hamidy (both from the Islamist political party PKS) and Amiruddin (from the secular Partai Demokrat) not only prioritized their Muslim identity but also refrained from bringing up their ethnicity. Similarly, the Mandailing Batak, the only Batak sub-group that is 99 percent Muslim downplayed their ethnicity and activated religion as a mobilization strategy. Overall, Damanik (2016: 77) finds that Muslim candidates emphasized religious identity first and ethnic identity second.

[111] This also holds for some of the Javanese candidates. For example, Prabowo Subianto found value in using both ethnic and religious mobilization strategies as he believed his main supporters were the Javanese but wanted to appeal to the Muslim majority in the city as well.

[112] For example, Medan has various *preman* (gangster) groups that have patronage networks connecting them to political parties and the ruling elite (Hadiz, 2010; Aspinall, 2011). One such example is the youth preman organization *Ikatan Pemuda Karya* (IPK) led by a Christian Toba Batak Olo Panggabean, who was powerful enough to have the appointed police chief Sutanto exchanged with another official that was more willing to turn a blind eye to his gambling empire in Medan. Candidates with such connections usually fare better in Medan, as exemplified in the 2010 election (Byl, 2014: 145).

ethnic group, most of the Javanese mayoral pairs in Medan did exactly what the CWC would have expected them to do and emphasized religion in a multiethnic coalition including Bataks. The Batak-led mayoral pair performed closer to the expectation of the MWC by first mobilizing ethnicity but even then aligned with the Malay to shore up their ethnic support. Furthermore, even this pair resorted to mobilizing a decidedly oversized religious coalition in the second round. Clearly, therefore, the CWC is a useful way to think about minority mobilizing strategies and the MWC seemingly is not a strategy that any of the candidates clung to very strongly.

6.9 CONCLUSION

The objective of this chapter was to probe the generalizability of the CWC prediction to electoral politics. Specifically, in the context of Indonesian politics, the question asked was whether there is evidence of relatively large marginalized ethnic minorities mobilizing in an oversized CWC the religious identity shared with the ethnic majority in an attempt to gain access to state institutions. Three cases at different administrative levels suggested that indeed the logic of the CWC does cast light on some regularities in minority electoral mobilization strategies in Indonesia. The evidence showed attempts at mobilizing the shared religious identity by the larger minority groups seeking access including the Javanese in gubernatorial elections in Kepri and in Mayoral elections in North Sumatra, and the Malay and Sundanese in presidential elections. However, one significant remaining question concerns the limited mobilization of the largest ethnic group, the Sundanese, in Indonesian politics at the national level.

6.9.1 The Sundanese

The Sundanese, who are mainly based in West Java, comprise 15.5 percent of the Indonesian population, which makes them the second-largest ethnic group in Indonesia, after the Javanese. Therefore, as per the theory in Chapter 3, we would have expected this group to feature prominently in mobilization of religious identity at the national level. What we found was that the Sundanese did attempt to secede in the 1950s after the struggle for independence. However, after the Javanese suppressed the secession, they successfully co-opted Sundanese leaders in subsequent periods, reducing Sundanese motivation for challenging Javanese control.

More specifically, during the independence war the Sundanese sided with the Javanese against Dutch colonialism. However, exploiting ethnic identities to weaken Indonesia's nationalist movement,[113] the Dutch colonial gov-

---

[113] van der Kroef (1950: 452) argues, Dutch sectionalist policies to divide and rule created resentment among the Sundanese against the Javanese leaders.

ernment supported an independent Sundanese state in their homeland on West Java (Bertrand, 2004: 32). Sukarno, however, repressed that initiative in the 1950s.[114]

Since then, the Sundanese have enjoyed great access to national-level politics. For example, Djuanda Kartawidjaja was the eleventh and final prime minister[115] of Indonesia when he passed away (Butcher and Elson, 2017). Before Sukarno's "Guided Democracy," Djuanda had served as Minister of Communications in seven cabinets from 1946 to 1953 as well as Minister of State and Minister of Welfare in other cabinets (Kahn, 2015: 127). Furthermore, between 1965 and 1998, Javanese and Sundanese governors ruled 73 percent of all provinces outside Java for at least one term. Moreover, "Half the provinces experienced more than 10 years of government by Javanese and Sundanese officials, and 23 percent witnessed more than 15 years of external rule" (Mietzner, 2014: 52). For instance, Sundanese Ali Sadikin (or Bang Ali) played important roles in local politics. Bang Ali, a former marine, was the longest-serving governor of Jakarta from 1966 to 1977, and was known for combating poverty in the city by issuing residence cards and banning migration into Jakarta (Aspinall, 2004).

At the local level, Bruner (2013) argues that in West Java where the overwhelming majority of the Sundanese live, the Sundanese have occupied key positions of power in administration such as occupying the position of the major of the capital city Bandung, while less well off Javanese migrants were merely laborers in the city. West Java is also one of the nation's wealthiest provinces. In fact, Java has long dominated the Indonesian economy. For example, in 2004, 61 percent of the country's total GDP originated in Java (Hill et al., 2013: 117) whereas Sumatra, Kalimantan, Sulawesi, and Eastern Indonesia follow Java in terms of wealth.[116] According to a 2014 report on regional competitiveness, West Java ranks third after Jakarta and East Java as a center of high economic vibrancy and is an attractor of foreign investment (Giap et al., 2015: 66). Local access or horizontal inequalities are consequently not a likely motivator for Sundanese mobilization in challenge to the Javanese.

Finally, like the Pashtuns in Pakistan, the Sundanese have enjoyed considerable access to the military. While the Javanese, mostly from East Java, dominate the Indonesian military making up 40 percent, Sundanese are the second comprising 8 percent of the military elite. In the top leadership of the military, "ethnic Javanese fill 25 posts (40 percent); another eight officers are either Sundanese or Madurese" (Rabasa and Haseman, 2002: 64).

[114] See Frakking (2017) for the fascinating story of how the Sundanese maneuvered between the Dutch and the Indonesian state during 1946–1950 to establish *Negara Pasundan* (Pasundan State), a distinct polity in West Java; however, the state got incorporated into the Republic of Indonesia in 1950.

[115] Subsequently, in 1959, under Sukarno's "Guided Democracy," Indonesia became a presidential system and the position of a prime minister ceased to exist.

[116] The two other consistently wealthy provinces are Jakarta and East Kalimantan (Hill et al., 2013: 120).

Despite sharing cultural and religious structures, there has been rivalry between Sundanese and Javanese (Bruner, 2013). However, the two groups have long coalesced to stay in power together. Therefore, despite their relatively large size, ethnic distinction, and orthodox religiosity, the Sundanese have rarely mobilized identity cleavages at the national level. The case of the Sundanese, therefore, reinforces an assumption made by the theory of *Alternatives in Mobilization* that access to power tempers the incentive for identity mobilization.

6.9.2 Lessons Learned

While examining the generalizability of the CWC to electoral politics was the first objective of this chapter, a second objective was to examine the internal validity of our theory, and reveal omitted variables and processes that the theory overlooks. The cases taught us a great deal in both domains. First, as our case narratives revealed in Chapter 5, the cases examined in this chapter reinforced our finding that ethnicity and religion are not the only politically salient identity cleavages, and this is definitely true in Indonesia. In particular, the *native versus migrant* identity cleavage has been and continues to be quite important in many locales within and outside Indonesia. Second, the Indonesia case drove home the point that each identity group often shares or is cross-cut by alternate identities in multiple ways that may matter for political mobilization. Therefore, accounting for context is extremely important when studying identity-based mobilization strategies.

Third, we learned much about political strategies of groups other than marginalized minorities. One of the most surprising revelations was how quickly majorities abandon their MWCs to join the mobilization of an over-sized coalition. For example, the winning candidates in Medan abandoned their emphasis on ethnicity in the second round when religious appeals to an oversized coalition seemed more promising. Similarly, following elections where minorities mobilized a religious CWC, majorities and plurality groups, Malay in the province of Kepri and the Javanese at the national level incorporated religion into their mobilization strategies – though at the national level, religion was not originally brought in by a CWC.

Why do Indonesian voters support CWCs? According to Allen (2018: 933), in Indonesian electoral politics "the conditions for strategic behavior, as laid out by Cox (1997, 76–80), are unlikely to exist." Allen cites among other reasons the fact that, at local level, information is still in short supply – especially because elections are recent and there has been limited learning. Allen adds that "Parties, for their part, are constrained by regional requirement rules from strategically exiting hopeless races.... [and] Indonesian voters are not instrumentally rational in the short term when it comes to their legislative choices. Rather, Indonesian elites and voters use the national legislative elections to accomplish goals that go beyond representation in the DPR." Allen's explanations ring true with respect to our findings. As discussed in the theory of *Alternatives in Mobilization* in Chapter 3, it is possible that in low information environments voters may not have enough information to trust that an MWC (such as the *native versus migrant* cleavage) is a viable option. The various institutional changes before every election also increase the difficulty of predicting electoral support accurately. Therefore, voters may be rationally choosing an oversized CWC coalition with overwhelming chances of winning over an MWC that they think has lower chances of election.

Clearly a multitude of factors in addition to ethnic and religious cleavages are at play in electoral mobilization in Indonesia. One empirical regularity, however, present in Indonesia (and in all the other cases we have covered in this book) is that the ethnic minority groups that engaged in alternative mobilization of CWCs within religious traditions, be it the Malay and Sundanese versus the Indonesian state, the Javanese in Kepri and Medan versus provincial majorities, likely did so in part because of demographic opportunities conditioned by institutions.

7

Conclusion

7.1 LESSONS LEARNED AND THE PATH FORWARD

If shared identities decrease political contestation, why is civil war common among ethnic groups that share religion? If the identity supporting a Minimum Winning Coalition (MWC) is the identity that gets mobilized politically, why are MWCs often unstable and less common than other types of identity coalitions? These are some of the principal questions asked in the introduction to this book. Chapter 2 contemplates whether identity demographics can answer these and some of the other questions scholars have raised about the political mobilization of identity. More specifically, this chapter suggests that the demographic context in which any given identity exists is an important variable to account for when seeking answers to the questions we posed in this book.

Building on this idea, Chapter 3 introduces the theory of *Alternatives in Mobilization*, a generalizable theory about identity mobilization as shaped by demographic context. The theory suggests that the relative size of identity groups and the way identities intersect in society shape mobilization strategies of all identity groups, majorities and minorities alike. The theory of *Alternatives in Mobilization* generates multiple insights, some of which propose useful explanations to the puzzles motivating the study. For example, it is plausible that in the aggregate – at the level of the country – shared identities have a stabilizing effect. The theory also clarifies that it is possible that at the same time, and in the same country, shared identities politically stabilize the interaction between some groups and destabilize others. For instance, in a country with many small and few large minorities, all of whom are segmented by one identity from the majority, sharing a second identity with the majority may stabilize their relationship with all of the small minorities but destabilize their relationship with the larger minorities. Therefore, in the aggregate, on average (because there are many more small minorities than there are large ones), the effect of sharing a second identity is stabilizing, but this effect is reversed in the subset of relationships between majorities and relatively large minorities that share a second identity.

This hypothesis about the destabilizing incentives engendered by a relative demographic balance between a majority and a large minority mobilizing a shared identity through the *Challenger's Winning Coalition* (CWC) suggests one answer to the question of why many ethnic groups that share a second identity mobilize this identity in a civil war. As ethnic minorities and majorities sharing faith become increasingly close in size, the probability of the minority attempting to mobilize religious identity across the ethnic divide to challenge the ruling coalition increases.

The CWC also addresses the second question motivating this project: Why are MWCs less common and more unstable than the theory of MWC would suggest? Specifically, one of the main contributions of the CWC argument is to highlight the limited role of the MWC, which is a first political move for power by leaders of an identity group that is large enough to beat out other groups, as long as the definition of the politically dominant identity remains constant. However, the predicted stability of the politically dominant identity rule often rests on the assumptions of availability of patronage resources and their equal distribution among supporters. In addition it likely assumes that supporters have ample information about the size of the MWC and other coalitions, and leaves aside rank and file substantive preferences unrelated to patronage. When considered in this perspective, and in light of the understanding that identities are constructed and malleable for political ends, it seems obvious that while a reasonable first move, many identity-based MWCs should not last. Instead, we should expect that as soon as an identity MWC has seized power, excluded political operatives will examine other available identity categories and attempt to redefine the relevant political identity as the one that they can lead to beat the status quo MWC.

Chapter 4 tests empirically the external validity of the CWC hypothesis at the national level, in ethnic civil wars across the world. According to the theory of *Alternatives in Mobilization*, there is no inherent sequence to the mobilization of identities, such as ethnicity and religion. However, historical trajectories involving colonial conflicts and global power politics in addition to underlying demographics that lend themselves better or worse to mobilization of some identities compared to others, likely influence which identity gets mobilized first in conflict in a given country. Whatever the specific reason is in each country, in the modern political era, ethnic war is the most common type of civil conflict. Furthermore, at least since the Iranian Revolution brought religion to the forefront in internal war, religious claim-making in civil war is increasingly common.

While the mobilization of religion across faiths is well understood, we know little about why religion is mobilized by competing groups within faith. Using the newly collected A-Religion data, which code religions and religious context of ethnic groups, in combination with Svensson and Nilsson's

(2018) RELAC data, which account for religious claim-making by civil war contestants, the analysis in Chapter 4 shows substantial support for the CWC hypothesis. This support for the CWC is robust to a number of statistical probes and disconfirms an alternative explanation, which suggests that within faith religious mobilization is evoked primarily in sectarian conflict.

Through in depth narratives of three cases that were randomly chosen from a stratified set of minority combatants that share religion with the majorities in their respective countries and make religious claims, Chapter 5 examines the internal validity of the CWC. Within Islam, the chapter explores the role of Pashtuns in civil war in Pakistan. The case examining religious claims made by Christian combatants focuses on the Holy Spirit Movement and Lord's Resistance Army (LRA), both led by the Acholi ethnic group in Uganda. The third narrative about religious claims in a Hindu conflict examines the Maoist People's Movement in Nepal. All these narratives support the idea that seeking access to power, leaders of relatively large excluded minority groups that share religious identity with the ruling majority mobilize religion across the segmenting identity (ethnicity and/or caste) in an oversized CWC to challenge the rule of a majority with whom they share religious family. The cases also suggest a number of refinements to the mechanisms proposed by the theory. One significant insight the cases provide is the idea that the selection of groups from which the leaders of the CWC recruit likely depends on the overall fragmentation of society on the first identity. Thus, in more homogeneous societies where majorities are large, leaders of the CWC will recruit across their own group and from the majority (Pakistan), whereas in more fragmented societies where majorities are small, leaders need not recruit from the majority but can build a CWC exclusively from among other excluded groups (Uganda, Nepal). Another is a reminder that mobilization around religion is not always for augmenting the role of religion in state affairs.

A fourth case was selected for an in depth narrative by convenience to examine a country (Turkey) where the outcome (religious claims in civil war) was not observed despite the presence of a relatively large minority sharing religion with the majority. An interesting pattern that emerged throughout the four cases that we examine in this book is how migration affects minority grievances and spurs the construction of new and resilient identity cleavages such as "immigrants" versus "natives" or "sons of the land." In Turkey, for example, forced migration of the Kurds, due to the decades-long armed conflict between the PKK and the state, changed the demographics of metropolitan cities like Istanbul and Diyarbakir, shifting political party strategies to appeal through religion to poor Kurds and Turks in shanty towns. In Nepal, the Terai region's demographics considerably changed as a result of the flow of migrants from India as well as the Hill people, making the Terai population very heterogeneous. In Uganda, the conflict between the HSM and LRA and the Museveni government over the last thirty years forcibly displaced the Acholi and other Northern ethnic groups into camps, which made recruitment easier for the LRA by way of abductions and aided in spreading the religious teachings of the LRA among those who voluntarily joined the organization. Similarly, as discussed in Chapter 6 in Indonesia, the transmigration policy that started in colonial times and lasted until re-democratization aimed at sending the majority Javanese to islands with less dense populations like Kepri. This changed the demographics, threatened the natives of the island, the Malay, and caused them to mobilize accordingly in local electoral politics. Overall, all the case narratives demonstrate that despite the differences in how and why it took place in each case, migration affected whether and then how the CWC was formed.and marginalization,

Yet another insight resulting from the case narratives emerged in the examination of the Kurds in Turkey. An in-depth exploration of this case suggests that examining mobilization in civil war in isolation from other types of political contestation may underestimate the extent to which groups with armed and peaceful political wings simultaneously adopt multiple divergent strategies – including the CWC – in their pursuit of access. Indeed, Kurds in Turkey have mobilized religion in electoral politics while simultaneously fighting an armed insurgency with the state. Furthermore, as the state increasingly opened the door to religious mobilization even the armed organization (PKK) has jumped on that bandwagon. This is likely a common story across many countries where groups contest elections while also engaging each other in deadly conflict, employing multiple mobilization strategies simultaneously.

Even so, existing work suggests that there is also merit to the idea that politics of war are distinct from politics of peace. Therefore, the final substantive Chapter 6 specifically asks whether the theory of *Alternatives in Mobilization* – and especially the testable hypothesis of the CWC – can be extended to explain identity mobilization in democratic electoral politics in the absence of war. To address this question, this chapter delves into the politics of one of the most ethno-religiously heterogeneous countries in the world, Indonesia. In addition to demographic diversity, Indonesia offers a complex institutional system with contested offices at multiple levels of administration. This chapter explains how the CWC can be expected to manifest in Indonesia's electoral politics and why. The chapter then offers three within-country case narratives that show conditions under which groups chose to mobilize a CWC in a competition for power with the majority, sometimes eschewing other salient identities that would have afforded mobilization of MWCs. Detailing the interaction of institutions and underlying demographics, the chapter offers anecdotal support for the internal validity of the CWC in electoral politics. Furthermore, this case clearly illustrates that even within the same country, mechanisms of identity mobilization vary across time, space, and institutional configurations.

7.2 FUTURE RESEARCH

While the theory and tests conducted in this book cast light on some of the questions motivating this project, including the rise of religious mobilization in civil war and the lifespan of MWCs, they unearth even more. The case narratives especially revealed many additional observations and questions that could and should be investigated and tested further. We highlight some of these below.

7.2.1 Identity Mobilization and Levels of Analysis

To begin with, the theory of *Alternatives in Mobilization* explains how the demographic incentive structures that shape political identity mobilization are affected by changing group size and identity overlap. Because opportunities for mobilization are conditioned by demography, the types of identity mobilization that materialize will tend to vary between countries, and within a country between groups, in predictable ways. Sketching some common demographic variants, the theory suggests several concomitant mobilization strategies that will likely emerge among groups whose demographic features correspond to one of the variants discussed.

The empirical chapters subsequently focus on outcomes as incentivized by one demographic variant in particular, that of relatively large ethnic minorities, which share a second identity with majorities. If, in countries with this demographic scenario, these large minorities are left out of a majority MWC, and the assumed requisites for the stability of the MWC are lacking, one mobilization strategy that is expected to emerge is the CWC capitalizing on the shared identity. Naturally, an argument about how opportunity structures shape mobilization is probabilistic. In some cases none of the leaders of a group will take advantage of this opportunity even if the group lacks access, and where they do take advantage of the opportunity, the timing may be influenced by strategy contagion and historical path dependence as discussed in Chapter 4. Even so, the empirical chapters also show that in ethnic civil war, many leaders do take advantage of this demographic incentive structure to empirically distinguish the mobilization of relatively large groups that share religion with the majority from that of others. Furthermore, Chapter 6, on the CWC in electoral politics, suggests that this strategy is common in electoral politics, when demographics allow.

At the same time, the case narratives in Chapter 5 show that the mechanisms of the theory can be further refined and tested, especially with respect to differences in recruitment for the CWC in low and high fractionalized societies. Furthermore, the CWC is only one of the alternative mobilization strategies that the theory of *Alternatives in Mobilization* implicates as a function of changing demographics and intersection of identity cleavage. For example, untested implications of the theory suggest that while the well-known outbidding story explains much conflict between fully segmented large majorities and small minorities, it may be less applicable in cases where the majority and minority are increasingly even in size. Therefore, at the group level, this book leaves for future research testing of the relationships between all of the other demographic incentive structure variants and the mobilization strategies predicted to emerge as a consequence. In that sense, this book is only the very beginning of the exploration of alternatives in mobilization of identity groups as a function of demographic size and identity overlap.

Furthermore, within any of the opportunity structures created by the divergent demographic profiles discussed in Chapter 3, groups are represented by leaders and organizations that compete for support of group members. Indeed, the case studies and anecdotes distributed throughout the book suggest substantial intra-group strategic maneuvering by political leaders. At the same time, there is also great variance in whether, and then which ones and how many, group leaders, as leaders of organizations or independent of organizations, take advantage of each demographic incentive structure by pursuing the corresponding mobilization strategy. Therefore, some of the important questions that are outside the scope of this study, but remain to be fully accounted for by research on identity mobilization include: Which leaders and organizations are more likely to take advantage of the demographic opportunity structures our project pinpoints, at what junctures and why? Multiple scholars have already explored and continue to produce informative work that focuses on contentious politics of organizations,[1] some of which are identity based.

Beyond the organization and political leaders, at the level of individual supporters recruited for contentious mobilization, several studies show that individuals do not so much follow as they choose to align with leaders whose goals stand to advance the objectives of the individual supporter – whatever these may be (Fearon and Laitin, 2000; Kalyvas, 2006). For example, with respect to religion we make the case in Chapter 4 that individual motives for supporting a CWC promoting religious identity over an ethnic one likely include instrumental objectives as well as motives of devotion.

This conversation about the relationship between individual identity and political mobilization is vibrant and ongoing, especially in the electoral literature. Some recent examples include Margolis (2018) who argues that in the United States individual choice in religion is driven by a marketplace of religious entrepreneurs who signal their political identity in religious practice, and to which the politically like-minded respond. In other words, she suggests that an individual's religious preferences follow their political mobilization (Margolis, 2017, 2018). Others suggest more of an endogenous sorting mechanism at work in US politics. Political parties pick up religious platforms, which in turn, induce constituency sorting into segmented blocks that are increasingly polarized on multiple identity dimensions including religion (Mason, 2018). Examining the relationship between religious preferences and mobilization more broadly, Livney (2020) shows that in Turkey informally shared Islamic

---

[1] See for instance Weinstein (2007); Asal and Wilkenfeld (2013); Fotini (2012); Staniland (2014); Cunningham (2014); Krause (2017). We thank especially Mimmi Söderberg Kovacs for excellent conversations about the role of organizations.

identity enhances inter-personal trust that helps overcome coordination failures, with consequences for multiple political and economic outcomes. At the same time, new experimental research conducted in Lebanon pinpoints the nuances in the relationship between cleavage content and outcomes, suggesting that the effect of sharing (or cross-cutting) of identities has divergent effects depending on the identity (Paler et al., 2020).

Further exploration of the origin and consequences of individual politically mobilized identity preferences across contexts is sure to elucidate and uncover additional nuances in the complexity, direction, and mechanism of the causal link between identity and mobilization. Furthermore, with a more solid grasp of the empirical regularities associated with mobilization at each level, scholars can better link analysis across levels for deeper and more comprehensive understanding of transgressive and contained political mobilization.

7.2.2 Group Size and Identifiability

Some of the questions we were left with as we neared completion of this book concern group size. One of the most vexing questions is, for example, how large does the minority group have to be relative to the majority to tip the scales of mobilization? Moreover, how do leaders and members of the group assess that the group is large enough to mobilize?[2]

The literature on identity politics commonly suggests that members of identity groups assess the size of the groups and the groups' consequent probability of success (Chandra, 2004). More generally, until recently, the literature has implicitly tended to assume that on average members of ethnic groups correctly identify in-group and out-group members based on physical characteristics and/or language and other features and make political decisions based on such identifications. However, emerging experimental work convincingly shows that overall individuals are seldom good at correctly identifying co-ethnics and members of the out-group although they tend to be marginally better at identifying the former (Harris and Findley, 2014; Harris et al., 2018).

If individuals are bad at correctly identifying co-ethnicity, it follows that they are likely not very accurate in identifying group size either. If this is true, then what are the political implications of this for group politics – especially mobilization? Take the example of mobilization for violent identity conflict, considering the implications at the level of the individual first. Anecdotal evidence suggests that individuals frequently escape targeting or conversely are killed because they are incorrectly identified as belonging to the in-group or out-group (Harris et al., 2018). Presumably one of the aims of identity

---

[2] The reader will recall that the equations in Chapter 3 set up the relationship between the size of the majority and the minority to calculate the benefit of mobilization given a particular group population balance. At the same time one long-standing critique of the MWC is that group members lack the information about relative sizes of groups, which would allow them to choose their preferred coalition.

war is to consolidate in-groups, and to drive out and/or kill members of out-groups. Therefore, if a person belongs to the in-group in ethnic war, they will likely try to clearly signal their in-group status among co-ethnics to avoid being targeted. Conversely, if an individual who belongs to the out-group finds themselves among members of the in-group in a conflict situation, they are likely going to try to hide their out-group status. How does individual behavior change if in-group members are being mistaken for out-group members in either scenario? The incentives for showing in-group membership are likely strengthened, and if the individual is an out-group member, their incentive for passing is similarly augmented. Thus, at the individual level the political aims of in-group consolidation and out-group terror are not undermined but possibly strengthened with mis-identification.

At the group level, implications for violent conflict, on the other hand, are less clear. If leaders over- or underestimate the size of their groups and that of the opponents, this potentially affects the outcome of the conflict. However, it is also possible that group size is not an entirely numerical construct but a composite assessment of capacity that includes numbers. Take the Pashtuns in Pakistan. The reader will recall that Pashtuns constitute between 15–20 percent of the population according to a 2010 population census, whereas the majority Punjabis constitute 46 percent of the country's population. Thus, in relative terms the numbers of Pashtuns are less than half that of Punjabis. However, Pashtuns are disproportionately represented in both the civil bureaucracy and the military where they constitute at least 19.5 percent of the army (Khan, 2005; Ahmed, 1998). Others put the number even higher at between 30 and 35 percent (Khan, 2005: 149). Possibly, this over-representation inculcates a strong sense of ownership and capacity among Pashtun leaders with respect to the state that translates into an "over-estimate" of size that is more of a measure of capacity in the conflict.[3]

What then about the effect of mis-identification in peaceful politics such as elections?[4] Seemingly, overestimating the size of a group for which one casts a vote could result in a wasted vote. However, "winning" in elections is only a binary outcome in majoritarian contests. In any contest where multiple

---

[3] The reader will recall the Acholi in Uganda were also over-represented in the military. Consequently, it is possible that they similarly over-estimate their relative group size/capacity.

[4] This question is relevant to many other areas such as public goods provision where sanctioning is a mechanism pinpointing the effect of ethnic diversity. By definition, the sanctioning mechanisms – and especially the deterrent of the credible threat of in-group sanction – depend on repeated interactions that over time allow for the creation of a norm of cooperation between co-ethnics who gradually sort into groups of co-ethnics and non-co-ethnics. For an overview of this literature, see Birnir (2017). The broader political implications of errors in identification then likely depend, for example, on whether the errors get sorted out over time. In the short term, multiple errors may undermine public goods provisions but if they are sorted out over time in the long run there should be no adverse effect on public goods provision. Only in cases where the errors never decrease would we expect to see a lasting effect.

parties can achieve access at the same time, votes for minority parties are often not "wasted" though the person casting the vote may be surprised that the total number of supporters is lower than anticipated, if she overestimated the size of the group supporting the party. Furthermore, entitlement and/or capacity may – rightfully or wrongfully – translate into political clout for the group that induces a following larger than the numbers alone would predict. Recall, for example, the Malay in Indonesia who constitute only 3.7 percent of the overall population but participated in a CWC at the national level. They also dominate politics in the provinces of Riau and in Kepri where they comprise about a third of the population but claim the title of "sons of the land" (Faucher, 2005, 2007). Numerically it is not evident that the Malay should play as large a role in Indonesian politics as they do but Malay leadership self-assessment suggests they should.

Perhaps, therefore, accuracy in identifiability of identity kin and concomitant assessments of the actual size of the group do not necessarily matter as much as whether individuals *think* they can correctly identify and assess group size. Furthermore, the assessment may not only depend on actual size but also on the perceived size as a function of visibility/claim/capacity, which, in turn, drives at least some group political activity. Sometimes errors may even strengthen rather than undermine the political processes underway including mobilization. Clearly, therefore, demographic size is only one of the indicators of a group's political power across contentious politics. We return to this idea at the end of this chapter.

7.2.3 Salience and Political Activation of Identity

Another set of questions that emerged in the research for this book concerns the clarity of conceptual constructs – and the testing of their effects, especially across contexts. One such concept is identity salience. What exactly is the meaning of this concept and how do differences in operationalization of this concept relate to outcomes?

The model in Chapter 3 incorporates the idea of identity salience. Briefly, the reader will recall that, across contexts, there is a proposed difference in identity salience, which makes any given identity more or less available for political mobilization. This seems reasonable because political mobilization of identity such as religion might seem like a more proximate choice for political leaders in Turkey and Pakistan, for instance, where religion plays a more overt role in public life than in Germany or Sweden where the role of religion is arguably less overt in public life.

The research in this book confirms the first part of the above observation. In many parts of the world identity such as ethnicity and religion are very salient in individuals' lives – seemingly independently of politics. The result of this salience is that "it isn't a matter of whether, only when each identity is activated in politics," as observed by one of the generous country study reviewers of this book.[5] Furthermore, research has shown that in political competition between segmented ethno-religious groups, the salience of religion varies with local incentives to compete over adherents (Isaacs, 2017). At the same time, it is less clear that identity salience varies sufficiently across contexts to fully explain differences in outcomes. Specifically, the thrust of the back-lash against secularization theory (Iannacone, 1991; Finke and Iannaccone, 1993; Gill, 2001; Broughton and ten Napel, 2000; Inglehart et al., 1998; Dalton, 2013)[6] is built on empirical evidence that shows inhabitants of the Western hemisphere, and Northern Europe in particular, have not necessarily become less devout over time though their church attendance has declined substantially in some cases. Thus, religion is not necessarily less salient in the West as much as it is more strongly reserved for private life and less easily activated politically. Importantly, the literature does find that identity that is politically activated, especially in violent conflict, "hardens" (Kaufman, 2001) and repression of public display has been found to consolidate identity (Gurr, 1969; Davenport et al., 2005).[7] In contrast, it has not been shown as conclusively that identity that is peacefully relegated to the private sphere becomes less salient. One question thus is, whether there is an interaction between how identity is moved between the public and the private sphere (repression or voluntary) and the salience of that identity. In a similar vein, if devotion in the Western and Northern hemispheres has moved from the public sphere to the private sphere but not necessarily diminished then salience cannot explain divergent mobilization of the identity across hemispheres. In other words rather than salience varying perhaps it is ease of political activation that varies? If salience is more constant than commonly assumed then what are the factors that differentiate the ease of activating identity mobilization in the Southern and Eastern hemispheres from the West, that may have been conflated with salience?

The case studies in this book, Turkey for example, revealed several pos-sible explanations. In many countries decreasing overt expression of both religion and ethnicity in politics is anecdotally correlated with state repression, as the literature would lead us to expect. In contrast, in many instances identity also came to be more commonly expressed in politics after country leaders explicitly mobilized the identity at the national level. For example, in both Pakistan and Turkey, state actors clearly led the way for politiciza-tion of religion in conflict and in electoral politics. In Nepal, the state was defined in religious terms and in Indonesia religion played an integral role in the state before and after re-democratization. If contentious politics is "[episodic, public, collective interaction among makers of claims and their

---

[5] We especially thank Nathan Allen for his feedback on our Indonesia case study.

[6] Secularization theory itself has a long history. For a recent overview of this debate as it pertains to mobilization, see Birnir and Overos (2019).

[7] Furthermore, Fox et al. (2009) show that when the state exclusively supports one religion, repression against ethno-religious minorities is more likely. See also Fox (2016).

objects]" (McAdam et al., 2001: 5), a question that results from the above anecdotal observations is: How commonly in contentious cycles is political activation of religion by non-state actors preceded by state politicization of religion? Concomitantly, is there an interaction between how identity is moved between the public and the private spheres (repression or voluntary) and subsequent availability for political activation of that identity when the state takes the lead in mobilizing the identity? For instance, where expression of identity has been relegated to the private sphere by way of the marketplace of religion (Iannacone, 1991; Finke and Iannaccone, 1993) as opposed to repression of religion (Fox, 2016), does that preclude future political activation of religion by the state, which in turn has ramifications for religious mobilization by non-state actors? If the answer to that line of thinking is positive, then the counterintuitive policy implication would be that if states want to move religion into the private sphere and out of the mobilization reach of non-state actors, they should fund religious organizations such as churches, synagogues, or mosques. The reason is that, according to the literature on the religious marketplace, funding of religious institutions decreases religious leadership entrepreneurial competition for adherents who then become dissatisfied with the options and are more likely to retreat into the private sphere for worship. Naturally, the answer will not be so simple – as shown in the cases of Pakistan and Turkey where the state did fund some religious activity. However, this line of thinking pinpoints the need for further clarification, theorizing, and testing of concepts and their correlates in the study of identity mobilization.

The case studies unearth many other questions with respect to political activation of identity. For example, if a religious identity shared across ethnicity is already co-opted by a majority, does that then affect minority ability to lead the mobilization of religion across the ethnic majority/minority divide? Finally, if the minority leads the political activation of identity, do political majorities join that bandwagon, and if so, how quickly, and do they manage to marginalize minority leaders? This project does not offer definitive answers to these questions but suggests much additional research is needed.

7.2.4 Intersectionality

Finally, the core idea in this book that political mobilization is better understood as a function of the multiple identity groups that an individual belongs to, owes an intellectual debt to the literature on intersectionality. As Collins and Bilge explain, "when it comes to social inequality, people's lives and the organization of power in a given society are better understood as being shaped not by a single axis of social division, be it race or gender or class, but by many axes that work together and influence each other" (2016: 2). Thus, a foundational idea of the intersectionality literature is that the position of those identities in the hierarchy of power is not value-neutral or equivalent across identities.

In this book, other than distinguishing between political majority and minority groups, we treat ethnicity and religion as content equivalent and do not theorize how intersecting vectors of power, oppression and marginalization, across different contexts, differentially intervene in the mobilization dynamics that we have proposed. We simply try to lay the foundations for an understanding of how demographic group size and identity overlap affects political opportunities for mobilization. The layering of status[8] associated with each identity and the concomitant political consequences of intersectionality is the future direction of our research.

---

[8] By status we are referring to the theoretical idea that differentiation in evaluation of individual "quality" is based on the individual's characteristics such as race or gender, rather than the actual performance evaluated. This, in turn, leads to biased perceptions/evaluations of individuals exhibiting this characteristic. For a discussion of this and other related literatures (i.e. backlash theory, stereotyping theory, role incongruity theory), as they relate to bias in evaluations of gender, see for example Bothelo et al. (2021).

Appendix A

AMAR Groups and the A-Religion Data Set

The information in this appendix supplements Chapter 2. First, Table A.1 details information about the AMAR groups not coded for religion in the A-Religion data, along with the reason for why these cases were not coded. Next, Table A.2 lists the groups where the religions of the group are coded, but we were not able to determine which of these is the primary religion. The following table, Table A.3, enumerates all AMAR groups, whose primary identity marker distinguishing it from all other groups is religion. Finally, Tables A.4 and A.5 list the country group details where religion of the politically dominant groups does not overlap perfectly with the religion coded as numerically the most common.

A.1 SUPPLEMENTARY TABLES

The A-Religion data code information about the religions of ethnic groups enumerated in the AMAR data. There are 1202 groups in the AMAR data. In contrast the A-Religion data code religions for 1199 groups as Taiwan is not included because of its disputed status as an independent country. Of the 1199 groups 12 groups remain not coded for religion for reasons detailed in Table A.1.[1]

In the A-Religion data we have also coded information about the primary religious family of 1171 groups. This information is missing for twenty-nine groups; the twelve groups listed in Table A.1, where there was insufficient information to reliably code religions, and an additional seventeen groups

---

[1] In addition we flagged for revision of the AMAR sample frame the Makhuwa/Metto in Madagascar (coded Animist) and Kabre/Kabiye in Togo. Our research into these groups suggests they may be a single group in each country rather than two separate groups in each country.

where we have information about group religions but cannot distinguish which group religion should be considered primary. Table A.2 lists the groups and their religions that we could code for religions but not distinguish the primary religion.

In most cases religion is only one of many identity markers that define a group. However, in some cases religion is the primary marker of a group that distinguishes it from all other groups. Table A.3 lists the countries and groups where this is the case.

TABLE A.1. *AMAR groups not coded in the A-Religion data*

Country	Group	Reason for exclusion
Angola	Nganguela	Missing info on religion
Burkina Faso	Nininsi	Missing info on religion
Cameroon	Eastern Nigritic	Missing info on the group
Central African Republic	Kare/Kari	Missing info on religion
Congo, Rep. of	Sanga	Missing info on religion
Gabon	Njebi	Missing info on religion
Gabon	Orungou and Nkomi	Sub-dialects of Myene. Missing info on groups.
Ghana	Assin	Missing info on religion
India	Officially Backward Classes	Umbrella group – not coded for religion
India	Forward Classes	Umbrella group – not coded for religion
Suriname	Mixed	Missing info on group
Taiwan	Aborigine	Taiwan not coded in
	Taiwanese	A-Religion
	Mainland Chinese	

TABLE A.2. *Groups whose primary religion is not coded in the A-Religion data*

Country	Group	Religions
Angola	Nkumbi	Christianity, Animism
	Nyaneka-Humbe	Christianity, Animism
Austria	Yugoslavs	Islam (Sunni), Christianity (Roman Catholic, Orthodox)
Burkina Faso	Busansi	Islam, Christianity (Roman Catholic, Protestant), Animism

Country	Group	Religions
	North-western Samo/Samo Matya	Christianity, Animism
Central African Republic	Riverene-Sango	Christianity, Animism
Democratic Republic of the Congo	Kivu	Islam, Christianity (Catholic, Protestant)
Ireland	Asians	Islam, Buddhism, Hinduism, Christianity
Republic of Congo	Mbete/Mbeti	Christianity, Animism
Spain	Eastern Europeans	Christianity (Roman Catholic, Orthodox), Islam (Sunni)
Switzerland	Spanish	Christianity (Roman Catholic), No religion
	Yugoslavs	Christianity (Roman Catholic, Orthodox), Islam (Sunni)
Tanzania	Rungwa	Christianity, Animism
	Subi	Animism, Christianity
Uganda	Rwenzururu	Christianity (Independent), Animism
	South Asians	Hinduism, Islam (Shi'i)
Yemen	South Asian	Christianity, Hinduism

TABLE A.3. *AMAR groups whose primary identity marker is religion*

Country	Group
Argentina	Jews
Armenia	Yazidi
Bahrain	Shi'i Bahraini/Baharna
	Sunni Bahraini
Bangladesh	Bengali Hindu
	Bengali Muslims
Belgium	Muslims
Bulgaria	Pomaks/Muslim Bulgarian
Denmark	Muslims
France	Jews
	Muslim
Germany	Jews
Greece	Thracian Muslims

(continued)

TABLE A.3. *(continued)*

Country	Group
India	Jains
	Kashmiri Muslims
	Muslims
	Sikhs
	Syrian/Malabar Christians
Iran	Baha'is
	Christians
Iraq	Arab Shi'i
	Christians
	Sunni-Arab
Israel	Druze
	Jewish
Jordan	Christians
Lebanon	Alawis
	Druze
	Greek Catholic
	Greek Orthodox
	Maronite
	Shi'is
	Sunni Muslims
Mauritius	Hindu
	Muslim
Montenegro	Bosniak/Muslim
Nepal	Muslim
Netherlands	Muslims
Norway	Muslims
Oman	Ibadhi Muslim
	Sunni
Pakistan	Hindus
Philippines	Lowland Christ. Malay
	Muslim Malay
Russia	Jewish
Saudi Arabia	Shi'is
	Sunni Arabs
Serbia	Sandzak Muslims/Bosniaks
Sri Lanka	Moor/Muslims
Sudan	Darfur Black Muslims
Suriname	Hindustani
Sweden	Muslims

Country	Group
Syria	Alawi
	Christians
	Druze
	Sunni-Arab
Thailand	Malay-Muslims
Ukraine	Jews
United Kingdom	Jews
(UK) Northern	Catholics
Ireland	Protestants
United States	Jewish
Yemen	Shi'i Arabs
	Sunni Arabs

TABLE A.4. *Politically dominant AMAR groups who differ in* Religious Family *from the demographic majority*

Country	Group	Dominant Group Religious Family (A-Religion)	Demographic Majority Religious Family (Brown and James, 2018)
China	Han Chinese	Syncretic (Animism, Buddhism, Taoism)	No religion
India	Forward Classes	Not coded	Hindu
Japan	Japanese	Syncretic (Buddhism and Shinto)	Buddhism
Laos	Lao Loum	Syncretic (Buddhism and Animism)	Buddhism
Lesotho	Sotho	Syncretic (Animism and Christianity Roman Catholic)	Christianity
N. Korea	Korean	Buddhism	No religion
Netherlands	Dutch	Christianity (Roman Catholic)	No religion
Singapore	Chinese	Syncretic (Buddhism and Taoism)	Buddhism
Vietnam	Vietnamese (Kinh)	Buddhism	No religion

Finally, Tables A.4 and A.5 respectively list the groups that are the single politically dominant group in a country, but do not share religious family or religious sect with the demographic majority population.

TABLE A.5. *Politically dominant AMAR groups who differ in* Religious Sect *from the demographic majority*

Country	Group	Dominant Group Religious Sect (A-Religion)	Demographic Majority Religious Sect (Brown and James, 2018)
Bahrain	Sunni Bahraini	(Islam) Sunni	(Islam) Shi'i
Oman	Ibadhi Muslim	(Islam) Ibadhi	(Islam) Sunni
Suriname	Creole	(Christianity) Roman Catholic	(Christianity) Protestant
Syria	Alawi	(Islam) Shi'i	(Islam) Sunni

Appendix B

Formal Representation of the Theory of *Alternatives in Mobilization*

This appendix accompanies the theory of *Alternatives in Mobilization* proposed in Chapter 3, showing the calculations of expected utilities and derivatives of expected utilities calculated to find endpoints, maxima and minima. Minority and majority utilities in identity mobilization are determined by the following factors:

1. The population balance (X) is defined as the politically dominant majority (hereafter majority) proportional demographic size (C_{maj}) minus the politically non-dominant minority (hereafter minority) proportional demographic size (C_{min}), or $C_{maj} - C_{min} = X$. For simplification $C_{maj} + C_{min} = 1$ though in reality there can be more than two groups in society. In turn, X ranges between $-1 < X < 1$. As the population balance increasingly favors one group over the other, the cost/benefit to each group changes in a non-linear fashion as specified by X^{α}. Finally, majority and minority utility deriving from the population balance mirror each other.
2. With respect to a new identity mobilization we assume both majorities and minorities are risk-averse but unequally so. Specifically, majority utility grows faster than does minority utility. Thus we take the square root of the absolute value[1] of the majority utility, while minority risk aversion is modeled as the log of minority utility plus one[2] because $\log(-X^{\alpha} + 1) < \mathrm{sqrt}(|X^{\alpha}|)$.
3. Furthermore, affecting the decision to engage in alternative mobilization, there is a social salience cost/benefit aspect (p) to identity mobilization that denotes how available each identity is for mobilization.

---

[1] We take the absolute value because the square root cannot be taken of a negative number.
[2] 1 is added so that the log can be taken if the minority is demographically larger than the majority and X is negative.

B.I SEGMENTED CLEAVAGES

Segmented identity cleavages are characterized by an additional feature that is a population balance tipping point Y.

1. The population balance tipping point ($Y = 1$) exists where internal outbidding challenges to majority leadership, targeting a segmented minority, changes between threatening and not threatening the majority group's absolute hold on power. This tipping point is:

$$\begin{cases} Y = 0 & \text{where } -1 < X \leq \mu \\ Y = 1 & \text{where } 1 > X \geq \mu \end{cases} \tag{B.1}$$

Thus the majority utility function for initiating a new identity mobilization when cleavages are segmented (*Se*) is defined as:

$$U(M_{maj}|Se) = \sqrt{|X^{\alpha} \times Y|} \tag{B.2}$$

and the minority utility function for initiating a new identity mobilization when cleavages are segmented (*Se*) is defined as:

$$U(M_{min}|Se) = \ln(-X^{\alpha} \times (1 - Y) + 1) \tag{B.3}$$

B.I.I Expected Utility

Where cleavages are segmented (*Se*) the majority expected utility for engaging in alternative identity mobilization is:

$$E(M_{maj}|Se) = p \times \sqrt{|X^{\alpha} \times Y|} + (1 - p) \times \ln(-X^{\alpha} \times (1 - Y) + 1) \tag{B.4}$$

When the majority is large compared to the minority so that Y is 1, this gives us:

$$E(M_{maj}|Se) = p \times \sqrt{|X^{\alpha}|} \text{ where } 1 > X \geq \mu \tag{B.5}$$

with a first simplified derivative of:

$$f'(X) = \frac{\alpha p \sqrt{|X^{\alpha}|}}{2X} \tag{B.6}$$

In turn where the minority is increasingly large so that Y is 0, the expectation for majority utility is:

$$E(M_{maj}|Se) = (1 - p) \times \ln(-X^{\alpha} + 1) \text{ where } -1 < X \leq \mu \tag{B.7}$$

with a simplified first derivative of:

$$f'(X) = \frac{\alpha(p - 1)X^{\alpha-1}}{X^{\alpha} - 1} \tag{B.8}$$

According to the functions the values at the endpoints are:

$E(M_{maj}|Se)$ approaches $p\sqrt{1}$ when X approaches 1

$E(M_{maj}|Se) = p\sqrt{\left(\frac{1}{3}\right)^3}$ at $X = \frac{1}{3}$ from the right

$E(M_{maj}|Se) = (1-p)\ln\left(\frac{26}{27}\right)$, at $X = \frac{1}{3}$ from the left

$E(M_{maj}|Se) = 0$ when $X = 0$

This means $E(M_{maj}|Se)$ has a global minimum at $X = -1$, a global maximum at $X = 1$, a local maximum at $X = 0$, and a jump at $X = \frac{1}{3}$
The jump in the utility at $X = \frac{1}{3}$ is:

$$p\sqrt{\left(\frac{1}{3}\right)^3} - \left((1-p)\ln\left(\frac{26}{27}\right)\right) \tag{B.9}$$

or

$$\left(\frac{1}{3}\right)^{\frac{3}{2}} p + (p-1)\ln\left(\frac{26}{27}\right) \tag{B.10}$$

B.2 SHARED IDENTITY AND MOBILIZATION

The shared identity that we focus on in this book can also be a cross-cutting identity provided that its cross-fragmentation fulfills the following condition:

$$R_{maj} + R_{min} \geq C_{maj} \tag{B.11}$$

Where R_{maj} and R_{min} respectively account for the majority and minority demographic shares of the largest secondary shared cleavage segment and C_{maj} accounts for the demographic share of the majority segment of the primary cleavage.

Provided that this condition is satisfied, the minority utility calculation is defined as the proportional population size of the minority (C_{min}) in relation to the majority/minority population balance X or $\frac{C_{min}}{X}$.

Thus, the minority utility in mobilization of the shared (alternatively cross-cutting) cleavage (Sh) then can be stated as:

$$U(M_{min}|Sh) = \ln\left(\left[-X^\alpha + \left(\frac{1-X}{2X}\right)\right] \times (1-Y) + 1\right) \tag{B.12}$$

Majority utility in mobilization of the shared cleavage (*Sh*) is:

$$U(M_{\mathrm{maj}}|Sh) = \sqrt{\left(\left|X^\alpha - \left(\frac{\mathrm{I} - X}{2X}\right)\right|\right)} \times Y \tag{B.13}$$

The minority likelihood of success in mobilizing the shared identity cleavage and accounting for the probability that this mobilization is not successful, the minority expected utility in mobilizing the alternative (challenger) cleavage coalition or the CWC is:

$$E(M_{\mathrm{min}}|Sh) = p \times \ln\left(\left[-X^\alpha + \left(\frac{\mathrm{I} - X}{2X}\right)\right] \times (\mathrm{I} - Y) + \mathrm{I}\right)$$
$$+ (\mathrm{I} - p) \times \sqrt{\left(\left|X^\alpha - \left(\frac{\mathrm{I} - X}{2X}\right)\right|\right)} \times Y \tag{B.14}$$

When *Y* is o because *X* is in the range $-\mathrm{I} < X \le \mu$, this gives the minority the following utility for mobilizing the alternative CW cleavage:

$$E(M_{\mathrm{min}}|Sh) = p \times \ln\left(\left[-X^\alpha + \left(\frac{\mathrm{I} - X}{2X}\right)\right] + \mathrm{I}\right) \tag{B.15}$$

The derivative of this function is:

$$f'(X) = \frac{p(2\alpha X^{\alpha+\mathrm{I}} + \mathrm{I})}{(2X^{\alpha+2} - X^2 - X)} \tag{B.16}$$

In contrast, when *Y* is I because *X* is in the interval $\mathrm{I} < X \ge \mu$ the minority utility in mobilizing the alternate CWC cleavage is:

$$E(M_{\mathrm{min}}|Sh) = (\mathrm{I} - p) \times \sqrt{\left|X^\alpha - \left(\frac{\mathrm{I} - X}{2X}\right)\right|} \tag{B.17}$$

The simplified derivative is:

$$f'(X) = -\frac{(p - \mathrm{I})(2X^{\alpha+\mathrm{I}} + X - \mathrm{I})(2\alpha X^{\alpha+\mathrm{I}} + \mathrm{I}}{8X^3|X^\alpha - \frac{\mathrm{I}-x}{2X}|^{\frac{3}{2}}} \tag{B.18}$$

The minority utility in mobilizing the CWC is highest where the minority population is increasingly equal in size to the majority population (*X* approaches o). Thus $E(M_{\mathrm{min}}|Sh)$ is decreasing in the interval $[\mathrm{o}, \frac{\mathrm{I}}{3}]$ as a function of *X*. There is a substantial discontinuity at $X = \frac{\mathrm{I}}{3}$ where the utility drops. Following the drop the minority utility in mobilizing CWC along the alternate cleavage is negative in the interval $[\frac{1}{3}, 1]$. This negative curve has a maximum at $X = 0.647799$ because of the absolute value necessitated by the square root, but the derivative does not exist (is infinite) at this point.

According to the functions where $\alpha = 3$ and $X = \frac{1}{3}$ the values at the endpoints are as follows:

$$E(M_{\min}|Sh) = \infty \text{ when } X = 0$$

$$E(M_{\min}|Sh) = p \times \ln\left(-\left(\tfrac{1}{3}\right)^3 + 2\right) \text{ or } p \times \ln\left(\tfrac{53}{27}\right) \text{ at } X = \tfrac{1}{3} \text{ from the left}$$

$$E(M_{\min}|Sh)$$
$$= (1 - p) \times \sqrt{\left|\left(\tfrac{1}{3}\right)^3 - 1\right|} \text{ or } (1 - p) \times \sqrt{\tfrac{26}{27}} \text{ at } X = \tfrac{1}{3} \text{ from the right}$$

Thus at $X = 1/3$ there is a drop from $(p) \times \ln\left(\tfrac{53}{27}\right)$ to $-(1 - p) \times \sqrt{\tfrac{26}{27}}$.

Finally, $E(M_{\min}|Sh) = (1 - p)$ where $X = 1$

B.3 MODEL VARIATIONS

A principal benefit of formalization is the clarity and internal validity of the argument where predictions necessarily follow from the assumptions made about properties of identity cleavages. This feature, however, begs the question of how the predictions would change if those assumptions were substantially altered.

Because the form makes clear statements about the inputs that affect the outcome it is simple to vary inputs into specific parts of the argument for the purpose of comparing predictions. In Chapter 3 in the section about segmented cleavages, for instance, we illustrated the comparative statics depicting change in the basic majority utility as a result of varying the exogenous costs and benefits of identity mobilization (captured by the probability of success or p).[3]

---

[3] One example of exogenous costs in our model is salience of identity that recent research shows has an important effect on outcomes (Isaacs, 2017) and changes over time and in response to prior political competition between identity groups, especially violent conflict (Kaufman, 2001), institutional changes (Posner, 2005), changes in historical conditions (Lipset and Rokkan, 1967; Kroneberg and Wimmer, 2012), or colonial institutions (Laitin, 1986). We explored further the role of exogenous costs and benefits, with a special emphasis on salience of identity and how this salience comes about, in the case accounts in Chapters 5 and 6. We then returned to this topic in the concluding chapter (Chapter 7) where we questioned the idea of varying salience and ask if the observed phenomenon is better described as activation rather than salience. Similarly, it is easy to see in the fully specified argument accounting for shared identity that exogenous factors – including salience of cleavages – likely have a substantial influence on the utility calculation of the minority. However, we leave the formalization of this idea for future research.

Another question concerns the presence of a tipping point (Y). When identity groups share at least one cleavage the literature suggests zero-sum contestations are reduced (Lipset, 1981; Rokkan, 1967; Lijphart, 1977, 1999; Selway, 2011a). Thus, when identities are shared, majority outbidding mechanisms are more difficult to activate presumably even when the minority is very small. Therefore, where at least one identity is shared, minority expected utility might better reflect reality without the tipping point – or with a different tipping point.

Similar questions arise with respect to the risk preferences of leaders of majority and minority groups. Decades of research suggest it is unlikely that minority leaders are always risk-taking (Birnir, 2011). However, their risk preferences might vary or their faith in the shared cleavage might render them risk-neutral with respect to majorities. Majority leaders, in turn, might be risk-takers if intra-majority competition is high and identity cleavage mobilization has worked well in the past or they might be risk-neutral because mixed strategies (identity and other types of mobilization) have worked equally well in the past.

Model choices including the selection of logarithm and square root to represent risk preferences of minorities versus majorities arbitrarily pertain to the story we think most accurately represents the change in incentives for mobilization as conditioned by sharing of identity and relative group size. The same is true for the setting of a tipping point where our utility calculations change. Therefore, it is useful to contemplate model variations and how conclusions might change with different choices.

Briefly, we selected logarithm and square root to represent divergent risk preferences because these are the simplest choices that we think most accurately illustrate divergent risk preferences of minorities and majorities on average. Similarly, taking the absolute value of the square root and adding 1 to the calculation of the logarithm to avoid creating uninformative singularities is a choice – though more mathematical in nature. Finally, the tipping point is a straightforward way to add the element of change to the story of incentives driven by segmentation or cross-cutting of cleavages and their respective sizes.

However, all of these choices are made with regard to each other. If we remove one element – such as the tipping point, the minority expected utility calculation becomes:

$$E(M_{min}|Sh) = (p) \times \ln\left(\left(-X^{\alpha} + \left(\frac{1-X}{2X}\right) + 1\right)\right)$$
$$+ (1-p) \times \sqrt{\left(\left|X^{\alpha} - \left(\frac{1-X}{2X}\right)\right|\right)} \qquad \text{(B.19)}$$

Alternatively if we remove only the risk assumptions the expected utility calculation for the minority when Y is 0 is:

$$E(M_{min}|Sh) = (p) \times \left(-X^{\alpha} + \left(\frac{1-X}{2X}\right)\right) \qquad \text{(B.20)}$$

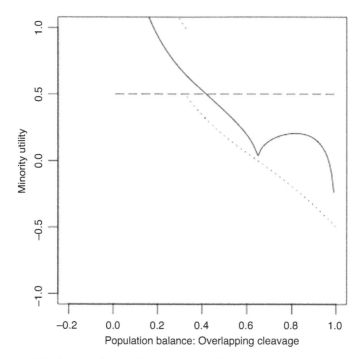

FIGURE B.1 Model variations. Minority expected utility without a tipping point (solid line), without risk assumptions (dotted lines), without tipping or risk (dashed line), as *Population Balance* changes from 0 to 1, among groups that share an identity

and

$$E(M_{\min}|Sh) = (1-p) \times \left(X^\alpha - \left(\frac{1-X}{2X}\right)\right) \tag{B.21}$$

when Y is 1.

Finally, without either the assumption of risk preferences or tipping the minority utility is:

$$E(M_{\min}|Sh) = (p) \times \left(-X^\alpha + \left(\frac{1-X}{2X}\right)\right) + (1-p) \times \left(X^\alpha - \left(\frac{1-X}{2X}\right)\right) \tag{B.22}$$

To compare our choices with these model alternatives, Figure B.1 graphs the alternative utility calculations setting $\alpha = 3$ and $p = 0.5$.

The figure nicely illustrates the utility of each assumption in conjunction with other assumptions. First, when excluding only the tipping point the risk assumptions jointly distort the picture away from the story we wish to tell. Specifically, in this variation while the minority utility is decreasing as the population balance approaches 1 (large majority) the apparent temporary increase is an artifact of the square root that is the risk assumption associated with the majority.

In turn, looking at the dotted lines only, excluding only the risk assumptions, this alternative most closely approximates our story but the change in utility is more abrupt and more linear than the change in incentives we believe occurs. Finally, the straight dashed line illustrates a model variant excluding both the risk assumptions and the tipping point, and is wholly uninformative. Therefore, we are satisfied that the model as we present it here is a good representation of our story about changing minority incentives as conditioned by sharing of identity and relative group size and that each assumption we make is appropriate for that purpose. However, we also see this model as a tool for exploring further how predictions about political outcomes, as a function of demography and identity intersection, change with different assumptions.

Appendix C

Transformation of RELAC Data to Group Level to Match with the A-Religion Data Set

The material in this appendix supports and expands upon the details of the analysis in Chapter 4. The first section addresses the ethnic coding and transformation of the RELAC data from the organizational to the group level. The second section addresses the translation of RELAC to the A-Religion data.

C.1 PROBING THE DATA: FROM ORGANIZATIONS TO GROUPS

C.1.1 Collapsing Organizations

Table C.1 lists the fifty-one ethnic groups that in any given year are represented by more than one organization and whose distinct organizational observations are, therefore, collapsed to the group level by year decreasing the number of observations in that year. Not all of the fifty-one groups are relevant to the inquiry as explained in Chapter 4. For instance, the regression analysis predicts claim making by political minorities only. However, table C.1.1 also shows politically dominant represented by more than one organization to give the reader a better sense of the full data. Specifically, the largest number of organizations representing a group is in 1984 when six organizations represented the Pashtuns in Afghanistan. One additional group (Palestinian Arabs) is represented by five organizations in any given year.[1] One additional group (the Somali) is represented by four organizations in additional four group years.[2] More commonly an additional nine groups are represented by three organizations over various numbers of group years each.[3] Among these, the

---

[1] Bringing the total of organization-group-years to ten observations in the data.

[2] This brings the total of organization group years to fourteen.

[3] For a total of forty-nine observations of organization-group-year or twenty-seven additional group-years.

TABLE C.1. *Groups represented by more than one organization in a given conflict and year*

Location	Group
Afghanistan	Pashtuns Tajiks Uzbeks
Algeria	Arabs
Angola	Bakongo Cabindan Mayombe
Argentina	Whites/mestizos
Bosnia-Herzegovina	Serbs
Burundi	Hutu
Cambodia	Khmer
Chad	Toubou Zaghawa, Bideyat
Congo	Lari/Bakongo
Croatia	Serbs
Ethiopia	Muslim Eritreans Somali (Ogaden) Tigray
Georgia	Georgians
Guatemala	Ladinos Maya
India	Indigenous Tripuri Manipuri
Iraq	Kurds Sunni Arabs
Israel	Palestinian Arabs
Lebanon	Maronite Christians Sunni Arab
Liberia	Gio Krahn (Guere) Mano
Libya	Arabs
Mali	Tuareg
Myanmar (Burma)	Kayin (Karens) Shan

Location	Group
Pakistan	Baluchis
	Pashtuns
Peru	Indigenous peoples
	Whites/mestizos
Philippines	Moro
Serbia (Yugoslavia)	Croats
Somalia	Somali
Sri Lanka	Sri Lankan Tamils
Sudan	Fur
	Masalit
	Nuer
	Zaghawa
Tajikistan	Tajiks
Uganda	Baganda
	Far North-west Nile
	(Kakwa-Nubian, Madi, Lugbara, Alur)
	Langi/Acholi
Zimbabwe (Rhodesia)	Africans

Khmer in Cambodia are represented by three organizations for the longest time period – ten group years, next are the Moro in the Philippines for five group years, and other groups for fewer years. Most commonly the remaining thirty-nine groups (out of fifty-one) are represented by two organizations in any given year.[4]

The following Table C.2[5] compares the proportions of groups claiming religious incompatibility by the above 51 groups represented by multiple organizations in the expanded RELAC data, to the proportion that claim religious incompatibility among the remaining 156 groups represented by a single organization in any given year during conflict. The cross-sectional table shows that minority groups represented by multiple organizations in the data are statistically significantly more likely to claim religious incompatibility with the state than are minorities represented by a single organization, and the difference in proportions is greater within religion.

Next, using the final collapsed data that includes population figures, we examined the size differences between groups that in the ethnically identified

[4] For an additional 205 organization-group-year observations and 124 group years.
[5] Because we wanted to check the RELAC data before matching with A-Religion, for this comparison we used RELAC information on SideA and SideB religion to separate out organizations representing groups of the same religion as the majority.

TABLE C.2. *Ethnically identified RELAC data: t-test of the differences in proportions of groups claiming religious incompatibility, by type of organizational representation*

	Claims of religious incompatibility	
Representation type	Across religion	Within religion
Single organization	0.320	0.144
Multiple organizations	0.490	0.333
p-value	0.037	0.053

TABLE C.3. *Final data: t-test of the differences in proportional group size, by type of organizational representation*

	Size	
Representation type	Across religion	Within religion
Single organization	0.163	0.138
Multiple organizations	0.266	0.155
p-value	0.033	0.684

RELAC data were represented by many organizations as opposed to groups represented by a single organization. Unsurprisingly, the *t*-tests in Table C.3 show that groups that are represented by multiple organizations tend to be larger though not significantly so within religion.

Taking these two observations together – groups that are represented by multiple organizations (to be collapsed) tend to be larger and more likely to claim religious incompatibility – we do not think collapsing organizations to the group level for groups represented by multiple organizations presents a problem for our analysis.

C.1.2 Expanding Group Observations

We next turn to the expansion of the data from the organizational to the group level. In the RELAC data forty-six organizations represent multiple groups to be expanded to the group level. Of those, the majority or twenty-three organizations represent two groups, an additional twelve organizations represent three groups, eight organizations represent four groups, one organization represents six groups, and one organization represents fourteen groups. This last organization, representing fourteen ethnic groups, is the Forces of the Caucasus Emirate. In the practice of putting together the final data this organization does not get fully expanded to all fourteen ethnic groups because of differences in group definition and inclusion in the ACD2 and A-Religion as discussed below. Specifically, in the A-Religion data, the Forces of the Caucasus Emirate represents ten socially relevant ethnic groups. Furthermore, because this organization claims religious incompatibility with the majority and none of the groups share religion with the majority, its expansion does not support the CWC hypothesis and we leave it as is in the data. Another high group count organization, the Islamic State (IS) over time representing multiple groups, is a multicountry organization and as such is not relevant here. Table C.4 lists all the multiethnic organizations and the groups they represent in a given country.[6]

Some of the organizations enumerated above do not get fully expanded in the final data because of thresholds for entry into the A-Religion data as explained below. Even so to ensure that the expansion from the organizational to the group level for groups in the multiethnic organization that are included does not unduly support the hypothesis we compared the proportions of groups claiming religious incompatibility between organizations representing multiple ethnic groups to that of organizations representing single ethnic groups and by sharing of religion. The *t*-tests are detailed in Table C.5. The table shows that groups represented in multiethnic organizations are statistically significantly more likely to claim religious incompatibility than are groups that are the sole groups represented by an organization, though this difference is not statistically significant within religion.

Next, using the final data we examine size differences between groups that are represented by multiethnic organizations to that of groups represented by single ethnic organizations. Perhaps unsurprisingly groups that are represented by multiethnic organizations tend to be smaller overall than groups that are the sole ethnic group represented by an organization. This is true overall and also within religion though the cross-sectional difference between groups within religion is not statistically significant.

Again taking together these two insights that groups in organizations to be expanded because they represent multiple groups are both smaller and more likely to claim religious incompatibility than are groups represented by single ethnic organizations suggests that this manipulation of the data is unlikely to manufacture a type one error. Notably these observations are not statistically significant within religion but the coefficients have the same relationship suggesting that the lack of significance is more to do with a lower number of cases than fundamentally different group characteristics. Even so, in the empirical analysis in Chapter 4 we run robustness tests accounting specifically for countries where expanded organizational groups support the hypothesis.

Group-Level Data: Connecting Ethnic RELAC Data to A-Religion Data Set
For the most part, the ACD2 and the A-Religion data enumerate groups in the same way because the A-Religion data is based on the AMAR data, and

---

[6] Some multiethnic organizations in the ethnically identified RELAC data are cross-national and are, therefore, not included in Table C.4.

TABLE C.4. *List of ethnically identified RELAC organizations representing more than one ethnic group, and the groups they represent*

Country	Organization	Group
Afghanistan	Jam'iyyat-i Islami-yi Afghanistan	Pashtuns
		Tajiks
		Uzbeks
	UIFSA	Hazara
		Pashtuns
		Tajiks
		Uzbeks
Angola	FLEC-R	Bakongo
		Cabindan Mayombe
	FLEC-FAC	Bakongo
		Cabindan Mayombe
Cambodia	KR	Khmer
		Khmer Loeu (various indigenous minorities)
Chad	FAP	Arabs
		Muslim Sahel groups
		Toubou
	GUNT	Arabs
		Muslim Sahel groups
		Sara
		Toubou
	MPS	Hadjerai
		Zaghawa, Bideyat
	UFDD	Arabs
		Toubou
		Zaghawa, Bideyat
	AN	Arabs
		Tamas
		Toubou
		Zaghawa, Bideyat
	UFR	Arabs
		Toubou
		Zaghawa, Bideyat
DR Congo (Zaire)	FLNC	Luba Shaba
		Lunda-Yeke

Country	Organization	Group
	MLC	Mbandja Mongo Ngbaka Ngbandi
Ethiopia	EDU	Amhara Tigray
	EPRDF	Amhara Oromo Tigray
	EPLF	Christian Eritreans Muslim Eritreans
	SALF	Oromo Somali (Ogaden)
India	CPI-Maoist	Other backward classes/castes Scheduled castes Scheduled tribes
	UNLFW	Assamese (non-SC/ST/OBCs) Bodo Manipuri Naga
Iraq	Ansar al-Islam	Kurds Sunni Arabs
Ivory Coast	FRCI	Northerners (Mande and Voltaic/Gur) Southern Mande
Lebanon	NSF	Druze Sunnis (Arab)
Liberia	NPFL	Gio Mano
	INPFL	Gio Mano
	LURD	Krahn (Guere) Mandingo
Myanmar (Burma)	CPB	Bamar (Barman) Buddhist Arakanese Chinese Wa

(continued)

TABLE C.4. *(continued)*

Country	Organization	Group
Nepal	CPN-M	Adibasi Janajati Caste Hill Hindu Elite Newars
Nicaragua	Contras/FDN	Afronicaraguans Miskitos Sumus Whites/mestizos
Peru	Sendero Luminoso	Indigenous peoples of the Andes Whites/mestizos
	MRTA	Indigenous peoples of the Andes Whites/mestizos
Russia (Soviet Union)	Forces of the Caucasus Emirate	Adyghe Avars Balkars Chechens Cherkess Dargins Ingush Kabardins Karachai Kumyks Laks Lezgins Nogai Tabasarans
Rwanda	ALiR	Hutu Tutsi
South Africa	ANC	Asians Blacks Coloreds
South Sudan	SSDM/A – Cobra Faction	Anyuak Murle
Sudan	SPLM/A	Beja Nuer Dinka Nuba Nuer Other Southern groups Shilluk

Country	Organization	Group
	SLM/A	Fur Masalit Zaghawa
	NRF	Fur Masalit Zaghawa
	SLM/A-Unity	Fur Masalit Zaghawa
	Republic of South Sudan	Dinka Nuer Other Southern groups Shilluk
Syria	Syrian insurgents	Kurds Sunni Arabs
Tajikistan	UTO	Pamiri Tajiks Tajiks
	IMU	Kyrgyz Tajiks Uzbeks
Uganda	NRA	Baganda South-westerners (Ankole, Banyoro, Toro, Banyarwanda)

	ADF	Far North-west Nile
		  (Kakwa-Nubian, Madi,
		  Lugbara, Alur)
		South-westerners (Ankole,
		  Banyoro, Toro)

Yemen (North)	NDF	Northerners Sunni Shafi'i (Arab)
	AQAP	Southerners Sunni Shafi'i (Arab)

the ACD2 is based on the EPR, which is conceptually an independent subset of ethnic groups in AMAR. However, there are a few instances where either AMAR groups are more or less disaggregated than EPR groups. This stems from the fact that the AMAR data code groups independent of their political mobilization, and the EPR codes groups only as they mobilize politically.

TABLE C.5. *Ethnically identified RELAC data: t-test of the differences in proportions of groups claiming religious incompatibility, by type of organizational representation*

	Claims of religious incompatibility	
Representation type	Across religion	Within religion
Single ethnic organizations	0.238	0.187
Multi ethnic organizations	0.490	0.196
p-value	0.000	0.902

TABLE C.6. *Final data: t-test of the differences in proportional group size, by type of organizational representation*

	Size	
Representation type	Across religion	Within religion
Single ethnic organizations	0.230	0.167
Multi ethnic organizations	0.137	0.120
p-value	0.009	0.195

In instances where the two, AMAR and EPR diverge, the A-Religion data, and thus the data used for testing in Chapter 4 follow the AMAR data listing of groups. Specifically where the AMAR data are more disaggregated, we add observations. An example is the case of Nepal. In the ethnically identified RELAC data the CPN-M in Nepal represents the Caste Hill Hindu Elite, the Adibasi Janajati, and the Newar. In AMAR the Adibasi Janajati are coded as eight different minorities. Only some of the Adibasi Janajati share religion with the majority while others do not. Even so we account specifically for Nepal in the empirical analysis to make sure that this transformation does not unduly support the CWC hypothesis. In a few cases the EPR is more disaggregated than AMAR. In those cases the ACD2 matches an organization with more than a single ethnic group. Then we carry over the RELAC data via the more aggregate AMAR group. One example is Sudan. ACD2 disaggregates the Fur, Zaghawa, and Masalit tribes that AMAR codes as Darfur Black Muslims. In ACD2 each of these is associated with the NRF, SLM/A, the SLM/AMM, and SLM/A-Unity. In addition, the Zaghawa are associated with JEM. For each group we collapse the organizational observations to the ACD2 group level. Furthermore, because the A-Religion data are coded for a single group representing the three, we collapse these three groups to the level of the single AMAR group, Darfur Black Muslims. Tables C.7 and C.10 respectively list the groups that are less aggregated in the A-Religion data (RELAC expanded to the A-Religion group level) and less aggregated in the ACD2 data (RELAC collapsed to the

TABLE C.7. *Groups that are more aggregate in the A-Religion data*

ACD2 Group Id	Country	ACD2 group	A-Religion numcode	A-Religion group
48405000	Congo	Lari/Bakongo	48406	Kongo
48409000	Congo	NA		
66601200	Israel	Palestinian Arabs	66603	Palestinian
66601000	Israel	Palestinians (Arab)		
9303000	Nicaragua	Miskitos	9302	Indigenous
9305000	Nicaragua	Sumus		Peoples
36543000	Russia (Soviet Union)	Balkars	36511	Karachay
36554000	Russia (Soviet Union)	Karachai		
36540000	Russia (Soviet Union)	Adyghe	36542	Circassians
36544000	Russia (Soviet Union)	Cherkess		
36528000	Russia (Soviet Union)	Kabardins		
45105060	Sierra Leone	Temne	45104	Temne
45105000	Sierra Leone	Northern groups (Temne, Limba)		
62504000	Sudan	Dinka	62501	Southern
62514000	Sudan	Masalit		Sudanese
62508000	Sudan	Nuer		
62511000	Sudan	Other Southern groups		
62513000	Sudan	Shilluk		
62505000	Sudan	Fur	62504	Darfur Black
62515000	Sudan	Zaghawa		Muslims
50011000	Uganda	South-westerners (Ankole, Banyoro, Toro, Banyarwanda)	50010	Banyoro
50011090	Uganda	South-westerners (Ankole, Banyoro, Toro)		
67806000	Yemen	Northern Shafi'i	67901	Sunni Arabs
67807000	Yemen	Southern Shafi'i		
67802200	Yemen	Sunni Shafi'i (Arab)		

TABLE C.8. *t-test of the differences in proportional size (within a country) between groups that are matched directly with a single group and groups that are collapsed to the A-Religion group (more aggregate in the A-Religion data)*

Group type	Prop. size
Direct match	0.190
Collapsed	0.162
p-value	0.504

TABLE C.9. *t-test of the differences in proportional size (within a country) between groups that are matched directly with a single group and groups that are expanded to multiple A-Religion groups (less aggregate in the A-Religion data)*

Group type	Prop. size
Direct match	0.211
Expanded	0.086
p-value	0.000

A-Religion group level). To examine whether and then how the groups that are expanded or collapsed differ significantly from the overall sample we again ran *t*-tests reported in Tables C.10 and C.8.

Since RELAC and A-Religion match includes numcodes and groups in A-Religion are coded for size, we can directly check the size differences between collapsed or expanded and all other groups.[7]

Table C.10 lists groups that are less aggregate in the A-Religion data than in the ACD2 data and are therefore expanded to the level of the A-Religion data (i.e. one ACD2 id is matched with more than one A-Religion numcode).

The analysis in Table C.9 of the size of groups in Table C.10 that are less aggregate in the A-Religion data and are therefore expanded, suggests that expanded groups are on average smaller.

As per the discussion of Type I error in Chapter 4, this discovery is potentially problematic if the small groups to be expanded are primarily peaceful and

---

[7] The difference in size checked in this test is absolute rather than relative to the largest group – which is the measure used in the test in the chapter – because we want to examine all units before they are collapsed or expanded to the group level.

do not share religious affiliation with the majority. Therefore, Table C.10 also includes columns accounting for whether the group claims religious incompatibility with the majority at any point in the data and whether it shares religious family with the majority. The table shows that seven of the (small) groups that share religion do claim religious incompatibility (contrary to our prediction), and three of the (small) groups that do not share family with the majority do claim religious incompatibility. Therefore, this transformation seems balanced (supporting and not supporting) and unproblematic. However, to be on the safe side, we run some robustness checks accounting separately for possibly problematic countries like Nepal and Uganda in the regression analysis in Chapter 4.

While we take every precaution here not to bias our results when combining different data sets, we also think that the mechanisms we propose should be studied further at the sub-national level, especially in large and diverse countries such as Nepal, Uganda, India, and Russia.

Finally, Table C.11 lists the remaining nineteen RELAC cases (countries and minority groups) that are coded by ACD2 as having ethnic actors but are excluded from the A-Religion data. The table also lists the reason for the exclusion, in addition to the group size and religion, and the majority religion.[8]

Two of the groups (the Anjouan (Nzwani) in Comoros and the Manipuri in India) do not meet AMAR ethnic group criteria. Both groups are geographically concentrated but internally diverse and do not clearly share a culture that makes them consider themselves ethnically distinct from their countrymen. Consequently, these cases are outside the scope of the study of identity mobilization conducted here. Two more (the backward classes and backward castes in India) are coded too differently in AMAR to match directly with ACD2.

Six cases, the Goula in CAR, the Tama in Chad, the Sahrawi in Mauritania, the Tobou in Niger, the Buddhist Arakanese in Myanmar, and Nogai in Russia are all very small groups, excluded because of AMAR population size criteria. This is a concern because the mechanism explored in this chapter focuses on group-relative size. We would reckon if this criteria systematically excludes cases that favor or contradict our hypothesis that large ethnic minority groups who share religion with politically dominant majorities are more likely to mobilize religion; the results we present here may not be accurate. Thus, we delve deeper into the cases to ensure that is not the case.

All of these small groups but the Nogai share religion with the majority. The Nogai are represented by the Forces of the Caucasus Emirate who do claim religious incompatibility with the state, but likely for reasons other than the CWC. While we do not test this implication directly in this book, the reader will recall that a separate implication of our theory pertained to the probability that

---

[8] Sources for our coding of group size for the groups in Table C.11 include the Encyclopedia Britannica, the CIA World Factbook, and Ethnologue. Both A-Religion and Svensson and Nilsson's (2018) RELAC data code religion. When the two differ, both group religions are noted. Religious incompatibility is coded by Svensson and Nilsson (2018).

TABLE C.10. *Groups that are less aggregate in the A-Religion data*

ACD2/ Group Id	Numcode	Country	Group name	Rel. Inc.	Shared/ Fam.
48405000	48406	Congo	Lari/Bakongo	I	I
	48401		Lari/Lali	I	I
75022000	75017	India	Scheduled tribes	O	I
	75024		Scheduled tribes of North India	O	I
	75023		Scheduled tribes of North-east India	O	I
	75026		Scheduled tribes of South India	O	I
	75025		Scheduled tribes of West India	O	I
43703000	43704	Ivory Coast	Gur	O	O
	43708		Northerners (Mande and Voltaic/Gur)	O	I
45003000	45005	Liberia	Gola	O	O
	45011		Loma	O	O
	45014		Vai	O	O
43201000	43202	Mali	Blacks (Mande, Peul, Voltaic, etc.)	O	I
	43203		Mande	O	I
	43213		Voltaiques/Gur	O	O
79002000	79020	Nepal	Adibasi Janajati	I	I
	79007		Dhanuk	I	I
	79009		Gharti/Bhujel	I	I
	79010		Gurung	I	O
	79016		Magar	I	I
	79002		Sherpa	I	O
	79024		Tamang	I	O
	79027		Tharu	I	I
45105000	45102	Sierra Leone	Northern groups (Temne, Limba)	O	O
	45104		Temne	O	O
56005000	56012	South Africa	Blacks	O	O
	56009		Ndebele	O	I
	56011		Sotho-Tswana	O	O

(continued)

ACD2// Group Id	Numcode	Country	Group name	Rel. Inc.	Shared/ Fam.
	56013		Tsonga	0	0
	56014		Venda	0	0
	56005		Xhosa	0	0
	56006		Zulu	0	0
62509000	62505	Sudan	Other Arab groups		
	62506		Baggara/Jahayna		
50011000	50009	Uganda	Banyarwanda	0	1
	50010		Banyoro	0	1
50009110	50012		Far North-west Nile (Kakwa-Nubian, Madi, Lugbara, Alur)	0	1
	50028		Kakwa	0	1
	50008		Lugbara	0	1
50011000	50010		South-westeners (Ankole, Banyoro, Toro, Banyarwanda)	0	1
	50027		Toro	0	1

Note: Eritrea is not listed here though there are significant aggregation differences between ACD2 and A-Religion because the correspondence of groups is complicated as explained in Chapter 4.

small ethnic minorities, segmented from the majority by ethnicity and religion, become engaged in conflict with the majority as a result of majority outbidding. The Nogai exemplify this separate type of conflict mobilization that neither supports nor contradicts the CWC hypothesis tested in this chapter and can be safely excluded. There is not enough information to accurately match the "Muslim Sahel" groups in Chad.

The Federal Republic of Yugoslavia (Serbia and Montenegro, 1992–2003), North Yemen (1962–1990), and Zimbabwe (Rhodesia, 1979) are not included separately in the AMAR data because all had run their course when the AMAR lists of contemporary country-groups were outlined (Birnir et al., 2015) and the pertinent ethnic groups are coded as parts of their current territories (Birnir et al., 2018). All are, therefore, excluded for reasons that are not systematically related to the outcome examined here, and the relevant groups are included as parts of different territories. Even so, a cursory look at current data on ethnic composition of Serbia and Montenegro separately suggests that Croats and Slovene groups are very small in these countries. While these groups share religious family with the majority, we would not have expected them to attempt mobilization of a religiously based CWC because of their size. The RELAC data confirms that Croats and Slovene groups in Serbia and Montenegro adhere to our expectation of not mobilizing religion – we would argue, in part, because of their small size – and can safely be excluded.

TABLE C.11. *ACD2 ethnic groups excluded from A-Religion data*

Country: Group	Reason for exclusion from A-Religion	Group religion	Majority religion
Central African Republic: Goula	AMAR size criteria	Christian	Christian
Chad: Tama	AMAR size criteria	Islam	Islam (Sunni)
Chad: Muslim Sahel groups	Insufficient information to match		Islam (Sunni)
Comoros: Anjouan (Nzwani)	AMAR ethnic criteria	Islam (Sunni)	Islam (Sunni)
India: Manipuri	AMAR ethnic criteria	Hindu	Hindu
India: Other backward classes/castes	AMAR ethnic criteria	Hindu	Hindu
India: Scheduled castes	AMAR ethnic criteria	Hindu	Hindu
Mauritania: Sahrawi	AMAR size criteria	Islam (Sunni)	Islam (Sunni)
Myanmar: Buddhist Arakanese	AMAR size criteria	Buddhism	Buddhism
Niger: Tobou	AMAR size criteria	Islam (Sunni)	Islam (Sunni)
Russia: Nogai	AMAR size criteria	Islam (Sunni)	Christian (Orthodox)
Serbia (Yugoslavia): Croats and Slovenes	Country (Yugoslavia) not coded in A-Religion		
South Sudan: Anyuak and Murle	Country not independent at time of AMAR coding		
South Sudan: Nuer	Country not independent at time of AMAR coding	Christian or Animist	Christian (Catholic and Anglican)
Yemen (North): Northerners and Southerners	Country not independent at time of coding of AMAR		
Zimbabwe (Rhodesia) Africans	Country not in AMAR		

Bibliography

Abdoellah, O. S. (1987). Transmigration policies in Indonesia: Government aims and popular response. In S. Morgen and E. Colson (Eds.), *People in Upheaval*, pp. 180–196. New York: Center for Migration Studies.

Acker, F. V. (2004). Uganda and the Lord's Resistance Army: The new order no one ordered. *African Affairs 103*(412), 335–357.

Adam, J. (2010). How ordinary folk became involved in the Ambonese conflict: Understanding private opportunities during communal violence. *Bijdragen tot de Taal, Landen Volkenkunde 16*(1), 25–48.

Adhikari, A. (2014). *The Bullet and the Ballot Box: The Story of Nepal's Maoist Revolution*. London: Verso.

Aditya, A. and T. K. Abraham (2019). Jokowi's poll fight shows Indonesia's Islam identity crisis. *The Bloomberg*.

Ahmed, A. (June 21, 2016). 39pc of Pakistanis live in poverty; Fata, Balochistan worst hit. *Dawn*, www.dawn.com/news/1266171, accessed December 16, 2021.

Ahmed, F. (1998). *Ethnicity and Politics in Pakistan*. Karachi: Oxford University Press.

Ahmed, I. (2013). *Pakistan the Garrison State: Origins, Evolution, Consequences, 1947–2011*. Karachi: Oxford University Press.

Akbaba, Y. and J. Fox (2011). The religion and state-minorities dataset. *Journal of Peace Research 48*(6), 807–816.

Akbaba, Y. and Z. Taydas (2011). Does religious discrimination promote dissent? A quantitative analysis. *Ethnopolitics 10*(3–4), 271–295.

Akbar, M. S. (January 3, 2015). The end of Pakistan's Baloch insurgency? *The Huffington Post*, www.huffpost.com/entry/the-end-of-pakistans-balo_b_6090920, accessed December 16, 2021.

Akdağ, G. A. (2015). *Ethnicity and Elections in Turkey: Party Politics and the Mobilization of Swing Voters*. New York: Routledge.

Akturk, S. (2018). One nation under Allah? Islamic multiculturalism, Muslim nationalism and Turkey's reforms for Kurds, Alevis, and non-Muslims. *Turkish Studies 19*(4), 523–551.

Alava, H. (2017). "Acholi youth are lost": Young, Christian and (a)political in Uganda. In E. Oinas, H. Onodera, and L. Suurpää (Eds.), *What Politics?: Youth and Political Engagement in Africa*, pp. 158–178. Leiden: Brill.

Alesina, A., C. Gennaioli, and S. Lovo (2018). Public goods and ethnic diversity: Evidence from deforestation in Indonesia. *Economica 86*(341), 32–66.

Ali, S. (April 1, 2017). Women literacy in FATA. *Daily Times*, https://dailytimes.com .pk/19882/women-literacy-in-fata/, accessed December 16, 2021.

Allen, N. W. (2012). *Dissertation: Diversity, Patronage and Parties: Parties and Party System Change in Indonesia*. British Columbia: University of British Columbia.

(2014). From patronage machine to partisan melee: Subnational corruption and the evolution of the Indonesian party system. *Pacific Affairs 87*(2), 221–245.

(2018). Effects of the electoral system. In E. S. Herron, R. J. Pekkanen, and M. S. Shugart (Eds.), *The Oxford Handbook of Electoral Systems*. New York: Oxford University Press.

Allen, T. (1991). Understanding Alice: Uganda's holy spirit movement in context. *Africa 61*(3), 370–399.

Altier, M. B., S. Martin, and L. B. Weinberg (Eds.) (2014). *Violence, Elections, and Party Politics*. New York and London: Routledge.

Amone, C. (2015). Constructivism, instrumentalism and the rise of Acholi ethnic identity in northern Uganda. *African Identities 13*(2), 129–143.

Ananta, A. (2006). Changing ethnic composition and potential violent conflict in Riau Archipelago, Indonesia: An early warning signal. *Population Review 45*(1), 48–68.

(2009). Newly found democracy in Indonesia: Religion and electoral behaviour. *Institute of Southeast Asian Studies* 1–23.

Ananta, A., E. N. Arifin, and Bakhtiar (2018). Chinese Indonesians in Indonesia and the Province of Riau Archipelago: A demographic analysis. In L. Suryadinata (Ed.), *Ethnic Chinese in Contemporary Indonesia*, pp. 17–47. Singapore: ISEAS–Yusof Ishak Institute.

Ananta, A., E. N. Arifin, M. S. Hasbullah, N. B. Handayani, and A. Pramono (2013). Changing ethnic composition: Indonesia, 2000–2010. In *Paper Prepared for the XXVII IUSSP International Population Conference*. Busan, South Korea: Routledge.

(2015). *Demography of Indonesia's Ethnicity*. Singapore: Institute of Southeast Asian Studies.

Ananta, A., E. N. Arifin, and L. Suryadinata (2004). *Indonesian Electoral Behaviour: A Statistical Perspective*. Singapore: Institute of Southeast Asian Studies.

Anderson, B. (2006). *Imagined Communities: Reflections on the Origin and Spread of Nationalism*. London: Verso.

Anshari, K. (2017). Indonesia's village fiscal transfers: A fiscal decentralisation review. *Jurnal Studi Pemerintahan (Journal of Government and Politics) 8*(3), 296–326.

Apuuli, K. P. (2011). Peace over justice: The Acholi Religious Leaders Peace Initiative (ARLPI) vs. the International Criminal Court (ICC) in Northern Uganda. *Studies in Ethnicity and Nationalism 11*(1), 116–129.

Arifin, E. N., A. Ananta, D. R. W. W. Utami, N. B. Handayani, and A. Pramono (2015). Quantifying Indonesia's ethnic diversity. *Asian Population Studies 11*(3), 233–256.

Arifin, E. N., E. Nurvidya, and A. Ananta (2013). Three mega-demographic trends in Indonesia. *Social Development Issues 3*(35), 109–126.

Arves, S., K. G. Cunningham, and C. McCulloch (2019). Rebel tactics and external public opinion. *Research & Politics* 6(3), 1–7.

Asal, V., M. Brown, and A. Dalton (2012). Why split? Organizational splits among ethnopolitical organizations in the Middle East. *Journal of Conflict Resolution* 56(1), 94–117.

Asal, V. and R. K. Rethemeyer (2008). The nature of the beast: Organizational structures and the lethality of terrorist attacks. *The Journal of Politics* 70(2), 437–449.

Asal, V. and J. Wilkenfeld (2013). Ethnic conflict: An organizational perspective. *Penn State Journal of Law & International Affairs* 2(1), 91–102.

Aspinall, E. (2004). Indonesia: Civil society and democratic breakthrough. In M. Alagappa (Ed.), *Civil Society and Political Change in Asia: Expanding and Contracting Democratic Space*, pp. 61–96. Stanford: Stanford University Press.

(2007a). The construction of grievance: Natural resources and identity in a separatist conflict. *Journal of Conflict Resolution* 51(6), 950–972.

(2007b). From Islamism to nationalism in Aceh, Indonesia. *Nations and Nationalism* 13(2), 245–263.

(2009). *Islam and Nation: Separatist Rebellion in Aceh, Indonesia*. Stanford: Stanford University Press.

(2011). Democratization and ethnic politics in Indonesia: Nine theses. *Journal of East Asian Studies* 11(2), 289–319.

(2018). Democratization: Travails and achievements. In R. W. Hefner (Ed.), *Routledge Handbook of Contemporary Indonesia*, pp. 83–94. New York: Routledge.

Aspinall, E. and W. Berenschot (2019). *Democracy for Sale: Elections, Clientelism, and the State in Indonesia*. Ithaca, NY: Cornell University Press.

Aspinall, E., S. Dettman, and E. Warburton (2011). When religion trumps ethnicity: A regional election case study from Indonesia. *South East Asia Research* 19(1), 27–58.

Aspinall, E. and G. Fealy (2003). *Local Power and Politics in Indonesia: Democratisation and Decentralisation*. Singapore: ISEAS–Yusof Ishak Institute.

Aspinall, E. and M. Sukmajati (Eds.) (2016). *Electoral Dynamics in Indonesia: Money Politics, Patronage and Clientelism at the Grassroots*. Singapore: National University of Singapore Press.

Atkinson, R. R. (1994). *The Roots of Ethnicity. The Origins of the Acholi of Uganda*. Kampala: Fountain Publishers.

(2015). *The Roots of Ethnicity. The Origins of the Acholi of Uganda before 1800*. Philadelphia: University of Pennsylvania Press.

(2018). Our friends at the bank? The adverse effects of neoliberalism in Acholi. In J. Weigratz, G. Martiniello, and E. Greco (Eds.), *Uganda: The Dynamics of Neoliberal Transformation*, pp. 60–77. London: Zed Books.

Azar, E. E. (1990). Protracted international conflicts: Ten propositions. In F. Dukes and J. Burton (Eds.), *Conflict: Readings in Management and Resolution*, pp. 145–155. London: Palgrave Macmillan.

Azra, A. (2004). Political Islam in post-Soeharto Indonesia. In V. Hooker and A. Saikal (Eds.), *Islamic Perspectives on the New Millennium*, pp. 133–149. Singapore: Institute of Southeast Asian Studies.

Bajoria, J. (April 20, 2011). Islam and politics in Pakistan. *Council on Foreign Relations*, www.cfr.org/backgrounder/islam-and-politics-pakistan, accessed December 16, 2021.

Balcells, L. and S. Kalyvas (n.d.). Revolutionary rebels and the Marxist paradox. Working paper, http://cpd.berkeley.edu/wp-content/uploads/2015/04/MarxIns_4_15.pdf, accessed January 29, 2020.

Baldwin, K. and J. D. Huber (2010). Economic versus cultural differences: Forms of ethnic diversity and public goods provision. *American Political Science Review* 104(4), 644–662.

Barnett, R. and A. Siddique (October 1, 2006). Resolving the Pakistan Afghanistan stalemate. Special report, United States Institute of Peace, www.usip.org/publications/2006/10/resolving-pakistan-afghanistan-stalemate, accessed December 15, 2021.

Barron, P., S. Jaffrey, and A. Varshney (2016). When large conflicts subside: The ebbs and flows of violence in post-Suharto Indonesia. *Journal of East Asian Studies* 16(2), 191–217.

Barter, S. J. (2011). The free Aceh elections? The 2009 legislative contests in Aceh. *Indonesia* 91(1), 113–130.

Barter, S. J. and I. Cote (2015). Strife of the soil? Unsettling transmigrant conflicts in Indonesia. *Journal of Southeast Asian Studies* 46(1), 60–85.

Barter, S. J. and I. Zatkin-Osburn (2016). Measuring religion in war: A response. *Journal for the Scientific Study of Religion* 55(1), 190–193.

Barth, F. (1969). *Ethnic Groups and Boundaries. The Social Organization of Culture Difference. [Results of a Symposium Held at the University of Bergen, 23rd to 26th February 1967]*. Little, Brown series in anthropology. Boston: Little, Brown.

Basedau, M., J. Fox, J. H. Pierskalla, G. Strüver, and J. Vüllers (2017). Does discrimination breed grievances – and do grievances breed violence? New evidence from an analysis of religious minorities in developing countries. *Conflict Management and Peace Science* 34(3), 217–239.

Basedau, M. and C. Koos (2015). When do religious leaders support faith-based violence? Evidence from a survey poll in South Sudan. *Political Research Quarterly* 68(4), 760–772.

Basedau, M., B. Pfeiffer, and J. Vüllers (2016). Bad religion? Religion, collective action, and the onset of armed conflict in developing countries. *Journal of Conflict Resolution* 60(2), 226–255.

Basedau, M. and J. Schaefer-Kehnert (2019). Religious discrimination and religious armed conflict in Sub-Saharan Africa: An obvious relationship? *Religion, State and Society* 47(1), 30–47.

Basedau, M., G. Struver, J. Vullers, and T. Wegenast (2011). Do religious factors impact armed conflict? Empirical evidence from sub-Saharan Africa. *Terrorism and Political Violence* 23(5), 752–779.

Bates, R. H. (1974). Ethnic competition and modernization in contemporary Africa. *Comparative Political Studies* 6(4), 457–484.

(1983a). Modernization, ethnic competition, and the rationality of politics in contemporary Africa. In D. Rothchild and V. A. Olunsorola (Eds.), *State versus Ethnic Claims: African Policy Dilemmas*. Boulder, CO: Westview Press.

(1983b). *Essays on the Political Economy of Rural Africa*. African studies series, no. 38. Cambridge [Cambridgeshire]: Cambridge University Press.

BBC (April 12, 2019). A short guide to Indonesia's election. *BBC News*.

Beaumont, P. (2012). The man who could determine whether the west is drawn into Mali's war. *The Guardian*, October 27, 2012.

Behrend, H. (1999). *Alice Lakwena & the Holy Spirits: War in Northern Uganda, 1985–97*. Oxford: J. Currey.

Behuria, A. K. (2007a). Fighting the Taliban: Pakistan at war with itself. *Australian Journal of International Affairs* 61(4), 529–543.

(2007b). The rise of Pakistani Taliban and the response of the state. *Strategic Analysis* 31(5), 699–724.

Belokrenitskii, V. and V. N. Moskalenko (2013). *A Political History of Pakistan, 1947–2007*. Karachi: Oxford University Press.

Berger, P. L. (1967). *The Sacred Canopy: Elements of a Sociological Theory of Religion* 1st ed. Garden City, NY: Doubleday.

Berger, P. L. and T. Luckmann (1967). *The Social Construction of Reality: A Treatise in the Sociology of Knowledge*, Anchor books ed. Anchor books. Garden City, NY: Doubleday.

Bertrand, J. (1997). "Business as usual" in Suharto's Indonesia. *Asian Survey* 37(5), 441–452.

(2004). *Nationalism and Ethnic Conflict in Indonesia*. Cambridge: Cambridge University Press.

(2008). Ethnic conflicts in Indonesia: National models, critical junctures, and the timing of violence. *Journal of East Asian Studies* 8(3), 425–449.

Beteille, A. (1965). *Caste, Class and Power: Changing Patterns of Stratiication in Tanjore Village*. California: University of California Press.

Birnir, J. K. and A. Hultquist (2017). Ethnic politics. In S. Maisel (Ed.), *Oxford Bibliographies in Political Science*, pp. 1–32. New York: Oxford University Press.

Birnir, J. K. (2004). Stabilizing party systems and excluding segments of society? The effects of formation costs on representation in Latin America. *Studies in Comparative International Development* 39(3), 3–28.

(2007). *Ethnicity and Electoral Politics*. Cambridge: Cambridge University Press.

(2011). The enduring theoretical relevance of Rabushka and Shepsle's Politics in plural societies. *Comparative Politics Newsletter* 22(1), 14–16.

Birnir, J. K. and P. Coronado-Castellanos (n.d.). Ethnic groups and geography: Introducing the GeoAMAR data. ilCSS working paper.

Birnir, J. K., D. D. Laitin, J. Wilkenfeld, D. M. Waguespack, A. S. Hultquist, and T. R. Gurr (2018). Introducing the AMAR (all minorities at Risk) data. *Journal of Conflict Resolution* 62(1), 203–226.

Birnir, J. K. and H. D. Overos (2019). Religion and political mobilization. In S. Ratuva (Ed.), *The Palgrave Handbook of Ethnicity*, pp. 1–18. Singapore: Palgrave Macmillan.

Birnir, J. K. and N. S. Satana (2013). Religion and coalition politics. *Comparative Political Studies* 46(1), 3–30.

Birnir, J. K, K. Sawyer, and N. S. Satana (n.d.). The effect of group size on the conflict potential of segmented ethno-religious groups. In David Backer and Paul Huth (Eds.), *Peace and Conflict 2019*.

Birnir, J. K., J. Wilkenfeld, J. D. Fearon, D. D. Laitin, T. R. Gurr, D. Brancati, et al. (2015). Socially relevant ethnic groups, ethnic structure, and AMAR. *Journal of Peace Research* 52(1), 110–115.

Bormann, N.-C. (2019). Uncertainty, cleavages, and ethnic coalitions. *The Journal of Politics* 81(2), 471–486.

Bormann, N.-C., L.-E. Cederman, and M. Vogt (2017). Language, religion, and ethnic civil war. *Journal of Conflict Resolution 61*(4), 744–771.

Bormann, N.-C. and M. Golder (2013). Democratic Electoral Systems around the world, 1946–2011. *Electoral Studies 32*(2), 360–369.

Bothelo, T., D. Waguespack, J. K. Birnir, and A. Gopal (2020). Gender effects in online evaluations: A large scale naturalexperiment. ILCSS working paper. ilcss.umd.edu.

Bozarslan, H. (1992). Political aspects of the Kurdish problem in contemporary Turkey. In P. G. Kreyenbroek and S. Perl (Eds.), *The Kurds: A Contemporary Overview*, pp. 99–101. New York: Routledge.

Brady, H. E. and C. S. Kaplan (2009). Conceptualizing and measuring ethnic identity. In R. Abdelal, Y. M. Herrera, A. I. Johnston, and R. McDermott (Eds.), *Measuring Identity: A Guide for Social Scientists*, pp. 33–71. Cambridge: Cambridge University Press.

Braithwaite, A., I. Salehyan, and B. Savun (2019). Refugees, forced migration, and conflict: Introduction to the special issue. *Journal of Peace Research 56*(1), 5–11.

Brancati, D. (2006). Decentralization: Fueling the fire or dampening the flames of ethnic conflict and secessionism? *International Organization 60*(3), 651–685.

Branch, K. (2020). Oklahoma's Native American Caucus focuses on bills, building partnerships amid gaming dispute. *The Oklahoman*, https://oklahoman.com/article/5655508/oklahomas–native–american–caucus–focuses–on--bills–building–partnerships–amid–gaming–dispute, accessed February 3, 2020.

Brandt, B. (2010). The Punjabi Taliban. *CTC Sentinel 3*(7), 6–9.

Brass, P. R. (1991). *Ethnicity and Nationalism: Theory and Comparison*. New Delhi; India: Sage Publications.

Brewer, M. B. (2001). The many faces of social identity: Implications for political psychology. *Political Psychology 22*(1), 115–125.

Brewer, M. B. and K. P. Pierce (2005). Social identity complexity and outgroup tolerance. *Personality and Social Psychology Bulletin 31*(3), 428–437.

Broughton, D. and H.-M. ten Napel (2000). *Religion and Mass Electoral Behaviour in Europe*, vol. 19. London: Routledge.

Brown, D. and P. James (2018). The religious characteristics of states: Classic themes and new evidence for international relations and comparative politics. *Journal of Conflict Resolution 62*(6), 1340–1376.

Brown, D. and I. Wilson (2007). Ethnicized violence in Indonesia: Where criminals and fanatics meet. *Nationalism and Ethnic Politics 13*(3), 367–403.

Brown, G. K. (2008). Horizontal inequalities and separatism in southeast Asia: A comparative perspective. In F. Stewart (Ed.), *Horizontal Inequalities and Conflict: Understanding Group Violence in Multiethnic Societies*, pp. 252–281. London: Palgrave Macmillan.

Brown, G. K. and A. Langer (2010). Conceptualizing and measuring ethnicity. *Oxford Development Studies 38*(4), 411–436.

Browne, E. C. (1971). Testing theories of coalition formation in the European context. *Comparative Political Studies 3*, 391–413.

Brubaker, R. (2015). Religious dimensions of political conflict and violence. *Sociological Theory 33*(1), 1–19.

Brumfield, B. (October 17, 2012). Who are the Pakistani Taliban? CNN, www.cnn.com/2012/10/17/world/asia/pakistan-taliban-profile/index.html, accessed December 16, 2021.

Bruner, E. M. (1974 [2013]). The expression of ethnicity in Indonesia. In C. Abner (Ed.), *Urban Ethnicity*. Oxon: Routledge.

Bueno de Mesquita, B. (2003). *The Logic of Political Survival*. Cambridge, MA: MIT Press.

Buhaug, H. and K. Gleditsch (2008). Contagion or confusion? why conflicts cluster in space. *International Studies Quarterly* 52(2), 215–233.

Bunker, P. L. (2016). The Lord's Resistance Army: A research note. In R. J. Bunker (Ed.), *Blood Sacrifices. Violent Non-State Actors and Dark Magico-Religious Activities*. Bloomington, IN: iUniverse.

Burke, P. J. and D. C. Reitzes (1981). The link between identity theory and role performance. *Social Psychology Quarterly* 44(2), 83–92.

Butcher, J. G. and R. Elson (2017). *Sovereignty and the Sea: How Indonesia Became an Archipelagic State*. Singapore: NUS Press.

Butt, S. (2017). The Constitutional Court and Indonesian Electoral Law. *Australian Journal of Asian Law* 16(2), 1–18.

(2018). Constitutions and constitutionalism. In R. W. Hefner (Ed.), *Routledge Handbook of Contemporary Indonesia*. New York: Routledge.

Byl, J. (2014). *Antiphonal Histories: Resonant Pasts in the Toba Batak Musical Present*. Middletown, CT: Wesleyan University Press.

Cailmail, B. (2008). *The Fall of a Hindu Monarchy: Maoists in Power in Nepal*. Number 12. The Institut Francais des Relations Internationales (IFRI).

Calderon, J. (1992). "Hispanic" and "Latino": The viability of categories for panethnic unity. *Latin American Perspectives* 19(4), 37–44.

Calhoun-Brown, A. (1998). The politics of black evangelicals: What hinders diversity in the christian right? *American Politics Quarterly* 26(1), 81–109.

Carter, D. B. and C. S. Signorino (2010). Back to the future: Modeling time dependence in binary data. *Political Analysis* 18(3), 271–292.

Cederman, L.-E., K. S. Gleditsch, and H. Buhaug (2013). *Inequality, Grievances, and Civil War*. Cambridge studies in contentious politics. New York: Cambridge University Press.

Cederman, L.-E., N. B. Weidmann, and K. S. Gleditsch (2011). Horizontal inequalities and ethnonationalist civil war: A global comparison. *American Political Science Review* 105(03), 478–495.

Central Bureau of Statistics (2014). *Population Monograph of Nepal*, vol. II. Kathmandu, Nepal: Multi Graphic Press.

Chandra, K. (2004). *Why Ethnic Parties Succeed: Patronage and Ethnic Head Counts in India*. Cambridge: Cambridge University Press.

(2005). Ethnic parties and democratic stability. *Perspectives on Politics* 3(2), 235–252.

(2012). *Constructivist Theories of Ethnic Politics*. New York: Oxford University Press.

Chandra, K. and C. Boulet (2012). A language for thinking about ethnic identity change. In K. Chandra (Ed.), *Constructivist Theories of Ethnic Politics*. New York: Oxford University Press.

Chandra, K. and S. Wilkinson (2008). Measuring the effect of "ethnicity". *Comparative Political Studies* 41(4–5), 515–563.

Chavar, A. (2014). Race and politics in Oklahoma. *New York Times*, www.nytimes.com/video/us/politics/100000002860180/race–and–politics–in–oklahoma.html?search ResultPosition=1, accessed February 3, 2021

Chenoweth, E. (2020). *Civil Resistance: What Everyone Needs to Know.* New York/London: Oxford University Press.

Chenoweth, E. and M. J. Stephan (2011). *Why Civil Resistance Works: The Strategic Logic of Nonviolent Conflict.* New York: Columbia University Press.

Choi, H. J. and D. Kim (2018). Coup, riot, war: How political institutions and ethnic politics shape alternative forms of political violence. *Terrorism and Political Violence* 30(4), 718–739.

Choi, N. (2007). Local elections and democracy in Indonesia: The Riau archipelago. *Journal of Contemporary Asia* 37(3), 326–345.

  (2011). *Local Politics in Indonesia. Pathways to Power.* New York: Routledge.

Cicek, C. (2017). *The Kurds of Turkey: National, Religious and Economic Identities.* London: I.B. Taurus.

Clark, J. N. (2010). The ICC, Uganda and the LRA: Re-framing the debate. *African Studies* 69(1), 141–160.

Cohen, S. P. (2004). *The Idea of Pakistan.* Washington, DC: Brookings Institution Press.

Collins, P. H. and S. Bilge (2016). *Intersectionality.* Malden, MA: John Wiley & Sons.

Corstange, D. (2016). *The Price of a Vote in the Middle East: Clientelism and Communal Politics in Lebanon and Yemen.* New York: Cambridge University Press.

  (2018). Clientelism in competitive and uncompetitive elections. *Comparative Political Studies* 51(1), 76–104.

Crenshaw, M. (2017). Transnational Jihadism & civil wars. *Daedalus* 146(4), 59–70.

Croatian Bureau of Statistics, R. o. C. (2011). Census of population, households and dwellings. https://www.dzs.hr/default_e.htm, accessed February 14, 2022.

Cunningham, K. (2014). *Inside the Politics of Self-determination.* New York: Oxford University Press.

Cunningham, K. and M. Lee (2016). Identity issues and civil war: Ethnic and religious divisions. In D. T. Mason and S. M. Mitchell (Eds.), *What Do We Know about Civil War.* New York: Rowman and Littlefield.

Dalton, R. J. (2013). *Citizen Politics: Public Opinion and Political Parties in Advanced Industrial Democracies.* Washington DC: CQ Press.

Damanik, A. T. (2016). Medan, North Sumatra: Between ethnic politics and money politics. In E. Aspinall and M. Sukmajati (Eds.), *Electoral Dynamics in Indonesia: Money Politics, Patronage and Clientelism at the Grassroots.* Singapore: National University of Singapore Press.

Davenport, C. (2014). *How Social Movements Die: Repression and Demobilization of the Republic of New Africa.* New York/London: Cambridge University Press.

Davenport, C., H. Johnston, and C. Mueller. (2005). *Repression and Political Mobilization.* Minnesota: University of Minnesota Press.

Davidson, J. S. (2008). *From Rebellion to Riots: Collective Violence on Indonesian Borneo.* Madison: The University of Wisconsin Press.

  (2009a). Dilemmas of democratic consolidation in Indonesia. *The Pacific Review* 22(3), 393–310.

  (2009b). Visual representations of ethnic violence: An Indonesian portrayal. *Asian Ethnicity* 10(2), 121–143.

Davis, P. K., E. V. Larson, Z. Haldeman, M. Oguz, and Y. Rana (2012). *Understanding and Influencing Public Support for Insurgency and Terrorism.* Arlington, VA: RAND Corporation.

de la Garza, R. O. (2004). Latino politics. *Annual Review of Political Science* 7(1), 91–123.

De-Soysa, I. and R. Nordas (2007). Islam's Bloody Innards? Religion and political terror. *International Studies Quarterly* 51(4), 927–943.

Denny, E. K. and B. F. Walter (2014). Ethnicity and civil war. *Journal of Peace Research* 51(2), 199–212.

Diani, M. (1992). The concept of social movement. *The Sociological Review* 40(1), 1–25.

Diani, M. and R. Eyerman (1992). *Studying collective action*. London: Sage.

Diprose, R. (2009). Decentralization, horizontal inequalities and conflict management in Indonesia. *Ethnopolitics* 8(1), 107–134.

Do, Q. T. and L. Iyer (2010). Geography, poverty and conflict in Nepal. *Journal of Peace Research* 47(6), 735–48.

Doniger, W. (2014). *On Hinduism*. New York: Oxford University Press.

Doom, R. and K. Vlassenroot (1999). Kony's message: A new Koine? The Lord's Resistance Army in Northern Uganda. *African Affairs* 98(390), 5–36.

Drexler, E. F. (2008). *Indonesia: Securing the Insecure State. Ethnography of Political Violence*. Philadelphia: University of Pennsylvania Press.

Drucza, K. (2017). Talking about inclusion: Attitudes and affirmative action in Nepal. *Development Policy Review* 35(2), 161–195.

Duran, B. (1998). Approaching the Kurdish question via *adil düzen*: An Islamist formula of the Welfare Party for ethnic coexistence. *Journal of Muslim Minority Affairs* 18(1), 111–128.

Effendy, B. (2003). *Islam and State in Indonesia*. Singapore: Institute of Southeast Asian Studies.

Eichstaedt, P. (2009). *First Kill Your Family: Child Soldiers of Uganda and the Lord's Resistance Army*. Chicago: Chicago Review Press, Incorporated.

Ellingsen, T. (1991). The Nepal constitution of 1990: Preliminary considerations. *Himalayan Research Bulletin* 11(1–3), 1–18.

(2005). Toward a Revival of Religion and Religious Clashes? *Terrorism and Political Violence* 17(3), 305–332.

Elmhirst, R. (1999). Space, identity politics and resource control in Indonesia's transmigration programme. *Political Geography* 18(7), 813–835.

Elson, R. E. (2009). Another look at the Jakarta Charter controversy of 1945. *Indonesia* 88, 105–130.

Esen, B. and S. Gumuscu (2016). Rising competitive authoritarianism in Turkey. *Third World Quarterly* 37(9), 1581–1606.

(2017). Turkey: How the coup failed. *Journal of Democracy* 28(1), 59–73.

Farkas, L. (2017). *Data Collection in the Field of Ethnicity*. European Union.

Faucher, C. (2005). Regional autonomy, malayness and power hierarchy in the Riau Archipelago. In M. Erb, P. Sulistiyanto, and C. Faucher (Eds.), *Regionalism in Post-Suharto Indonesia*, pp. 125–140. London/New York: Routledge Curzon.

(2007). Contesting boundaries in the Riau Archipelago. In H. G. C. Schulte and G. van Klinken (Eds.), *Renegotiating Boundaries. Local Politics in Post-Suharto Indonesia*, pp. 199–227. The Netherlands: Brill.

Fearon, J. D. (1999). Why ethnic politics and "Pork" tend to go together. In *SSRC-MacArthur Sponsored Conference*. University of Chicago.

(2008). Ethnic mobilization and ethnic violence. *The Oxford Handbook of Political Economy*, www.oxfordhandbooks.com/view/10.1093/oxfordhb/9780199548477 .001.0001/oxfordhb-9780199548477-e-047, accessed December 16, 2021.

Fearon, J. D. and D. D. Laitin (2000). Violence and the social construction of ethnic identity. *International Organization 54*, 845–877.

(2003). Ethnicity, insurgency and civil war. *American Political Science Review 97*(1), 75–90.

(2011). Integrating qualitative and quantitative methods. putting it together again. pp. 1–22. Oxford University Press.

Feenstra, R. C., R. Inklaar, and M. P. Timmer (2015). The next generation of the Penn World Table. *American Economic Review 105*(10), 3150–3182.

Feith, H. (1957). *The Indonesian Elections of 1955*. Ithaca, NY: Cornell Modern Indonesia Project.

Felder, B. (2016). Evangelical voting bloc remains a force in Oklahoma. *The Oklahoman*, https://oklahoman.com/article/5524535/evangelical–voting–bloc–remains–-a–force–in–oklahoma, accessed February 3, 2021.

(2019). Growing black caucus in Oklahoma legislature expands its voice. *The Oklahoman January*(21), https://oklahoman.com/article/5620779/growing–black–caucus–expands–its–voice, accessed May 10, 2020.

Finke, and L. Iannaccone (1993). Supply-side explanations for religious change. *527*(1), 27–39.

Finnstrom, S. (2008). *Living with Bad Surroundings: War, History, and Everyday Moments in Northern Uganda*. Durham: Duke University Press.

Fisher, R., W. L. Ury, and B. Patton. (1981). *Getting to Yes: Negotiating Agreement without Giving In*. New York: Penguin Books.

Fjelde, H. and K. Höglund (2014). Electoral institutions and electoral violence in sub-Saharan Africa. *British Journal of Political Science 46*(2), 297–320.

Flesken, A. (2018). Ethnic parties, ethnic tensions? Results of an original election panel study. *American Journal of Political Science 62*(4), 967–981.

Ford, M. (2003). Who are the Orang Riau? Negotiating identity across geographic and ethnic divides. In E. Aspinall and G. Fealy (Eds.), *Local Power and Politics in Indonesia: Patterns and Issues*, pp. 132–147. Singapore: Institute of Southeast Asian Studies.

Forsberg, E. (2005). Conflict diffusion : Ethnic kin as a transmitter of internal conflict. *DIVA*, 24.

(2014). Transnational transmitters: Ethnic kinship ties and conflict contagion 1946–2009. *International Interactions 40*(2), 143–165.

Forsberg, E., J. K. Birnir, and C. Davenport (2017). *Ethno-Political Violence: State of the Field and New Directions for Research*. London: Routledge.

Fotini, C. (2012). *Alliance Formation in Civil Wars*. Cambridge: Cambridge University Press.

Fox, C. A. and J. Menchik (2011). The politics of identity in Indonesia: Results from political campaign advertisements. *APSA 2011 Annual Meeting Paper*, 1–29.

Fox, J. (2002). *Ethnoreligious Conflict in the Late Twentieth Century: A General Theory*. Lanham, MD: Lexington Books.

(2003). Are religious minorities more militant than other ethnic minorities? *Alternatives: Global, Local, Political 28*(1), 91–114.

(2004a). Is ethnoreligious conflict a contagious disease? *Studies in Conflict & Terrorism* 27(2), 89–106.

(2004b). *Religion, Civilization, and Civil War: 1945 through the Millennium.* Lanham, MD: Lexington Books.

(2006). World separation of religion and state into the 21st century. *Comparative Political Studies* 39(5), 537–569.

(2008). *A World Survey of Religion and the State.* Cambridge: Cambridge University Press.

(2012). *Religion, Politics, Society, and the State.* Boulder, CO: Paradigm Publishers.

(2013). *An Introduction to Religion and Politics: Theory and Practice.* New York: Routledge.

(2015). *Political Secularism, Religion, and the State: A Time Series Analysis of Worldwide Data.* New York: Cambridge University Press.

(2016). *The Unfree Exercise of Religion: A World Survey of Discrimination against Religious Minorities.* Cambridge: Cambridge University Press.

(2020). *Thou Shalt Have No Other Gods before Me: Why Governments Discriminate against Religious Minorities.* Cambridge: Cambridge University Press.

Fox, J., P. James, and Y. Li (2009). State religion and discrimination against ethnic minorities. *Nationalism and Ethnic Politics* 15(2), 189–210.

Frakking, R. (2017). "Gathered on the point of a bayonet": The Negara Pasundan and the colonial defence of Indonesia, 1946–50. *The International History Review* 39(1), 30–47.

Freedman, A. and R. Tiburzi (2012). Progress and caution: Indonesia's democracy. *Asian Affairs An American Review* 39(3), 131–156.

Gaddie, R. K. and S. E. Buchanan (1998). Shifting partisan alignments in Oklahoma. *Oklahoma Politics* 6, 25–32.

Gallagher Cunningham, K. (2014). *Inside the Politics of Self-determination.* Oxford: Oxford University Press.

Gartzke, E. and K. S. Gleditsch (2006). Identity and conflict: Ties that bind and differences that divide. *European Journal of International Relations* 12(1), 53–88.

George, A. L. and A. Bennett (2005). *Case Studies and Theory Development in the Social Sciences.* Cambridge, MA: MIT Press.

Gerring, J., M. Hoffman, and D. Zarecki (2018). The diverse effects of diversity on democracy. *British Journal of Political Science* 48(2), 283–314.

Giap, K. T., M. Nurina, and A. Mulya (2015). *2014 Provincial and Inaugural Regional Competitiveness Analysis. Safeguarding Indonesia's growth momentum.* Singapore: World Scientific.

Gill, A. (2001). Religion and comparative politics. *Annual Review of Political Science* 4(1), 117–138.

(2004). Weber in Latin America: Is protestant growth enabling the consolidation of democratic capitalism? *Democratization* 11(4), 42–65.

Gleditsch, N. P., E. Melander, and H. Urdal (2016). Patterns of armed conflict since 1945. In T. D. Mason and S. M. Mitchell (Eds.), *What Do We Know about Civil Wars?*, pp. 15–32. Lanham, MD: Rowman & Littlefield.

Gleditsch, N. P. and I. Rudolfsen (2016). Are Muslim countries more prone to violence? *Research & Politics* 3(2), 1–9.

Goldstone, J. A., E. Kauffman, and M. D. Toft (2011). *Political Demography: How Population Changes Are Reshaping International Security and National Politics.* Boulder, CO: Paradigm.

Gooszen, H. (1999). *A Demographic History of the Indonesian Archipelago, 1880–1942.* Singapore: Institute of Southeast Asian Studies.

Gordon, S. C., P. L. Bihan, and D. Landa (2015). Crosscutting cleavages and political conflicts. *Institute for Advanced Study in Toulouse* (15–30), 1–35.

Görmüş, S. (2015). Anket şirketleri 30 Mart testini geçti mi? *Uluslararası Politik Araştırmalar Dergisi 1*(1), 35–53.

Green, M. (2009). *The Wizard of the Nile: The Hunt for Africa's Most Wanted.* Northampton, MA: Olive Branch Press.

Grzymala-Busse, A. (2012). Why comparative politics should take religion (more) seriously. *Annual Review of Political Science 15*(1), 421–442.

Gubler, J. R., J. S. Selway, and A. Varshney (2016). Crosscutting cleavages and ethno-communal violence evidence from Indonesia in the post-Suharto era. WIDER working Paper 2016/129. Helsinki: UNU-WIDER.

Guerin, B. (2002). Indonesia: The enemy within. *Asia Times*, October 15.

Gunes, C. (2013). Explaining the PKK's mobilization of the Kurds in Turkey: Hegemony, myth and violence. *Ethnopolitics 12*(3), 247–267.

Gurr, T. R. (1969). A comparative study of civil strife. In H. Graham and T. Gurr (Eds.), *Violence in America: Historical and Comparative Perspectives*, vol. 2, pp. 443–486. New York: Praeger.

(1970). *Why Men Rebel.* Princeton, NJ: Published for the Center of International Studies, Princeton University [by] Princeton University Press.

(1993a). *Minorities at Risk: A Global View of Ethnopolitical Conflicts.* Washington, DC: U.S. Institute of Peace Press.

(1993b). Why minorities rebel: A global analysis of communal mobilization and conflict since 1945. *International Political Science Review / Revue internationale de science politique 14*(2), 161–201.

(2000). *Peoples versus States: Minorities at Risk in the New Century.* Washington, DC: U.S. Institute of Peace Press.

Gurses, M. and A. E. Ozturk (2020). Religion and armed conflict: Evidence from the Kurdish conflict in Turkey. *Journal for the Scientific Study of Religion 59*(2), 327–340.

Hachhethu, K. (2008). Maoist insurgency in Nepal: An overview. In P. V. Ramana (Ed.), *The Naxal Challenge: Causes, Linkages, and Policy Options*, pp. 136–162. New Delhi: Dorling Kindersley.

Hackett, C. and M. Stonawski (2017). *The Changing Global Religious Landscape.* Washington, DC: Pew Research Center.

Hadiz, V. R. (2010). *Localising Power in Post-Authoritarian Indonesia: A Southeast Asia Perspective.* Stanford, CA: Stanford University Press.

(2016). *Islamic Populism in Indonesia and the Middle East.* Cambridge: Cambridge University Press.

Hale, H. E. (2004). Explaining ethnicity. *Comparative Political Studies 37*(4), 458–485.

Handloff, R. E. (1988). *Ivory Coast: A Country Study.* Washington, DC: GPO for the Library of Congress.

Hanioglu, S. (2012). The historical roots of Kemalism. In A. Kuru and A. Stepan (Eds.), *Democracy, Islam and Secularism in Turkey*, pp. 32–60. New York: Columbia University Press.

Hansen, H. B. (1977). *Ethnicity and Military Rule in Uganda*. Uppsala: Scandinavian Institute of African Affairs.

Hardjono, J. M. (1977). *Transmigration in Indonesia*. Kuala Lumpur: Oxford University Press.

Harris, A. and M. Findley (2014). Is ethnicity identifiable? Lessons from an experiment in South Africa. *Journal of Conflict Resolution 58*(1), 4–33.

Harris, A., D. L. Nielson, L. Medina, C. Bicahlo, M. Correia, M. G. Findley, et al. (2018). Experimental evidence from Uganda, South Africa, and the United States on ethnic identification and ethnic deception. Prepared for the APSA Annual Conference, Boston.

Harsono, A. (2019). *Race, Islam and Power: Ethnic and Religious Violence in Post-Suharto Indonesia*. Australia: Monash University Publishing.

Hasenclever, A. and V. Rittberger (2000). Does religion make a difference? Theoretical approaches to the impact of faith on political conflict. *Journal of International Studies 29*(3), 641–674.

Haynes, J. (2007). Religion, ethnicity and civil war in Africa: The cases of Uganda and Sudan. *The Round Table 96*(390), 305–317.

Hefner, R. W. (2018). The religious field: Plural legacies and contemporary contestations. In R. W. Hefner (Ed.), *Routledge Handbook of Contemporary Indonesia*. New York: Routledge.

Hermann, R. (2003). Political Islam in secular Turkey. *Islam and Christian-Muslim Relations 14*(3), 265–276.

Hicken, A. and Y. Kasuya (2003). A guide to the constitutional structures and electoral systems of east, south and southeast Asia. *Electoral Studies 22*(1), 121–151.

Hicks, J. (2012). The missing link: Explaining the political mobilisation of Islam in Indonesia. *Journal of Contemporary Asia 42*(1), 39–66.

Hidayat, R. (2017). Political devolution: Lessons from a decentralized mode of government in Indonesia. *SAGE Open 7*(1), 1–11.

Hill, H., B. R. Resosudarmo, and Y. Vidyattama (1974 [2013]). Economic geography of Indonesia: Location, connectivity, and resources. In Y. Huang and B. A. Magnoli (Eds.), *Reshaping Economic Geography in East Asia*. Washington, DC: The World Bank.

Hirschman, A. O. (1970). *Exit, Voice, and Loyalty: Responses to Decline in Firms, Organizations, and States*. Cambridge, MA: Harvard University Press.

Hlavac, M. (2018). *stargazer: Well-Formatted Regression and Summary Statistics Tables*. R package version 5.2.2.

Hoffman, B. (1995). "Holy terror": The implications of terrorism motivated by a religious imperative. *Studies in Conflict & Terrorism 18*(4), 271–284.

(2006). *Inside Terrorism*, rev. and exp. ed. New York: Columbia University Press.

Horowitz, D. L. (1985). *Ethnic Groups in Conflict*. Berkeley: University of California Press.

(1990). Making moderation pay: The comparative politics of ethnic conflict management. In J. V. Montville (Ed.), *Conflict and Peacemaking in Multiethnic Societies*, pp. 451–75. Lexington, MA: Lexington Books.

(2013). *Constitutional Change and Democracy in Indonesia.* Problems of international politics. Cambridge: Cambridge University Press.

House of Representatives. (2021). Mapping-Congress. Office of the Historian and the Clerk of the House's Office of Art and Archives. https://history.house .gov/Map/Mapping-Congress, accessed February 5, 2021.

Houston, C. (2001). *Islam, Kurds and the Turkish Nation-State.* Oxford: Berg Press.

Huang, R. (2020). Religious instrumentalism in violent conflict. *Ethnopolitics 19*(2), 150–161.

Hug, S. (2013). The use and misuse of the "minorities at risk" project. *Annual Review of Political Science 16*(1), 191–208.

Hugo, G. (2000). The patterns and trends of Indonesian migration during the last three decades. In *Proceedings of the Symposium on Current Policy Issues on Population Mobility, Urbanisation and Transition.* Indonesia: Ministry of Transmigration and Population in Collaboration with Lembaga Demografi FEUI and UNFPA, Indonesia.

Hugo, G. (2002). Pengungsi – Indonesia's internally displaced persons. *Asian and Pacific Migration Journal 11*(3), 297–331.

(2006). Forced migration in Indonesia: Historical perspectives. *Asian and Pacific Migration Journal 15*(1), 53–92.

Iannacone, L. R. (1991). The consequences of religious market structure. *3*(2), 156–177.

ICG (2011). *Nepal: Identity Politics and Federalism.* Number 199. International Crisis Group Asia Report.

Inglehart, R., M. Basanez, and A. Moren (1998). *Human Values and Beliefs: A Cross-Cultural Sourcebook.* Ann Arbor: University of Michigan Press.

Intan, B. F. (2006). *"Public Religion" and the Pancasila-Based State of Indonesia: An Ethical and Sociological Analysis.* New York: Peter Lang.

Iqtidar, H. and D. Gilmartin (2011). Secularism and the state in Pakistan: Introduction. *Modern Asian Studies 45*(3), 491–499.

Isaacs, M. (2017). Faith in contention: Explaining the salience of religion in ethnic conflict. *Comparative Political Studies 50*(2), 200–231.

Izady, M. (1992). *The Kurds: A Concise History And Fact Book.* Washington: Taylor & Francis.

Jaffrelot, C. and C. Schoch (2015). *The Pakistan Paradox: Instability and Resilience.* The CERI series in comparative politics and international studies. New York: Oxford University Press.

Janson, M. and B. Meyer (2016). Introduction: Towards a framework for the study of Christian-Muslim encounters in Africa. *Africa 86*(4), 615–619.

Jelen, T. (1993). The concept of fundamentalism applied to non-western settings. *Review of Religious Research 35*(1), 68–71.

Jelen, T. G. and C. Wilcox (2002). *Religion and Politics in Comparative Perspective: The One, the Few, and the Many.* Cambridge: Cambridge University Press.

Jones, B. (2007). The Teso insurgency remembered: Churches, burials and propriety. *Africa: Journal of the International African Institute 77*(4), 500–516.

Jones, Z. and Y. Lupu (2018). Is there more violence in the middle. *American Journal of Political Science 62*(3), 652–667.

Juan, A. D. and A. Hasenclever (2015). Framing political violence: Success and failure of religious mobilization in the Philippines and Thailand. *Civil Wars 17*(2), 201–221.

Juergensmeyer, M. (2003). *Terror in the Mind of God: The Global Rise of Religious Violence,* 3rd ed., rev. and updated ed. Berkeley: University of California Press.

Kahfi, K. (2019). Elections largely peaceful despite glitches. The Jakarta Post, April 17, 2019. https://www.thejakartapost.com/news/2019/04/17/elections-largely-peaceful-despite-glitches.html, accessed December 17, 2021.

Kahin, G. M. (1952). *Nationalism and Revolution in Indonesia.* Ithaca, NY: Cornell University Press.

Kahn, A. (2015). *Historical Dictionary of Indonesia.* Lanham, MD: Rowman & Littlefield.

Kalyvas, S. N. (1996). *The Rise of Christian Democracy in Europe.* Ithaca, NY: Cornell University Press.

(2000). Commitment problems in emerging democracies: The case of religious parties. *Comparative Politics* 32(4), 379.

(2006). *The Logic of Violence in Civil War.* Cambridge: Cambridge University Press.

(2009). Civil wars. In *The Oxford Handbook of Comparative Politics.* Oxford: Oxford University Press.

Karakoc, E. and Z. Sarigil (2020). Why religious people support ethnic insurgency? Kurds, religion and support for the PKK. *Religion and Politics* 13(2), 245–272.

Karam, J. T. (2007). *Another Arabesque: Syrian-Lebanese Ethnicity in Neoliberal Brazil.* Philadelphia, PA: Temple University Press.

Karaosmanoğlu, A. (1992). *Türkiye'de Demokrasinin Uluslar Arası Koşulları.* Ankara: Yeni Forum Yayinlari.

Karpat, K. (2010). *Türk Demokrasi Tarihi.* Istanbul: Timas Yayinlari.

Kasozi, A. (1994). *Social Origins of Violence in Uganda, 1964–1985.* Quebec, Canada: McGill-Queen's University Press.

Kathman, J. (2011). Civil war diffusion and regional motivations for intervention. *The Journal of Conflict Resolution* 55(6), 847–876.

Kaufman, S. J. (2001). *Modern Hatreds. The Symbolic Politics of Ethnic War.* Ithaca, NY: Cornell University Press.

(2015). *Nationalist Passions.* Ithaca, NY: Cornell University Press.

Kaya, Z. N. and M. Whiting (2019). The HDP, the AKP and the battle for Turkish democracy. *Ethnopolitics* 18(1), 92–106.

Khadka, N. (1986). Crisis in Nepal's partyless Panchayat system: The case for more democracy. *Pacific Affairs* 59(3), 429–454.

Khan, A. (2005). *Politics of Identity: Ethnic Nationalism and the State in Pakistan.* Thousand Oaks, CA: Sage.

Kimura, E. (2013). *Political Change and Territoriality in Indonesia: Provincial Proliferation.* Routledge Contemporary Southeast Asia Series. New York: Routledge.

Kingsbury, D. (2003). *Power Politics and the Indonesian Military.* London: Routledge Curzon.

Kintu, D. (2018). *The Ugandan Morality Crusade: The Brutal Campaign Against Homosexuality and Pornography under Yoweri Museveni.* Jefferson, NC: McFarland.

Kirisci, K. and G. Winrow (1997). *The Kurdish Question and Turkey: An Example of a Trans-state Ethnic Conflict.* London: Frank Cass.

Koc, I., A. Hancioglu, and A. Çavlin (2008). Demographic differentials and demographic integration of Turkish and Kurdish populations in Turkey. *Population Research and Policy Review* 27, 447–457.

Koopmans, R. (2004). Migrant mobilisation and political opportunities: Variation among German cities and a comparison with the United Kingdom and the Netherlands. *Journal of Ethnic and Migration Studies* 30(3), 449–470.

Koopmans, R. and P. Statham (1999). Challenging the liberal nation-state? postnationalism, multiculturalism, and the collective claims making of migrants and ethnic minorities in Britain and Germany. *American Journal of Sociology* 105(3), 652–696.

Krause, P. (2017). *Rebel Power: Why National Movements Compete, Fight, and Win.* Ithaca, NY: Cornell University Press.

Krehbiel, R. (2017). Rural-urban divide has a long history in Oklahoma politics. *Tulsa World*, https://tulsaworld.com/news/local/rural-urban-divide-has-a-long-history-in-oklahoma-politics/article_2e4b23a5-33d4-55ea-bec1-7d6c1cf76543.html, accessed December 16, 2021

Kroneberg, C. and A. Wimmer (2012). Struggling over the boundaries of belonging: A formal model of nation building, ethnic closure, and populism. *American Journal of Sociology* 118(1), 176–230.

Kumar, D. (2005). Proximate causes of conflict in Nepal. *Contributions to Nepalese Studies* 32(1), 51–92.

Kuran, T. (1991). Now out of never: The element of surprise in the East European Revolution of 1989. *World Politics* 44(1), 7–48.

Kurban, D. and M. Yeğen (2012). *Adaletin Kıyısında, Zorunlu Göç Sonrasında Devlet ve Kürtler/5233 Sayılı Tazminat Yasası'nın Bir Değerlendirmesi – Van örneği.* Istanbul: TESEV.

Kurt, M. (2017). *Kurdish Hizbullah in Turkey. Islamism, Violence and the State.* London: Pluto Press.

Lackmeyer, S. (2004). Mayoral voters explain how choices were made. *NewsOK.com*, https://oklahoman.com/article/1892141/mayoral–voters–explain–how–choices–were–made, accessed February 3, 2021.

Laitin, D. D. (1986). *Hegemony and Culture: Politics and Religious Change among the Yoruba.* Chicago: University of Chicago Press.

(1998). *Identity in Formation: The Russian Speaking Populations in the near Abroad.* Ithaca and London: Cornell University Press.

(2002). Comparative politics: The state of the subdiscipline. In I. Katznelson and H. V. Milner (Eds.), *Political Science: The State of the Discipline*, pp. 630–659. New York: W. W. Norton.

Laitin, D. and K. Chandra (2002). A constructivist framework for thinking about identity change. *Unpublished Manuscript*, Stanford University and New York University.

Lamberson, P. J. and S. E. Page (2012). Tipping points. *Quarterly Journal of Political Science* 7(2), 175–208.

Lawoti, M. (2005). *Towards a Democratic Nepal. Inclusive Political Institutions for a Multicultural Society.* New Delhi: Sage.

(2007). Contentious politics in democratizing Nepal. In M. Lawoti (Ed.), *Contentious Politics and Democratization in Nepal*, pp. 17–48. New Delhi: Sage.

(2013). Transforming ethnic politics, transforming the Nepali polity. from peaceful nationalist mobilization to the rise of armed separatist groups. In M. Lawoti and S. I. Hangen (Eds.), *Nationalism and Ethnic Conflict in Nepal: Identities and Mobilization after 1990*, pp. 226–256. Oxon: Routledge.

(2015). Competing nationhood and constitutional instability: Representation, regime, and resistance in Nepal. In M. Tushnet and M. Khosla (Eds.), *Unstable Constitutionalism: Law and Politics in South Asia*, pp. 86–124. New York: Cambridge University Press.

Lawoti, M. and S. I. Hangen (2013). *Nationalism and Ethnic Conflict in Nepal: Identities and Mobilization after 1990*. Oxon: Routledge.

Leeper, T. J. (2018). *margins: Marginal Effects for Model Objects*. R package version 0.3.23.

Levinson, D. (1995). *The Encyclopedia of World Cultures, Volume 9: Africa and the Middle East*. Farmington Hills, MI: Prentice Hall International.

Lewis, B. D. (2015). Decentralising to villages in Indonesia: Money (and other) mistakes. *Public Administration and Development* 35(5), 347–359.

Lichbach, M. I. (1994). Rethinking rationality and rebellion theories of collective action and problems of collective dissent. *Rationality and Society* 6(1), 8–39.

(1998). Contending theories of contentious politics and the structure-action problem of social order. *Annual Review of Political Science* 1(1), 401–424.

Liddle, W. R. and S. Mujani (2007). Leadership, party, and religion: Explaining voting behavior in Indonesia. *Comparative Political Studies* 40(7), 832–857.

Lijphart, A. (1977). *Democracy in Plural Societies: A Comparative exploration*. New Haven: Yale University Press.

(1984). *Democracies: Patterns of Majoritarian and Consensus Government in Twenty-One Countries*. New Haven: Yale University Press.

(1999). *Patterns of Democracy: Government Forms and Performance in Thirty-Six Countries*. New Haven: Yale University Press.

Lindberg, J.-E. (2008). *Running on Faith?: A Quantitative Analysis of the Effect of Religious Cleavages on the Duration and Intensity of Internal Conflicts*. MA thesis, University of Oslo.

Lipset, S. M. (1981). *Political Man: The Social Bases of Politics*, exp. ed. Baltimore: Johns Hopkins University Press.

Lipset, S. M. and S. Rokkan (1967). *Party Systems and Voter Alignments: Cross-National Perspectives*, Robert R. Alford and others. International yearbook of political behavior research, vol. 7. New York: Free Press.

Livney, A. (2020). *Trust and the Islamic Advantage in Turkey and the Muslim World*. Cambridge: Cambridge University Press.

Lohmann, S. (1994). The dynamics of informational cascades: The monday demonstrations in Leipzig, East Germany, 1989–91. *World Politics* 47, 42–101.

Lynch, C. (2014). A Neo-Weberian approach to studying religion and violence. *Millennium* 43(1), 273–290.

Madrid, R. (2008). The rise of ethnopopulism in Latin America. *World Politics* 60(3), 475–508.

(2012). *The Rise of Ethnic Politics in Latin America*. London/New York: Cambridge University Press.

Major, B., A. Blodorn, and G. Major Blascovich (2018). The threat of increasing diversity: Why many White Americans support Trump in the 2016 presidential election. *Group Processes & Intergroup Relations* 21(6), 931–940.

Margolis, M. F. (2017). How politics affects religion: Partisanship, socialization, and religiosity in America. *80*(1), 30–43.

(2018). *From Politics to the Pews: How Partisanship and the Political Environment Shape Religious Identity*. Chicago: University of Chicago Press.

Markus, H. (1977). Self-schemata and processing information about the self. *Journal of Personality and Social Psychology* 35, 63–78.

Marquardt, K. L. and Y. M. Herrera (2015). Ethnicity as a variable: An assessment of measures and data sets of ethnicity and related identities. *Social Science Quarterly* 96(3), 689–716.

Mason, L. (2018). *Uncivil Agreement: How Politics Became Our Identity*. Chicago, IL: University of Chicago Press.

Mason, T. D. and S. M. Mitchell (2016). *What Do We Know about Civil Wars?* Lanham, MD: Rowman & Littlefield.

Mazzei, P. (June 30, 2018). "The Blue Wave Came": Win for non-Hispanic democrat signals big shift in Miami. *The New York Times*, www.nytimes.com/2018/06/30/us/miami-little-havana-cuban.html, accessed December 17, 2021.

McAdam, D. and S. Tarrow (2000). Nonviolence as contentious interaction. *PS: Political Science & Politics* 33(2), 149–154.

McAdam, D., S. G. Tarrow, and C. Tilly (2001). *Dynamics of Contention*. Cambridge, MA: Cambridge University Press.

McCauley, J. F. (2014). The political mobilization of ethnic and religious identities in Africa. *American Political Science Review* 108(4), 801–816.

  (2017). *The Logic of Ethnic and Religious Conflict in Africa*. Cambridge: Cambridge University Press.

McDonald, H. (2015). *Demokrasi. Indonesia in the 21st Century*. New York: Palgrave Macmillan.

McDowall, D. (2007[1996]). *A Modern History of the Kurds*. London: I. B. Tauris.

McKenzie, B. D. and S. M. Rouse (2013). Shades of faith: Religious foundations of political attitudes among african americans, latinos, and whites. *American Journal of Political Science* 57(1), 218–235.

Mecham, Q. (2017). *Institutional Origins of Islamist Political Mobilization*. New York: Cambridge University Press.

Melvin, J. (2018). *The Army and the Indonesian Genocide: Mechanics of Mass Murder*. New York: Routledge.

Menchik, J. (2006). *Islam and Democracy in Indonesia: Tolerance without Liberalism*. Cambridge: Cambridge University Press.

Mietzner, M. (2014). Indonesia's decentralization: The rise of local identities and the survival of the nation-state. In H. Hill (Ed.), *Regional Dynamics in a Decentralized Indonesia*, pp. 45–67. Singapore: Institute of Southeast Asian Studies.

Miklian, J. (2009). Nepal's Terai: Constructing an ethnic conflict. In *South Asia Briefing Paper*. Oslo, Norway: International Peace Research Institute.

Miran-Guyon, M. (2012). Native conversions to Islam in Southern Côte d'Ivoire: The perils of double identity. *Journal of Religion in Africa* 42(12), 95–117.

Moroff, A. and M. Basedau (2010). An effective measure of institutional engineering? Ethnic party bans in Africa. *Democratization* 17(4), 666–686.

Mujani, S. and R. W. Liddle (2010). Personalities, parties, and voters. *Journal of Democracy* 21(2), 35–49.

Mujani, S., R. W. Liddle, and K. Ambardi (2018). *Voting Behaviour in Indonesia since Democratization: Critical Democrats*. Cambridge: Cambridge University Press.

Mukasa, N. (2017). War-child mothers in northern Uganda: The civil war forgotten legacy. *Development in Practice* 27(3), 354–367.

Murshed, S. M. and S. Gates (2005). Spatial-horizontal inequality and the Maoist insurgency in Nepal. *Review of Development Economics* 9(1), 121–134.

Nasution, A. (2014). Ethnicity, democracy and decentralization: Explaining the ethnic political participation of direct election in Medan 2010. *Procedia Environmental* 20, 496–505.

Nasution, I. K. (2016). Government decentralization program in Indonesia. Asian Development Bank Institute (ADBI) Working Paper Series 601, 496–505.

Nayak, N. (2011). The Madhesi movement in Nepal: Implications for India. *Strategic Analysis* 35(4), 640–660.

Nedelmann, B. (1987). Individuals and parties-changes in processes of political mobilization. *European Sociological Review* 3(3), 181–202.

Neethling, T. (2013). The Lord's resistance army in the DRC. *Africa Insight* 43(1), 32–44.

Nellis, G. and N. Siddiqui (2018). Secular party rule and religious violence in Pakistan. *American Political Science Review* 112(1), 49–67.

Neto, O. A. and G. W. Cox (1997). Electoral institutions, cleavage structures, and the number of parties. *American Journal of Political Science* 41(1), 149–174.

Noel, K. (2016). Understanding the roots of conflict in South Sudan. Council on Foreign Relations, September 14, 2016. www.cfr.org/interview/understanding-roots-conflict-south-sudan, accessed May 8, 2021.

Nolte, I., R. Jones, K. Taiyari, and G. Occhiali (2016). Research note: Exploring survey data for historical and anthropological research: Muslim-Christian relations in south-west Nigeria. *African Affairs* 115(460), 541–561.

Nordas, R. (2014a). Gunning for god? Religion and conflict severity. Presented at the Annual Meeting of the International Studies Association, Toronto, Canada. Typescript.

(2014b). Religious demography and conflict: Lessons from Côte d'Ivoire and Ghana. *International Area Studies Review* 17(2), 146–166.

(2015). Beyond religious diversity: Religious state repression and intrastate armed conflict. PRIO (Peace Research Institute Oslo) Working paper. Typescript.

Oboler, S. (1995). *Ethnic Labels, Latino Lives: Identity and the Politics of (Re)presentation in the United States*. Minneapolis: University of Minnesota Press.

Ofcansky, T. P. (2018). *Uganda. Tarnished Pearl of Africa*. New York: Routledge.

Oklahoma Coalition of Tribes (2016). The Native American Caucus of Oklahoma House of Representatives. www.okcoalitiontribes.org/resources/ok+tribal+caucus.pdf, accessed December 16, 2021.

Okuku, J. (2002). Ethnicity, state power and the democratisation process in Uganda. Nordic Africa Institute Discussion Paper 17, 1–42.

Olson, M. (1971). *The Logic of Collective Action; Public Goods and the Theory of Groups*. Harvard economic studies, vol. 124. Cambridge, MA: Harvard University Press.

Olzak, S. (1983). Contemporary ethnic mobilization. *Annual Review of Sociology* 9(1), 355–374.

(1992). *The Dynamics of Ethnic Competition and Conflict*. Stanford, CA: Stanford University Press.

(2006). *The Global Dynamics of Racial and Ethnic Mobilization*. Studies in social inequality. Stanford, CA: Stanford University Press.

Orcés, D. (2021). Black, white, and born again: How race affects opinions among evangelicals. *Public Religion Research Institute*, https://www.prri.org/spotlight/black–white–and–born–again–how–race–affects–opinions–among–evangelicals/ last accessed March 15, 2021.

Ordeshook, P. C. and O. V. Shvetsova (1994). Ethnic heterogeneity, district magnitude, and the number of parties. *American Journal of Political Science* 38(1), 100–123.

Ostby, G. (2008). Polarization, horizontal inequalities and violent civil conflict. *Journal of Peace Research* 45(2), 143–162.

Öztürk, A. E. (2016). Turkey's Diyanet under Akp rule: From protector to imposer of state ideology? *Journal of Southeast European and Black Sea Studies* 16(4), 619–635.

Özkan, A. E. (2017). PKK terrorism and 2015 elections in Turkey. In *International Studies Association (ISA) 58th Annual Convention*. Baltimore: ISA.

Ozsoy, A. E., I. Koc, and A. Toros (1992). Ethnic structure in Turkey as implied by the analysis of census data on mother tongue. *Turkish Journal of Population Studies* 14, 101–114.

Paik, A. and L. Navarre-Jackson (2011). Social networks, recruitment, and volunteering: Are social capital effects conditional on recruitment? *Nonprofit and Voluntary Sector Quarterly* 40(3), 476–496.

Paler, Laura, L. Marshall, and S. Atallah (2020). How cross-cutting discussion shapes support for ethnic politics: Evidence from an experiment in Lebanon. *Quarterly Journal of Political Science* 15(1), 33–71.

Pandey, N. N. (2010). *New Nepal: The Fault Lines*. New Delhi: Sage.

Paudel, D. (2016). Ethnic identity politics in Nepal: Liberation from, or restoration of, elite interest? *Asian Ethnicity* 17(4), 548–565.

Pelt, M. (2008). Adnan Menderes, Islam, and his conflict with the one-party era establishment. In D. Jung and C. Raudvere (Eds.), *Religion, Politics, and Turkey's EU Accession* pp. 91–113. New York: Palgrave Macmillan.

Pepinsky, T. B., W. Liddle, and S. Mujani (2018). *Piety and Public Opinion. Understanding Indonesian Islam*. Oxford: Oxford University Press.

Pepinsky, T. B. and M. M. Wihardja (2011). Decentralization and economic performance in Indonesia. *Journal of East Asian Studies* 11(3), 337–371.

Petersen, R. D. (2002). *Understanding Ethnic Violence: Fear, Hatred, and Resentment in Twentieth-Century Eastern Europe*. Cambridge studies in comparative politics. Cambridge: Cambridge University Press.

Pettersson, T., S. Högbladh, and M. Öberg (2019). Organized violence, 1989–2018 and peace agreements. *Journal of Peace Research* 56(4), 589–603.

Pettersson, T. and P. Wallensteen (2015). Armed conflicts, 1946–2014. *Journal of Peace Research* 52(4), 536–550.

Pfaff, S. and A. Gill (2006). Will a million Muslims March?: Muslim interest organizations and political integration in Europe. *Comparative Political Studies* 39(7), 803–828.

Philpott, D. (2007). Explaining the political ambivalence of religion. *American Political Science Review* 101(3), 505–525.

Piazza, J. A. (2009). Is Islamist terrorism more dangerous?: An empirical study of group ideology, organization, and goal structure. *Terrorism and Political Violence* 21(1), 62–88.

Piccone, T. (2016). *Five Rising Democracies and the Fate of the International Liberal Order*. Washington, DC: Brookings Institution Press.

Pierskalla, J. H. (2016). Splitting the Difference? The Politics of District Creation in Indonesia. *Comparative Politics* 48(2), 249–268.

Pierskalla, J. H. and A. Sacks (2017). Unpacking the effect of decentralized governance on routine violence: Lessons from Indonesia. *World Development* 90, 213–228.

Pirouet, L. M. (1980). Religion in Uganda under Amin. *Journal of Religion in Africa* 11(1), 13–29.

Piscopo, J. M. and K. N. Wylie (2020). Gender, race, and political representation. In H. Vanden and G. Prevost (Eds.), *Encyclopedia of Latin American Politics*. New York: Oxford University Press.

Posner, D. N. (2004). Measuring ethnic fractionalization in Africa. *American Journal of Political Science* 48(4).

(2005). *Institutions and Ethnic Politics in Africa*. Cambridge: Cambridge University Press.

(2017). When and why do some social cleavages become politically salient rather than others? *Ethnic and Racial Studies* 40(12), 2001–2019.

Potter, L. (2012). New transmigration "paradigm" in Indonesia. *Asian Pacific Viewpoint* 53(3), 272–287.

Power, T. P. (2018). Jokowi's authoritarian turn and Indonesia's democratic decline. *Bulletin of Indonesian Economic Studies* 54(3), 307–338.

Putnam, R. D. (1995). Bowling alone: America's declining social capital. *Journal of Democracy* 6(1), 65–78.

Rabasa, A. and J. Haseman (2002). *The Military and Democracy in Indonesia*. Santa Monica, CA: RAND.

Rabushka, A. and K. A. Shepsle (1972). *Politics in Plural Societies: A Theory of Democratic Instability*. Columbus, OH: Merrill.

Radon, J. and S. Logan (2014). South Sudan: Governance arrangements, war, and peace. *Journal of International Affairs* 68(1), 149–167.

Rae, D. W. and M. Taylor (1970). *The Analysis of Political Cleavages*. New Haven: Yale University Press.

Raphaeli, N. (2003). Financing of terrorism: Sources, methods and channels. *Terrorism and Political Violence* 15(4), 59–82.

Rausch Jr, J. D. (1994). Religion and political participation in Oklahoma City. *Oklahoma Politics* 3(0), 15–30.

Reid, A. (2010). *Imperial Alchemy: Nationalism and Political Identity in Soitheast Asia*. Cambridge: Cambridge University Press.

Reilly, B. (2006). *Democracy and Diversity: Political Engineering in the Asia-Pacific*. Oxford: Oxford University Press.

(2007a). Electoral systems and party systems in East Asia. *Journal of East Asian Studies* 7(2), 185–202.

(2007b). Political engineering in the Asia-Pacific. *Journal of Democracy* 18(1), 58–72.

Ricks, J. I. and A. H. Liu (2018). Process-tracing research designs: A practical guide. *PS: Political Science & Politics* 51(4), 842–846.

Riker, W. H. (1962). *The Theory of Political Coalitions*. New Haven: Yale University Press.

(1986). *The Art of Political Manipulation*. New Haven: Yale University Press.

Robinson, G. B. (1998). Rawan is as Rawan does: The origins of disorder in New Order Aceh. *Indonesia* 66, 125–157.

(2018). *The Killing Season. A History of the Indonesian Massacres, 1965–66*. Princeton: Princeton University Press.

Roccas, S. and M. B. Brewer (2002). Social identity complexity. *Personality and Social Psychology Review* 6(2), 88–106.

Rokkan, S. (1967). Geography, religion, and social class: Crosscutting cleavages in Norwegian politics. In S. Rokkan and S. M. Lipset (Eds.), *Party Systems and Voter Alignment*. New York: Free Press.

Rondonuwu, O. and E. Davies (September 23, 2008). Indonesia's Wiranto wants wealth spread more widely. Reuters, www.reuters.com/article/idINIndia-35614720080923, accessed December 17, 2021.

Rothchild, D. (1983). Collective demands for improved distribution. In D. Rothchild and V. A. Olorunsola (Eds.), *State versus Ethnic Claims: African Policy Dilemmas*. Boulder, CO: Westview.

Rubin, J. Z., D. G. Pruitt, and S. H. Kim (1994). *Social Conflict: Escalation, Stalemate, and Settlement*. London: McGraw-Hill.

Rudy, R., Y. Hasyimzum, H. Heryandi, and S. Khoiriah (2017). 18 years of decentralization experiment in Indonesia: Institutional and democratic evaluation. *Journal of Politics and Law* 10(5), 1913–9055.

Sakallioglu-Cizre, U. (1998). Kurdish nationalism from an Islamist perspective: The discourses of Turkish Islamist writers. *Journal of Muslim Minority Affairs* 18(1), 73–89.

Sambanis, N. (2001). Do ethnic and nonethnic civil wars have the same causes?: A theoretical and empirical inquiry (part 1). *The Journal of Conflict Resolution* 45(3), 259–282.

Sambanis, N. (2020). Power sharing and peace building. ERF Working Paper No. 1396, 1–30.

Sambanis, N., M. Germann, and A. Schädel (2018). SDM: A new data set on self-determination movements with an application to the reputational theory of conflict. *Journal of Conflict Resolution* 62(3), 656–686.

Sarigil, Z. (2018). *Ethnic Boundaries in Turkish Politics: The Secular Kurdish Movement and Islam*. New York: NYU Press.

Sarigil, Z. and O. Fazlioglu (2013). Religion and ethno-nationalism: Turkey's Kurdish issue. *Nations and Nationalism* 19(3), 551–571.

Sarkissian, A. (2015). *The Varieties of Religious Repression: Why Governments Restrict Religion*. New York: Oxford University Press.

Satana, N. S. and B. B. Özpek (November 2020). Civil-military relations and the demise of Turkish democracy. In Gunes Tezcur (Ed.), *The Oxford Handbook of Turkish Politics*. November 2020. www.oxfordhandbooks.com/view/10.1093/oxfordhb/9780190064891.001.0001/oxfordhb-9780190064891-e-15, accessed December 17, 2021.

Satana, N. S. and T. Demirel-Pegg (2020). Military counterterrorism measures, civil-military relations, and democracy: The cases of Turkey and the United States. *Studies in Conflict & Terrorism* 43(9), 815–836.

Satana, N. S., A. Özkan, and J. K. Birnir (2019). Religion, social constituency representation and interest articulation. In J. Haynes (Ed.), *The Routledge Handbook to Religion and Political Parties*, pp. 92–104. London: Routledge.

Satana, N. S., M. Inman, and J. K. Birnir (2013). Religion, government coalitions, and terrorism. *Terrorism and Political Violence* 25(1), 29–52.

Satana, N. S. (2008). Transformation of the Turkish military and the path to democracy. *Armed Forces & Society* 18(7), 357–388.

Schock, K. (2005). *Unarmed Insurrections: People Power Movements in Nondemocracies. Social movements, protest, and contention*, vol. 22. Minneapolis: University of Minnesota Press.

Schomerus, E. M. and L. Aalen (2016). Considering the state perspectives on South Sudan's subdivision and federalism debate. Report. Overseas Development Institute. and CHR Michelsen Institute, odi.org, accessed December 16, 2021.

Schulte Nordholt, H. and G. van Klinken (2007). *Renegotiating Boundaries: Local Politics in Post-Suharto Indonesia*. Leiden: KITLV Press.

Schulze, K. E. (2017). The "ethnic" in Indonesia's communal conflicts: violence in Ambon, Poso, and Sambas. *Ethnic and Racial Studies 40*(12), 2096–2114.

Schumpeter, J. A. (1992). *Capitalism, Socialism, and Democracy*. London: Routledge.

Seawright, J. (2016). *Multi-Method Social Science: Combining Qualitative and Quantitative Tools*. Cambridge: Cambridge University Press.

Seawright, J. and J. Gerring (2008). Case selection techniques in case study research: A menu of qualitative and quantitative options. *Political Research Quarterly 61*(2), 294–308.

Selway, J. S. (2011a). Cross-cuttingness, cleavage structures and civil war onset. *British Journal of Political Science 41*(1), 111–138.

(2011b). The measurement of cross-cutting cleavages and other multidimensional cleavage structures. *Political Analysis 19*(1), 48–65.

(2015). *Coalitions of the Well-Being: How Electoral Rules and Ethnic Politics Shape Health Policy in Developing Countries*. New York: Cambridge University Press.

Selway, J. S. and K. Templeman (2012). The myth of consociationalism? Conflict reduction in divided societies. *Comparative Political Studies 45*(12), 1542–1571.

Seul, J. R. (1999). "Ours is the way of god": Religion, identity, and intergroup conflict. *Journal of Peace Research 36*(5), 553–569.

Shah, S. A. (2016). 144 militants including four commanders surrender in Balochistan. *The Dawn*, www.dawn.com/news/1252887, accessed December 17, 2021.

Shair-Rosenfield, S. (2012). The alternative incumbency effect: Electing women legislators in Indonesia. *Electoral Studies 31*(3), 576–587.

Sharma, K. (2006). The political economy of civil war in Nepal. *World Development 34*(7), 1237–1253.

(2016). Foreign aid, development and civil war in Nepal. In A. Ware (Ed.), *Development in Difficult Sociopolitical Contexts: Fragile, Failed, Paroah* pp. 163–179. London: Palgrave Macmillan.

Sharp, G., J. Paulson, and CIAO (Organization) (2005). *Waging Nonviolent Struggle: 20th Century Practice and 21st Century Potential*. Boston: Extending Horizons Books.

Shaykhutdinov, R. (2010). Give peace a chance: Nonviolent protest and the creation of territorial autonomy arrangements. *Journal of Peace Research 47*(2), 179–191.

Sheikh, M. K. (2012). Sacred pillars of violence: Findings from a study of the Pakistani Taliban. *Politics, Religion & Ideology 13*(4), 439–454.

(2016). *Guardians of God: Inside the Religious Mind of the Pakistani Taliban*. London: Oxford University Press.

Shepsle, K. A. (1974). On the size of winning coalitions. *American Political Science Review 68*(2), 505–518.

Siddique, A. (2014). *The Pashtun Question: The Unresolved Key to the Future of Pakistan and Afghanistan*. London: Hurst.

Sidel, J. (2006). *Riots, Pogroms, Jihad: Religious Violence in Indonesia.* Ithaca, NY: Cornell University Press.

Sikander (March 2, 2017). Federal cabinet approves FATA's merger with K-P, repeal of FCR – The Express Tribune, https://tribune.com.pk/story/1343825/federal-cabinet-approves-fata-reforms, accessed December 17, 2021.

Singh, B. (2007). *The Talibanization of Southeast Asia: Losing the War on Terror to Islamist Extremists.* Westport, CT: Praeger Security International.

Siroky, D. and M. Hechter (2016). Ethnicity, class, and civil war: The role of hierarchy, segmentation, and cross-cutting cleavages. *Civil Wars 18*(1), 91–107.

Sisk, T. D. (1996). *Power Sharing and International Mediation in Ethnic Conflicts.* Perspectives series. Washington, DC: United States Institute of Peace Press.

Smith, G. (2015). *Americas Changing Religious Landscape.* Washington, DC: Pew Research Center.

Soares, B. F. (2006). *Muslim-Christian Encounters in Africa.* Leiden: Brill.

Soedirgo, J. (2018). Informal networks and religious intolerance: How clientelism incentivizes the discrimination of the Ahmadiyah in Indonesia. *Citizenship Studies 22*(2), 191–207.

Sofjan, D. (2016). Religious diversity and politico-religious intolerance in Indonesia and Malaysia. *The Review of Faith & International Affairs 14*(4), 53–64.

Solahudin (2013). *The Roots of Terrorism in Indonesia: From Darul Islam to Jem'ah Islamiyah.* Ithaca, NY: Cornell University Press.

Somer, M. and G. Glupker-Kesebir (2016). Is Islam the solution? Comparing Turkish Islamic and secular thinking toward ethnic and religious minorities. *Journal of Church and State 58*(3), 529–555.

Somer, M. and E. G. Liaras (2010). Turkey's new Kurdish opening: Religion and ethnicity in Turkey's Kurdish conflict. *Middle East Policy 17*(2), 152–165.

Staniland, P. (2014). *Networks of Rebellion: Explaining Insurgent Cohesion and Collapse.* Ithaca, NY: Cornell University Press.

  (2015). Armed groups and militarized elections. *International Studies Quarterly 59*(4), 694–705.

Stark, R. and R. Finke (2002). Beyond church and sect: Dynamics and stability in religious economics. In T. Jelen (Ed.), *Sacred Markets, Sacred Canopies: Essays on Religious Markets and Religious Pluralism.* Lanham, MD: Rowman & Littlefield.

Stephan, M. J. and E. Chenoweth (2008). Why civil resistance works: The strategic logic of nonviolent conflict. *International Security 33*(1), 7–44.

Stewart, F. (Ed.) (2008). *Horizontal Inequalities and Conflict: Understanding Group Violence in Multiethnic Societies.* Conflict, inequality and ethnicity. London: Palgrave Macmillan.

Stewart, F. (2012). Religion versus ethnicity as a source of mobilization: Are there differences? In Y. Guichaoua (Ed.), *Understanding Collective Political Violence,* pp. 196–221. London: Palgrave Macmillan.

Stewart, F., G. Brown, and A. Cobham (2009). The implications of horizontal and vertical inequalities for tax and expenditure policies. CRISE Working Paper No. 65, February 2009. Oxford: University of Oxford.

Subedi, M. (2010). Caste system: Theories and practices in Nepal. *Himalayan Journal of Sociology & Anthropology IV*, 134–159.

Suhartono, M. and D. Victor (May 22, 2019). Violence erupts in Indonesia's capital in wake of presidential election results. *The New York Times*, www.nytimes .com/2019/05/22/world/asia/indonesia-election-riots.html, accessed December 17, 2021.

Suryadinata, L., A. E. Nurvidya, and A. Ananta (2003). *Indonesia's Population. Ethnicity and Religion in a Changing Political Landscape*. Singapore: Institute of Southeast Asian Studies.

Svensson, I. (2007). Fighting with faith. *Journal of Conflict Resolution 51*(6), 930–949.

  (2012). *Ending Holy Wars : Religion and Conflict Resolution in Civil Wars*. Australia: University of Queensland Press.

  (2016). Conceptualizing the religious dimensions of armed conflicts: A response to "Shrouded: Islam, War, and Holy War in Southeast Asia". *Journal for the Scientific Study of Religion 55*(1), 185–189.

Svensson, I. and D. Nilsson (2018). Disputes over the divine: Introducing the religion and armed conflict (RELAC) data, 1975 to 2015. *Journal of Conflict Resolution 62*(5), 1127–1148.

Sweijs, T., J. Ginn, and S. de Spiegeleire (2015). *Barbarism and Religion: The Resurgence of Holy Violence*. The Hague Centre for Strategic Studies. Netherlands: The Hague.

Taştekin (May 20, 2015). Kurds abandon AKP. *Al Monitor*, www.al-monitor.com/ originals/2015/05/turkey-pious-kurds-abandon-akp-in-droves-hdp.html, accessed December 17, 2021.

Tadjoeddin, M. Z. (2013). Educated but poor: Explaining localized ethnic violence during Indonesia's democratic transition. *International Area Studies Review 16*(1), 24–49.

Tajfel, H. (1978). *Differentiation between Social Groups: Studies in the Social Psychology of Intergroup Relations*. London: Academic Press.

Tajfel, H. and J. C. Turner (1979). An integrative theory of intergroup conflict. In W. G. Austin and S. Worchel (Eds.), *The Social Psychology of Intergroup Relations*, pp. 33–37. Monterey, CA: Brooks/Cole.

  (1986). The social identity theory of intergroup behavior. In W. G. Austin and S. Worchel (Eds.), *Psychology of Inter-group Relations*, pp. 7–24. Chicago: Nelson-Hall.

Tajima, Y., K. Samphantharak, and K. Ostwald (2018). Ethnic segregation and public goods: Evidence from Indonesia. *American Political Science Review 112*(3), 637–653.

Talitha, T., T. Firman, and D. Hudalah (2020). Welcoming two decades of decentralization in Indonesia: A regional development perspective. *Territory, Politics, Governance 8*(5), 690–708.

Tanuwidjaja, S. (2010). Political Islam and Islamic parties in Indonesia: Critically assessing the evidence of Islam's political decline. *Contemporary Southeast Asia: A Journal of International and Strategic Affairs 32*(1), 29–49.

Tarrow, S. (2011). *Power in Movement: Social Movements and Contentious Politics*. Cambridge: Cambridge University Press.

The Economist (2019). To win re-election, Indonesia's president has betrayed his principles – There's more to life than infrastructure.

Themner, L. and P. Wallenstein (2014). Armed conflicts 1946–2011. *Journal of Peace Research 51*(4), 541–554.

Thiong, D. A. (2018). How the politics of fear generated chaos in South Sudan. *African Affairs* 117(469), 613–635.

Tilly, C. (1978). *From Mobilization to Revolution*. Reading, MA: Addison-Wesley.

(1993). Social movements as historically specific clusters of Political performances. *Berkeley Journal of Sociology* 38, 1–30.

(2004). *Social Movements 1768–2004*. Boulder: Paradigm.

Tirtosudarmo, R. (1997). Economic development, migration, and ethnic conflict in Indonesia: A preliminary observation. *Sojourn: Journal of Social Issues in Southeast Asia* 12(2), 293–328.

(2001). Demography and security: Transmigration policy in Indonesia. In M. Weiner and S. Stanton Russell (Eds.), *Demography and National Security*, pp. 199–227. New York: Berghan Books.

Toft, M. D. (2002, 12). Indivisible territory, geographic concentration, and ethnic war. *Security Studies* 12, 82–119.

(2003). *The Geography of Ethnic Violence: Identity, Interests, and the Indivisibility of Territory*. Princeton, NJ: Princeton University Press.

(2006). *Religion, Civil War, and International Order: Discussion Paper 2006–03*. Cambridge, MA: Belfer Center for Science and International Affairs, John F. Kennedy School of Government, Harvard University.

(2007). Getting religion? The puzzling Case of Islam and Civil War. *International Security* 31(4), 97–131.

(2013). The politics of religious outbidding. *The Review of Faith & International Affairs* 11(3), 10–19.

Toft, M. D., D. Philpott, and T. S. Shah (2011). *God's Century. Resurgent Religion and Global Politics*. New York: W. W. Norton.

Toha, R. (2021). *Rioting for Representation: Local Ethnic Mobilization in Democratizing Countries*. New York/London: Cambridge University Press.

Tom, P. (2006). The Acholi traditional approach to justice and the war in Northern Uganda. www.beyondintractability.org/casestudy/tom-acholi, accessed December 17, 2021.

Tomsa, D. (2018). Parties and party politics in the post-reformasi era. In R. W. Hefner (Ed.), *Routledge Handbook of Contemporary Indonesia*, pp. 95–105. New York: Routledge.

Tribes, O. C. o. (2006). The Native American Caucus of the Oklahoma House of Representatives. www.okcoalitiontribes.org/resources/ok+tribal+caucus.pdf, accessed February 3, 2021.

Trivedi, H. and M. A. Naqvi (Directors) (2016). Among the Believers [Film]. Manjusha Films.

Türkmen, G. (2018). Negotiating symbolic boundaries in conflict resolution: Religion and ethnicity in "Turkey's Kurdish" conflict. *Qualitative Sociology* 41(4), 569–591.

Turner, J. C. (1985). Social categorization and the self-concept: A social cognitivetheory of group behavior. In E. J. Lawler (Ed.), *Advances in Group Processes*, vol. 2, pp. 77–121. New York: JAI Press.

Tusicisny, A. (2004). Civilizational conflicts: More frequent, longer, and bloodier? *Journal of Peace Research* (4), 485–498.

Twesigye, E. (2010). *Religion, Politics and Cults in East Africa: God's Warriors and Mary's Saints*. New York: Peter Lang.

Tyson, S. A. and A. Smith (2018). Dual-layered coordination and political instability: Repression, co-optation, and the role of information. *The Journal of Politics 80*(1), 44–58.

UCDP (2021). India: Tripura. In www.ucdp.uu.se (Ed.), *Conflict Encyclopedia*. Conflict Data Program. https://ucdp.uu.se/conflict/335, accessed March 11, 2021.

Ufen, A. (2008). From aliran to dealignment: Political parties in Post-Suharto Indonesia. *South East Asia Research 16*(1), 5–41.

Unal, M. C. (2014). Strategist or pragmatist: A challenging look at Ocalan's retrospective classification and definition of PKK's strategic periods between 1973 and 2012. *Terrorism and Political Violence 26*(3), 419–448.

United Nations Population Division (2018). 2018 world population by country. https://worldpopulationreview.com/, accessed March 6, 2018.

US Census (2020a). Race and ethnicity: Oklahoma. In *Population Survey*. New York: United States Census Bureau. https://data.census.gov/cedsci/pro_le?g=0400000US40, accessed February 3, 2021.

(2020b). Race and ethnicity: Oklahoma. In *Population Survey*. New York: United States Census Bureau. https://data.census.gov/cedsci/pro_le?g=1600000US4055000, accessed February 3, 2021.

US House of Representatives (2021). *Mapping-Congress*. Office of the Historian and the Clerk of the House's Office of Art and Archives.

van Acker, F. (2004). Uganda and The Lord's Resistance Army: The new order no one ordered. *African Affairs 103*(412), 335–357.

van Bruinessen, M. (1992). *Agha, Shaikh and State: On the Social and Political Organization of Kurdistan*. London: Routledge.

(2000). Religion in Kurdistan. In *Mullas, Sufis and Heretics: The Role of Religion in Kurdish Society*. Istanbul: The Isis Press.

van der Kroef, J. M. (1950). Social conflict and minority aspirations in Indonesia. *American Journal of Sociology 55*(5), 450–463.

van der Veen, M. and D. D. Laitin (2012). *Modeling the Evolution of Ethnic Demography*, pp. 277–311. New York: Oxford University Press.

van Klinken, G. (2003). Ethnicity in Indonesia. In C. Mackerras (Ed.), *Ethnicity in Asia*, pp. 64–87. New York: Routledge/Curzon.

(2007). *Communal Violence and Democratization in Indonesia: Small Town Wars*. New York: Routledge.

Varshney, A. (2002). *Ethnic Conflict and Civic Life: Hindus and Muslims in India*. New Haven, CT: Yale University Press.

(2008). The idea of Pakistan. *India International Centre Quarterly 35*(3/4), 2–21.

Varshney, A., M. Z. Tadjoeddin, and R. Panggabean (2008). Creating datasets in information-poor environments: Patterns of collective violence in Indonesia, 1990–2003. *Journal of East Asian Studies 8*, 361–394.

Vel, J., W. Berenschot, and R. D. Minarchek (2016). New law, new villages? Changing rural Indonesia. In *Workshop by KITLV, Leiden University's Van Vollenhoven Institute, the Asian Modernities and Traditions program (AMT), and the Norwegian Centre for Human Rights at the University of Oslo (NCHR)*. Leiden: KITLV.

Vermeersch, P. (2012). Theories of ethnic mobilization: Overview and recent trends. In G. K. Brown and A. Langer (Eds.), *Elgar Handbook of Civil War and Fragile States*. Cheltenham: Edward Elgar.

Vinci, A. (2007). Existential motivations in the Lord's Resistance Army's continuing conflict. *Studies in Conflict & Terrorism 30*(4), 337–352.

Vogt, M. (2019). *Mobilization and Conflict in Multiethnic States*. Oxford: Oxford University Press.

Vogt, M., N.-C. Bormann, S. Ruegger, L.-E. Cederman, P. Hunziker, and L. Girardin (2015). Integrating data on ethnicity, geography, and conflict: The ethnic power relations data set family. *Journal of Conflict Resolution 59*(7), 1327–1342.

Voll, J. (2006). African Muslims and Christians in World History: The irrelevance of the "Clash of Civilizations". In B. F. Soares (Ed.), *Muslim-Christian Encounters in Africa*. Leiden and Boston: Brill Academic.

von Einsiedel, S., D. Malone, and S. Pradhan (2012). *Nepal in Transition: From People's War to Fragile Peace*. Cambridge: Cambridge University Press.

Vreeland, J. R. (2008). The effect of political regime on civil war: Unpacking anocracy. *Journal of Conflict Resolution 52*(3), 401–425.

Wald, K. D. (2014). *Religion and Politics in the United States*. Lanham, MD Rowman & Littlefield.

Ward, K. (2010). Soeharto's Javanese Pancasila. In E. Aspinall and G. Fealy (Eds.), *Soeharto's New Order and Its Legacy: Essays in Honour of Walter Crouch*. Australia: ANU Press.

Weinberg, L., A. Pedahzur, and A. Perliger (2008). *Political Parties and Terrorist Groups*. London/New York: Taylor & Francis.

Weiner, M. (1971). Political demography: An inquiry into the consequences of population change. In S. C. of the Office of the Foreign Secretary: National Academy of the Sciences (Ed.), *Rapid Population Growth: Consequences and Policy Implications*. Baltimore: Johns Hopkins University Press.

Weiner, M. and M. S. Teitelbaum (2001). *Political Demography, Demographic Engineering*. New York: Berghahn Books.

Weinstein, J. M. (2007). *Inside Rebellion: The Politics of Insurgent Violence*. New York: Cambridge University Press.

Whelpton, J. (2004). *History of Nepal*. New York: Cambridge University Press.

Whiting, M. and Z. N. Kaya (2021). Autocratization, permanent emergency rule and local politics: Lessons from the Kurds in Turkey. *Democratization 28*(4), 821–839.

Wickham, H., R. François, L. Henry, and K. Müller (2018). dplyr: A Grammar of Data Manipulation. R package version 0.7.6.

Wilkinson, S. (2004). *Votes and Violence: Electoral Competition and Ethnic Riots in India*. Cambridge studies in comparative politics. Cambridge: Cambridge University Press.

Wimmer, A. (1997). Who owns the state? Understanding ethnic conflict in post-colonial societies. *Nations and Nationalism 3*(4), 631–666.

(2013). *Ethnic Boundary Making*. Oxford/New York: Oxford University Press.

Wimmer, A., L.-E. Cederman, and B. Min (2009). Ethnic politics and armed conflict: A configurational analysis of a new global data set. *American Sociological Review 74*(2), 316–337.

Wong, J. (2018). *Immigrants, Evangelicals and Politics in an Era of Demographic Change*. New York: Russell Sage Foundation.

(2019). Race, evangelicals, and immigration. *The Forum 17*(3), 403–419.

Worden, R. L. and W. H. Frederick (1993). *Indonesia: A Country Study*. Washington, DC: Federal Research Division, Library of Congress.

Wucherpfennig, J., N. Weidmann, L. Girardin, L.-E. Cederman, and A. Wimmer (2011). Politically relevant ethnic groups across space and time: Introducing the GeoEPR Dataset1. *Conflict Management and Peace Science 28*(5), 423–437.

Xue, S. (2018). Ethnic mobilization in 2015 local elections in North Sumatra, Indonesia. *Asian Ethnicity 19*(4), 509–527.

Yavuz, H. M. (2001). Five stages of the construction of Kurdish nationalism in Turkey. *Nationalism and Ethnic Politics 7*(3), 1–24.

Yavuz, H. M. and N. A. Ozcan (2006). The Kurdish question and Turkey's Justice and Development Party. *Middle East Policy 13*(1), 102–120.

Young, C. (1976). *The Politics of Cultural Pluralism*. Madison, WI: University of Wisconsin Press.

Yüceşahin, M. and E. Ozgur (2008). Regional fertility differences in Turkey: Persistent high fertility in the Southeast. *Population Space and Place 14*(2), 135–158.

Zeileis, A. (2006). A (2006), Object-oriented computation of sandwich estimators. *Journal of Statistical Software 16*(9), 1–16.

Zink, J. A. (2018). *Christianity and Catastrophe in South Sudan: Civil War, Migration, and the Rise of Dinka Anglicanism*. Waco, TX: Baylor University Press.

Index

Hizb-i Demokratik-i Khalq-i Afghanistan or
    People's Democratic Party of
    Afghanistan (PDPA), 105
Hizb-i Islami-yi Afghanistan (Islamic Party of
    Afghanistan), 105
Hizb-i Islami-yi Afghanistan-Khalis faction
    (Islamic Party of Afghanistan Khalis
    faction), 105
Holy Spirit Movement (HSM), 137, 140, 142,
    143, 145, 146, 217
horizontal inequalities, 4, 212

identifiability, 221, 223
identity, 216
    cleavage, 2, 6, 10, 12, 13, 20, 23, 25, 56, 57,
        60, 62, 66, 67, 71, 74, 79, 81, 83, 85,
        86, 93, 94, 153, 168–170, 172, 178,
        198, 209, 213, 217, 219, 236–238
    interaction, 6
    intersection, 7, 13, 25, 27, 55, 67, 207
    mobilization, 1, 3, 4, 7, 10, 11, 13, 14, 17,
        20, 21, 24, 26, 27, 33, 38, 48, 56, 92,
        93, 96, 126, 136, 155–157, 161, 167,
        168, 173, 185, 191, 192, 206, 213, 253
    political activation of, 223, 224
    segmented, 2–4, 6, 7, 12–14, 35, 40, 47, 55,
        56, 65, 74, 75, 82, 85, 92, 124, 177,
        192, 196, 197, 215, 219, 220, 234, 255
    cleavage, 20, 56, 60, 64, 79–81, 86, 90,
        167, 234, 237
    ethnic majority, 59
    groups, 4, 12–14, 21, 26, 37, 46, 47,
        57–60, 66, 67, 75, 85, 93, 95, 224
    majority, 193
    minority, 4, 59, 79, 90, 115, 168, 177,
        192, 234
    shared, 13, 14, 17, 56, 60, 62, 64, 65, 67, 68,
        72, 74, 81, 82, 90, 92, 119, 120, 124,
        126, 130, 167, 170, 177, 192, 193, 207,
        216, 219, 235, 237
India, 33–35, 55, 61, 133, 150, 153, 217, 253
Indonesia, 2, 3, 12, 15, 16, 21, 23, 34, 44, 61,
        92, 93, 96, 159, 161, 163, 168–172,
        174, 175, 177, 179, 180, 185–188,
        190–192, 195, 196, 198, 200–203, 209,
        211–214, 218, 223, 224
    abangan (syncretic masses), 174
    asas tunggal (sole basis), 173, 175
    bupati, 173, 181
    bupati (regent), 184
    Central Java, 176, 188, 193, 201, 205
    Demokrasi Terpimpin (Guided Democracy,
        170, 172, 173, 212

East Java, 188, 196, 212
Eastern Java, 188
Jakarta, 169, 173, 175, 176, 190, 193, 196,
    198, 201, 203, 212
Javanization, 202
Kepri (Kepulauan Riau), 188, 197–200,
    204–206, 211, 213, 214, 218, 223
Medan, 206–208, 210, 211, 214
New Order, 173, 177, 178, 207
North Maluku, 175, 197
North Sumatra, 175, 196, 197, 199, 202,
    206–211
Pancasila, 157, 170–173, 175–177
pendatang (migrant), 199
pengungsi (refugees and internally displaced
    persons), 175
People's Representative Council (*Dewan
    Perwakilan Rakyat*, DPR), 183, 185
People's Representative Council (*Dewan
    Perwakilan Rakyat*, DPR), 171, 179,
    188, 207, 213
preman (gangster), 210
putra daerah (sons of the land), 198, 206,
    217, 223
Reformasi (Reform), 170, 171, 175, 177,
    182
transmigration, 187, 198, 201, 202, 218
walikota (mayor), 184
West Java, 176, 188, 201, 205, 211, 212
Indonesian National Party (*Partai Nasional
    Indonesia*, PNI), 171
Indonesian Ulema Council, 2
internal majority fissures, 59, 77
internal validity of the CWC, 15, 21–23, 126,
    127, 131, 167, 169, 213, 217, 218, 237
intersectionality, 225
Iran, 46
Iraq, 61, 120
Islam, 16, 21, 22, 26–30, 32, 35, 36, 39, 40,
    42–46, 49, 50, 53, 112, 127, 129, 136,
    140, 144, 155, 156, 158, 160, 163, 165,
    170, 171, 175, 176, 191, 196, 203, 210
    Alevi, 160
    Druze, 43
    Ibadhi, 43
    Shi'i, 43, 46, 112, 122, 158
    Sunni, 39–41, 43, 46, 97, 98, 108, 112, 122,
        133, 155, 156, 158, 160, 162, 165
Islamic
    brotherhood, 163
    Caliphate, the, 157, 162
    cleric, 2, 165
    coalition, 200

Ingram Content Group UK Ltd.
Milton Keynes UK
UKHW010646050723
424457UK00013B/269